Inverse Images

Inverse Images:
The Meaning of Culture, Ethnicity and Family in Postcolonial Guatemala

John Hawkins
Foreword by Manning Nash

University of New Mexico Press
Albuquerque

Library of Congress Cataloging in Publication Data

Hawkins, John, 1946–
  Inverse images.

  Bibliography: p.
  Includes index.
  1. Indians of Central America—Guatemala. 2. Indians of Central America—Guatemala—Kinship. 3. Indians of Central America—Guatemala—Ethnic identity. 4. Ethnicity—Guatemala. 5. Family—Guatemala. 6. Guatemala—Civilization. I. Title.
  F1465.H29   1984   305.8'97'07281   84-11855
  ISBN 0-8263-0774-4
  ISBN 0-8263-0775-2 (pbk.)

© 1984 by the University of New Mexico Press.
All rights reserved. Manufactured in the United States of America.
First edition

Material from Waldemar R. Smith, *The Fiesta System and Economic Change,* © 1977, Columbia University Press, reprinted by permission.

*To those who saw less of me
than they deserved because of "the book":
Carol Lee and our children Claire, Suzie, Abby, and Richard.*

Contents

Tables	x
Figures	xi
Plates	xi
Maps	xii
Foreword, by Manning Nash	xiii
Acknowledgments	xvii

Part 1: *Theory and History for the Understanding of Guatemala*   1

1   Perspectives on Guatemala   3

    Culture: An Ideological System   5
    The Structure of Guatemalan Culture   9
    Ethnicity as Origin Symbolism   14
    Guatemala: An Overview   15

2   The Historical Context of Guatemalan Culture and Society   23

    Preconquest Spain   24
    Preconquest Mesoamerica   39
    Precursors of the Conquest of Guatemala   44
    The Conquest Period: 1524-1542   50
    The Colonial Institutions: 1542–1821   54
    Colonial Society   63
    Colonial Society in San Marcos and San Pedro   67
    Independence—Minimum Structural Change (1821-1944)   80
    The Modern Period: From 1944 to Today   84

Part 2: *The National Domain and Present-Day San Marcos and San Pedro: Culture and Symbolism in Polity, Economy, and Social Status*   89

3   The Political Positions of San Marcos and San Pedro Sacatepéquez   91

	The Structure of Government in Guatemala	91
	Municipal, Departmental, and National Linkages	97
	The Municipality of San Marcos	100
	The Municipality of San Pedro Sacatepéquez	113
	Case Studies of the Material and Social Implications of Inverse Status Ideologies	117
4	The Economic Oppositions of San Pedro Sacatepéquez and San Marcos	135
	The Economic System of San Pedro	138
	The Economic System of San Marcos	157
	The Household Division of Labor and Ethnic Symbolism	164
	Class Identity and Status Difference	166
5	The Conceptual Organization of Status and Ethnicity	173
	Ethnic Categories: Ideal Types and Institutional Continua	173
	Ethnic Concepts in San Pedro and San Marcos	176
	Categories of Institutional Placement	195
6	Institutional Congruence, the Individual, and Ethnic Change	201

Part 3: *The Domestic Domains in San Marcos and San Pedro: The Impact of Inverse Ideologies* — 213

7	The Kinship System	215
	The Kinship System in San Pedro Sacatepéquez	217
	The Kinship System in San Marcos	229
	Comparisons	237
	Status Inequalities and the Permutations of Kinship	240
8	Courtship and Marriage	243
	San Pedro Sacatepéquez	243
	San Marcos	253
	Comparisons	261
9	Postmarital Residence	267
	San Pedro Sacatepéquez	268
	San Marcos	278

	Comitancillo	286
	Notes on the Wider Ethnography	295
	Functional Explanations: Marriage, Inheritance, and Lastborn Residence	296
10	Divorce, Separation, and Abandonment	301
	Categories of Alliance Termination	301
	The Causes of Conjugal Breakdown among San Marcos Non-Indians	305
	The Causes of Marital Dissolution in San Pedro	313
	Conclusion	324
11	Death and Inheritance	327
	The Funeral	327
	Funeral Expenses versus Inheritance	330
	Inheritance	332
	After Inheritance	335
	Summary	336
12	The Developmental Cycle of the Household	337
	The Impact of Cultural Premises on the Developmental Cycle	341
	Conclusion	343
13	Inverse Images: A Comparison of Postcolonial Societies and Cultures	349
	Peru: Social Structure and Ideological Inversion in the Andes	350
	The Philippines: Colonial Experience at the Limits of Spanish Control	363
	Jamaica: Colonial Inversions with a British Twist	368
	Inverse Images and Postcolonial Instability	377
Appendix 1.A:	Ethnic Inversion among the Pocomam of Eastern Guatemala	379
Appendix 1.B:	Ethnic Inversion among the Cakchiquel of Central Guatemala	382
Appendix 2.A:	Principal Occupation of Urban Household Heads	385

Appendix 2.B: Value of Agricultural Land Owned
   by Household   389

Appendix 2.C: Total Monthly Household Income   392

Appendix 3:   Ethnic Definitions   395

Appendix 4:   Prospects for Further Research   403
               Topics and Sites in Guatemala   404
               Beyond Guatemala   407

Notes   411
References   447
Index   461

Tables

Table	1	National, Regional, and Departmental Population and Land Data (1973 Census)	94
Table	2	Municipal Responsibilities of the Courts of Initial Jurisdiction Serving the Department of San Marcos	104
Table	3	Relative Importance of All Crafts in Urban San Pedro and San Marcos	148
Table	4	Agricultural Land per Household in San Pedro and San Marcos	154
Table	5	Relative Importance of Government Employment and Professional Jobs in Urban San Marcos and San Pedro	159
Table	6	Professional Services in San Marcos and San Pedro	163
Table	7	Household and Per Capita Monthly Incomes in Urban San Marcos and San Pedro	167
Table	8	Kinds of Symbolism Used to Define Indian, Ladino, and Self	191
Table	9	Household and Per Capita Monthly Incomes and Land Values for Each Ethnic Sector of Urban San Marcos and San Pedro	207
Table	10	Legal Status of Household Head's Domestic Alliance in Urban San Pedro Sacatepéquez	249

Table 11	Relation of Current Household Income to the Legal Status of Co-Resident Domestic Alliances of Household Heads in Urban San Pedro	250
Table 12	Legal Status of Household Head's Domestic Alliance in Urban San Marcos	255
Table 13	Relation of Current Household Income to the Legal Status of Co-Resident Domestic Alliances of Household Heads in Urban San Marcos	257
Table 14	San Pedro: Urban Stem Household Monthly Income	273
Table 15	San Pedro: Urban Stem Household Land Values	275
Table 16	San Marcos: Urban Stem Household Monthly Income	281
Table 17	San Marcos: Urban Stem Household Land Values	283
Table 18	Reported Types of Most Recent Conjugal Failure	306
Table 19	Economics of Separation	314
Table 20	Mean Male and Female Incomes at Time of Conjugal Dissolution	314
Table 21	Notes of Serial Reunion (All Conjugal Types)	317
Table 22	Divorce or Separation Timing since Conjugal Union	318
Table 23	Volunteered Reasons for Conjugal Failure	320
Table 24	Elicited Causes of Conjugal Breakdown	323

Figures

Figure 1	San Pedro Composite Genealogy	226
Figure 2	San Marcos Composite Genealogy	227
Figure 3	The Relationship of Ethnicity to Household Size	344
Figure 4	The Relationship of Income to Household Size	345

Plates

Plate 1	An Eighteenth-Century Map of San Marcos and San Pedro	68
Plate 2	Aerial view, San Marcos and San Pedro	101
Plate 3	Urban center of San Marcos	102
Plate 4	San Marcos	103

Plate 5	Typical San Marcos house	105
Plate 6	The Palacio Maya	106
Plate 7	A parade, San Marcos	112
Plate 8	A religious procession, San Marcos	113
Plate 9	San Pedro on market day	114
Plate 10	San Pedro market	120
Plate 11	San Pedro's new market building	121
Plate 12	San Marcos, new market building	122
Plate 13	Home of a *patrono,* San Pedro	138
Plate 14	Weavers' work area, San Pedro	139
Plate 15	Footloom weaving, San Pedro	140
Plate 16	Household weaving production, San Pedro	142
Plate 17	Husband weaving, San Pedro	143
Plate 18	Wife sewing, San Pedro	144
Plate 19	Knitting, San Pedro	146
Plate 20	Candle making, San Pedro	147
Plate 21	A household shop, San Pedro	151
Plate 22	Heavy transport, San Pedro	152
Plate 23	Rural home and milpa, San Pedro	153
Plate 24	Church wedding, San Marcos	222
Plate 25	Indians, Comitancillo	287
Plate 26	Funeral procession, San Pedro	329

Maps

Map 1	Western Guatemala	16
Map 2	Topography of Western Guatemala	17

Foreword

In *Inverse Images* John Hawkins challenges an ethnological tradition that has governed Mesoamerican studies for more than fifty years. He challenges that corpus of reporting and interpretation on the fundamental grounds of the unit of ethnographic study, on the interpretation of cultural diversity, on the meaning of Indian and non-Indian in the region, and finally on how to account for the observed differences in culture and social structure throughout the area of Mesoamerica.

Such a broad and sweeping assault on the wide consensus that usually pervades reports and interpretations of Mesoamerican societies and cultures must of course rest on a series of concepts, ideas, and modes of interpretation which, in some deep sense, is at odds with the theory and conceptual apparatus that produced the body of interpretation that Hawkins confronts.

First, Hawkins uses the current notion of "culture" to focus his observations. His use of the concept of culture intends a semiotic stance—attention to a set of meanings held by actors rather than to behaviors or artifacts used and displayed by the people studied. This use of culture as meaning, as man-made meaning, and as somehow finally definitive, if not wholly so, of action systems is certainly the regnant idea in contemporary anthropology. But Hawkins errs when he excoriates earlier anthropologists for holding a "behavioral" view of culture. He describes Redfield's idea of culture as centering on "act and artifact," i.e., a materialist or behavioralist conceptual stance. But this is only half so. Redfield in fact defined culture as "conventional understandings *manifest* in act and artifact." "Conventional understandings," though the term is not 1980s trendy, certainly focuses on meanings, on the social construction of reality out of the historical materials available. In any event, Hawkins's rigorous attention to culture as meaning is salutary (whatever his unclear position on symbols is) and certainly makes clear the base of his argument.

On the unit of study in Mesoamerica, Hawkins says the community study, treated as a social isolate, is inadequate to illuminate cultural and social diversity. Certainly, he argues, using communities as units of comparison for generalization will lead and has led to spurious or empty generalization. This criticism has some force, and there are ethnologists who have mechanically used the community study as though it were a tribal entity, just as there have been ethnologists like Schultze-Jena who have invented social entities like the "Quiché" on the basis of extracting traits from a series of Quiché-speaking Indians *municipios* that had no social existence in common. But, again, Hawkins is a bit overzealous, as all reformers must be, in overlooking those ethnologists who did not confuse the locus of study with the focus of the problem studied.

The problem turns on what sense an investigator assigns to separate communities (culturally distinct-socially bounded) which are nonetheless interconnected. Or the extent to which distinct local units are part of a larger social and perhaps cultural system. The vexed problem of *pars pro toto* is not solved by Hawkins but restated in a manner sure to generate interest and new formulation.

The boldest, and hence most startling and controversial, ideas of this book are the positions taken on the terms "Indian" and "Ladino" and their interconnections, and, in fact, the origin and maintenance of these terms. Hawkins's radical position is that now Indian and Ladino form a single continuum, not distinct or separate cultural traditions. The "culture" of the Indians is seen as a status culture of the exploited and the oppressed. The analogy Hawkins uses is that of a "status dictionary" in which everybody has the same grammar and structure but there are lexical differences stemming from position in an agreed upon and well-defined hierarchy. This works for language, i.e., a single language has status variants, regional variants, and discernible isoglosses. The question is, Does the analogy fit the facts, data, observations, and self-images of the people of Mesoamerica? I have strong doubts about the utility of the analogy, and I would hold that even if (say) Quiché and Spanish have words in common (through loans and some pidginization), they are clearly separate languages. Just so with Indian communities: they certainly have much in common in the sense of cold hammered cultural traits or face-sheet social data with Ladinos, but this does not diminish the separateness (socially) nor the distinctiveness (culturally) of Indians from Ladinos in objective fact and in subjective apprehension by the people of Mesoamerica.

But there is no sense arguing categories. The proof is the productive generation of ideas, concepts and testable hypotheses. It is in the area of explanation (or interpretation) that Hawkins is at both his most novel and his most speculative. The differences between Indians and Ladinos in Mesoamerica stem from the colonial situation and the processes set in motion by the Spanish conquest and domination of the Indian populations. The "inferiority" of Indians was established by Spanish ideology that imputed to Indians cultural traits, attitudes, motivations, and characters which were the exact opposite of those of the dominant and exploitative Spaniards whose descendants in the main are today's Ladinos. The Indians came to accept this ideology, and the differences between Indians and Ladinos rest on this use of symbols of ethnic origins to perpetuate a set of hierarchical relations.

The sweep of this hypothesis (or interpretation) leaves one breathless. Hawkins takes the interpretation to the Andes, and it seems to be powerful in accounting for the Indian-Mestizo division in Peru. He also does a brief comparative review against Jamaica, where, it seems, the black population is the inverse of the English settler dominant group. The differences in Jamaica seem to be other than Mesoamerican and to be explained not by differences in native or indigenous cultures but by the image of opposites foisted by the dominant on the subordinate peoples. The Philippines, in his terms, will be a test case of the inverse image of colonial domination making for ethnic categories. Indonesia and a host of other places are also possible testing grounds for Hawkins's sweeping reinterpretation of historical and cultural processes in Mesoamerica.

I think a clear distinction among ideology, stereotype and culture would go a long way toward clearing up many of the ambiguities, inconsistencies, and apparent paradoxes in Hawkins's formation. However, a bold, outrageous hypothesis based on careful field work can stir the juices in ethnologists and even cause the reexamination and perhaps reaffirmation of a long tradition.

Manning Nash
University of Chicago

Acknowledgments

Scholarship, like art, creates in relationship to the existing works of others. I thus owe much to those cited in the references to this book and in a prior discussion of the literature (Hawkins 1983). On a more personal basis, I thank Ruth Benedict, whose lucid *Patterns of Culture* attracted me to anthropology; Merlin Myers, whose masterful teaching charged my undergraduate years with the excitement and insight of social anthropology; Raymond T. Smith, whose publications, teaching, counsel, and criticism anchored my graduate work; and Manning Nash, likewise, for guidance, teaching, and encouragement.

Raymond Smith, Rex Cooper, Leslie Dow, Norman B. Schwartz, Carl Kendall, Barbara Tedlock, and Jim Taggart have each read the manuscript at various stages in its development and sent me criticism and encouragement. In particular, both Norman B. Schwartz and Carl Kendall have been enormously supportive.

Marshall Craig's faculty writing seminar at Brigham Young University gave me valuable insights into the craft of writing and rewriting. Suzie Goodfellow assisted by reading and critiquing from an editor's point of view, and Jan Lowman read page proofs. Marilyn Webb supervised the typing and revision process in the college word processing center. Sandra Stein Poore had a splendid talent for consistent copy editing in two languages.

Jim Logan, of the Brigham Young University computing services division, spent the better part of two days rescuing my data file from oblivion when the university sold one system and adopted another. Howard Christensen, Brigham Young University Statistics Department, helped me more correctly phrase some of the statistical inferences. Merrill K. Ridd, professor of geography at the University of Utah, and Renee M. Ridd entered the data necessary for creating the topographic projection of part of western Guatemala. They used the Harvard ASPEX Mapping Program.

Fieldwork became a family affair. Carol Lee Hawkins gained the confidence of many women. Her interviews, casually gleaned native comments, and resulting insights add appreciably to this study, as have her encouragement, editorial efforts, and sporadic typing. Our blonde three year old, Claire, was known and loved throughout San Pedro and San Marcos. Indeed, I was readily welcomed into home after home, once they realized I was "el papá de Clarita." This proved most valuable in my census work, where only three houses in San Pedro and one house in San Marcos refused to let her (and me) in for a census discussion.

My greatest debt is to the Guatemalans who shared their lives with me. In addition, one assistant typed several hundred pages of colonial records, and four local college students helped me faithfully in census work. Political events in Guatemala have made the possible consequences of thanking these friends by name uncertain. So they go unnamed but not unappreciated.

Several institutions financially supported my work. A National Science Foundation graduate fellowship allowed me to prepare for study in Guatemala. The University of Chicago Department of Anthropology and Committee on Latin American Studies funded preliminary research in Guatemala during the summer of 1971 and absorbed a fairly large computer bill. The National Institute of Mental Health supported the main field research, conducted in Guatemala between February 13, 1973, and June 12, 1974. Employment at Brigham Young University enabled me to write and refine my thinking on various topics. Brigham Young University also apportioned generous sums for computer work, for typing the now numberless drafts, and for three trips to Guatemala in 1975, 1978, and 1979.

At Brigham Young University, Merlin Myers and John Sorenson, successive chairpersons of the Department of Anthropology; Stan Taylor, director of the Center for International and Area Studies; and Martin Hickman, dean of the College of Family, Home, and Social Sciences, have all been supportive.

I have supplied all the translations of archival documents, informant statements, and Spanish publications. Though trite, those who have written will understand: the errors and shortcomings of this work are entirely my own, while its strengths, such as they may be, had their genesis in others.

Part I

Theory and History for the Understanding of Guatemala

1
Perspectives on Guatemala

Guatemala challenges anthropological theories with an extraordinary mosaic of social contrasts. The most obvious expression of this diversity exists among the Indians, whose "non-Western" clothing, crafts, agricultural practices, and even language vary from town to town and from region to region as the colored tiles vary in a mosaic. Additional diversity comes from the Ladinos, the country's symbolically "Westernized" and politically dominant ethnic sector.[1] Unlike the Indians, Ladinos, through their shared "Western" clothing style and a single language, display a commonality with each other that varies through class distinctions more than by regional differences. But throughout the country, people of each ethnic category conform their lives to different tempos and premises, bringing marked contrasts into even the small towns and countryside where the preponderance of Indians may at first glance give the appearance of homogeneity. How does one deal with such diversity? What is the nature of Guatemalan society?

Anthropologists have supplied answers to these questions in a few rather distinctive ways, each way conditioned by a particular theoretical focus. Thus, to evaluate our understanding of Guatemala, we must look closely at the issue of theory and ferret out the implications of the assumptions that underlie the theories. To be sure, the focus of this book is on Guatemala. But the theories that have been brought to bear on Guatemalan life were not developed exclusively within the bounds of that nation. Rather, they have largely come from outside Guatemala.

There are several reasons why this should be so. First, the original Spanish colony, the Kingdom of Guatemala, included both Chiapas and Guatemala as well as the rest of Central America. Chiapas, therefore, is a relatively recent accession to Mexico and is, sociologically, more like most of Guatemala than it is like most of Mexico. As a result, anthropological studies of Chiapas, especially Mayan Chiapas, shed valuable light on Guatemala. Second, Mesoamerica—

essentially the homeland of the once high Indian civilizations—and not Guatemala has been the early conceptual unit of the anthropologists. As a consequence, the development of anthropological thought emerges with some clarity if one links studies from throughout Mesoamerica. Again there is historical and sociological reasonableness to the concept of Mesoamerica, in spite of the region's obvious diversity. There were the commonalities of pre-Columbian state systems, as well as much communication, and there was the essentially similar mode of Spanish conquest and control throughout the region. Thus, while this book is *focused* on two towns in Guatemala—San Marcos and San Pedro Sacatepéquez—it is theoretically *rooted* in Mesoamerica. Understanding the complexity of Guatemala obligates me to treat briefly more than just Guatemala, especially with regard to the sources of theory.

The early anthropology of Mesoamerica and Guatemala tended to focus on the community. Within the community, the anthropologists explored the lifeways of one of the two ethnic segments in any community or region: the Ladinos and the Indians. For the most part, the anthropologists concentrated their studies on the Indians. Indians were, after all, a people with a distinctive lifeway, a culture. There are, of course, recent valuable works in the community-study style focused on the Indian. But the focus on Indians, as I show in *Heritage of Conquest: Thirty Years Later* (Hawkins 1983), was a product of a definition of culture that identified behavior—"act and artifact" (Redfield 1941:152)—as culture, the source of distinctiveness. This concentration on distinctiveness led to a conceptual separation of the Ladino and the Indian. Thus, Redfield, in his monumental regional study, *The Folk Culture of Yucatán* (1941), came to see Ladino-Indian relations as an acculturation or flow of act and artifact assimilation across a cultural gulf bridged by the continuum of acculturative change. The initial assumption that culture is behavior—a lifeway—separated Indians and Ladinos because Indians and Ladinos behaved differently and looked different. But the separation was counterproductive, for in important ways Ladinos and Indians were intimately bound together.

Thus a changed focus emerged in anthropology. Indians and Ladinos, though different, were next seen as essentially intertwined because Ladinos hold political power and economic advantage over the Indians. Anthropologists explored these linkages between Indians and Ladinos with several models. For example, Aguirre Beltrán (1967) sees the Indians as cultural refugees, who preserve where possible their behavioral distinctiveness through isolation in mountainous redoubts of Chiapas and Guatemala. Colby and van den Berghe (1969) see the Indians as a segment of a plural society: they keep their autonomy in their distinctive family institutions and in some distinctive ritual but are otherwise subordinate in politics, economics, and orthodox Catholic institutions. Stavenhagen (1970) sees the Indians as an internal colony, maintained as underdeveloped dependents by the Ladino overlords in the interests of national and international capitalism.

These studies more accurately portray the circumstances and consequences of the political, economic, and social subordination of the Indians. Yet, paradoxically, while these studies identify the Indian as distinctive because of traditional behavior, the Indian tends to disappear, especially in the internal-colonialism analyses; the emphasis on structural subordination and underprivilege dissolves the Indians into a vast underclass. Situationally, this emphasis makes the Indians like other powerless peasant agriculturalists.[2]

The plural-society model, though, escapes this conflation by simultaneously highlighting the ethnic distinction and behavioral difference of Indians, especially in the domestic domains of their lives. But are the domestic lives of Indians and Ladinos separate just because they are distinctive? Or is plural-society separation induced by the definition that culture is behavior? In this book, I suggest that the continued use of a behavioral definition of culture has forced the plural-society analysts to see the domestic difference when there is in fact functional complementarity in the many domains of the domestic, political, economic, and social lives of Ladinos and Indians. More important, I will show that the Indians and Ladinos are not only socially interlocked—in political, economic, and ecclesiastic institutions—but that Indians and Ladinos are culturally interlocked. They hold inverse ethnic ideologies and as such are co-participants in an encompassing culture. Conceptualizing Ladinos and Indians within a single culture depends, however, on a nonbehavioral definition of culture.[3]

Culture: An Ideological System

Culture is at once the guiding concept of anthropology and the source of many of anthropology's weaknesses. As James Boon (1973:1) put it, the culture concept is a center "of and for debate, . . . difficult to talk about and impossible to agree upon." To avoid the liabilities of the behavioral view of culture, I use a more restricted definition of culture—one that focuses on ideas. *Culture* is here defined as "a structured system of ideas." This definition of culture can be more clearly understood by comparing and contrasting it with those of David Schneider, Raymond Smith, Clifford Geertz, and Ward Goodenough.

In Schneider's work, culture is defined as a "system of symbols and meanings." Schneider elaborates this phrase. For "symbols and meanings" he offers "ultimate values, the collective representations" (Schneider 1976:208), the "basic premises," the "units" of life, their "order or classification," and the "parts" and "premises" with which the world is structured (Schneider 1972:38). Schneider has been a major source of my definition of culture.

The word *symbols,* however, is present in Schneider's definition but absent in mine. Throughout his writings on culture, Schneider persuasively asserts that behavior must be kept analytically separate from culture. Unfortunately, the word *symbol* frequently refers to behavior that is patterned and meaningful, what Milton Singer (1972) has termed "cultural performances." However, the idea that symbols are a part of culture focuses our attention on the devices used to portray a system of ideas rather than on the system of ideas itself. If used in this way, the inclusion of symbols in the definition of culture contradicts Schneider's dictum of the separation of behavior and culture.

This conflation in symbols of culture and behavior appears to be the central issue behind Raymond Smith's concern with culture as a system of ideas and not with the particular forms by which the system is represented. Lauding Schneider (1968) for his "fruitful" separation of "cultural symbols" from "norms," Smith affirms that the cultural level consists of "the most basic ideas about the nature of kinship"; thus, Smith sees "the idea" of "the nuclear family as a cultural symbolic system" standing as a "fundamental assumption" or "conception" that is "embodied in religious doctrine and symbolism." But Smith separates the "idea" from its "vivid images," so that "cultural symbol" "refer[s] to the very elementary ideas which define what kinship is" (Smith 1970:57-58). One can see here an attempt to disentangle the idea or conceptual system from the symbolic or presentational system, although the attempt is partially obscured by Smith's use of the phrase "cultural symbol" to refer to the ideas rather than the symbols.

By contrast, Clifford Geertz's definition of culture sometimes focuses directly on the performance aspect of symbols. Thus, culture is "meanings embodied in symbols," the symbols being "forms by means of which men communicate" (Geertz 1973:89). Too much emphasis on the performance aspect of culture (as symbol) may lead to the dismembering of different statuses within a society.[4] If the members of a particular status perform differently to represent the idea of their differing positions, they might be construed as separate cultures. As we have seen, precisely this tactic dismembered Guatemalan society into the culture of the Ladinos and the many cultures of the Indians. Moreover, the focus on symbolic forms makes it very difficult to compare systems or to speak of, say, a "Mediterranean culture" (Peristiani 1976:1)—a region where parallel ideas are presented through distinct symbols from country to country. To be sure, Geertz elsewhere emphasizes the idea matrix by means of which performances are interpreted, seeing his approach as "semiotic," where "man is an animal suspended in webs of significance," "culture" being "those webs." Thus, the elucidation of culture is "interpretive"; the anthropologist is in search of meaning (Geertz 1973:5). In this perspective Schneider, Smith, Geertz, and Goodenough are in essential agreement. I would simply add that the meanings arise out of the structuring of ideas. Symbols merely help us to perceive the structure by objectifying the relations among the ideas that are tagged to different portions of the symbol, ritual, or cultural performance. But the same structure of ideas may be acknowledged by one segment of a society through reverence for the Holy Family and by another segment through regular attention to the Walton family.[5] In short, I must assert, as Saussure (1959:122) did for language, that culture "is a form and not a substance."

It is precisely a structural and systematic concept of meaning that Redfield lacked, for meaning, or in his words "significance" or "understanding," was attached to individual things, whether acts or objects. This approach deprives ideas of structural relations to each other. Saussure, however, provides the roots of a structural approach to meaning.[6]

According to Saussure, the meaning of a linguistic sign is not intrinsic to a single sign but arises out of a system of relations within the entire corpus of other signs. Furthermore, the sense or "value" of a term is a product of a kind of negation. Meanings often arise out of binary opposition. In more complex sets of signs, the meaning of one term is a kind of leftover or remainder in relation to the other terms. Thus, Saussure (1959:14) observes, "language is a system of interdependent terms in which the value of each term results solely from the simultaneous presence of the others." In the process, "words used to express related ideas limit each other reciprocally" (Saussure 1959:116). In discussing French synonyms, Saussure notes that *"redouter* 'dread,' *craindre* 'fear,' and *avoir peur* 'be afraid,' " "have value only through their opposition: if *redouter* did not exist, all its content would go to its competitors" (Saussure 1959:116). Moreover, Saussure observes the reverse process: in English, the adoption of *mutton* took the food aspect away from the meanings once attached to *sheep*. "Concepts are purely differential and defined not by their positive content but negatively by their relations with the other terms of the system. Their most precise characteristic is in being what the others are not" (Saussure 1959:117). If I may use my own metaphor, the value of a sign is achieved in a process that parallels the expansion of several small balloons within a larger container, each balloon inflating into the unoccupied semantic space. The space becomes wholly occupied, and the balloons shape each other in a single system.

Subsequent research has shown that even binary opposition is a highly complex phenomenon. In dealing with two-term paradigmatically opposite signs (high-low, white-black, man-woman, and the like), Linda Waugh (n.d.), following Jakobson, has noted that distinctive-feature opposition in the Lévi-Straussian sense of plus and minus features is not usually correct. Rather, one member of the polar opposition is either unmarked or negatively marked, while the other term is positively marked. Thus, in the set [man, woman], [man] in its unmarked, superordinate status may refer to either a male or a female person. [Woman] is the marked or restricted term, referring only to a female. [Man] used in the environment of [woman] takes negative marking as the opposite of the positively restricted term, in short, a [non-woman]. These are exemplified, for example, in "Man cannot live by bread alone" versus "First a woman ascended in the elevator and then a man." The latter sentence is marked by opposition; in the former there is no marking. Further, we note that the unmarked form of the ambiguous term (either unmarked or opposite of marked) may often be replaced by an explicitly neutral term, in this case [person].

A second source of meaning consists of the syntagmatic relations generated by language. Syntactic rules bring lexical concepts into relationships with each other. Sometimes the relationships may be anomalous because of incompatible feature structures of the syntactically joined lexical items. Thus, "He is a good man" is permissible, while "He is a good woman" is usually not permissible.[7] It is usually discordant. Yet it is sayable, and, if it is ungrammatical, it is ungrammatical in quite a different sense from "Man good a is he."

These notes do not pretend to be a full explication of meaning. Yet it is certain that meanings are not individually attached to single-sign vehicles. Rather, meanings or ideas arise out of oppositions among a set of ideas. This is the essential Saussurian notion: though each term and each context are different and unique, no term and no context have meaning or significance in and of themselves. The meaning of any term derives from the paradigmatic oppositions and syntagmatic contexts considered as a total system.

The Structure of Guatemalan Culture

The Saussurian approach to meaning can be applied to Guatemala, though the overview of Guatemalan culture and society in the remainder of this chapter must be considered merely a sketch. First, the people are subdivided into the basic social categories of *ladino* and *indígena*. The categories are conceptual opposites in several senses: race, social status, occupation, and education. Each ethnic sector is frequently defined as those people bearing the opposite or negation of some characteristic of the other. While the term *ladino* in its unmarked form does not encompass *indígena*, its relation of markedness with respect to *indígena* is interesting. In its general sense, *ladino* is unmarked for status. Thus, a ladino can be either high or low status, a president or a peasant. *Indian*, however, is marked as low status. Nevertheless, in the environment of a discussion of Indians, Ladino is the opposite of the marked low status. Thus, Ladino is also high status, especially in the western half of the country, where Indians are more contrastively present.

A similar pattern emerges in the concept of urban affiliation. Ladinos are unmarked as to urban residence and may be either city-wise urbanites or country peasants. This is most obviously the case in eastern Guatemala, where Ladino peasants abound. Indians, however, are marked as peasants, as rural, uneducated, manual laborers.[8] In the environment of a discussion of Indians, Ladinos are urban, urbane, and professional, depending on whether the rural residence, the education, or the agricultural occupation of the peasant is the issue in focus.

This conceptual structure carries several social implications. First, the city itself is the symbolic manifestation of the urban ideology attached to high status. Thus, the city, especially the capital city, guts the hinterland of its human resources as individuals move to capture the symbols of central high status. This is manifest in absentee *finca* landlordism at one end of the social scale, where high-status Ladinos can hardly bear to live on their rural estates. It is manifest in the vacant-town phenomenon at the other of the social scale, where low-status Indians move to the rural lands and outer edges of even the tiny villages. The oppositional marking within the entire system is further manifest in the process of ladinoization that tends to affect the Indians who leave their marginal *municipios*[9] and move to the larger town centers. Finally, those who no longer wish to be Indian move, usually toward a larger urban center or to the symbolically Ladino lowlands. In each case, people are integrating their categorical social status with their symbolic productions in actual circumstance.

Attached to these opposed social statuses of Indian and Ladino is a system of inverse ideologies. The inversions of ideology correspond to the mutual negations of Ladino and Indian as marked categories. The Ladino orients toward the city, to the center, to power, and despises manual labor. The Indian orients to the field, the *campo*, the periphery. He flees power and sees manual labor not only as his lot but as his preference. To be sure, the wealthy Indian may hire others to add to the work accomplished, but the result is to hire others to work with him as much as to work for him. There is no added shame in a return to the earth with implement in hand.

The ideological oppositions run deeper yet. Attached to Ladino status is an ideology of social interconnection. The Ladinos both tend to have and intend to seek out protections and favors through a system of friends. Indians, on the other hand, are more apt to isolate themselves. Ruben Reina (1959), for example, has noted the inability of Indians to form multiple or enduring friendships, in contrast with the multiple linkages among Ladinos. Indeed, Indians evince an ideology of disconnection or atomization, preferring to do things on their own, as separate family households and as politically unprotected and largely unassisted local communities. Ladinos, by contrast, involve the government, seek out help, and cultivate many personal ties.

Indians are not only the marked category; they are also restricted.

To be sure, the restrictions on the Indians were worse in the colonial period, yet sharp constraints remain. At least in western Guatemala, the Indians of the peripheral agricultural communities are forcibly recruited for nonofficer military service. Such is not the fate of the Ladinos, except, perhaps, the near derelict. The restrictedness of Indians is further manifest in the political domain in the Indian's orientation to a closed corporate community. In the domestic domain, Indian restrictedness is manifest in community endogamy and in precise rules of postmarital residence. In the domain of religion, Indian men participate more than Ladino men. Whether as orthodox or as unorthodox Catholics, Indian men and women have manifested their restrictive submission (Warren 1978) to Catholic government through symbols of suffering. As individuals they have traditionally supported the fiesta system in a structural parallel of *encomienda* taxation and *repartimiento* labor service.

Ladinos, by contrast, conceive of themselves as fluid and adaptable. They are unrestricted and ideally (but only in contrast with Indians) above the law. Ladino friendships are open; Ladino political affiliations span the nation; Ladino marriages link communities; Ladino postmarital residence is conditional upon self-interest. Ladino religious participation—a symbol of subordination as well as of restrictedness—is considerably downplayed among the Ladino men, though thoroughly appropriate to the subordinate and submissive status of Ladino women.

The system of ideologies is symbolically manifest in the patterns of indexical behavior such as clothing use and language preference. In clothing, Indians are, at the first level of categorization, uniform from individual to individual and varied from community to community.[10] Ladinos, on the other hand, are varied from individual to individual within a community and uniform from community to community. Similarly, Ladinos speak one language across many communities, while Indians speak distinct languages from region to region and, at least for the Mams, each *municipio* community is distinguishable by subtle dialect differences. Taken as a whole, the system symbolizes the underlying ideologies of Ladino interconnection versus Indian atomization. The inversions of Ladino and Indian are pervasive and systematic.

Certainly I am not the first to note such contrasts between Ladino and Indian. John Gillin's (1952) *Heritage of Conquest* article, "Ethos and Cultural Aspects of Personality," is a masterful display of such ideological oppositions. For convenience I present the many points of contrast in his analysis in tabular form in Appendix 1.A. Here, suffice it to say that Gillin found multiple oppositions in politics, economics, family, and religion. Indeed, his language is laced with words connoting structural opposition: "in contrast," "on the other hand," "quite the opposite is true of." Other sentences balance on a comma, contrasting one group with the other. Yet he maintained that the cultures were distinct. Gillin presumably did not see the single-system implications of the pattern because, like Redfield, he treated the meanings of each ethnic segment in isolation, as attributes attached to objects or behavior (Gillin 1952:205). Furthermore, for Gillin, behavior was typed, discrete, and elemental, and diacritically characterized a culture's participants. "San Luís," he says, "happens to be a community which contains both Indians and Ladinos, each still preserving separate and distinguishable cultures" (Gillin 1952:195).

Others have seen the oppositions, too. Manning Nash, for example, speaks of the sharp distinction between the national perspective of Ladinos and the local perspective of Indians and further develops the idea in his "Political Relations in Guatemala" (1958b). What presumably prevented Nash from viewing diverse political interests as systems of inverse-status ideologies is his assumption that the differences come from "two distinct cultural traditions." Thus, the too easy assumption of origins, the idea of a "cultural cleavage," and the apparent equation of *distinct* and *different* with *separate* precluded the observation of a single cultural system that systematically relates the different ethnic perspectives and behavior. In these respects, Nash fell heir to the limitations that had blocked Redfield from seeing a single system in the beliefs of the supposedly dual cultures. Even Alexander Moore, in his excellent comparative study of Atchalán ethnicity in the national context, did not capitalize on the inversions he detailed between the Ladino's track to social glory through patronage networks and social interconnection among individuals versus the Indian's track to prestige through categorical advancement as a disconnected member of a group (Moore 1973). It appears that Moore did not perceive the unity in the oppositions in his monograph because he, too, focused on culture in the behavioral sense of "careers" and "lifelong processes" rather than on the "premises" or "images" to which he also attends (Moore 1973:1, 4, 5, 70).[11]

But the Saussurian perspective of meaning analysis forces us to a quite different conclusion. First, culture is a system of meanings. Second, meaning arises from a system of oppositions. Therefore, categories of opposite meaning are elements of the same culture. Since Indian and Ladino are opposed categories and take meaning by reference to each other, they are elements of the same culture. Moreover, these categories are structured in a status hierarchy. Associated with these status-linked positions of Indian and Ladino are two sets of basic premises about how to live one's life. These I have called *status ideologies*. According to Schneider's definition of culture, status ideologies constitute a portion of the cultural system, for they establish the basic premises of world view. Inasmuch as these status ideologies are also opposed to each other in a systematic pattern of inversions or negations, they, too, constitute elements in the same culture. They take their meaning from their relationship to each other.

The apparent variability of Guatemalan institutions arises from the differentiating impact of the inverse-status ideologies on the various institutions of each status group. Thus, as we shall see later in this book, the Ladino ideology penetrates their domestic institutions, giving them extension and flexibility. On the other hand, the Indian ideology penetrates their domestic system, giving it narrowed, inflexible, and restrictive characteristics. But the resulting differences are parts of a single system. Not in spite of their differences, but rather because their differences are opposed and structured as they are, Ladinos and Indians are distinctive and yet members of a single culture.

In this book, I attempt to unravel some of the enigmas of Guatemalan society by exploring the structures that exist among the ideas, social relations, and behavior of Ladinos and Indians, considered as a whole. While the fieldwork and therefore the main example of this book comes from two towns in western Guatemala—San Marcos and San Pedro Sacatepéquez—the argument is intended to be general. To support the assertion of generality, I have included an extensive presentation of similar inversions between the Ladinos and the Pocomam Indians of eastern Guatemala (Appendix 1.A), and between the Ladinos and Cakchiquel Indians of central Guatemala (Appendix 1.B). In addition, in several chapters, I show parallels between the area I studied and other reports in the literature on Guatemala and, more generally, on Mesoamerica. In the vocabulary of Saussure, I shall show that we can understand more of Guatemala by analyzing the two ethnic sectors together as a "form," rather than separately as "substances." To proceed on firm footing, though, I must define what is meant by *ethnic* and *ethnicity* in this book.

Ethnicity as Origin Symbolism

Ethnicity, as Max Weber long ago emphasized, is subjective. It is a meaning system rather than an objective condition of life. In his view, ethnic groups are

> human groups that entertain a subjective belief in their common descent because of similarities of physical type or of customs or both, or because of memories of colonization and migration; this belief must be important for the propagation of group formation. (Weber 1968:I:389)

Clearly, we must follow Weber's lead and focus on the subjective, mental aspects of ethnicity rather than concentrate on the objective conditions. But Weber's focus on subjective "belief in . . . common descent" is problematic. One grants that there must be belief in distinctiveness and that such belief is subjective since the truth or falsity of the claimed descent or origin is irrelevant.

But what is the status of the "belief" of a Guatemalan who in one breath says he is a pure descendant of the Conquistadors and Ladino, and in the next asserts he has Indian blood? Moreover, Guatemalans frequently make claims about their blood and origins that they also admit are not objectively true. Yet other Guatemalans subjectively switch their ethnic affiliation entirely, changing from Indian to Ladino.

One avoids the problem of having to decide whether stated beliefs are actually believed if one asserts that the critical subjective feature is not the *belief* in origins but the *use* of those origins as *symbols*. The question is, symbols of what? I define *ethnicity* as the use of origin-linked symbols to claim or attribute place and ideology in a social-status hierarchy.

Armed with two ideas—of culture as a structure of ideas and of ethnicity as the use of origin symbols for hierarchical relations—I can now explore the cultural order and ethnic nature of Guatemalan society. To do so, I shall first describe briefly the physical environment, agricultural conditions, and social setting of Guatemala. This sketch provides the essential staging for an understanding of my particular field site of San Marcos and San Pedro, for to understand these towns one must see their placement in the country as a whole and especially their relation to the capital city and to the rich southern coast.

Guatemala: An Overview

PHYSICAL GEOGRAPHY, CLIMATE, AND
AGRICULTURAL RELATIONS

Guatemala sits like a misshapen boot at the foot of southern Mexico. Traversed from west to east by a belt of mountains, the country divides reasonably well into three zones: the south coast lowlands, the central highlands, and the northern Petén lowlands.

Guatemala City, the country's capital, almost exactly divides the eastern and western halves of the mountain belt. Like most Latin American capitals, Guatemala City has grown at a phenomenal rate, at the social and economic expense of the hinterland. Indeed, the city has captured more than 20 percent of the country's population. Having used up the flat land of the valley floor and engulfed towns to the east and west on the hillsides, the city fingers its way along the ridge tops to the north and south, the poor building cardboard-and-tin shantytowns in the otherwise unwanted ravines.

Guatemala City is the focus of the country: the center of government, the center of industry, the center of commerce, the center of education, the center of roads and transportation, the center of prestige. As the center, Guatemala City reaches out and impacts upon the country's hinterland regions—indeed, the whole country is a hinterland colony of the capital city. Thus, Guatemala City, its political apparatus, economy, and the intervening road network have a decided impact upon San Marcos and San Pedro Sacatepéquez, located in the mountains of the westernmost Department of San Marcos.

The main axis of western-highland transportation is a single paved road extending from Guatemala City to Quezaltenango, Huehuetenango, and the Mexican border. Paved spurs connect to most department centers and to a few other towns. The longest of these spurs extends fifty kilometers from Quezaltenango to my field site of San Pedro Sacatepéquez and nearby San Marcos. Beyond these few paved highways, gravel roads and jeep tracks connect almost every highland community, most often to a departmental government center or to the closest town on the road to the center.

The western highlands is the principal redoubt of today's Indian

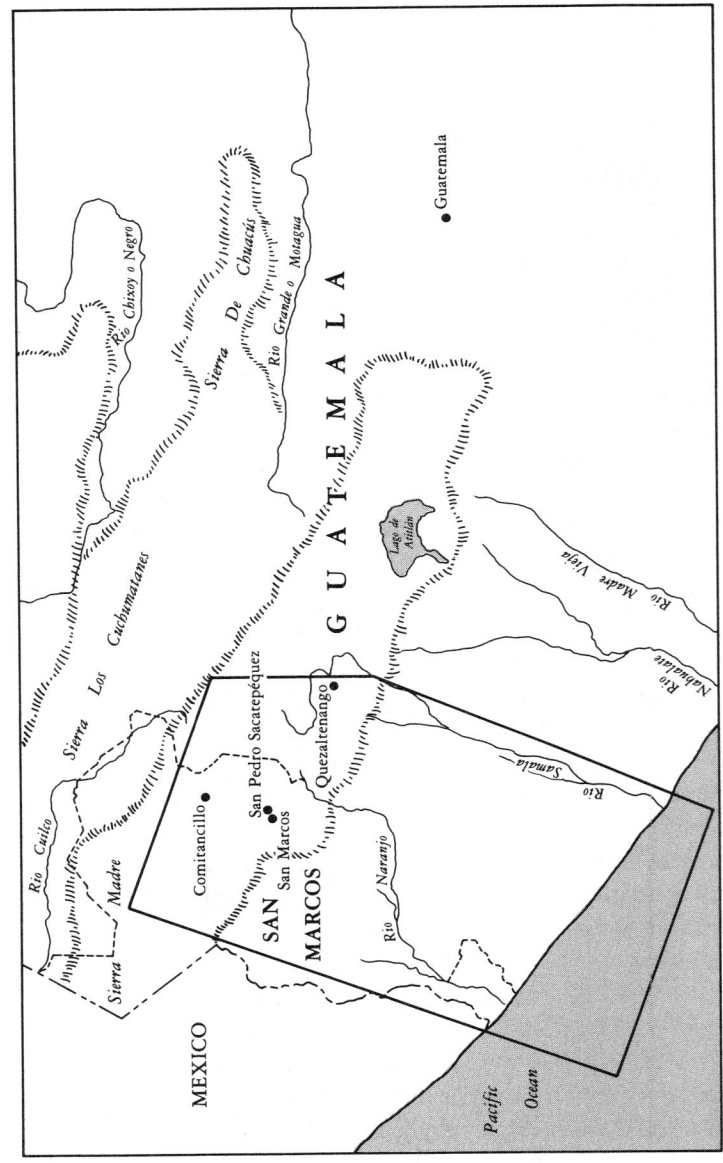

Map 1. Western Guatemala (see Map 2 for inset area).

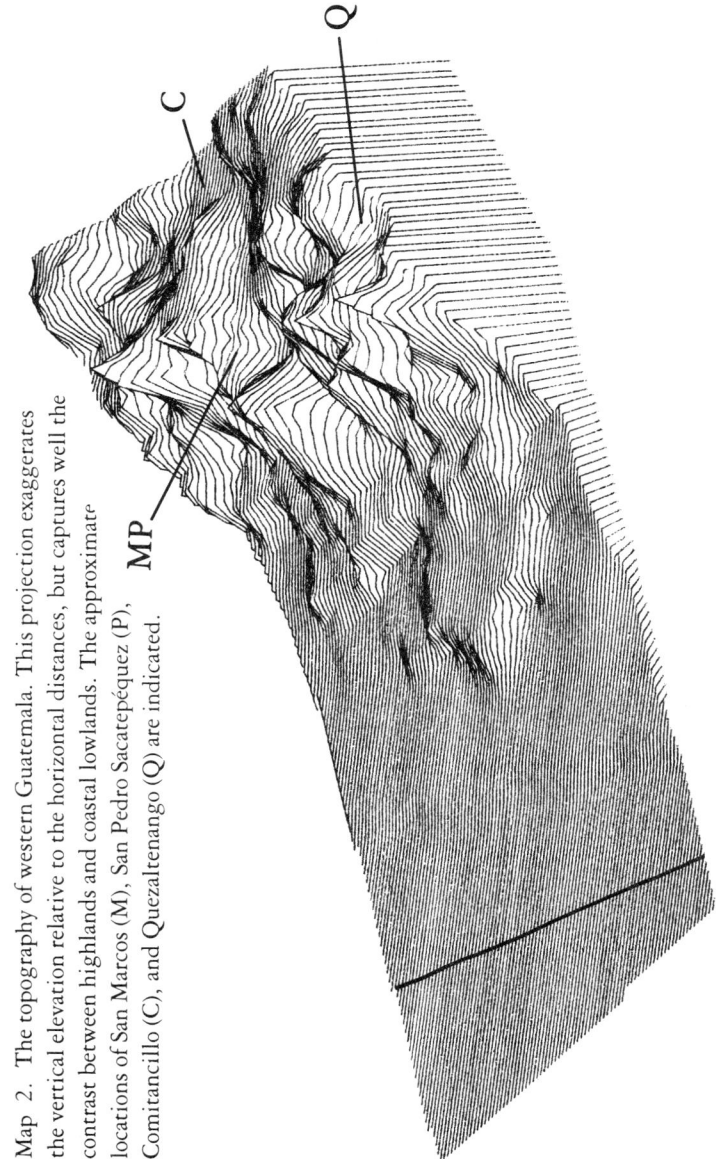

Map 2. The topography of western Guatemala. This projection exaggerates the vertical elevation relative to the horizontal distances, but captures well the contrast between highlands and coastal lowlands. The approximate locations of San Marcos (M), San Pedro Sacatepéquez (P), Comitancillo (C), and Quezaltenango (Q) are indicated.

peoples. Within this zone, a diversity of languages in addition to Spanish and a variety of clothing styles in addition to what is conveniently termed "Western" uniquely identify the many *municipios*. There are pockets of Indian population beyond this region—on the south coast, to the east of the capital, and in the Petén. But in these regions, Indians do not constitute a numerical majority of the population as they do in the western highlands.

In addition to the nation's capital, one other region of the country has a major impact on San Marcos and San Pedro, as well as on the rest of the mountainous "Indian" western highlands: the south coast. The south coast contrasts sharply with the mountainous highlands. The region is relatively flat (especially toward the Pacific Ocean), tropically humid, and hot. The entire region is extensively served by paved highways, gravel roads, jeep tracks, and paths. Indeed, the south coast region is much more densely interconnected than the starburst hierarchy of one-road access that links Indian communities in the highlands, where a community usually connects to the center by only one road and offers connection to its hinterland or to more remote municipalities by a starburst of trails and one or two roads.[12]

The westernmost two-thirds of the coastal plain supports an intensive export agriculture because of its high rainfall and tropical temperature. Near the seashore, the great estates produce cotton and raise cattle. Between the coastal flats and the volcanoes, cattle and sugarcane occupy the undulating alluvial fans. Interspersed with these cattle and sugar estates are a few rubber plantations; citrus, pineapple, and banana groves; and the ubiquitous plots of corn. Close to the volcanic upthrust, where the elevation exceeds three hundred meters, and continuing up the mountainsides to an elevation of about fifteen hundred meters, lucrative coffee plantations predominate. This region is known as the *boca costa*.

The lowland rural area is well populated, with large estates *(fincas)* predominating throughout. Most of these support the full-time or part-time residence of the owners *(dueños)* and a sometimes sizable collection of resident laborer/sharecroppers *(colonos)*. The *fincas* are serviced by two types of communities. One type provides major services and government and is usually a department capital. The other provides labor and consists of proletarian laborers, freeholders, petty-service operators, and shopkeepers. Occasionally, one finds an Indian hamlet inhabited by the descendants of a particular highland community that purchased or occupied the land, usually in the last one hundred years.[13]

Two paved roads give access to the western and central highlands from the south coast. Each road rises steeply to the highland plateau. In addition, eight secondary roads, as well as numerous foot trails, connect the highlands and the coast. These roads channel the main interactions between the south coast and the highlands, for down them flow the truckloads of Indian laborers that pick coffee and cotton on the Ladino *fincas* or plant their own corn on rented plots. In return, the Indians take back some cash, some corn, some material goods, and some diseases, the last being the price of making ends meet on the too-small highland Indian plots.

The other regions of the country have had a lesser effect on the Indians of the western highlands. To be sure, where the northern mountains descend into the Petén, coffee picking supplements Indian subsistence much as it does in the south. Farther north, however, the Guatemalan Petén extends over a vast, relatively uninhabited tropical flatland, an area of little consequence to the western highlands.[14] Finally, the eastern, predominantly Ladino region of the country appears to have little discernible impact on society in the western highlands.

HIGHLIGHTS OF WESTERN GUATEMALAN SOCIETY

In this context, Guatemalan highland society unfolds in intriguing complexity. Basic to the society, as already noted, is a status division between one sector of the population called *ladino* and another called *indígena*. The division is ethnically marked. The superior Ladinos claim to be of European ancestry and life-style, while the Indians claim to be autochthonous in origin.

Among the Ladinos throughout Guatemala there are class divisions based on wealth and occupation. Yet these Ladinos constitute a social class relatively connected throughout the nation. There are wealth differences among Indians, too, and these differences in wealth make possible the differences in ritual and political service to the community. Yet the focus among Indians is less on wealth than on service. The idea that they are generally poor is conceptually more prominent than the fact that there are differences among them. In practice, the fiesta system, the town religious festivals sponsored by a few appointed individuals, apparently functioned to stabilize class relations among Indians by consuming the excess wealth of the sponsors. Nowadays, the fiesta system, centered around a civil-religious hierarchy of offices, is breaking down in many towns. Partly as a result of this breakdown, wealth differences are becoming more pronounced. But against the larger system, Indians are still considered similar and poor.

So, within the "traditional" Indian community, Indians are of a kind. However, Indians are of a kind only in reference to a particular community; differences in dress, language, and custom divide and distinguish the residents of one community from those of another almost as colorfully as the plumage of birds in a tropical aviary. In contrast to birds, however, Indian women are the more colorful and distinctive, the men in most towns being more subdued.[15]

Politically, Ladinos operate the national institutions. Indians tend to participate only up to the level of the local community and, until recently, only through the mechanism of the civil-religious hierarchy.

Indians are the principal agricultural laborers in the western region. While many hire out to farm the lands of others, most of the Indians also work at least some of their own lands. Their highland crops are substantially different from those of the lowland, partly as a result of the climate and partly as a result of the land-tenure system of predominantly small-plot agriculture. The Indians plant cash-crop vegetables along the south face of the escarpment. Panajachel, Zunil, and Almolonga are well-known centers of this vegetable production. But corn is the predominant crop of most of the highlands. It is often planted with beans. The leguminous beans fertilize the soil while they benefit by climbing the cornstalks. Squash is also planted among the corn and beans. It has been suggested that squash provides ground cover against erosion in a triple symbiosis with corn and beans (Guzmán Böckler 1975:13–14, n. 5), while its broad, ground-covering leaves are recognized by some natives as valuable weed control (Norman B. Schwartz: personal communication). At the higher elevations, wheat competes with corn and serves as a cash crop. The cash sale of wheat has increased dramatically since the introduction of a regional wheat cooperative that buys and stores the crop. Selling wheat makes possible the cash purchase of corn. Above twenty-seven hundred meters, potatoes supplant corn as the principal crop, and sheep graze the uncroppable pastures.

Although the Indians gain a measure of economic independence through their subsistence farming, in other regards they are subordinate to Ladinos in the economic domain. Ladinos control import distribution to the retail level and much of the fixed-location retail in the country. Moreover, Indians have engaged only in partial subsistence agriculture. Whether as a result of legal requirement (in the past) or of land shortage (in the present), Indians have always been constrained to make their labor available to the Ladinos. Indians have also sustained a regional market system, often a weekly rotation around a dominant market and political center. The varied products are carried by foot or mule, and, more and more of late, by truck or bus.

In religion, Ladinos and Indians share Catholicism, though they have distinct differences. Unfortunately, there is no penetrating, theoretically satisfying study of religion and religious symbolism of Guatemala taken as a whole. For Ladinos, the anthropologists make brief reference to the well-known Latin American variety of international Catholicism and determine that it therefore needs no further comment. The anthropologists turn quickly to the more strange and varied practices of the Indians. Thus, from sociologically similar Chiapas, we have excellent descriptions of the civil-religious hierarchy (for example, Cancian [1965]) and of aspects of Indian ritual and symbolism. Moreover, Gary Gossen (1974), Evon Vogt (1976), and others have begun to show the logic in the Indian belief systems. But the degree to which Indian religion interlocks with Ladino religion is not well explored. Yet the possibilities emerge. Indian symbolism often shows their submission to or fear of Ladinolike Earth Lords, a theme expanded on in Kay Warren's *Symbolism of Subordination* (1978).

Family and kinship constitute a further domain of difference. Relatively little work has been done on kinship and not much more on household organization in Guatemala (Gross 1974; Gross and Kendall 1983). It has been observed that Ladinos have a greater interest in kinship connections, yet these phenomena have remained largely unexplained in the Mesoamerican literature.[16]

Compadrazgo is a system of ties established between the parents of a child being initiated to a new social or ritual status and a set of "sponsors" or "godparents" to the child. These relationships bind households to one another in each ethnic sector. Where the ties cross the ethnic boundary, they subordinate Indians to Ladinos in the moral and religious contexts and thus parallel the structure of subordination in politics and economics.

These are the major features of Guatemalan society.[17] Though shorn of detail, this description points to the broad diversity and complexity of the Guatemalan milieu. It is this very complexity that has challenged anthropological analysis both in Guatemala and throughout Mesoamerica. The weakness in meeting the challenge, I suggest, is rooted in the view that culture is behavior, a view that is unable to handle complexities of meaning. To see if the meaning-oriented approach to culture outlined earlier will help, let us return to the beginning and see what we discover using the new perspective.

2
The Historical Context of Guatemalan Culture and Society

The culture and society of present-day Guatemala are foreshadowed in the country's historical origins. Traditionally anthropologists have suggested that these origins are twofold: the Iberian-colonial Spanish source, and the pre-Columbian Mayan influence. These sources of distinctive culture and society were brought together by the Spanish conquest of Latin America. As a result, the cultures mixed. Sometimes this mixing is seen as a fusion or syncretism of cultural elements that led to new social or cultural forms. Sometimes this mixing is seen more as an agglomeration of cultural components, each of which retained its symbolic integrity or formal similarity to its distinctive Spanish or Mayan sources. In either case, some relatively pure Mayan beliefs and practices are said to have devolved to modern times among the Indians, the descendants of the preconquest societies.

This chapter argues against simple notions of cultural syncretism, cultural separatism, or pre-Hispanic cultural continuity among the Indians by suggesting that many of the unique and un-Spanish aspects of Indian culture are an inverse creation of the overlord culture brought to America by the Spaniards. The deep premises of Indian life are a conceptual system primarily forged in response to Conquistador thought and action, rather than a system largely derived from the pristine Mayans and corrupted by subsequent Spanish influence. To continue the metaphor, I suggest that the concepts and ideology of the *conquistadores* were the mold in which Indian concepts and ideology were reshaped, for the Spaniards thought the Indians were different, opposite, and even nonhuman. Thus, as in the foundry, the structure of Indian ideology is a reversal of the structure etched in the Spanish crucible-mold: where one is concave, the other is convex; where one indents, the other protrudes. If Spanish ideology was the mold, the conquest and colonial institutions of *encomienda, reducción,* and *repartimiento* were the fire that melted down the aboriginal culture and society, enabling them to be recast as the Indian culture. The Indian, Martínez Peláez asserts, is a Spanish creation, nonexistent prior to the conquest of the aborigines (1971).

Now there are at least three kinds of evidence necessary if the foundry-mold metaphor is reasonably valid for thinking about Guatemalan culture. First, there must be evidence of social pressure sufficient to cause a softening or meltdown in the aboriginal cultures. Second, there must be enough aspects of point-counterpoint relationship between the two cultures that the mold metaphor is appropriate. Finally, if there is evidence that distinctly different aboriginal cultures became substantially similar under Spanish rule, then the metaphor of the mold is irresistible. All three points are treated in this chapter. The final issue is explored again in the conclusion, where I examine variants of the Spanish conquest in Peru, as well as the meltdown inversion of Jamaican slaves and their modern-day cultural descendants.

Since a casting, however imperfect, has a definite relation to its mold—the mold being temporally, causally, and logically prior—we shall look first to preconquest Spain for insight into the cultural background of present-day Guatemala.

Preconquest Spain

The cultural and social roots of the Spanish colonial enterprise in America lie exposed in the history of fifteenth-century Spain. Although one could trace these roots deep into Spanish history, to the bedrock preliterate period, I will not attempt to press beyond what is needed to picture the Spain that conquered America. Nor will I attempt to tease that Spain's cultural and symbolic systems out of original documents. For an introduction to present-day Guatemala, the central features of culture and society in Spain emerge sufficiently from secondary sources that focus on the period just prior to the discovery of the New World or during its early colonization. Regrettably, one pays a price for easy access to the large number of materials boiled down in secondary sources: the distinctions between category, ideology, symbol, and practice are usually lost. We must, therefore, make do with a more global and less precise notion of culture than that laid out in the previous chapter as we examine the social relations and ideas of the Christian Spaniards.

THE RECONQUEST AND CHRISTIAN SOCIETY

The reconquest of Moorish Spain, *la reconquista,* dominated the ideology and institutions of preconquest Christian Spain. Beginning in A.D. 711, the Islamic Moors *(moros)* invaded Spain and quickly expanded their empire on the Iberian Peninsula (O'Callaghan 1975: 91). Although the idea and goal of a reconquest no doubt appeared shortly after the Islamic invasion, the Moors dominated the battlefields and consolidated their influence until the beginning of the eleventh century. With their victories early in the eleventh century, the Christians began to advance; the balance of power began to shift. For two hundred years more, the two sides felt both victory and defeat. The northern frontier undulated, but time strengthened the Christians while it weakened the Moors. The Spanish Christians consolidated politically and developed the institutions that would conquer. The Moors, on the other hand, increasingly fragmented. Thus, from the turning-point battle of Las Navas de Tolosa in 1212 until the fall of Granada in 1492, successful political, economic, and military institutions backed the consuming ideology of Christian Spain: the long-held dream of *la reconquista* (O'Callaghan 1975). But the task involved more than just reconquering; it required conquering, converting, and then governing the "infidels," the Moorish race. Thus, the reconquest's ideology complexly linked race, religion, ancestry, and political legitimacy.

In contrast with the relative peace and religious freedom of Christians under the Moors, the Christian conquerors introduced religious strife by making religion the crucial symbol of political position. Christianity came to mean superiority and political power. As a result, the Jews and the *muwalladun,* the Iberians who had accepted or been born into Islam during the centuries of Moorish rule, become *(conversos* "converts"). Wealthy Jews and Moors, whether converted or not, entered the Spanish nobility by marriage. Jewish and Islamic adherents who were not so wealthy suffered persecution and pogroms. Thus, social pressures forced the Jews and Moors to become Christians or to otherwise hide. This trend toward conversion began to obscure the once clean separations of race and religion as the basis of political legitimacy.

In part, the Inquisition was an attempt to clarify and restore the structural parallels of race (light and dark), religion (Christian and infidel), and political access (lord and subject). Thus, in the last half of the fourteenth century the Inquisition sought to make Christianity—which had been the motivating symbol of the reconquest—into the pure core of social legitimacy. Indeed, Kamen shows the degree to which the Inquisition was an instrument of political value and concludes that "the Inquisition was neither more nor less than a class weapon, used to impose on all communities of the peninsula the ideology of one class—the lay and ecclesiastical aristocracy" (Kamen 1965:17).[1] The Inquisition brought the ideological order of Catholicism and the political order of Spanish aristocracy into closer structural parallel. According to Kamen, the Inquisition did not create a new cultural or social order among the Christians; it merely purified and consolidated and coordinated ideas and institutions already present.

Thus, the centuries-long penetration of Jewish and Moorish families into the Spanish elite became the dominant concern of the Inquisition. The object was to root out the impurities, especially those of Jewish origins. As a result Spain convulsed, like a patient made sick by the administration of an antibiotic: purified but sterilized and therefore rendered incapable, deprived of those alien life forms that digest the hard substances and cleanse the inner but crucial passages. Spain, too, had her odious tasks and a need for the diversity provided by the Jews and Moors. As a world power Spain died, albeit slowly, in part from her self-administered Inquisitorial purge.

The source of the problem and yet the heart of Spain lay in the use of Christianity as the primary symbol of political orthodoxy and elite status. Of course, this Christianity meant orthodox Spanish Catholicism. Other brands of Christianity were heretical. Thus, the conversion of Jews and Moors to Catholic Christianity quickly became a symbol as well as a requirement of political submission to the Spanish crown. But those who were "old Christians," who had participated through their ancestry in the reconquest, were a more privileged group. Thus, at the same time that Christianity became a symbol of submission, "old Christian" became a distinctive symbol of centrality and right to political access. Beginning in 1483, only "old Christians" could hold office in the Inquisition (Kamen 1965:124). Subsequently, all political offices were restricted to certifiable "old Christians," which further enhanced the value of origins. One needed proof of genealogical purity, documentation that one's ancestry was "old Christian." Such a condition was called "blood purity—*limpieza de sangre.*"

Elements of this complex are manifest in the surviving cultural documents.

> I am a man
> And though of village caste
> I am of pure blood
> And without Jewish or Moorish stain.²

Significantly, the term *villana,* which refers to village status, also links to villainy—*villanía.* Here the impropriety of a scoundrel is closely tied to the nonurban environment. Furthermore, the village link is low in status; otherwise there would be no contradiction that would necessitate "And though . . ." prior to "pure blood." In *Don Quixote,* another piece of period literature, Kamen notes Sancho Panza saying, "I am an old Christian, and to become an earl, that is sufficient." Don Quixote replies, "And more than sufficient" (Kamen 1965:11). In these passages one sees the cultural linkages between "old Christianity" and earldom and between origin, religion, and political office.

But the requirement of racial *cum* religious purity precipitated a crisis within Spain. Long before the Inquisition established the requirement of genealogical proofs for political office, rich Jewish *conversos* had married into the aristocratic Christian families. Many of their noble descendants were blocked from rising within government while peasants, whose genealogies were untraceable, were able to rise (Kamen 1965:121–39). Thus, racial impurity brought about political and social marginalization. This phenomenon of falling lords and rising peasants tended to homogenize the Spanish Catholics. Through the Inquisition, the elite were brought down by the taint of Jewish intrusion, while the humble people were able to rise within the system. However, the Inquisition merely accelerated and institutionalized the consequences of an ideology of social equality that had already been present in Spain. Kamen cites several sources for this characteristically egalitarian aspect of Spanish society. For example:

> Particularly after the elimination of the more dynamic sector of the urban middle class—the Jews—there remained little to separate a lord from his peasant. By the time of Cervantes it was possible to

observe with Don Quixote that "there are two kinds of classes in the world: those who draw and derive their descent from princes and monarchs, and whom time undoes bit by bit until they are totally ruined; and others who take their beginnings from the common people and rise from rank to rank until they become great lords; the difference being that some were what they are no longer and others are what they once were not." With such great social mobility between these two classes, it is not surprising that the lower classes should have considered themselves as good as their betters. As the maiden Dorotea says to her noble lover Fernando in *Don Quixote,* "although a peasant and laboring girl, I consider myself the equal of you who are a lord and knight." (Kamen 1965:18)[3]

Such equality applied only among the "old Christians." Thus, the "old Christians" of Spain were of a piece. Vis-à-vis the Jews and Moors, they were the undifferentiated superiors. Among themselves, there were differences of nobility and class, but these differences were less significant.

In spite of the egalitarian spirit among the Spanish citizens evidenced in the various contemporary sources, these records also show that the Spaniards enshrined and accepted the values of the nobility (Kamen 1965:18). The Spanish peasants strove toward, or at least esteemed, the values of the center as expressed in nobility. Several period sources note that Spain focused on the attributes of the nobility. Thus, honor, disdain for manual labor, the place of "old Christians," and position in high office are the desired ends within the whole society. As Cervantes had his characters remark in the passage cited earlier, "to be an earl is more than sufficient." O'Callaghan's history of Spain also notes this focus on the noble stratum in the Spain of this period.

> Many members of the petty nobility, however, who were dependent upon the revenues of their estates for sustenance, were impoverished; some had to abandon their condition as *hidalgos* or members of the noble class in order to survive, but most preferred to retain their dignity and honor in the midst of poverty, rather than defile themselves by engaging in trade or crafts. Here is the model of the broken-down knight caricatured by Cervantes in Don Quixote.
>
> Despite the example of poverty-stricken knights, the ascendency of the nobility and their dominance of nearly every aspect of life

created a pro-aristocratic mentality in the kingdom of Castille. Disdain for manual labor, a desire to share in the esteem enjoyed by the nobles, and especially to be exempt from taxation, caused many men to aspire to the privileged status of *hidalguía*. (O'Callaghan 1975:611–12)

Kamen argues similarly and cogently that, with the destruction of the Jewish middle class and in the absence of serfdom, the lower and upper classes were quite mobile and assimilated to a single idea of nobility and honor. Thus, the "narrow concepts of the governing class became, for good or ill, the accepted code of conduct" (Kamen 1965:122; see also 11–21). Disdain for manual labor characterized the honor of Castilian nobility.

> Their task was to fight and not to labour. *Hidalguía* would not permit a nobleman, even the lowest rank of nobleman, to labor or to trade. . . . The noble concept of "honour" also involved a disdain for manual labour and commerce, and in a country where "honour" was the touchstone, work and productivity became relegated to a dishonourable position. (Kamen 1965:122)

The relation of "work is to honor" matched the relation of "race is to honor" in such a way that eventually work and race could symbolize each other. The focus on origins (the oldness of one's Christianity, the blood basis of one's purity, and the village birth giving rise to one's caste) is clearly manifest and thoroughly fused in these passages. As time progressed, the racial categories increasingly lost their religious character and assumed additional symbolic values. Kamen notes a document dated 1788 in which a Spanish high official speaks of "limpieza de sangre." The phrase is used, Kamen observes,

> in the sense of purity from any taint of servile office or trade, so that the synonymous term *limpieza de oficios* also came into existence by the end of the century. Here we have the term used in a purely class context: the upper classes were pure, and the lower servile, the distinction being grounded on a racialist dogma whose origins had almost been forgotten. (Kamen 1965:138–139)

Economic class and political position are here expressed through a symbol of biological origins. Race had become a symbolic idiom for discussing occupational and social class as well as political structure.

The high status of the nobleman presupposed its opposite in the low status of the commoner. This division in status paralleled the dichotomies between "old Christian" and "new Christian," or "non-Christian"; between urban and rural; between Spaniard and Moor; between leisure and labor; between ownership and nonownership; between governing and governed.

Add to these the further opposition of urban center to rural margins, implied by the passage from Lope de Vega quoted previously. To be from a village is to be of a lowly caste. The oppositions repeat the structure, strengthening the social fabric as they intertwine, like strands of hemp in a seaman's cordage.

During the reconquest and thereafter, Spain ruled the Muslim peoples indirectly, through a council of Islamic elders, "according to their own law" (O'Callaghan 1975:462). Nevertheless, taken as a whole, Kamen's work implies that the Inquisition tended to transform the Moorish communities toward a conformity with Christian principles. For instance, both before and during the colonization of Latin America, the conquering Spaniards isolated the religiously distinct Moorish people. Indeed, this isolation was in part achieved by the system of indirect rule. Moreover, the reconquered Moors had to abide a number of behavioral restrictions. Moors could not have Christian employees. They could not give their children to be nursed by Christian women, and sexual relations with Christian women were strictly prohibited (O'Callaghan 1975:463).

The *encomienda* and *repartimiento* institutions were present and flourishing by A.D. 1212. (González 1951:234 passim). These further isolated and restricted the Moors. The reconquest *encomiendas* were towns granted to the monastic military orders, principal agents in the reconquest of Spain. *Repartimiento,* at this time, appears to have been a simple division of spoils and land. The taxation and tribute of the Moors based in the *encomienda* and the desire for exemption from taxation among the nobles and commoners suggest further oppositions between the unrestricted, nontaxed *encomendero* and the restricted, taxed, tributed Moor.

Moreover, a small percentage of the Spaniards owned the bulk of the land. Kamen, citing Spanish sources, suggests that less than 2 percent of the population controlled 97 percent of the land in Spain by A.D. 1482. (Kamen 1965:13–14). Whether these figures are precisely accurate or not is immaterial: the elite controlled the land.

So Christian Spain developed an ideology in which conquest was a duty and Christianization a service that both justified conquest and symbolized political affiliation. The Spanish ideology tied religion, race, politics, and status together as mutually substitutable symbols. And the ideology linked high status with disdain for labor, genealogical interest, the pursuit of high office, urban centrality, and orthodox Catholicism.

THE RECONQUEST AND MOORISH SOCIETY

Thus far the discussion has centered on the reconquest from the perspective of Christian Spain. But to understand more fully the impact of Spanish ideology and institutions, we must examine what happened to the Moors who were captured and brought under Spanish control. The changes that occurred among the Moors as a result of the reconquest, however, will be more apparent against the background of the prior period of Islamic rule in Spain.

As the Moors captured Spanish towns, they established a system of indirect administration. Where Spanish towns submitted peacefully, the Moors allowed the town's existing rulers to govern, virtually as a separate estate, provided they paid the requisite taxations and did not attack either Islamic belief or Muslim women (Chejne 1974:27–28). If the captured towns were inhabited by more than one religious, racial, or ethnic group, the different groups were separated internally by walls and gates. However, there was freedom of movement for all groups between towns and subdivisions (Imamuddin 1965:53). The Arabic nobility preferred living in the rural villages and on country estates. Converts to Islam and Mozarabs (persons who remained Christian while adopting the Arabic culture in other respects) inhabited the towns (Imamuddin 1965:23).

The Mozarabs were taxed and "in some instances subjected to stiff regulations" (Chejne 1974:115). Even during the collapse of Muslim Spain, the Mozarabs suffered less persecution than did the Mudejars under the Christians. As Chejne phrases it, "on the whole, Islam remained faithful to a policy of scrupulous tolerance" (1974:116). The Mozarabs administered their own judicial arrangements, according to their customary practice. This, however, applied to cases or administrative matters internal to the non-Muslims. A Muslim judge tried any case involving Muslims and non-Muslims (Imamuddin 1965:51, 193).

Nevertheless, remaining Christian in Muslim Spain does not appear to have resulted in oppression. The Moors considered Christians "People of the Book" and accorded them an honorable place in the society. Yet there were advantages in conversion to Islam. In spite of the reasonable rights accorded those who remained Christian, the full social equality given neo-Muslims as well as their exemption from the higher taxes precipitated a rapid adoption of Islamic culture. "The Islamization of the neo-Muslims seems to have been very rapid and after some generations it was difficult to make any distinction at first sight between them and the Muslim emigrants in Spain" (Imamuddin 1965:27).

The Christians also adopted Arabic language and custom, becoming Mozarabs. They intermarried with the Muslims. They held military and civil offices in the Muslim government. They could trade with and correspond with Christians in the exterior. Christians attended either Muslim schools or their own schools and monasteries.

While these facts indicate both official and public tolerance of the now minority Christians, there were cases of the expression of prejudice (Imamuddin 1965:36–38). Perhaps one evidence of a degree of prejudice is the maintenance of a category, *muwalladun,* for the descendants of the neo-Muslims.

The degree of Arabization, of intermarriage, and of participation in the government is quite remarkable and deserves comment, for the process took place with such vigor that it "was soon hardly possible to distinguish ethnically the elements of foreign origin from the natives" (Imamuddin 1965:29). Islamic culture—by according both Christians and Jews the status of People of the Book, or People of the Covenant—demonstrated an ideology that allowed social integration along classlike lines and avoided a sharp division along ethnic, religious, or racial lines. Islamic Spain did not manifest the dualism, the colonial structure of oppositions, that Christian Spain subsequently imposed on the peninsula.

As one might suspect, however, with the increasing success of the Christian reconquest, the Muslims' tolerance of the Christians within their empire wore somewhat thin. First, the presence of Christians implied the possibility of internal treason. Second, conversion and reconversion, as the tides of conquerer and reconquerer ebbed and flowed across the land, cast doubt on religious profession. Coupled with the knowledge of the harsh fate of captured Muslims, these processes hurt the social position of the Arabized Christians. Religious problems increased, and there were further restrictions placed on the Mozarabs, although these were much less constraining than the restrictions placed on Muslims incorporated into Christian Spain (Chejne 1974:119–20).

The Historical Context of Guatemalan Culture and Society

Once the Christians securely gained control of regions long held by Moors, the social atmosphere changed sharply. If the Arabs were rather tolerant of religious diversity and managed to integrate their society, the Spaniards both before and after the reconquest were quite intolerant and created a condition of internal colonialism. Indeed, by 1526 all Moors were forced to become Christians and were designated by the term Morisco. A letter from one anonymous Morisco manifests the extent of the intolerance and duplicity.

37. Then their Sultan and grandee said to us: "What you have stipulated is granted to you in more than its entirety,"
38. Showing us documents containing a pact and a treaty, saying so us: "This is my amnesty and my protection [over you],
39. So remain in enjoyment of your possessions and homes as you were before, unharmed."
40. Yet when we came under their treaty of protection, their treachery towards us became apparent for [he] broke the agreement.
41. He broke the compacts he had deceived us with and converted us to Christianity by force, with harshness and severity,
42. Burning the books we had and mixing them with dung or with filth. (Monroe 1966:297)

The Morisco then details the punishments for the practice of Islamic religion and the forced disparagement of the prophet Muhammad. He further laments:

54. [They committed] many other similar, shameful deeds, as well as numerous wicked acts.
55. Our names were changed and given a new form with neither our consent nor our desire.
56. Therefore, alas, for the exchanging of Muhammad's religion for that of the Christian dogs, the worst of creatures!
57. Alas for our names when they were exchanged for those of ignorant non-Arabs!
58. Alas for our sons and daughters who go off every morning to a priest
59. Who teaches them unbelief, idolatry, and falsehood while they are entirely unable to circumvent [the Christians] by any trick! (. . .)
64. We have become slaves; not captives who may be ransomed, nor even Muslims who pronounce their declaration of faith!

65. Hence, were your eyes to see what has become of our lot, they would overflow with abundant tears.
66. So alas! Alas for us! Alas for the misfortune that struck us, namely harm, sorrow and the robe of oppression! (Monroe 1966:298–9)

This was the fate of the Muslims, though, to be sure, until 1526 not all Muslims were immediately required to adopt Christianity.

Indeed, the term *mudéjar* referred to professing Muslims living within the Christian kingdom. However, the Mudejars' social position among Christians differed substantially from that of the Christians living under the Muslims. The Mudejars were legally "a foreign body," tolerated under the personal protection of the crown. As Ladero Quesada notes, this foreign body was "a different cultural entity . . . in large part counterpoised to that of the Castilians, . . . in consequence of which the Mudejar had had to be treated in such a manner as to not 'contaminate' the Castilian culture with this other" (1969:16). But Mudejars were not simply different. Their "counterposition" entailed a reversal of things Castilian. Over several generations, Moors in Spanish Christendom adopted an ideology inverse to that of their lords.

From an early period, the Mudejars were segregated into towns. Robert Burns implies that during the thirteenth century some towns were formally known as "Saracen," and that others were predominantly of Saracen or Muslim composition (1975:140–41). Some two centuries later, in 1480, Isabella I notes that her laws "accentuated the firmness of the dispositions to require the Muslims and Jews to [live in] wards separated from the rest of the population" (Ladero Quesada 1969:21). Thus, Christian Spain sought to segregate and isolate the ethnically second-class infidel Moors.

Of course, Spain taxed the Mudejars and exacted labor service from them. Robert Burns's monograph on the structure of taxation among the Moors from 1200 to 1300 describes the prelude to later and more demanding forms of taxation. He notes that fees were required for the transaction of government business. There were taxes by virtue of state monopoly on salt and other products. Finally, for the Mudejars there were personal head taxes and community taxes (Burns 1975).

Beyond these taxes, Spain required the Mudejars to give labor service *(sofra)*. Burns notes that labor services in the thirteenth century meant working from one day per month up to as much as one day per week. These services included delivery of wood and water to the household of Spanish lords and the requirement of carrying Spanish goods. Listed out of context, the taxes and services appear oppressive. Burns, however, suggests that the taxes and services were not so severe since many of the taxes also applied to Christians (Burns 1975:344–45, 347).

Among the few surviving original documents on the social conditions of Mudejars, tax records showing changes in the amounts collected in different tax categories help Burns to identify and reconstruct social shifts. Burns notes that the early Mudejars had a much more complex economy than the later Mudejars. Burns speaks of the

> subsequent . . . relegation of subject Muslims to agricultural hinterlands. Mudejar Valencia only later devolved into a peasant-farmer class, losing its nation of shopkeepers and merchants; the rural-urban dichotomy only gradually strengthened, replacing a more subtle symbiosis of the two. (Burns 1975:345)

Thus, Christian society pressed its Moorish enclaves into agricultural homogeneity, collapsing a once complex spectrum of social levels and occupations into a dichotomous opposition.

At the same time that the diverse economy of the Mudejars was changing toward one of agricultural dominance, other restrictions on Mudejar life gradually increased. In the latter part of the fifteenth century, but before acceptance of Christianity was legally required and before Moorish culture had substantially disappeared, Mudejars were required "to use identifying signs on their clothing." In addition, they were forbidden to use Christian given names, to eat with Christians, or to visit them when they were sick. Moreover, "sexual relations with Christian women were absolutely prohibited, since these were spiritual wives of Our Lord Jesus Christ, by reason of faith and the baptism they received in His name" (Ladero Quesada 1969:22). More significantly, both Jews and Mudejars were prohibited from holding offices in the government. Finally, as of 1407, "Mudejares not only could not leave the kingdom, but also they could not change residence within it" (Ladero Quesada 1969:22–25). Mudejars thus suffered social isolation, political alienation, and residential restriction.

Although Burns feels that the thirteenth-century Moors were reasonably treated in matters of taxation and service obligation, he evaluates the fate of the Moors of the sixteenth century more harshly. "By the sixteenth century," he asserts, "the complex of services" owed by the Moriscos "rendered" them "almost servile" (Burns 1975:172). The *moriscos* mentioned in this quote were descendants of Muslim Spaniards and Arabs who had accepted Christianity by choice or by force. They represent the final stage in the transformation of Moorish Spain. Importantly, the Moriscos also appear to have dropped a great deal of their Islamic culture and custom, for "harsh measures aiming at de-islamizing and de-arabizing the Mudejares contributed not only to the decline and disappearance of their cultural heritage, as expressed in religious practices, customs, and language, but to their eventual extermination and expulsion" (Chejne 1974:120). "Expulsion" refers to the fact that persons of Moorish, Mudejar, and eventually Morisco descent were forcibly expelled from Spain after 1600.

As has been noted, the Moriscos were restricted to particular communities, prohibited to intermarry, and, at least in the Valencia area, were bound as near-serfs to the large estates of the Spanish overlords. According to Imamuddin, the Moriscos were "the main tillers of the soil in Aragón" (1969:310–11). Indeed, in Valencia and Aragon, the Moriscos appear to have been almost the only agricultural laborers, for they were protected by their lords from the effects of the Inquisition in an effort to maintain the estates. When the Inquisition got the upper hand and the Moriscos were tried and expelled from Aragon, "the fields fell into a wretched state" (Imamuddin 1969:311).

> The Moriscos were known for their hard work and skill. Hurtado de Mendaza *{sic},* in appreciation of their skill in agriculture, writes that every piece of Alpujarra which was naturally sterile and hard was used for cultivation because of their diligence. They were not in the habit of begging but were always busy with some employment and excelled in manual work hated by the Christians. They were diligent cultivators and skillful in the manual trades. . . . In 1638 the historian Bermudez de la Pedraza . . . wrote, ". . . they were little given to idleness; all worked." (Imamuddin 1969:303–4, citing Florencio Janer, *Condición social de los Moriscos* 1857:159, 162)

We see here the tendency toward an association between the Moriscos and agricultural trades and manual labor, as well as an allusion to the fact that they worked the sterile and hard marginal lands. Hard work was their lot.

The implications of Moriscos *excelling* in manual labor *hated* by the Spaniards suggest a reversal or inversion of ideologies arising out of the reconquest colonial system. The Spaniards themselves were quite explicit about this inverse relationship with the subject Moriscos. After the reconquest of Granada in 1492, the first archbishop of the region noted that the Moriscos were known for their work and the Christians for their faith. He suggested that they partially exchange these qualities so as to end the difference between the Moriscos, who were "work without faith," and the Christians, who were "faith without work" (Imamuddin 1969:305). The description of the Moriscos by an anonymous Aragonese Spaniard sheds yet more light on the matter:

> They were given to trades of little work, weavers, tailors, rope makers, sandal makers, potters, shoemakers, *albeytares,* mattress makers, gardeners, muleteers, and retailers of oil, fish, honey, raisins, sugar, cloth, eggs, sandals, and woolens for children; in short they had trades that required help in the house and that permitted them to travel about to different places seeing what happened of peace and war, so that they were ordinarily idle, vagabonds, out in the sun in the dry months with their jug at their sides, and on their porches in the wet months, engaged with great passion in their trades the few hours they worked at them, or they were in their fields, greatly concerned for their fruits, crops, and vegetables; but few, indeed, very few of them had trades in metal, or iron or stone, or wood (except that they had a few smiths engaged among themselves due to the great love they had for their beasts), in order to avoid being contracted by the Christians for the hatred which they had for us. (García-Arenal 1975:232)

It would appear that the Moriscos were "given to trades of little work" because, in addition to a few hours at their trades each day, they were also quite dedicated to their fields. One also notes that the Spanish author calls the Moriscos lazy only when he refers to their travel as traders. Morisco movement beyond the limits of their community and their involvement in anything except rural activity elicits the sharp criticism, indicating the Spaniard's expectation that they confine themselves to the local community and the nearby soil.

The same author becomes even more disparaging when his description of the Moriscos relies on the implicit contrast with the ways and beliefs of the Spaniards:

They were a vile people, unkempt, the enemies of letters and illustrious science (these the companions of virtue), and consequently indifferent to all things urban, courteous, and political.

They were beasts at their meals, always eating in the dirt (for such they were) without a table, without other utensils proper to humans, sleeping in the same fashion, on the ground, on pads.

They spent very little, either for food or clothing, although they had to pay much in tributes to their lords. (García-Arenal 1975:29–31)

It seems odd that the descendants of the Spanish Moors—creators of a civilization famed for the best universities and libraries in all of Europe and North Africa, renowned for its bathhouses to which the faithful were called by law and religious precept, and praised for its lavish public works, its generosity to the poor, and the expenditures of its persons—should be described as dirty, unkempt, indifferent to literacy and politics, and tight with money unless the conditions of the reconquest worked an immense change upon them. Indeed, Spanish institutions forced Moorish descendants to accept an ideology opposite to that of their lords. *Moros* became beasts of burden on the margins of Spanish humanity.

The many changes in the Moors suggest that Spanish culture and institutions had a strongly shaping effect. Moreover, the changes came to be oppositional: Spaniards disclaimed labor, Moros excelled at it; Spaniards were pure Christians, Moros impure; Spaniards took up government and moved across the land, while Moros gave up trades and withdrew to closed, corporate agricultural communities. Certainly there is evidence of the kind of colonial pressure that could cause a substantial meltdown of the precolonial culture. And there are several evidences of point-counterpoint inversions between Spanish overlord and postreconquest Moor. Indeed, Louis Cardaillac (1979) and Mercedes García-Arenal (1978) demonstrate that the Moriscos rejected the fundamental Islamic precepts of Mary's virgin birth and Jesus's prophetic calling, presumably to contrast themselves more precisely from the overlord Catholics. The Moriscos became something new in response to the molding of the Spaniards.

If the Spanish colonial program had such a shaping and molding impact on the Moors, it should have a similar impact on colonized New World peoples. The parallels and continuities should be especially interesting since the conquest of the New World largely took place in the fifty years immediately following the fall of Moorish Granada in 1492. Indeed, the end of the Moorish conquest coincided with the beginning of the Indian conquest, as though the momentum of the reconquest endeavor flowed across the sea without letup, with conquest substituted for reconquest and Indians substituted for Moors. Thus, Bernal Díaz del Castillo remarked that the Spaniards "went about robbing the native peoples, taking from them their women and chickens and clothing, just as they did in Moorish lands" (Hanke 1974:6).[4] Indeed, Hanke claims to be a member of "the school that interprets the beginning of the conquest of America in 1492 as but the continuation of the medieval reconquista that ended at Granada the same year" (Hanke 1974:5).

The similarities are extensive. Both colonized peoples—Indians and Moors—were infidels. Both experienced the fusion of Christian ideology with political allegiance and the joining of clergy and crown in government. Both peoples felt the urban focus of the elite Spanish Christians, in contrast with the rural placement of the nonpolitical and pagan (or heretical because corrupt) beliefs and practices of the colonial subjects at the margins of society. In response to the elite Spaniard aversion to manual labor, both Moros and Indios acquired (or continued) an ethic of work; indeed, both groups achieved notoriety on account of their love of agricultural labor and petty craftsmanship. Both Moors and Indians were restricted in their movements between towns and were unable to change their residences. Both married endogamously, were prohibited from sexual access to Spanish females, and were subjected to privileged access by Spanish males. Thus, both peoples became endogamous, heretical, agricultural, taxed, servile labor pools in closed communities. They acquired or maintained these similar characteristics under the pressure of the same Spanish ideology and closely similar institutions: the *encomienda*, the *reducción*, and the *repartimiento*.

Preconquest Mesoamerica

By comparison with what we know of preconquest Spain, the cultural categories, symbols, and institutional arrangements of the preconquest aborigines of Mesoamerica are little understood. Sadly, the Spanish burned many of the booklike records that they found as they conquered. The three or four pre-Columbian Mayan texts that did survive appear to be calendrical almanacs with little other cultural information.

There are some postconquest documents rendered by priests or Indians who early became literate in the Spanish alphabet. But modern sociological studies on peoples undergoing stressful economic and political colonization indicate that a native people may very quickly adjust their social and religious premises, even before the arrival of the first colonizers (Lawrence 1967; Worsley 1968; Burridge 1969). Given the internal evidence of millenarian adjustments in the postconquest texts—and our knowledge of the early population collapse, economic enslavement, and political stress that would make such changes expectable—the postconquest texts must be used with great caution.

Lacking richly descriptive writings by the preconquest Mayas, anthropologists conjecturally reconstruct much of what they understand about the ancient Mayas from the ethnographic present. Sanders and Price (1968) provide a clear example of how this is done. In one section of their book, they briefly review the available ethnographic literature on the social functions of the political-religious hierarchy or fiesta system among present-day (or recently studied) Mesoamericans. The fiesta system, they conclude, disperses wealth and prevents a challenge to the position of the overlords. Sanders and Price then go on to say that although the data on which the analysis of Marvin Harris (1964) is based and from which Sanders and Price draw are "post-Hispanic,"

> The pre-Hispanic situation of social stratification was remarkably similar structurally. It is, therefore, highly likely that an institution similar to the fiesta-cargo system existed, with similar functions, in pre-conquest times. Such an institution seems to us to be ideally suited to the inferred sociological picture of the Lowland Classic Maya. (Sanders and Price 1968:143)

The passage reveals the inferential reasoning underlying much of what is claimed about preconquest Mayan culture and society.

There is evidence that this pattern of dependence on the ethnographic present is changing. For example, although Robert Carmack claims that "many details about ancient Quiché culture in this book derive from my ethnographic experience in the highlands" (1981:xv), it appears that he does not impute the present to the past in the style I have outlined. Rather, there is much closer attention to ethnohistorical documents. For Carmack, present-day activities are seldom the source for what must have been, but a clarification of matters at least hinted at in the early postcolonial annals.[5] Moreover, Carmack does not attempt complete social and cultural reconstruction; "there is much groundwork to be laid" before such a task can be accomplished (Carmack 1981:10). Rather, Carmack limits himself to tracing out the emergence of state relations and the development of material civilization, though the treatment of religious ideas figures prominently. Indeed, religious symbolism and lineage organizations are the fundamental "survivals" in present-day culture.

Yet there is an unresolved ambivalence toward both cultural continuity and cultural change. On the one hand, Carmack's "understanding of Quiché culture" "was greatly enriched by [his] eight months' residence in Santa Cruz," which became "the foundation on which this book was built" (Carmack 1981:xvii). Though changes have occurred, one can still discover aspects of the "Utatlán culture" that have not yet passed away, even though it be only "important fragments" (Carmack 1981:367, 408). The tenor of Carmack's book suggests that the postcolonial period was characterized more by cultural continuity than discontinuity. Traditional Quiché community life "was not drastically changed by the forces of modernization" until the reforms of 1944 (Carmack 1981:347), of which the most important were "the elimination of forced labor, the introduction of elections, and the formation of peasant groups" (Carmack 1981:360). On the other hand, even as early as 1930, a community like Santa Cruz had "lost many of its traditional cultural features" and was "no longer the traditional community it was in the days of Stephens" (that is, the 1840s) (Carmack 1981:356, xvi).

The idea of a traditional community even in the nineteenth century is deceptive, though. With the fall of Utatlán to the Spanish, "Quiché culture began changing radically" (Carmack 1981:7). Thus Fray Francisco Ximénez, for example, "failed to appreciate sufficiently how much of the elite culture had been lost" (Carmack 1981:24). Indeed, "the documents dramatize . . . how much a culture can change over time" in a way that "can be unsettling for the ethnohistorian" and that even "change in ecology had greatly altered Quiché culture" (Carmack 1981:75, 108). One might surmise that if the removal of forced labor was a major impetus for cultural change, then surely the imposition of forced labor from the beginning of the colony brought about even greater change.

Given the degree to which Carmack is aware of change among the Quiché, we may speculate on his method of using ethnographic data. If the form of a given behavior appears to be the same today as in the immediate postconquest or subsequent documents, then the present-day meaning may be imputed to the earlier form. But such a procedure would violate the contextual set theory of meaning that emerges from Saussure. For Saussure, the first corollary of a change of context is a change of meaning. This approach to meaning weakens one's trust in a book that attributes meaning to a form that has changed context; the great strength of Carmack's impressive book is that he does it so seldom.[6]

Richard E. W. Adams is also cautious in his recent study (1977). But Adams devotes less than two pages to the preconquest highland Maya. In his material we are told that the highland area was divided into small political states and that its people placed an emphasis upon lineage (R. E. W. Adams, 1977:267–68). Adams's work is, however, a synthetic and introductory overview of Mesoamerican prehistory. It is therefore partially unfair to attach too much significance to the fact that only two pages of commentary are given on a major region within the zone of discourse, for Adams posits a regional culture within Mesoamerica, and he underlines the similarities from Mexico through Guatemala. In a final, synthetic chapter, Adams brings together the knowledge that we have from the various excavations and the chronicles from the preconquest. Clearly, from a cultural point of view, what he is able to say by conjoining all the cultural information from the entire region is minimal.

There is a further and more substantial difficulty deriving from a circularity of argument. Adams devotes a small section to the Mesoamerican cultural continuities into the colonial period. He implies that the tributary system, the predominance of the large estates, the system of rule through native *caciques* or leaders, and the focus on particular municipalities and their subdivisions were adopted or absorbed by the Spaniards from the Mesoamerican aboriginal system. However, each of these characteristics has been shown to exist in Spain well before the conquest. Furthermore, the documentation of the Spanish context for these institutions is much more thorough and convincing. Thus, while these institutions may have existed prior to the conquest, their continuity seems best explained by their fit with Spanish preconceptions.

Moreover, speaking of the preconquest aborigines generally, Adams himself notes the destruction of the elite-class culture (1977:299), the "reformulation of culture" (1977:329), and "cultural failure" (1977:329). In the face of such discontinuities and transformations in the Mayan system, the assertion of cultural continuities to the present is not a simple matter.

Finally, the logical status of Mayan continuities among the present-day Indians is made especially doubtful when the former conditions of the Maya are guessed at by using the current conditions of the Indians as a model. The circularity of using cultural continuities to explain the present when the present was used to arrive at the preconquest conditions by cultural upstreaming is obvious. Unfortunately, it is also endemic to the literature of the preconquest period. Thus, the interpretation of present-day Indian peculiarities as preconquest Mayan derivatives seems fatally flawed.[7]

To be sure, there are many aspects of the Mayan aboriginal life that were carried over into the conquest and modern periods. The Mayan languages, for example, are largely derived from the preconquest aboriginal systems. However, the meaning of using a Mayan language has been substantially altered by imposing the Spanish language of the overlords. Speaking Mayan became an index of servile status.

Furthermore, the maintenance of the Indian tongues appears to be related more to the outcome of conflicts within Spanish colonial society than to the weight of cultural continuity. Shirley Heath has shown in *Telling Tongues* that the policy of the Spanish crown was to eliminate the Indian languages in order to consolidate its administrative control over the empire (Heath 1972:7). Indeed, the Indians showed both skill and interest in learning Spanish as well as Latin, and those who were taught to write learned quickly. When the early schools were terminated, Indian leaders sent petitions and delegations requesting more Spanish instruction (Heath 1972:44–45).

But Indian and crown interests in learning Spanish were consistently and successfully thwarted by the resident Creoles and the clergy. "For the functional purpose it served them as members of the closed Indian villages" and because it "enabled these religious isolates [the friars] to live in harmony with the natives and to exclude any outside Spaniards," the friars "ardently defended the indigenous language retention of their charges" (Heath 1972:34–35). Indian language retention served not only "to protect their positions and put the prelates from Spain at a distinct disadvantage among the

Indians" (Heath 1972:35). In addition, according to the seventeenth century phrasing, it is better that the Indians not "learn the Spanish tongue and become ladinos, which is the first step toward their becoming impudent; . . . while they speak their own language, they are more humble" (Heath 1972:43). Indeed, "the Spaniards viewed those Indians who learned Spanish as crafty rascals who wanted to work around the rules of the socially prescribed system" (Heath 1972:43). The Spaniards called such Indians *ladinos,* a term which Heath and others have shown meant "cunning" and was both "applied in Spain to Moors who learned Castilian," and as a "derogatory tag the colonists gave these Indians" (Heath 1972:43). The colony needed a labor source that was freely available and divided internally, exactly the condition enhanced by multiple Indian languages. So the *criollos* won out over the desires of the crown and the early Indian leaders. Thus, Spanish society gave new parameters to the meaning and maintenance of the Indian languages. In general, we may suspect that Spanish culture similarly broke down other elements of the aboriginal culture and created the Indians from the pieces.

Thus, this chapter establishes the perspective that the aboriginal culture and society were substantially altered by the imposition of ideologies on the Indian through the *encomienda,* the *reducción,* and the *repartimiento.* In the view of Severo Martínez Peláez (1971), the Indian did not exist until the Spaniard subjugated the aborigine. Martínez Peláez, though, takes a Marxian view, for he contends that the newly created Indians took form in response to the technological superiority of the Spaniards and to the Indian position in the productive enterprise that the Spanish imposed on them. By contrast, the data presented in this book indicate a dual response to the Spaniards. The essential characteristics of Indian ideology and position arose both from the imposition of an ideology and from the institutions by which ideology and social positions were imposed. But postconquest Indian culture was largely recast in the inverse image of the Spanish culture through the institutional mold that encompassed and constrained the human raw material. If so, a fruitful interpretation of present-day Indian ideology would lie in its inverse, opposed relation to Spanish and, more recently, to *ladino* ideology.

Precursors of the Conquest of Guatemala

The Guatemalan conquest was among the later of the New World campaigns. Earlier, in subjugating the Aztec kingdom and its dependents, Spain had established a model of conquest and control.

We may therefore shed light on the nature of the Guatemalan conquest by examining its precursors in the conquest of the Aztecs.

Private armies conquered the New World. Many of the leaders of the *conquistadores* were *hidalgos*—*hijos de algo* or "sons of substance." To be sure, they were the dispossessed sons, the second and later sons who were blocked from inheriting their established estates in Spain. Had they had a claim on their Spanish family estates, they might not have ventured to the New World and put up their own funds to finance the expeditions. But with the customary severance monies, they became adventurers, soldiers of fortune, and capitalists. In return for exposure to financial risk and personal danger, the *conquistadores* expected personal gain (Díaz del Castillo 1967). They had in mind *encomienda* rights to taxation and the *repartimiento* or distribution of spoils—the same mechanisms that rewarded and financed the military-religious orders that had reconquered Spain.

What did the Spaniards of the time think about the New World residents they would control and mold through these institutions? Two extreme positions on the nature of the Indian emerged in Spanish thought.

On one side, represented by Juan Ginés de Sepúlveda, were those Spaniards who thought the Indians, like the Moors, were barely human and incapable of the civility that was the natural state of the Spaniard.

> Shall we doubt that these peoples, so uncivilized, so barbarous, so wicked, contaminated with so many evils and wicked religious practices, have been justly subjugated by an excellent, pious, and most just King, such as was Ferdinand and the Caesar Charles is now, and by a most civilized nation that is outstanding in every kind of virtue? (Hanke 1974:86)

Sepúlveda's words resonate with opposites. Hanke quotes him again:

> Now compare their [the Spaniards'] gifts of prudence, talent, magnanimity, temperance, humanity, and religion with those little men in whom you will scarcely find traces of humanity. . . . If you deal with the virtues, if you look for temperance or meekness, what can you expect from men who were involved in every kind of intemperance and wicked lust and who used to eat human flesh? (Hanke 1974:85)

And again:

> In prudence, talent, virtue, and humanity, they are as inferior to the Spaniards as children to adults, women to men, as the wild and

cruel to the most meek, as the prodigiously intemperate to the continent and temperate, that I have almost said, as monkeys to men. (Hanke 1974:84)

Concerning the appropriateness of the animal analogy, Sepúlveda expounds:

> But even though some of them show a talent for certain handicrafts, this is not an argument in favor of a more human skill, since we see that some small animals, both birds and spiders, make things which no human industry can imitate completely. (Hanke 1974:85)

Nor was Sepúlveda alone in his thinking. Domingo de Betanzos, founder of the Dominican order in New Spain, is quoted, "I have spoken somewhat on Indian capacity in general, not saying that they were wholly incapable, because I have never said that, but rather that they have very little capacity, like children" (Hanke 1974:19).

I am not concerned here with whether these statements concerning the Indians are true or not. My only concern is to show that the Spaniards at that time thought of the Indians as a kind of opposite.

There were, of course, a few Spaniards who thought better of the Indians. Antonio de Montesinos, a Dominican, observed in a 1511 sermon on Hispaniola, "Are these Indians not men? Do they not have rational souls?" Hanke observes that "Montesinos evidently astounded and shocked the colonists" (Hanke 1974:4). Among those who listened to Montesinos was Fray Bartolomé de las Casas, who would become Defender of the Indians, but who at the time was an ecclesiastic in Hispaniola owning both estates and slaves whom he worked in the mines. Hanke observes that "the sermon of Montesinos evidently did not disturb" las Casas, since he received "as reward both land and an encomienda" for participating in the conquest of Cuba (Hanke 1974:7). Only in 1515 did las Casas change, give up his *encomienda,* and begin to crusade.

But even as las Casas defended the Indians, he and others did so within the fundamental premise that Spaniards and Indians were opposites. In the words of las Casas,

> Now if Christians unsettle everything by wars, burnings, fury, rashness, fierceness, sedition, plunder, and insurrection, where is meekness? Where is moderation? . . . Where is humanity? (Hanke 1974:97)

To quote Hanke summarizing las Casas, "Preaching the faith by massacres and terror was an Islamic practice that must not be emulated by Christians" (Hanke 1974:97). By contrast, of the Indians, las Casas affirmed:

> The creator . . . has not so despised these peoples . . . that he willed them to lack reason and made them like brute animals, so that they should be called barbarians, savages, wildmen, and brutes as they [most New World Spaniards, and Sepúlvedistas in particular] think or imagine. On the contrary, they are of such gentleness and decency that they are, more than the other nations of the entire world . . . supremely fitted . . . [for] the Word of God." (Hanke 1974:82)

Nor was las Casas alone in defending the Indians as virtuous while holding them essentially opposite of the Spanish. Reacting to renewed proposals for further violent and essentially cruel measures (such as more branding) to subjugate the Indians, Vascode Quiroga, as an *Audiencia* judge, observed, "I believe firmly that all the people of this land and of the New World are almost all of one quality, very mild and humble, timid and obedient" (Hanke 1974:16). Again, the issue is not whether the Indians or Spaniards in reality had these virtues or vices. The important fact is that even the defenders of the Indians thought of them as opposite of the Spaniards.

Through a vociferous alliance with the crown, some churchmen sought to establish at least minimal protections for the Indian, so that both church and crown would have at least someone to administer to. This suggests, however, that the dominant ideology among the New World's colonialists was closest to that of Juan Ginés de Sepúlveda. The Indians, barely human infidels, were virtually the opposite of all things Spanish and properly elite. This would be the key idea that shaped the reconstruction of Indian culture.

Indeed, Charles Gibson attributes a characteristic personality to these *conquistadores*. In *Spain in America* he calls them "valiant, cruel, indefatigable, ferocious, courageous, and villainous," mixing "material and spiritual goals . . . lust and sentimentality . . . honorable and base conduct" (Gibson 1966:36). He wonders why they should have mixed such qualities. But these hero-villain attributes are quite intelligible in the context of conquest society. The *conquistadores* were shorn of social position and hence of social risks in the Iberian fatherland. They had invested personal fortunes in a chance for a portion of whatever booty they might acquire. Indeed, *conquistador* ideology justified any action that might subjugate the heathens and thereby bring them to Christianity: if the Indians were brought to Christianity, *conquistador* wealth was deserved. Under such conditions, what other kind of personality might we expect? Violence brought booty in the name of "Our Lord."

Pedro de Alvarado presumably shared some of these personality traits, as well as the ideas on the nature of the Indians and the proper institutions with which to govern them, when he captained the conquest of Guatemala. He had participated with Hernán Cortés in the subjugation of the Aztec empire. This experience likely served as a model to Alvarado and to other lieutenants of Cortés (Gibson 1966: 29). In such campaigns, both leaders and followers expected to gain from their participation. The leaders financed the conquest and therefore deserved the most spoil, as well as special privileges, *encomiendas*, and lands. Subordinate officers hoped to acquire enough wealth to finance their own expeditions into new corners of the unconquered land and thus acquire their own privileged domains.

Alvarado had seen it before. When Cortés's immediate superior became engrossed in managing his newly acquired holdings in the Caribbean islands, Cortés, wanting more than a continued subordinate relationship, abandoned him and financed his own expedition to the recently discovered mainland (Díaz del Castillo 1967). When Cortés in turn halted and began to extract the available wealth in his new Mexican kingdom, Alvarado, one of Cortés's principal lieutenants, organized and led troops to the aboriginal kingdoms on the new frontier, Guatemala.

Cortés's conquest of Mexico must have been an instructive model for Alvarado. First, Alvarado had seen that a giant Indian empire could be undermined by making alliances with nearby rival states or with unwilling subjects. Such alliances enabled the Spaniards to acquire mercenaries and to incite rebellion by exploiting the internal divisions and political interests of the aborigines. Indeed, the conquest of Aztec Mexico largely succeeded because of the alliances that Cortés readily formed with the Tlaxcalans and others. Indian porters, builders, mercenaries, and spies made Cortés's small corps of cavalry and foot soldiers a specialized and supremely effective weapon (Díaz del Castillo 1967; Gibson 1966:35).

Second, Alvarado saw that the responsibility of Christianization incumbent upon the *conquistadores* could be used to justify any action that quashed Indian resistance. In the Spanish ideological system, derived from the reconquest of Moorish Spain, conquest made possible the imposition of Christianity, the highest moral good; and the end came to justify the means.

Third, Alvarado would have experienced and come to understand the relation between the conquistadors, the Spanish crown, and the Catholic priesthood. The crown took a fifth of the conquest booty. In return, and in order to collect it, the crown sent the fleets to resupply the conquistadors. The crown provided priests sufficient to justify conquest activities in the highest moral framework. The crown legalized the system of stewardships *(encomiendas)* and other grants that were accorded to the conquerers as a means of recouping their investments of capital and personal risk. This legalization tied the *conquistadores* to the Iberian social and cultural scheme. Disputes among the *conquistadores* were referred to the crown judiciary rather than to the battlefield.

Finally, Alvarado would have been familiar with the forms of the *encomienda* that had been imposed on the Indians in the Caribbean islands and on the Mexican mainland. To be sure, these social institutions were prefigured in the reconquest of the Moors, as well as in the conquest of the Canary Islands. In its initial forms in the Caribbean, the Spaniards compelled the Indians to reside among the Christians and provide them with labor. The Indians were assigned to particular Spaniards and were forced to work, preferably in mines, but if there were none, on the land. Perhaps the distinguishing feature of the Caribbean and mainland *encomienda* in the early period was the crown's total lack of control over the use of the Indians by the *encomenderos*. The system amounted to chattel slavery with no restraining cost of investment. The end result: the islands depopulated rapidly from disease and from overwork (Simpson 1950:chap. 1 and 2).

Guatemala experienced this same social process. Pedro de Alvarado left Cortés and led his own expedition to the south. Collecting his soldiers and priests, as well as a small contingent of Mexican mercenaries, Alvarado set out to acquire gold, Indians, and land for himself. He thus introduced to Guatemala the same rapacious conquest exploitation that the Aztecs and the islanders had experienced before. More important, Alvarado and his band introduced the Spanish cultural categories that the aborigines would adopt, the Iberian status ideology that the aborigines would invert, and many of the symbolic oppositions that the aborigines would employ to define their existence within the imposed institutions of enslavement. In the process, the aborigines would make themselves Indians.

The Conquest Period: 1524–1542

Some time after the conquest, the Indians of the towns of San Juan Ostuncalco, Concepción Chiquirichapa, and San Martín Sacatepéquez in western Guatemala petitioned the Spanish crown for special privileges. The document, located in the national archives, relates briefly that the Mams had had longstanding conflicts with the Quiché and Achí Indian nations with whom they bordered. These Mams asserted that, as a consequence of their prior contentions, they had helped Pedro de Alvarado in the conquest of the Quiché nation. Moreover, a

> . . . privilege which the Indians of the Town of San Pedro Sacatepéquez have presented your Graces (the Corregidor and Oidor of the Audiencia) was conceded by the King our Lord to the Indians of the *Mame* nation in said town because on behalf of the King in his conquest of the Indies they sided with and [illegible word] the Adelantado don Pedro de Alvarado to conquer and overcome the Indians of the QUICHE nation. (AGG leg. 226, exp. 4086 [emphasis in MSS])

Because they gave help to Alvarado, Fray Luis Zapata affirmed in 1676 that the king promised never to "alienate *(enajenar)*" these Indians from the crown.

Another highly valued colonial document stands framed in the municipal archives of San Pedro Sacatepéquez. This document grants special privileges to the municipality of San Pedro as a consequence of its citizens having participated in the campaign for the reduction of what was then called *"tierra de guerra*—the war zone." This war zone was later to be called *Vera Paz* or "True Peace" because the priestly orders succeeded in pacifying it by peaceful missions where combat had earlier failed. These two documents suggest rather strongly that the southern Mams allied themselves with Alvarado in the conquest of the other Guatemalan Indians.

We may speculate on how this might have come about. We know from Bernal Díaz del Castillo that Pedro de Alvarado left Tenochtitlán (now Mexico City) and went southwest to Oaxaca. There he resubjugated some communities that had rebelled. We may presume that

Alvarado then reprovisioned. According to Castillo, Alvarado left Oaxaca with 120 horsemen, 300 foot soldiers, 4 artillery pieces, and 300 Mexican allies (Alvarado 1525b:24 n.5; Díaz del Castillo 1967:379).

Alvarado entered Guatemala from the coastal plain, having traversed Soconusco. The first letters to Cortés from this part of his march have been lost, for in the first letter that we have, which was written after the conquest of the Quiché highlands, Alvarado writes,

> Sir: From Soconusco I wrote to Your Grace all that had happened to me as far as that place and even something of what was expected to happen further on. And after having sent my messengers to this country, informing them of how I was to come to conquer and pacify the provinces that might not be willing to place themselves under the dominion of His Majesty, I asked of them as his vassals (for as such they had offered themselves to Your Grace) the favor and assistance and passage through their country; that by so doing, they would act as good and loyal vassals of His Majesty and that they would be greatly favored and supported in all justice by me and the Spaniards in my company; and if not, I threatened to make war on them as on traitors rising in rebellion against the service of our Lord the Emperor. (Alvarado 1525a:53)

The next day he left and engaged the Quiché at Zapotitlán, situated at the opening of the gorge that leads to Quezaltenango. Now, we might ask, how did Alvarado know of what he expected to see ahead? He probably made contact with coastal populations of the southern Mams, or with delegations from the highlands along the volcanic escarpment out of which San Pedro Sacatepéquez was later created. This contact would not be difficult as it is only a few hours' march to the center of the coastal plain from the present town center, and all of it is downhill. Whoever they were, these natives offered themselves "as the King's vassals." At this point, or shortly thereafter, the southern Mams, or at least those from the region that was later to be called San Pedro Sacatepéquez and San Martín Sacatepéquez, probably joined Alvarado's small contingent of Mexican Indians. Perhaps these Mams were indeed motivated by the prospect of putting down their Quiché enemies once and for all. In any case, Díaz del Castillo reports that in Soconusco the Spaniards were received in peace by the "more than 15,000 residents" of this region just before they began to battle with the advance guard of the Quiché at Zapotitlán (Díaz del Castillo 1967:380).

How did they know Alvarado was coming, so that they were ready to make contact with him? Through ambassadors, merchants, and no doubt other sources, the Indian leaders apprised themselves of a matter of great importance to the native empires (Alvarado 1525a: 11). Bernal Díaz del Castillo describes the ambassadors and the various kinds of alertings that were evident in the Mexican campaign. The Guatemalan nations knew what was coming by virtue of what had happened in Mexico.

Alvarado's account gives other, though less direct, evidence of collaboration from the Mams. Alvarado left Zapotitlán and climbed the very steep gorge leading to Quezaltenango. His forces were met by three or four thousand of the enemy, "and they fell upon the people of our friends" (Alvarado 1525b:26) pushing them back. Later the Spanish contingent met and broke up an army of thirty thousand above the gorge. Finally, on the plains around Quezaltenango, "one Thursday at midday, there appeared a great multitude of people in many lines *(cabos)*, that according as I learned from they themselves, numbered 12,000 from within this town, and from surrounding towns of which they say cannot be counted. And after seeing them, I put the people in order." (Alvarado 1525b:27–28) Would he have spoken of "putting in order" his three hundred Tlaxcalan Mexican allies who had campaigned with him repeatedly even prior to the conquest of Mexico City? It appears that Alvarado had acquired inexperienced new allies. Once the allies were ready, the Spanish horsemen set upon the Quiché, disorganizing them thoroughly, whereupon "our friends and the foot soldiers worked the greatest destruction in the world," forcing many up into a mountain where they were killed or taken prisoner. "That day were killed or taken, many people." This does not sound like the kind of mop-up tactics that three hundred foot soldiers and three hundred Mexicans could have handled. "Our friends" were probably a sizable contingent of Mam Indians from San Pedro Sacatepéquez, San Martín Sacatepéquez, Concepción Chiquirichapa, San Juan Ostuncalco, and possibly other southern Mam towns.

Such an alliance virtually duplicates the strategy of Cortés in his alliances with the Tlaxcalans prior to the conquest of the central Aztecs (Gibson 1966:27). Alvarado must surely have welcomed this and wished for it, if not suggested it, in his diplomatic contacts at Oaxaca with the ambassadors sent to New Spain from Guatemala. Furthermore, we note that Alvarado turned eastward after the Quiché encounters, reducing the Cakchiquels and others around Lake Atitlán, then moving to Escuintla, El Salvador, and Honduras. From Honduras, in his second letter, Alvarado notes he had 100 horsemen, 150 *peóns* (Spanish footmen), and "about five or six thousand Indian friends of ours" (Alvarado 1525b:42). Some of these might have been from San Pedro Sacatepéquez, in addition to the Cakchiquels he is reported to have used (MacLeod 1973:40–42). This alliance would explain why the Mam area was not reduced until 1533, why Alvarado went first to the east of the Quiché, and why the Indians of San Pedro have a document granting them protection in return for having participated in the other conquests of Alvarado.

In 1533, the Spanish returned to the Quiché area and then set about the conquest of the northern Mams. Under the command of a Juan de León Cardona, they laid seige to Zaculeu. The attack and subjugation of present-day Huehuetenango through the fall of Zaculeu is important here in that it establishes the date of 1533 for the return of the Spaniards to the general area of the Mam enclave.

But the southern Mams are nowhere mentioned in these chronicles of war; it is indeed probable that they submitted their region peaceably. Oral tradition (now fixed in writing) from both towns asserts that San Pedro either surrendered, if told by a Ladino of San Marcos, or allowed the Spaniards to reside nearby, if told by an Indian of San Pedro.

Unfortunately, there is no written record of how the southern Mams switched from a posture of subordinate alliance to a position of subservience. It seems probable that this did not occur until after the conquest of the northern Mams in 1533. Furthermore, it seems unlikely that the southern Mams would have resisted. Having helped Alvarado in several campaigns, the Mams would have seen the futility of resistance. The southern Mams probably had been promised special concessions from the Spanish, as an incentive to alliance; as Alvarado had said, those who had "offered themselves" were to be "greatly favored and supported." In any event, the San Pedro charter shows they had acquired a statement of special privilege from the Spanish crown by 1543.

This San Pedro "privilege" is worth quoting substantially:

> Don Carlos by Divine Grace [and] Doña Juana his mother . . . by the same grace Kings of Castile . . . [thirty-four additional titles of their rule over portions of the kingdom omitted] . . . wherefore

> on behalf of You *(Vos)* [the] *Caciques* of the towns of Sacatepéquez an account has been made to us in which we learned how You had served by joining together with Fray Pedro de Angula and with other clergy of the Dominican Order in bringing peace and knowledge of Our Holy Catholic Faith [to] the natives of the provinces of [illegible] and Lacandon and their environs . . . [and in bringing] all the other natives under Our Government and Royal Crown we ask that in remuneration to your Lords that it be [granted] unto you that neither now nor at any time may you or the other towns be estranged or separated from Our Royal Crown by any person placed between. (various signatures, dated 1543) (Framed manuscript sheet, mayor's office, San Pedro Sacatepéquez)

The critical point is that in return for having participated with the Spaniards, the Spanish crown granted that San Pedro Sacatepéquez would never be "estranged" *(enajenado)* from rule by the crown. In other words, no individual would be its master; San Pedro would be, in some degree, protected by the crown. But the privilege did not mean protection from the exploitation of its labor resources; rather, it meant that San Pedro's labor would be managed by the crown rather than by private *encomenderos*. San Pedro was not unique in having sought and acquired this status. Gibson records that Tlaxcalan towns also petitioned the crown (1966:37–38). These details of the conquest period establish a historical basis for certain unusual aspects of San Pedro society and culture, although the context of colonial institutions left the San Pedranos recognizably Indian.

Thus, the conquest brought together four social categories throughout Latin America: conquistador, crown, priest, and aboriginal inhabitant. To see how, in Martínez Peláez's phrasing, the aborigines were made into Indians, we must examine the linkage of conquistador, crown, and priest to the institutions of colonial rule.

The Colonial Institutions: 1542–1821

THE *ENCOMIENDA*

In repayment for their conquest efforts, the crown granted the *conquistadores* concessions to portions of towns or whole towns of Indians. In terms of the grants, the *conquistadores* took tribute from the townsmen and had some claim to their labor. The grants also entailed a responsibility for Christianization, though this was often ignored or hired out to the clergy, and from this ministerial responsibility comes the name *encomienda* or "stewardship."

The Spaniards at first felt themselves entitled to extract wealth from their charges by any means whatever. In the earliest period (in Guatemala, between 1525 and 1542), the conquistadors operated the *encomienda* system. They had direct dominion over the Indians in the towns assigned to them by Pedro de Alvarado or by the Spanish crown. Moreover, anyone resisting the conquest could be enslaved as the personal property of the *conquistadores*. Since the conquistadors wanted to return to Spain in wealth, and since there had been no effective restrictions on the ways that the Indians were to be treated, it is not surprising that the early years of the conquest are best characterized as a period of unmitigated exploitation and abandon.

The priestly orders very quickly saw that their interests in the New World would be rapidly terminated by the uncontrolled *conquistadores*. Bartolomé de las Casas and others therefore went to Spain in an effort to secure the crown's support for protecting and preserving the Indians. Under the advice of las Casas, the crown framed the New Laws and issued them in 1542. These laws would restrict the *conquistadores* and *encomenderos* in the New World and would benefit the Indians—and the clergy.

In theory, the New Laws significantly altered the *encomienda* system. First, slavery was abolished. Indians could no longer be attached to Spaniards as property; rather, they were attached to their own Indian towns. Second, the towns themselves were removed from the direct control and dominion of the person holding the *encomienda*. Third, the *encomendero* was not allowed to live in the town or to acquire direct personal service from the Indians. Fourth, the inheritance of *encomiendas* was to be limited to the second descending generation of the current *encomendero*. In practice, however, the provisions of the New Laws were never fully implemented as stated. To have done so would have deprived the *conquistadores* of their reason for serving the crown. As a result, the New Laws were implemented with a number of accommodations and understood dilutions in the intensity of their provisions.

More important than the facts of actual practice, though, the New Laws established the crown's intent to exert political control. The crown began to make use of the clergy for information and advice as well as for the political administration of some of the towns that were returned to the crown from *encomendero* control.[8] Thus, from a very early date the institutional linkage of civil government and clergy was established.

Under the New Laws the *encomienda* was limited to "a concession," which the King granted to a Spaniard who participated in the conquest and colonization, "consisting in the receipt of tributes from an Indian group, levied by the Audiencia and collected by the Corregidores or their dependents" (Martínez Peláez 1971:93). Prior to the New Laws, the *encomienda* entailed a direct stewardship responsibility for the Christianization of the Indians. However, the New Laws shifted this responsibility from the *encomendero* to the priestly orders. The religious orders then charged the *encomendero* for the Christianizing services they rendered. Thus, the church and the Spanish crown were involved in the governance and administration of the Indian townships. The *encomendero* now only received a stipend and was prohibited access to the community. An *encomienda* therefore consisted in the rights to a percentage of the tribute from a given Indian town.

Landholding was not an attribute of the *encomienda*. Rather, land was acquired by petitioning the crown either to grant rights to unused land or to validate a title deriving from prior use *(composición)* (Martinez Pelaez 1971:92–93). Nevertheless, *encomenderos* did attempt to acquire land, especially land near their own *encomienda* villages. The system, which allotted Indian labor to paying petitioners, allowed the landowning *encomenderos* not only to use a portion of the taxes or tribute from the village allotted to them by *encomienda* but also to use the labor of their Indians on *encomendero* estates *(haciendas)*. For example, in one case reported by MacLeod (1973:129–32), a certain Juan de León Cardona had a large *hacienda* near his *encomiendas*. *Repartimiento* labor from these *encomienda* villages herded his sheep and cattle. The animals were sold to the capital or to other Spanish users for meat. The Indians were forced to buy the wool and wheat produced on the landholdings and to convert the wool into the cloth products with which they paid their *encomienda* tribute.

In many places *encomienda* tribute was required in cash or in cacao, the preconquest native currency. This forced the Indians to become migratory wage laborers, for few except the Spanish-owned cacao plantations on the Pacific littoral paid laborers in cash or in cacao. The system of tributes forced Indians to migrate to the coastal lands in search of work. Thus, from the beginning of the colonial period, the Indian villagers had been disciplined to labor either on the nearby landholdings of Spanish overlords or on the coast (MacLeod 1973:140).

By 1600 the *encomienda* system of private Spanish stewardships over the Indians had effectively collapsed. On the deaths of the second inheritors the privately held *encomiendas* reverted one by one to the crown. In many instances these *encomiendas* were then given to the religious orders to administer. In addition, MacLeod (1973) attributes the collapse to Indian depopulation and to "royal interference." So the personal *encomiendas* became relatively insignificant. But this does not mean that the village-based tributes were terminated. On the contrary, until 1821 the Indian towns were required to pay tribute according to each town's population of adult males, but the tribute went to the crown rather than to the conquistadors and their descendants.

As the *encomiendas* passed to the crown, the basic two-level political structure of township versus central government was established. Although there were administrative subdivisions of the kingdom of Guatemala, called *Alcaldías Mayores,* these territorial subdivisions were not separate governing entities but merely administrative arms of the central government.

THE *ENCOMIENDA* IN SAN PEDRO SACATEPÉQUEZ

There is ample evidence in the colonial documents in the Guatemalan National Archives that the *Pueblo de Indios* of San Pedro Sacatepéquez was a town held in *encomienda*.

Unfortunately, a record of the initial *encomienda* grant could not be located. But in 1646, the crown paid the Mercedarian order for "spiritual administration" in San Pedro Sacatepéquez (AGG leg. 600, exp. 11786). This document arises from the New Laws requirement that *encomenderos* pay the clergy for the Christianization of the *encomendero's* stewardship. It thus suggests strongly that the town of San Pedro was held in *encomienda* by the crown. But in 1656 and again in 1688, documents show that San Pedro was held in *encomienda* by a certain Señor Don Diego de Cardona. As *encomendero,* this individual paid the Mercedarian order for "the doctrine and administration of the holy sacraments" (AGG leg. 5900, exp. 49986; leg. 1074, exp. 19472). Subsequent colonial documents indicate that San Pedro was not held for long as a personal *encomienda,* though there is neither a date nor a reason for the change. Most likely the *encomienda* of San Pedro reverted to the crown or to the Mercedarian order. Whichever the case, tribute appears to have been levied on the community for the entire colonial period. An 1810 document in the possession of the San Pedro municipality shows that on this date there were 417 tributaries or assessed males in the community (a "tributary" is a working-age male). For this number of persons, 1,522 *tostónes* and one *real* were levied, or a total of 17 *reales* for each tributary (San Pedro Sacatepéquez, Treasurer's Office, document 27). On the basis of these documents we know that Sacatepéquez participated in the *encomienda* system that, we may assume, defined the social relations and work ideology of San Pedro, much as it did the rest of the country.

REDUCCIÓN AND *REALENGA:* THE POLITICS OF SETTLEMENT AND LANDOWNERSHIP

Prior to the conquest and for a short period thereafter, most of the Indians had been living dispersed over the countryside, farming their agricultural lands. But following the conquest and at the insistence of the clerical orders, the Spanish crown announced a system of roundups *(reducciones)* or congregations *(congregaciones)*. Orders were issued in 1542 to round up the Indians and place them in concentrated town centers. Most of the current Indian townships were founded as a result of this order (MacLeod 1973:120–22). The *reducción* program benefited virtually all Spaniards and was greatly desired by them. For the priests, *reducción* provided a compact, easy means of reaching the people to be Christianized. For the Spanish crown, *reducción* facilitated the administration of the Indians and the collection of the tribute to be sent to Spain. For the Spaniards born in the New World and called *criollos, reducción* removed the smallholders from the land. These lands could then be appropriated to Creole use through land claims before the crown. Finally, *reducción* made possible the recruitment of laborers from the villages, under the rotating labor allotments called *repartimiento*.

MacLeod suggests that, while the system of congregations left the land free for Spanish occupation and use, it also had the effect of making land a surplus commodity. From this surplus-commodity aspect MacLeod assumes that the land was relatively valueless. On the contrary, documentation from the San Pedro-San Marcos region suggests that land was valued and frequently under dispute. With this position Martinez Pelaez also concurs. He suggests that in the *Recordación Florida,* the earliest chronicle by a Guatemalan Creole, the text is virtually lyrical when it refers to the land. From this he concludes that land was highly valued. However, the value of land did not lie in its relative scarcity or abundance but in its relation to the social hierarchy. Land was valuable by virtue of its productive capacity. Land was only productive and hence valuable to those Spaniards who had consignments of Indian labor through the *repartimiento* or to those who would work it themselves—the Indians. In either case, to understand the value of land we must look to the Indian *reducción* town, the *Pueblo de Indios*.

Each Indian town was assigned a parcel of *ejido* lands. The amount of land varied somewhat, but it was supposed to extend one-half league or approximately two kilometers in all directions from the town center (Martínez Peláez 1971:166–72). These *ejidos* were village properties. Some portions were communal lands to which all Indian townsmen had access, usually for pasturage or forest products. Other areas were given in inheritable usufruct to specific persons. In theory, such *ejido* lands were inalienable, but in practice it was only necessary to show that the lands were not being used by the community in question in order for an outsider to acquire them. Thus, a well-connected Spaniard could usurp the land either by colluding with an Indian leader or by pursuing bureaucratic paperwork to declare that the lands were insufficiently used.

Apart from the village *ejidos,* all land not properly titled to individuals was owned by the crown. An individual desiring land could, for a price, petition the crown for a grant from *realenga* or crown land. But there were also cases of land being used without title. Under crown law, long-term use could be regularized with a title issued under a process called *composición,* again for a fee given to the Spanish crown through its local agents. This composition of irregularly possessed land was a major source of revenue for the crown. More significantly, local government officials were given a 2 percent commission on the fees that were gathered. As Martinez Pelaez points out, the commission increased the local officials' interest in matters of state revenue while it closed their eyes to the original illegality of the land-grabbing (1971:153–55). The net result was an extreme degree of land predation, especially in the vicinity of the Indian villages where a supply of labor was readily available. To be sure, the crown did attempt to protect the Indians so that they would have sufficient lands to maintain themselves. But the Indians were unsure of the nature of their rights under Spanish land law. Thus, individual Indians and Indian towns paid for the *composición* of their lands repeatedly, turning the registration-fee procedure into a regular Indian property tax. And the local officials had a 2 percent incentive not to correct the misinterpretation.

REDUCCIÓN AND REALENGA IN SAN PEDRO

Specific details on the initial *reducción* of San Pedro are not available. Nevertheless, the town does display the square-grid pattern that suggests that it was subjected to the ordering process of *reducción*. Furthermore, the populations of the towns surrounding San Pedro on the north, west, and south are all Ladino. Concerning the land, available colonial documents show first that much of the coast piedmont and mountain slope toward the south was royal land (*realenga*) and, second, that the lands were being petitioned and composed from time to time, mostly by Spaniards. Furthermore, there are a number of documents concerning the *haciendas* or large landholdings that were in the vicinity of San Pedro (AGG leg. 6043, exp. 53332; leg. 6039, exp. 53293). Evidences of land pressure on Indian San Pedro, arising from the surrounding Spanish people, are present in a number of documents, two of which are cited in detail later in this chapter. Essentially, in one case, a brother of the principal *cacique* of San Pedro sold land that the *cacique* held to be inalienable. In two other cases, San Pedranos complained about the usurpation of their lands by the Ladinos living in the area. Thus, San Pedro suffered the same land problems documented in other Indian towns.

REPARTIMIENTO

The third major institution of Spanish colonial practice was called *repartimiento*. The early and fairly rapid decline of the Indian population reduced the tribute value of *encomiendas* and left the *repartimiento* system as the primary institution of colonial control over the Indians. At first, the word *repartimiento* referred to a system in which one-fourth of the Indians of each town, on a rotation basis, were required to report for work to the persons to whom the labor supply had been allocated. The Indians were supposed to be paid a nominal sum for their work, which, including the transportation time, was not supposed to last more than one week out of every month. However, Martinez Pelaez shows that both pay and the work limits of the system were frequently infringed upon. By approximately 1760 and thereafter, the labor system shifted slightly from an allocation on a weekly rotation to a seasonal general call-up by the Spaniards during the prime agricultural periods. Under this latter system, often called *mandamiento* ("consignment," "commandment"), the Indians were called primarily at harvest and planting times (Martinez Pelaez 1971:506–7).

While many of the Indians labored on consignment at *haciendas* close to their *pueblo,* there was also a constant stream of Indians who were also assigned to go down to the coast. Early in the conquest, the Pacific coastal area called Soconusco was a center of cacao production. For the Indians, cacao was both a desired drink and a recognized medium of exchange. The Spaniards quickly took over the cacao production, requiring a great many Indians to work the plantations in various tasks. *Repartimiento* satisfied this labor need. And, as noted earlier, many *encomiendas* demanded cacao as tribute, thereby forcing other Indians to the coast to acquire this medium of exchange. Though the cacao industry collapsed in the first century of the colony, it was followed by the coastal indigo industry, which developed principally between 1580 and 1720 (MacLeod 1973:176–88). Again Indians were required on the coast. Indigo production was particularly detrimental to the health of the Indians because it required long exposure in water. As a result, the crown, fearing the loss of its Indians, prohibited their involvement in indigo. Without other labor, the embargo on Indians was unreasonable, and the inspecting officials were bribed. Thus, indigo production was carried on with Indian assistance and, indeed, with the de facto approbation of the governing authorities, since they benefited from both the fines and bribery that resulted from the law (MacLeod 1973:176–88).

The *repartimiento* system was not entirely satisfying to the overlords. First of all, the Creole Spaniards felt that they did not get enough labor from the Indians. And the crown felt shortchanged on royalties from the rental of Indian labor. Moreover, depopulation and labor abuse caused food production in the Indian villages to fall. As a result, food prices rose in the cities because the Indians were not exporting. Indeed, the Indians were not producing sufficient food for themselves; there was even starvation in the Indian *pueblos* that were subjected to *repartimiento* (MacLeod 1973:204–8). To insure that the Indians planted sufficient crops and took care of their lands, the crown created new officers, the *jueces de milpas* or "field judges" (MacLeod 1973:210). Whether or not the field judges were successful in raising production, the example shows the degree to which Spaniards made an industry of managing the Indians.

REPARTIMIENTO IN SAN PEDRO

To be sure, San Pedranos were assigned to *repartimiento* shifts. In 1778, a certain Prudencio Tovar, a resident and subsequent mayor of San Marcos, petitioned the crown representatives in Guatemala City and requested forty Indians in *repartimiento*. Tovar requested that they be assigned from San Cristóbal Cucho, a town near San Pedro, and that those Indians that Cucho could not supply be assigned from San Pedro Sacatepéquez. San Pedro's leadership resisted this request in a document now in the National Archives.

The San Pedro argument against the petition is most instructive. San Pedro's leaders did not deny the rightful allocation of their citizens under the system of *repartimiento*. Rather, they argued that Prudencio Tovar was not an *"español"*; they argued that he was but a *"mestizo"* and thus was not entitled to a consignment of Indians. San Pedranos therefore petitioned the crown representatives that

> neither the corregidor of Quezaltenango nor anyone else . . . be able to compel them to work in repartimiento in the service of the aforementioned Prudencio or of anyone else of a similar class (AGG leg. 226, exp. 4048).

Thus, the San Pedranos did not claim that they should not be issued in *repartimiento*. Rather, they objected to being consigned to anyone of improper status. Furthermore, the San Pedranos also pointed out, their original charter from 1543 asserted that San Pedranos would never be estranged from the crown and that assignment to Tovar would constitute a form of estrangement.

The court responded by observing that San Pedranos were not estranged if the crown administered their issuance under *repartimiento*. Nevertheless, the crown authorities in Guatemala City rejected Tovar's request because

> San Pedro Sacatepéquez finds itself reduced to the number of 180 tributaries and San Cristobal Cucho to the number 32, all of whom in both towns are assigned to public works projects in conformity with the New Laws. (AGG leg. 226, exp. 4086)

This passage is the only evidence available to me that San Pedro participated in the *repartimiento* system. However, it displays the characteristics of *repartimiento* labor demand documented for the rest of Guatemala, except that San Pedranos were assigned by the crown to the crown. The document implies that present-day San Pedro was conditioned by approximately three hundred years of institutionalized *repartimiento* social interaction.

Colonial Society

Thus far, the focus of this chapter has been on the Indians and on the institutional context within which the Indians lived out their lives. It is quite apparent that the Indians were not isolated. Indeed, the definition of the Indian's place in the social system always involved a relationship to the government, which was controlled by the Spaniards. Thus, to understand the Indian, one must thoroughly understand the other components of the social system.

Members of the highest status group or sector of the colony were called *blancos,* or *españoles*. These *españoles* (Spaniards) were subdivided into several political interest groups. First, there were the *criollos* (Creoles), those persons claiming European descent but who were born in the Americas. Second, there were the *peninsulares,* also called *gachupines*. These were the *españoles* who had been born in Spain. Most of them came to the New World as crown officials. The third political interest group was the clergy. Interstitial to the Indians and *españoles* were the *ladinos*. This term was applied to the miscegenated newborn as well as to those Indians who acquired facility in Spanish, many of whom had left their native villages.

Throughout the colonial period there existed a sharp conflict between the *criollo* and the *peninsular*. The *criollos* were the descendants of the original Spanish *conquistadores* and first settlers, as well as descendants of *peninsulares* who had assimilated into the New World's social milieu. In essence, *criollos* contested with the Spanish crown for control of the fruits of their ancestors' labor, bridling at the efforts of the Spanish crown to restrict *criollo* exploitation of the Indian population. From the establishment of the New Laws in 1542 to independence in 1821, the crown attempted to assert control in the New World by sending waves of appointees to serve as governors and other officers. Family, kin, and friends accompanied the high officers and were given subordinate positions in the New World government. Charged with the interest of the crown, the *peninsulares* thus came into conflict with the native Creoles, who were desirous of extracting as much wealth as possible with a minimum of restraints. Crown and Creole disagreed not only on the issue of just how to use or how much to conserve the Indians. They also fought over who was to use them: the crown needed the remaining Indians for public works, construction, road repair, and porterage; the Creoles wanted them allotted to productive labors as peóns in the agricultural estates and processing plants. Creole and *peninsular* also competed for power and privilege within the bureaucracy of the New World government.

Several mechanisms somewhat reduced the conflict. First, the *criollos* could partially compromise the *peninsulares* by weaving them into the system of social relations through astutely arranged marriages or choice as *compadres*. Second, *peninsulares* profited from *criollo* excesses, for the *peninsulares* generally collected a percentage of the fines imposed. But they could collect even more from the *criollos* by agreeing, for a fee, not to impose the fines at all. Altogether, it was a profitable arrangement for both. Finally, *peninsulares* compromised themselves when they sought the available wealth of the New World, putting themselves at odds with the crown they were sent to represent.

So the crown found it necessary to replace its representatives from time to time. As each wave of peninsular Spaniards came to the New World to enforce the crown's wishes, they replaced the previous *peninsulares* and installed their own network of friends and relatives into the governmental posts. This pushed the Creoles and the previous peninsular Spaniards down in the governmental structure. *Encomiendas* that had been held by Creoles were given to *peninsulares*. Offices that were held by Creoles were reapportioned to *peninsulares*. *Peninsulares* were pushed out and came to identify with the *criollos*. As a result, there developed a considerable population of *déclassé*[9] whites or Spaniards. These people's déclassé political and economic status was in conflict with their racially and culturally elite social status. Indeed, out of this Creole ferment arose the major class base for the independence movements in the 1820s.

A second fissure existed in the Hispanic society, between the Creoles and the clergy. Martinez Pelaez demonstrates the *criollo* ambivalence toward the priestly orders by analyzing the writings of Francisco Antonio de Fuentes y Guzmán, the early *criollo* chronicler. On the one hand, Fuentes y Guzmán is vituperative when he talks about the clergy, because they helped to instigate the New Laws that shackled the *encomienda* system and restrained the Creoles. On the other hand, he is appreciative and full of praise when he discusses the church's service to the Creoles through Christianization. Indeed, the priestly orders facilitated the symbolic domination of the Indians. Church participation, initially by baptism, was the symbol of submission to the new social order.

The church's involvement in governing the Indians was not just symbolic. Throughout the colonial period, the Catholic priesthood advised the crown and administered many of the crown's *encomiendas*. There was a fusion of crown and clerical interests in the governing of the Indian peoples: the government acquired a secure administrative arm, while the church acquired access to and power within the Indian communities. Both agreed that the Indians must be conserved: the crown wanted Indians to tax; the church wanted Indians to evangelize and to provide revenue. Thus, the Catholic friars were a source of physical and social protection for the Indians as well as the symbolic basis for Indian submission.

Then as now, religious piety symbolized political submission. With the clergy operating on behalf of the crown in Indian governance, through imposing and collecting tribute and personal labor service and by managing the municipal level of the colonial occupation, it is not surprising that the civil-religious hierarchy became the most outstanding institution in many Indian communities.[10]

From the time of the conquest, the social system had two primary status categories and two primary social groupings. On the one hand, there were the Spaniards, linked by kinship connection, birthplace, and ideology to Spain. On the other hand, there were the Indians, linked by legal definition to a particular hinterland community. Very quickly, however, there arose an interstitial sector of the populace. The Spanish *conquistadores* brought very few Spanish women with them. As part of the spoils of conquest, the conquerors availed themselves of the Indian women. In doing so, they established an ideology that which continues to the present: that status superiors have sexual access to status inferiors.

Given the racial-origin symbolism of the early colonists, sexual access also created a new kind of person, neither European conqueror nor Indian subject. Biologically, these persons were miscegenated. *Mestizo* is one of the words used to refer to them in the colonial period. *Castas* is a more general term, with subdivisions referring to many of the possible combinations of miscegenation between white, Indian, and black slave.[11] *Pardos* or "browns" also refers to the racial cross between Indian and white (Martinez Pelaez 1971:259 n. 1, 267–70, 289). The interstitial and contradictory character of these *castas* is indicated by the phrase that they were *"gente de color quebrado*—people of broken color" (Martinez Pelaez 1971:269).

Another significant term used in the early part of the conquest was *ladino*. Initially, this word applied to any individual of Indian or Mestizo extraction who could speak Spanish. However, by the last decades of the 1700s, the word was used to refer to politically marginal individuals in the Spanish-speaking community. The reason for this shift is simple. Spaniards and Indians were integral to the system. The *castas*—the *mestizos, mulatos, zambos,* and a score of other *casta* combinations—were not; they were ideologically marginal, broken, incomplete, and anomalous. Hence one could put down provincial townsmen by calling them *ladinos españoles,* as the central government often did when it referred to the people of San Marcos.

Not all the *mestizos* or *ladinos* were racially mixed. The *déclassé* Creoles who had been pushed downward by the continuing influx of *peninsulares* were always in some danger of being identified with this sector of the society. One finds numerous colonial documents of persons pleading their inappropriate poverty and citing their illustrious ancestry that links them to the original conquest and settlement of the country (Martinez Pelaez 1971:106–7). As MacLeod points out, the changes in Spanish governors, the deaths of kings, and the consequent alteration of networks of friendship led to the deposing of peninsular Spaniards into Creoles and brought Creoles to the margin of respectability as Spaniards (MacLeod 1973:319–21).

Legally, the *castas* or interstitial persons in the society were barred from residence within the Indian towns. In fact, however, there were always *castas* or *mestizos* who were in contact with the Indians. These Mestizos or Ladinos were the petty tradesmen, the artisans, the mule skinners, the ranch hands of the society.[12] In short, they were everything that the Indians and the Spaniards were not. On the one hand, the Indians were restricted legally, linked to towns and subjected to tribute. By contrast, the *castas* were not linked to communities; they were highly mobile, and they were not subject to tribute. They were the Spanish speakers who were not connected to Spain or to local tribute towns. On the other hand, the Spaniards, whether Creole or peninsular, were in command, in power, of high status; and they were essentially unfettered by legal restraint. By contrast, the *castas* and *ladinos* were equally unfettered but they were out of power. While the Indians were the basic agricultural providers and the source of the Spaniards' wealth in taxation and labor services and the Spaniards were the source of government power, the *castas* and *ladinos* became whatever else was left. They were neither high status nor low, neither fixed to towns nor linked to power, neither legally required to labor nor authorized to tap Indian labor, neither white nor Indian. Throughout the colonial period, the Mestizos appear to have been in an adaptive flux, partaking of neither the fixity of the Indians nor the status of the Spaniards.

Like the mortar between the foundation and the bricks, Mestizos came into contact with both Indians and Spaniard and were the medium by means of which the one supported the other. As MacLeod has shown (1973:191–193), the *castas* were chosen from a very early period to be the labor gang bosses over the Indians working on the coastal plantations. And as merchants and transporters, Mestizos brought goods and information back and forth between the Indian and the Spanish groups.

As a result of their ideologically induced and socially secured mobility, the *castas* were virtually above the law and were a scourge both to the Indian villages and to the Spaniards' peace of mind. The source of the problem is that the *castas* were ideologically anomalous to the basic two-division system. *Castas* were neither connected to Spain nor to the Indian villages. Their violence and shiftlessness, then, were a result of their ideological marginality. The *castas*, whether *mestizo* or *ladino* and regardless of their actual racial composition, were like the cloven-hoofed nonruminants and the single-hoofed ruminants of the Jews (Douglas 1966:54–72). They were dangerous. From the point of view of the Spaniards, it was the *castas* who disaffected the Indians, who carried them into rebellion, who showed them how to fend for themselves outside their villages, and, in general, who severed them from the system of tribute and *repartimiento* in their restricted village context (Martinez Pelaez 1971: 430–33).

Colonial Society in San Marcos and San Pedro

We have seen San Pedro Sacatepéquez as an Indian town, participating and evolving in the context of the colonial institutions of *encomienda, reducción* and *repartimiento*. Indeed, the San Pedranos looked to the crown and to the church for government and protection, particularly for protection from the Spaniards living next to them in San Marcos. Thus, it is not possible to divorce San Pedro from the

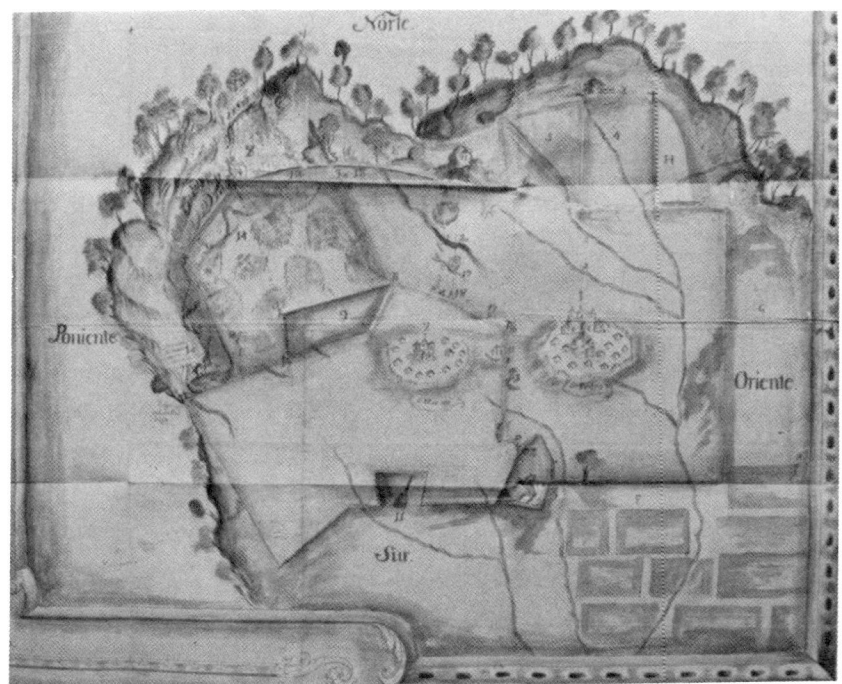

Plate 1. An eighteenth-century map of San Marcos and San Pedro. The exact date is unknown, but a copy of the map is referred to in September 1783 in connection with a dispute over land ownership. San Marcos and San Pedro are the two circles in the middle of the map.

surrounding ideological and sociological context of *ladinos* and colonial Spaniards.

Nor is it possible to describe San Pedro without major reference to the community of San Marcos, since San Marcos has been the focus of the *ladinos* (formerly *españoles*) most intimately connected to San Pedro. But, thus far, there has been a de-emphasis of the discussion of the community of San Marcos. To see San Pedro in its total social situation, we must fit San Pedro and San Marcos together and show in what ways San Marcos specifically supplied the *españoles* and *ladinos* generally described earlier.

The founding of San Marcos in relation to San Pedro is of first consequence. The residents of San Marcos today assert, through their "town chronicler," that San Marcos was founded as an encampment of armed conquistadors in the fields adjacent to the community of San Pedro. The conquistadors had arrived in force, but San Pedro surrendered peacefully, willingly, and wisely. By contrast, the origin myth in San Pedro asserts that land near San Pedro was usurped by indigent travelers who sought a temporary place to stay and then remained permanently. Historical documentation does not deny either of these claims but places them in a significantly different light. In February 1676, the *Audiencia* in Guatemala issued the crown's orders that the titles for all house sites be presented to the governing authorities in the provinces to ascertain whether they were properly legalized. The order suggested that, if titles were not presented, the sites would be turned over to the crown administrators or to the Indian towns *(Pueblos de Indios)* in which they stood. In September 1676, six named residents "and other citizens *(vecinos)*" from the *Barrio de San Marcos* presented themselves before the visiting representative of the *Audiencia* in Quezaltenango and affirmed,

> in the name of the other residents *(vecinos)* and natives of said Barrio of San Marcos and families which are there residing, we have come to make manifest and exhibit a Royal Provision made out by the *Señores Presidentes y Oydores* of said Royal *Audiencia*, dated 30 July 1631 and one [illegible word] by Andres de Escobar, head secretary of it [the *Audiencia*] in which it seems that said Indios of San Pedro Sacatepéquez having attempted to expel from among them [selves] the residents of said Barrio and [the latter] having requested [it] through you, it was ordered that they be removed, without disturbing the former arrangements [of the town of San Pedro] in that the Spaniards leave said town of San Pedro, not to be understood as leaving said barrio [that is, they partitioned administratively but did not move physically] and in this aspect they were upheld in the possessions which they have had, and in this arrangement they have been. At present, for the greater security of the persons that inhabit said Barrio they solicit to compose [that is, legitimate their possession] with Your Majesty the lands occupied by the houses and *solares* of the families which are now there . . . bearing in mind that they are vassals of Your Majesty (God safeguard him) and that they have resided in this place since time immemorial in these parts, and that they support themselves with their work, and that they lend themselves to all that is of service to the Crown, and pay their taxes, on account of all of which they ask the fulfillment of justice. (AGG leg. 5483, exp. 47183)

The documentation shows that San Marcos first offered fifty *reales* to compose the lands. The central authorities rejected this offer. However, a subsequent offer of a hundred *reales* was accepted on September 26, 1676. From this document we learn that, prior to 1631, San Marcos had been a subdivision or ward within the Indian community of San Pedro Sacatepéquez. Given the laws prohibiting the residence of *castas* or Spaniards in Indian towns, the predivision arrangement probably was illegal.

Worse, it was inconsistent with the ideological system. In another part of the document, residents of San Marcos complained (and a clerk recorded) that the residents of San Pedro "raise their canes of authority against them [the Spaniards]." Such a complaint would not have been meaningful except for an ideology of Spanish authority over Indians. Under such circumstances, a division was inevitable.

For a century more, until municipal incorporation after 1752, the place continued to be called the "Barrio of San Marcos," the "Barrio and Pueblo of San Marcos Sacatepéquez," or just the "Barrio." The Barrio of San Marcos was governed by a judge or military officer "appointed by the *alcalde mayor* of the territory." The petition for municipal formation is most instructive. In it, the residents of San Marcos affirmed that

> from time immemorial to us, said Barrio is founded of Spaniards from among the First Conquerors of this kingdom, and as such, and as soldiers, which they have always been, they have lifted up the flag, residing in the service of your Majesty as the occasions offered, as in the controversies of Tequila and Berrospe [place names? illegible] so widely known in this kingdom, there being in this plaza the armed men that were requested. [And also] that in a certain uprising or rebellion that arose among the Indians of the town of Quezaltenango there was a prompt remedy in the men at arms of said Barrio of San Marcos, who cut down the pride of the Indios with their [that is, San Marcos's] respect [that is, forcefulness] as well as when, in the vicinity of said Barrio, the town of San Pedro Sacatepéquez gave evidence of shortly bursting into an uprising which was being introduced among the Indians of said town, and when later they attempted new tumults in the vicinity, [San Marcos] came to the rescue and attacked them until they were reduced to peaceful tranquility, which services have been well known to the Royal Audiencia. (AGG leg. 196, exp. 3980)

This document, dated March 1754, is accompanied by a request from the central authorities for a census of the town of San Marcos, in preparation for municipal status and elected local government. In response, the *corregidor* noted that San Marcos requested the right to form its own elected government "to the benefit of the public cause, peace, and tranquility of its residents, the better administration of justice, and removal of vices."

San Marcos was elevated from categorization as a *pueblo* to categorization as a *villa* in 1825. The term denoted its increased urbanity, though in terms of governmental rather than population significance. It was made headquarters of the newly formed Territorial District of San Marcos in 1832. In 1866, this and the other territorial districts were dissolved and reconstituted as departments. The municipality of San Marcos was made the department capital. In October 1897, however, its status as headquarters of the Department of San Marcos was rescinded and given to San Pedro Sacatepéquez. The department governorship remained in San Pedro until February 1898, a period of approximately four months, after which it was returned to San Marcos by administrative edict, where it has remained to the present.

The social-status categories in San Marcos and San Pedro follow the colonial pattern. The documents refer to Spaniards and Indians, with obviously primary interest, and they label the interstitial sector by using the words *ladinos, mestizos, castas,* and *mulatos* in about that order of frequency. As one example, in 1740 the crown gave orders for a complete census and geographical reconnaissance and report on the country. In this report, San Pedro Sacatepéquez was listed as having 418 tributaries. The subdivisions in the listing are quite interesting.

Married *naturales*	169
Indios married with *Indias* of other towns	50
Indios from other towns	51
Indias married with *mestizo*	2
Indios married with *mulata*	2
Indio married with *española*	1
Indio widowers	32
India widows	39
Single *Indios*	51
Single *Indias*	16
Indios married with non-tribute paying women	5
(AGG leg. 210, exp. 5009)	

The document then gives the heading of *españoles* living in San Pedro, after which each resident is named in nuclear family groups, with children's ages specified. Following the listing, a single paragraph describes San Pedro:

> This town is administered by the Mercedarian doctrinal priest. It is twelve leagues from the headquarters of Quezaltenango. These natives have a minor part to play. Their harvest is wheat and corn; their land [illegible word] and flat. Fog abounds and the ambience is humid but healthy for those natives. There are no mines except a sulfur mine. The natives are workers and inclined to buying and selling. A bit out of the town of San Pedro Sacatepéquez there is a town of Spaniards named the Barrio of our Lord San Marcos. They have no priest of their own, being ministered to by the *doctrinero* of San Pedro Sacatepéquez. It lies about one quarter of a league from said Sacatepéquez. They say that this barrio of San Marcos was formed by the first Spaniards who conquered the province and in it there are the following Spaniards. (AGG leg. 210, exp. 5009)

Thereupon, all of the San Marcos Spaniards are named, under the heading "Barrio of San Marcos," again giving the nuclear family groups with children's names and ages.[13] At the end of the census listing the document says,

> This town of San Marcos is of Spaniards, all laborers. They are poor and short of land on account of their closeness to the town of natives. The placement of said town is on a flat, but near the mountains. (AGG leg. 210, exp. 5009)

While the social statuses and categories of the people are fairly clear-cut in this document, they are much less clear-cut in other documents from the colonial period. For example, a 1752 document refers to San Pedro's Spanish-speaking town crier as an *"Indio ladino"* (AGG leg. 6036, exp. 53238). On the one hand, this reference shows that the word *ladino* refers to a Spanish speaker. However, it is clear in the context of this document that this particular Spanish speaker is an employee of the government by virtue of his Spanish-speaking capacity. He is the colonial government's official *"pregonero"* or crier. In this case, *ladino* shows not just facility with Spanish but also some degree of proximity to the central institutions and the values of the Spanish overlords.

More interesting examples of this phenomenon occur in the documentation in which San Marcos, San Pedro, and the central government vie for land or other privilege. Whenever San Pedro writes the central authorities concerning San Marcos, San Pedro calls the Marquenses *"ladinos"* or a *"town of ladinos."* The San Pedranos call themselves "Indians." Whenever San Marcos writes the central government concerning its land disputes, the Marquenses claim to be a "town of Spaniards" and assert that San Pedro is "Indian." Finally, when officers of the central government in Guatemala City (or its representatives in Quezaltenango) refer to San Marcos, they call it a *"Población de gente ladina*—a settlement of *ladino* people" (AGG leg. 196, exp. 3980). In the context of this document, one can see that, from the view of the *Audiencia* in Guatemala City, which is the ideological and institutional center (excepting Spain), San Marcos is peripheral, being twelve leagues beyond one of the most distant provincial capitals, Quezaltenango. It is not Indian, but it is marginal and disconnected and is therefore labeled *ladino*. The San Pedranos use the same tactic in referring to San Marcos. By calling San Marcos *ladino,* San Pedranos try to remove it further from close contact with the central government. By contrast, San Marcos sought to assert its connection in terms of loyalty, payment of taxes, and defense of the interests of the crown. Thus, when San Marcos's representatives claimed that the town was "founded of Spaniards from among the First Conquerors of this kingdom, and as such, and as soldiers," they were asserting their connection and hence their symbolic legitimacy as Spaniards. In doing so, they were using origins as symbols of social place—the defining feature of ethnicity. For the most part, biological reference was the symbol of social status and political standing within the system. It was not the case that racial biology determined one's standing in the society.

When Indians are named in documents, they are usually identified as being *naturales* ("natives") of a particular Indian town, in this case, San Pedro. Natives of Indian towns were legally Indians regardless of their racial heritage. By contrast, when Spaniards are identified, they are usually identified only by title and by their designation as Spaniard. When they are linked to a town, it is rarely with the words *natural de,* but, rather, as *"vecino de*—resident [or] citizen of" a particular place, which connotes the notion of neighbor and social interaction. In this manner, the documents emphasize the narrow, restricted, local focus imposed on the Indians as natives of their place, while they highlight the more mobile and temporary ideology of the *españoles* by calling them just citizens and neighbors, in spite of the fact that many were also natives of the place.

I have suggested earlier that Spanish and Indian world views or status ideologies are in many respects the inverse, opposite, or counterpoint transformations of each other. But there are also core concepts and values that Indians and Spaniards share. Land is one of these. The members of both communities considered the land to be socially and symbolically important. For this reason, they constantly disputed over the surrounding lands.

In 1699, a certain Don Jorge González, "a principal Indian and native of this town of San Pedro Sacatepéquez," attempted to get title to lands he was using. He said,

> I stand before your Grace and say that I have a piece of land in which I sow wheat. The land was inherited from my grandfather, and I bought some from different persons. In order to hold it with greater security, it should serve Your Grace to measure it and mark its boundaries, and allow me to compose it in order to pay what is due Your Majesty. (AGG leg. 5971, exp. 52439)

This passage illustrates several important facts. First, the first-person account shows a San Pedro Indian speaking Spanish ably at an early date, for translated testimony is usually written down as *"dijo que*—he said that." Second, it shows the possibility of private possession and ownership of land outside the community's *ejidos*. Third, the passage "in order to hold it with greater security" suggests that mere possession was not sufficient and that without other protections one might be subject to removal by someone acquiring proper title. Finally, it shows the value of land to these Indians.

The manner in which disputes over land were resolved illustrates the differing social and political access of the two communities in the colonial period. To the south and west of both San Marcos and San Pedro, on the piedmont and coastal region that is now coffee country, there was a large section of land that was believed to be a crown holding or *realenga*. The San Pedranos determined that this land would be an appropriate addition to their *ejido* holdings, and consequently, in 1793, they petitioned the *Audiencia* to have the region measured and the boundary marked so that it could be composed into the municipal holdings. The land judge, a resident of San Marcos, was ordered to proceed with the measuring task. A party of San Pedrano Indians, some "Spanish" assistants, the judge, and other San Marcos residents made their way toward the coast. They sent announcements to the various *haciendas* and surrounding communities in the region, and began with the measurement. As was customary in such actions, the party of measurers and interested persons proceeded around the designated territory, marking the corner points, the mountain peaks, and the passes with crosses. The crosses were constructed in appropriate places, carved on trees, or scratched into rocks. On completion of the circuit, the party of measurers and interested persons returned to San Marcos and San Pedro. The documents were drawn up: the measurements were calculated and multiplied to give the land area. Testimony was taken of various residents and members of the measuring group as to the approximate value of such land. By this means, a base price was arranged for the petitioners from San Pedro.

However, crown lands were not simply given at cost to the petitioners but were auctioned. Public announcement had to be made to give interested persons the opportunity to contest the actuality of the crown holding. They could do this by establishing title or by declaring that they had been in continuous and useful possession of portions of the land. Public announcements were cried throughout the town of San Pedro. Following each announcement, called the *pregón,* the land judge awaited the arrival of persons who might wish to bid up the base price that was settled upon for San Pedro. Six of the nine required days of announcement were made in San Pedro, with no increment in the base value of the land being offered. The three final days of public announcement were declared in San Marcos. On the day of the first announcement in San Marcos, authorities of that community raised the price by 25 percent. This increment was not improved by San Pedro. Therefore, on the ninth day the land was granted in favor of San Marcos.

San Pedro's leaders then wrote a letter of complaint to the land judge and through him to higher authorities.[14] They argued that San Pedro had started and financed the measurement and that now,

> knowingly the inhabitants of the Barrio want to thrust us out and deprive us of our town and lands. They want to be owners of all the lands, indeed they have us surrounded; and in a few days they will want to put their haciendas in the San Pedro cemetery. They want that they only eat; they want to cast us out yonder. [But] being that we are *criollos* and natives, bearing privileges from His Majesty, we have no further patience for putting up with the many distasteful events, prejudices, and harms which they commit upon us. (AGG leg. 6039, exp. 53293)

In this document, the San Pedranos further complain that they had asked for the land first, that they are in need, and that San Marcos could always offer more than San Pedro: "Those of the barrio could pay more than ten pesos inasmuch as they have earned too much money." San Marcos had more money, but it also had better connections to the land judge and other officials.

The original calculations on the land concluded that the piece of land to be composed was 39 *caballerías*[15] in size. According to my calculations from the side measurements of the land in question, this figure is very close to correct. However, when the dispute was reviewed by higher authorities, it was declared that the figure was incorrect, that there were not 39 *caballerías* but rather 406. In the light of this incorrect figure, it was determined that the piece of land was far too large for an Indian community. The central government declared that allotting it to San Pedro would restrict the growth of coastal towns and would interfere with the free passage of muleteers through the province of Soconusco. Whether this shift from 39 to 406 *caballerías* was a Machiavellian "error" that the Indians could not catch because they did not understand the mechanics of land-area calculation in the Spanish system or an honest mistake, we will probably never know. But the effect was the same. If a 25 percent increase in the bid price on 39 units buckled San Pedro, imagine the effect of a tenfold increase in the number of units that had to be purchased. San Pedro was squeezed out.

San Marcos, although labeled by the central government as a community of *ladinos,* reasserted its Spanish descent and redoubled its effort to secure the lands in order to enhance its agricultural pursuits. The residents of San Marcos pointed out that, in the 1790 census, San Pedro had only 241 tributaries. This would suggest not more than 241 households and probably less—perhaps one thousand and certainly no more than two thousand residents. By contrast, San Marcos declared itself to have five thousand inhabitants. At this point in the folio, a considerable number of years elapses without any reference to the land. Notes are included to the effect that San Pedro diverted its attention to rebuilding its town following a series of earthquakes.

In 1809, San Pedro reasserted its interest in the lands and declared that there was a folio of documentation regarding the matter. The central government then declared that it had lost the records. As a result, the *corregidor* of Quezaltenango ordered a review of San Pedro's landholdings. A document was made out to that effect, though it is not sewn into the case record, and then the same order was reissued in September 1809. Between this 1809 document and one dated 1816 stands an undated petition:

> Señor Minister and Governor:
>
> José López and José Orozco, Indians *(indígenes)* from the town of San Pedro Sacatepéquez, on behalf of the town, with the appropriate solemnity we accompany these documents and with due respect I manifest that in the Land Archives there exists a documentation of measurements and, moreover, of *ejidos,* and we beg *(suplicamos)* that you be good enough to order that the chief clerk look for said documentation and that we be given a title, an authentic one, since it concerns land, and we ask and beg that you not act maliciously, Your Lordship.
>
> Signatures
(AGG leg. 6039, exp. 53293)

The lack of dates, not uncommon on individual petitions (I have discovered three such undated petitions in the San Pedro records), perhaps indicates a certain timelessness, or a detachment from the implications of time. More certainly, the passage manifests an Indian fearfulness of Spanish duplicity when they "ask and beg" that the officials in control of the records "not act maliciously." Perhaps as a result of the petition, sometime in 1816 the case record was discovered in the archive box for San Marcos's legal documents.

So the contest for land was again taken up, with San Marcos asserting that it was not desirable for San Pedro to have lands on both San Marco's east and west sides. In 1817, the special protector or legal defender of the Indians suggested that the lands in dispute be parted half-and-half between San Marcos and San Pedro. However, in 1819 and again in 1820 and 1823, priests from the area were consulted as to the social conditions in the department, and it was determined that "it is proper that San Marcos have its *ejidos,* although it is not of *Indios,* so that its inhabitants not have need of renting lands from their neighbors." Following this decision, a new judge was installed who ruled in favor of San Marcos and certain coastal *ladino* towns, and in favor of the commercial interests of free transport on the coast. Thus, after thirty years, San Pedro lost the case (AGG leg. 6039, exp. 53293).[16]

Tension over land has persisted to the present and has occupied much of the attention of the people in the two towns. For example, in 1772, San Marcos held an auction sale to raise funds for "the lengthy litigations which they have maintained with the community of Sacatepéquez" (AGG leg. 2793, exp. 40421). Later, in 1784, a dispute over land between the two communities was resolved principally in favor of San Marcos, although San Pedro got "good mountain land." However, at the termination of this dispute over lands, San Pedro was told to keep quiet: the *Audiencia* finished the documentation with an order "placing upon them as was done, perpetual silence upon the community, the *Indios* of the Pueblo of San Pedro Sacatepéquez" (Archives of the municipality of San Pedro Sacatepéquez, Document No. 44, 1776). So San Pedro further lost its ability to communicate with the central institutions.

This lack of social connection was exacerbated by the patterns of ethnic residence. From a very early date, the officials of the regional government resided in San Marcos, the place where they also conducted most of their official business. In the style of the Roman legal system, most official and legal matters were disposed of by taking depositions of witnesses or interested parties. When a person presented himself (or more rarely, herself) for official business, the person's name and other identifying information was written into the document. The difference in the way Indians and non-Indians were written up highlights the differences in social connection. When a Marquense appears in the official record, the presiding official usually records the witness's name, followed by a statement that the official or someone else "knows and identifies [him] to be an Español (or Ladino) and resident of San Marcos." By contrast, a San Pedrano who appears in the official record is named and immediately labeled "*Indio* of San Pedro." No reference is given to knowledge or certification of the San Pedrano's social status as other than derived from his or her town. An Indian is not "certified as known by" the official. Thus, in the formerly mentioned case, when Prudencio Tovar sought to have a *repartimiento* of San Pedro Indians and his request was challenged by San Pedro on the grounds that he was a *mestizo*, Tovar presented evidence in the form of testimony from persons of San Marcos to the effect that he was Spanish. The various witnesses named his father, mother, grandfathers, and grandmothers and asserted that they were "known and esteemed in these parts to be Spaniards." The term *Español* does not denote what one is biologically or physically. Rather, it is a symbol, drawn from the biological-origin idiom, of what one is "esteemed" to be. For the Indians, status derived ideologically and sociologically from community residence and from the social connections that bind one into that community. One only reads of so-and-so, *Indio de San Pedro.* By contrast, the condition and status of both Spaniard and, to a degree, of the *ladino,* derive from social connection. One reads officials naming so-and-so, "whom I know and certify to be *español."* Spaniards are supposed to be known socially; Indians are not. That is why the 1740 census of the region (pp. 2–58) recorded San Pedranos numerically, by marital-status category, and by birth within or outside the town. However, in the same census, all Spaniards, both parents and children, were personally named.

Throughout these episodes, we see the Spaniards and the Indians differentiating themselves and their behavior in terms of a consistent and pervasive set of opposed ideologies. Moreover, the transformation followed a pattern that had been set in the Old World. *Naturales* replaced Moros as the marginal beasts of burden, confined to sterile mountain agriculture, cottage industries, and petty trade; Christianized by force; submissive, distinctively dressed, community-oriented, and believed to practice secretly a pagan religion behind the guise of their acceptance of Christianity—the enemies of all things civilized. Thus, the Spaniards brought a model of social dichotomy (Christian and infidel), hierarchy (lord and servant), and opposition (good and bad), which made the division of Spaniard and Indian meaningful. It would appear that much of what the American aboriginal cultures had that fit this model was retained or even enhanced, and that much of what did not fit was shorn off. In either case, the Spaniards called the tune and re-created the Indian according to their own cultural image. One concludes with some assurance that the major features of category, social institution, and ethnic structure of the colonial New World were prefigured on the Iberian Peninsula and carried to the modern Mayans through postindependence colonial institutions and colonial ideology.

The social and cultural characteristics of the Indians, then, are not derivatives of a pre-Columbian culture. Nor are they simple products of the fusion of Indian and Spanish cultural systems. Rather, the characteristics of the Indians are a consistent component deriving from the larger colonial social system. As MacLeod has phrased it,

> the demands of the encomienda, above all tribute in cash or useful goods, introduced the European money economy to Indian society and drove Indians to the coastal plantations, usually of cacao, to

get money. Thus we have the transformation of a varied and cultured people into a kind of peasantry. The Indians were to be part of the economy, influenced and depressed by the alien Spanish cities, yet dependent on them and not sharing in their profits.

Highly complex and stratified Indian societies had been reduced to a common denominator. There were still a few rich Indians. There were still some differences among Indians because of prestige, office, or religion but in general variety had gone, and the Indian survivors of these terrible years had become the peasantry of the newly formed agrarian society. (MacLeod 1973:142)

Martinez Pelaez has also argued that the Indian is a product of the conquest. In his words, "oppression made the Indian and has conserved him as such" (Martinez Pelaez 1971:568): the Indian is a product of the colonial social system. Thus, Martinez Pelaez asserts that Pedro de Alvarado never saw Indians, only aborigines. The Indian is the product of a much longer sequence of conquest domination than Alvarado lived to witness.

In some analyses, such as Martinez Pelaez's for the colonial period and Stavenhagen's for the modern period, political force and economic necessity determine the Indian character. In my view, the system is not this economically or politically determinant. To be sure, exploitation, pressure, economic difference, and a particular relation to the means of production affect the Indian significantly. But the Spanish overlords brought with them from Spain a colonial ideology. They established a social system based on that ideology. So the economic and political pressure applied to the Indians arose from the ideology brought by the Spaniards. But more than that, the Indians forged many aspects of their ideology in precise counterpoint to the ideology of their overlords. In many respects, as we shall see, the Indian world view is the inverse, a negative transformation, of the Spanish ideology or world view. To be sure, some aspects of Indian ideology are identical to those of the Spanish overlords, and a few may be totally unrelated to the Spanish impact. But in generally opposite ideology as well as in subordinate position, the Indian is a component in a single, integrated sociocultural system.

Independence—Minimum Structural Change (1821–1944)

Postcolonial Guatemala extends the basic social structure established in the colonial period. On September 15, 1821, Guatemala peacefully assumed its independence from Spain. However, the postindependence history of Guatemala turns Byzantine. Mexico sent troops to bring the Central American region under its influence, but, by July 1823, the Mexican leader ordering the campaign had been deposed. This freed the Central American region, though Chiapas cast its lot with Mexico (Contreras R. 1951:90–96).

A federal government of the remaining Central American states was attempted, first under Jose Arce and then Francisco Morazán, though this federation progressively weakened until the breakup began with Nicaragua's secession in 1838. Guatemala pulled out of the now nonexistent federation in 1847, having been preceded by Nicaragua, Honduras, Costa Rica, and El Salvador (Contreras R. 1951:97).

Nevertheless, under the guidance of Dr. Mariano Gálvez (the histories repeat the title often), between 1831 and 1838, the federated state of Guatemala made important social reforms including the beginnings of public education, secularization by reducing fiesta days and by imposing other restraints on the church, establishment of a citizen militia, municipal reform, and other matters.

But the period between independence and the reforms of the 1870s was still restrictive upon the Indians. While there may have been some slackening of the demands imposed on the Indians as the dyestuff industry withered after the discovery of analine dyes, the rise of coffee quickly brought on new demands. Thus, Jones observes that "as the new industry [coffee] spread the demand for labor steadily increased, and problems of supply and control took on greater acuteness. Forced labor was still the rule. Slavery had been abolished but little more had been done to change the well-entrenched labor system" (Jones 1940:149).

Rafael Carrera stands as the principal figure between the deposition of Gálvez (1838) and the rise of Barrios (1873). Contreras characterizes the period as conservative, as "a return to colonial customs and practices" (Contreras R. 1951:109), including a restoration of ecclesiastical rights. But revolutionary tensions mounted, as well as the states' suppression of them.

Among the surviving revolutionaries, Justo Rufino Barrios and Miguel García Granados launched a successful attack in 1871. By midyear, they had captured Guatemala City and thus launched the period that Guatemalans call *La Reforma*.

García Granados, the first reform president, stepped down after two years (1871–1873). Thus, Barrios is remembered as the principal architect of the reform period. He democratized and secularized the schools, nationalized church properties, and "stimulated agriculture and industry," by, among other things, founding a national bank, establishing the monetary system, and beginning the nation's railroad and telegraph systems. Barrios died in 1885 while conducting an unsuccessful military campaign aimed at reuniting Central America.

But again, the reforms impacted harshly on the Indians. For example, on November 3, 1876, Barrios informed the *jefes políticos*. or district administrators,

> If we abandon the farmers to their own resources and do not give them strong and energetic aid, they will be unable to make any progress, for all their efforts will be doomed to failure due to the deceit of the Indians. You should therefore see to it: *First:* that the Indian villages in your jurisdiction be forced to give the number of hands to the farmers that the latter ask for, even to the number of fifty or a hundred to a single farmer if his enterprise warrants this number. *Second:* when one set of Indians has not been able to finish the work in hand in a period of two weeks, a second . . . should be sent to relieve the first, so that the work may not be delayed. *Third:* the two weeks work shall be paid for ahead of time by [through?] the mayor of the Indian town, thus avoiding the loss of time involved in paying every day. *Fourth:* above all else see to it that any Indian who seeks to evade his duty is punished to the full extent of the law, that the farmers are fully protected and that each Indian is forced to do a full day's work while in service. (Jones 1940:150).[17]

This hardly eased life for the Indians.

Although slavery and the forced labor of *mandamiento* were gone, in its place, the practice of advancing partial wages against a labor contract emerged. Moreover, the contracting plantation owners could further indebt their laborers with supplies issued at the plantation. This practice of debt peonage emerged as the principal form of labor recruitment, and the full force of the government supported the system and punished Indians who tried to evade their contracts. The preface to the 1894 labor laws inform us they were

> "to guarantee the supply of native workers to the fincas formed and fostered under the mandamientos" and "to assure the permanent residence of the workers in the agricultural exploitations by

indirect means which should not be in conflict with the freedom of labor." The system of obligations entailed in cash "advances without limit of quantity . . . might establish the equilibrium broken by the suppression of mandamientos" (Jones 1940:153).[18]

Manuel Estrada Cabrera governed from 1898 to 1920, after which six successively imposed governments held on tentatively until Jorge Ubico was elected in 1931. His thirteen years in office (to 1944) brought economic gains to the country but continued the dictatorship and the constraints on the Indians.

Ubico abolished debt peonage, although landowners could still give Indians small but legally binding cash advances against future work. Although Ubico terminated the *mandamiento* system (except for continued road-maintenance obligations), he imposed the Vagrancy Laws (Dombrowski et al. 1970:30–31). The Vagrancy Laws required an Indian to work on the coastal plantations between 100 and 150 days per year, depending on the size of his own personal landholdings. Such holdings, as well as the work performed, were certified in a labor book, which the Indians were required to carry and have signed. To avoid any labor requirement, an Indian had to have four *manzanas* of highland or three *manzanas* of lowland fields under cultivation. A *manzana* is approximately sixteen *cuerdas*. If he had less than sixteen but more than ten *cuerdas,* he had to work 100 days per year on the coast. With less than ten *cuerdas* of land, he had to work 150 days per year on the coast. Few Indians had enough land to avoid the 100-day obligation. This work was to be signed off in the labor book by the *finquero,* the plantation owner. An Indian was to be paid a wage for his labor.

However, the requirement of signature and the severity of the penalty if the book were unsigned left the Indian subject to considerable manipulation and exploitation. In numerous cases, the books were not signed, but the wage was paid, resulting in the enslavement of the Indian on the *finca*. Alternatively, the book was signed, but the wage was not paid. In either case, the *finquero* was supplied with Indian labor as a result of legislation issued from the central government (Martinez Pelaez 1971:577–81). This legislation forced Indian labor from the highlands to the coast until the laws were voided by the reform movement of 1944. For more than four hundred years, the Indians had been legally bound in labor servitude to their status superiors.

The Modern Period: From 1944 to Today

The year 1944, then, is a crucial turning point in the social history of the Indian. Only since then has Guatemala systematically eliminated the legislative distinction between Indian, Ladino, or other ethnically defined sectors of the society. Laws could no longer apply exclusively to the Indians, and, as a result, the Indian's social position has considerably loosened. But the legal loosening has only had thirty years to affect the communities, though the period from 1944 to the present (1974) has brought great change to many Indian communities. Nevertheless, these legal reforms and economic changes have not undone the social positioning or the ideological imprinting that four hundred years of servitude had built into Indian society. Political control is still virtually non-Indian. And in the domains of social esteem, conceptual orientation, political enfranchisement, and social-network access to the central institutions of the society, the distinction between Indian and non-Indian *(ladino)* today is firm. Moreover, Indians occupy a restricted sector of the economy, tending toward agricultural independence, seasonal labor, and petty village crafts.

Yet, once Indian social status was cut loose from its legal straitjacket, the flux of economic, educational, and transportational changes, to name but a few, has decreased the congruence of the several components of the social system. Ideological, categorical, social, political, and economic institutions and rankings are no longer as tightly redundant as they once were. As a result, perhaps at no time since the conquest have the Indians undergone such extraordinary change as since 1944. Both individuals and towns have become acculturated and notably "ladinoized." But the reason for this change is not increased contact with *ladinos* nor economic opportunity. Ladinoization proceeds because the system is unpacking institutionally. Whether *ladino* or Indian, one's place and one's behavior in each institution has a ranked, central-versus-peripheral symbolic value. But one's ranking may now be different in the various institutions since the laws restricting Indians have been eliminated, for it was these laws that kept individuals at roughly the same place in the various institutions. With the institutional unpacking comes symbolic incongruence, which makes some Indians more Ladino. As a result, the ethnic categories have recently become quite complex, with the reappearance of interstitial categories such as *mestizo* and the denial of ethnic categories by some. Ladinoization has speeded up, and since the Spanish, urbane, connective ideology has always been the prestige element of the counterpoint ideologies, the flux and flow of personal and group change proceed in that direction.

Nevertheless, the correspondence between status category, ideology, power, and social connection is sufficient that even the most acculturated and economically viable community may remain categorically Indian. That is the theoretical interest of San Pedro: it is, on the surface, quite Ladino in appearance, yet San Pedro is classed as Indian. In Chapters 3 and 4, I explore why this is so. But first I must contemplate what happened to the terms for certain social categories that were once common among the colonial Spaniards.

While the social milieu of the Indian is relatively enduring, one asks, what happened to the non-Indians: the *español*, the *peninsular*, the *criollo*, the *mestizo*, the *ladino?* The question is an interesting one. Why is it that *ladino* now predominates and the rest are little used, except for *mestizo* (whose active use appears to be a recent reintroduction) and *español* (which is often a way of redefining *ladino*)? Sol Tax commented on the lack of an explanation for this shift in his article on ethnic relations in Guatemala (Tax 1942:45). He was at a loss to explain what he called the mystery of the disappearance of the *criollo*.

The mystery need not remain, though my answer is necessarily speculative. The independence movement brought about the removal of the Spanish crown from the immediate national affairs of Guatemala. While independence did not take a violent course in Guatemala, it did so in a number of other countries, and the news of this violence and of the Creole opposition to the Spanish crown was well known and supported within the Guatemalan milieu. The Creole takeover in Guatemala was more of a palace revolt than a social revolution. It is Martinez Pelaez's view (1971:576–78) that the independence movement was merely a substitution of the Creoles for the *peninsulares*. The old, colonial social structure was maintained. Since, however, *criollo* and peninsular were subdivisions of the basic category of *español*, the subdivisions were only relevant in the colonial context of competition and displacement of native-born by Spanish crown appointees. Thus, with the elimination of the Spanish crown's control, the opposition between *peninsular* and *criollo* would be expected to fade and the superordinate term *español* would be sufficient.

But, I hypothesize, the independence that the *criollos* sought may well have unleashed the contradictions that led to their own displacement. The Creole Spaniard, throughout the colonial period, had supported himself by Indian labor and tribute stipends from the *encomiendas* and *repartimientos*. But independence changed the economic situation of Guatemala significantly. The forced extraction of wealth, to the benefit of the Creole-Spaniard and the prior crown, could no longer be sustained, for without Spain, the colonial export economy was untenable.

On the other hand, internal trade, which had been controlled by the Ladino-Mestizo muleteers and artisans, must have become significantly more important by 1820. Thus the Creole-Spaniard class was doomed. The necessary social reorientation probably was at the heart of the reform of 1871. The most famous leader of the reform movement, Justo Rufino Barrios, came from the periphery of Guatemala, from a hamlet that was then in the Ladino municipality of San Marcos. Given the economic reorientation of the country toward internal commerce and wealth, the substitution of *ladino* for *español* would express a recognition that the *ladino* dominated internal trade throughout the colonial period.

The change seems to communicate a major societal reorientation. The non-Indian sector of Guatemala still depended in a large measure on extraction of wealth from the Indians. But the support of the non-Indian was no longer by tribute, a colonial enterprise symbolized by *español*. Now, rather, the support of the non-Indian depended on direct labor relations and commercial management with respect to the Indians. Also deriving from the conquest, these were and are essentially *ladino* enterprises. *Español* seems to have become a high-status subdivision of *ladino*, rather than a separate and more prestigious category. *Español*, as well as the now seldom-used *criollo*, seems to have been encompassed by *ladino*.

The shift from *español* to *ladino* for the primary category of high social status did more than just reflect the class background of the new economic and political focus in the Guatemalan nation. The changes returned the status system to its original two-category structure of status superiors and status inferiors, rulers and subjects, that had been the basic conceptual order at the conquest. The *tertium quid* Ladino disappeared by emerging supreme.

The conclusions of this chapter are drawn from the historical study of the *municipios* of San Marcos and San Pedro Sacatepéquez, but have been viewed within the larger context of social process in Guatemala.

Thus, they are generally applicable to Guatemala. Indeed, the arguments may be fruitfully extended both to Mexico and Andean South America in those regions where sizable autochthonous peasant populations submitted to the Spanish *encomienda* colonial regime. The region might conveniently be styled "Encomienda America," paralleling Wagley's "Plantation America" (1957). This would appropriately identify the *encomienda-reducción* as the institution central to the development of social structural similarities throughout the Hispanic mainland, and the insistent force behind the development of cultural inversion.

Today, San Marcos and San Pedro are products of this colonial drama, modernized by the events of independence in 1821, reform in 1871, revolution in 1944, and reaction in 1954. Against this long and richly textured tradition, we can now examine the current political, economic, and social-status relations of San Marcos and San Pedro. We shall discover that the cultural categories, the attached status ideologies, and much of the structure of social relations that originated in the colonial enterprise in fact continue to the present. To be sure, the social relations defining Indians and Ladinos have become less rigid. Guatemalan law now refuses to recognize the ethnic categories so that law no longer maintains the place of the Indians. Because laws no longer serve to define ethnicity, I look in Chapter 3 to the de facto social-network processes of politics to explore why the Indian epithet is still applied to San Pedro and its inhabitants. In addition to changes in law, since the 1940s there have been changes in economics. San Pedro substance is not based on the same sleepy agricultural and petty-trade economy it once was. To this end, Chapter 4 shows colonial economic structure persisting to the present day, though it shows as well the results of economic flexibility from 1944 to the modern period. Chapters 5 and 6 explore the consequences of economic changes and institutional incongruence for the system of ethnic-status terms today, noting the ways in which present-day flexibility generates individual ethnic mobility. But since the individual moves in a context of structure, I begin with the modern structure of government and the culture of political ideology.

Part 2

The National Domain and Present-Day
San Marcos and San Pedro:
Culture and Symbolism
in Polity, Economy, and Social Status

3
The Political Positions of San Marcos and San Pedro Sacatepéquez

The historical events outlined in the preceding chapter, and the system of categories and ideologies that guided them, have given present-day Guatemala its highly centralized, two-tiered system of government, a government intent on controlling rather than serving the nonelite masses. To see San Marcos and San Pedro in the modern context, I begin with the structure of government at the national level.

The Structure of Government in Guatemala

At the national level, Guatemala is managed by a formally tripartite government consisting of executive, legislative, and judicial branches. Most Guatemalans, however, do not think of the system as three branches but as a single unit: *el gobierno* ("the government"). They view it as highly centralized, with the president giving administrative commands, the ministries and local offices carrying out the president's orders and arranging the details, the courts making decisions about individual compliance, and the police enforcing the administrative and punitive decisions of the whole.

In practice, the people's view seems largely correct, since the legislative branch, a unicameral congress of deputies elected from each of the twenty-two departments or states, appears to be largely subordinate to the wishes of the executive branch.[1] Indeed, legislative actions generally are rubber-stamp legitimizations of executive policy. Thus, in its official capacity, the congress has no distinctive impact on the local communities. Unofficially, however, personal ties to congressional deputies are important to the local elite as a means of access to the central administrative machinery. Since the congressmen (*diputados*) are elected from among the local elite, and most frequently from among the Ladinos, local elites are strengthened when one of their number is elected and builds friendships within the congress and the central government.

The judicial branch is composed of a supreme court having powers of review over congressional law and executive activity, several national courts with special domains of legal responsibility, a regional appellate-court system, and local courts. However, as one lawyer put it, the supreme court serves as a brake on executive excess "only in theory."

Indeed, politically knowledgeable informants laughed at the idea of the court blocking the president on constitutional grounds, recounting an episode in which a supreme court justice publicly thanked the president for his appointment and vowed court cooperation. In fact, congress elects the judges; but this episode merely confirms the presidential control of congress. Moreover, an uncooperative justice's tenure is insecure because he must be elected for four terms. Only on the fourth election do they acquire tenure until retirement at age seventy.

The local courts are called *Juzgados de Primera Instancia* ("Courts of Initial Jurisdiction"). At least one is present in each province (*departamento;* hereafter, "department") in the municipality that hosts the province's administrative offices. Where more than one court exists within a department, the department's municipalities are distributed into each court's respective jurisdiction. The Courts of Initial Jurisdiction try the criminal, civil, and familial cases (the three branches of Guatemalan law provided legislatively) that arise within their departmental jurisdiction. Minor infractions and disorderliness are handled by a justice of the peace in each municipality.

All Guatemalans have legal access to court protection and court action. As of 1964, Guatemalan law provides either court-appointed lawyers or court clerks to act on behalf of the needy. As a result, Guatemalans enjoy a reasonable measure of protection in criminal and familial legal issues. On the other hand, the local people feel that political offenses are dealt with outside the protections of the courts.

Because the congress and the court system effectively support the ministrations of the president, the executive branch dominates the national government. Supported by his personal staff, the vice-president, and other councils, the chief executive administers the country through a series of decrees, which are implemented by various ministries. The ministries deliver the government to the people.

Typically, a ministry is further subdivided into offices or bureaus (often called *Dirección General de* . . .; "Directorate General of . . .") with specific responsibilities. Finally, the national government bureaucracy penetrates and affects the local scene through the actions of regional and local staffs of the ministries and their subdivisions.

Guatemala is divided into twenty-two departments. This excludes Belize, over which Guatemala exercises a claim but not political hegemony. These departments have an average size of 4,950 square kilometers and an average population of 234,556 each in 1973. By comparison, the Department of San Marcos has an area of 3,791 square kilometers and a population of 389,760 in 1973 (Dirección General de Estadística 1974).

From Table 1, one can note certain characteristics of the Department of San Marcos by comparison with the average departments of Guatemala and with the highland, heavily Indian departments. By excluding the Petén, which is exceptional as an undeveloped hinterland, and by excluding the Department of Guatemala, which is exceptional as a disproportionately urban zone, one can explore the average provinces, the Indian provinces, and the San Marcos department. First, the San Marcos department is slightly larger than average but only insignificantly so. San Marcos has, however, a much larger than average department population with a much higher population density, being 83 percent denser than the regular provinces and 42 percent denser than the western highland departments. Finally, the Department of San Marcos has more municipalities than average, though they tend to be somewhat smaller in average size than those of the rest of the country.

The Ministerio de Gobernación (Ministry of Government) is responsible for political and legal process in the departments; department government is thus a bureaucratic extension of the central government. As such, department government is structurally equivalent to any bureaucratic office stemming from the other ministries that also extend services to the hinterland departments. A department governor does not control the heads of other offices in his department, though he may influence them personally. Governors are appointed by the president and supervised by the central ministry with the president's approval. All are expected to follow the orders and guidelines issued by the central government, and none have any power or any basis for independent policymaking outside the ministry's demands.

Table 1. National, Regional, and Departmental Population and Land Data (1973 Census)

	Country[a]	Country, excluding El Petén and Guatemala	Western Highland Departments[b]	San Marcos Department
Number of departments	22	20	7	1
Total area (sq. km.)	108,892	70,921	25,630	3,791
Average area (sq. km.) per dept.	4,950	3,546	3,661	3,791
Total number of inhabitants	5,160,221	3,987,921	1,858,612	389,760
Average inhabitants per dept.	234,556	199,396	265,516	389,760
Average inhabitants per sq. km.	47.4	56.2	72.5	102.8
Percent increase since 1964	20.4	15.6	19.1	15.6
Total number of *municipios*	325	296	145	29
Average number of *municipios* per dept.	14.8	14.8	20.7	29
Average inhabitants per *municipio*	15,878	13,473	12,818	13,440
Average area (sq. km.) per *municipio*	336.1	239.6	176.7	130.7

SOURCES: Morales Urrutia 1961; Dirección General de Cartografía 1961; Dirección General de Estadística 1971b, 1974.
[a]Excludes Belize.
[b]San Marcos, Huehuetenango, Quezaltenango, El Quiché, Solalá, Chimaltenango, and Totonicapán.

Like the other department governors, the San Marcos governor is an appointed figurehead representing the central government's presence in the peripheral provinces. He is a conduit for information from the provinces to the central government, and he is a useful link to the capital for some people living in these provinces.[2]

In his figurehead capacity, the governor opens municipal fairs (*ferias*) and inaugurates projects that the central government has funded, provided that the project or the municipality is not of sufficient importance to be attended by a minister of the central government or perhaps even by the president. The governor presides over the region's inaugural ceremonies—of fairs, of hamlet or village schools, and of wells or culinary water-piping projects in the hinterland municipalities in default of interested visitors from the central officialdom. Moreover, the governor has no responsibility for administering funds and manages only a small staff (a *secretario* or executive assistant, four *oficiales* or secretarial clerks, and a personal chauffeur), further underscoring his figurehead capacity.

In his information-conducting capacity, the governor of San Marcos routes information on conditions in the department to the central government. Some residents aver that the governors have a system of paid informants (*orejas;* "ears"), outside of the normal official channels, but it was impossible to verify this. In general, gossip about political matters is likely to cross one or another officer of the government and be passed on to the governor. If deemed significant, such gossip presumably goes on to the central ministries. From time to time, central authorities ask the governor to report on specific issues.

As a contact man, the governor escorts central government officials on their visits to the towns and villages and makes local introductions where necessary. He may also introduce local officers and personal friends to the officials he knows in the central government. This is done by personal escort or letter or through conversation. However, since the last three governors have been poorly connected, retired, out-of-favor army colonels, the San Marcos elite has not cultivated the governor beyond the necessity of courtesy.

The next level of geopolitical subdivision is the municipality. In fact, since the departmental divisions are an administrative convenience of the central government, the municipalities are actually the second and only independent lower level of government. They therefore merit careful description.

The Guatemalan municipality has a number of generalizable physical and social characteristics beyond the mere fact that it is a political subdivision of the department. First, the municipality generally has a territorial base of between 40 and 400 square kilometers, though there are exceptional municipalities with areas as low as 8 square kilometers or as high as 1,112 square kilometers. Second, the municipality has a town center, usually focused on a park or plaza, surrounded by civil offices, ecclesiastical buildings, a market building, a school, and a few shops. Around these, one finds a nucleus of houses, sometimes densely packed, sometimes a bit interspersed with small fieldplots. The town center, called the *cabezera municipal* ("municipal headquarters"), is often serviced with public drainage and electricity. Third, the municipalities manifest two basic forms of residential distribution. On the one hand, many municipalities have a residential population that clusters around the town plaza. Of course, the size of the cluster varies enormously, from the massive concentration of Guatemala City to the small nuclei of the hinterland towns. On the other hand, one finds many examples of what Sol Tax early identified as the "vacant town type" (Tax 1937). In these municipalities, a significant proportion of the houses in the town-center cluster are owned by Indians who reside in them only on market or fiesta days or during an entire year that the owner serves in a civil or religious office. Undoubtedly, the ebb and flow of the weekly residential cycle and the longer-term fiesta-cycle residential variation were more pronounced and more general in the 1930s and 1940s than they are today. But the word "vacant" exaggerates the impact of the movement on the town centers, for the word diverts attention from the presence of the continuously resident Ladinos and Indians, detectable even in the monographs on the towns used to exemplify the vacant type (see Bunzel 1952:1–14). But, whether or not these towns are seen as relatively vacant, the residents in the town centers of the rural highlands are usually a minority in the municipality. The hinterland municipalities are indeed rural.

Thus, fourth, except for some of the topographically restricted Lake Atitlán municipalities, the hinterland municipalities usually contain a sizable, scattered, rural population.[3] The rural area of a municipality is divided administratively into hamlets *(aldeas)*. The hamlet often has a distinct center near a road or trail. Depending on the size of the hamlet, one may find a school, a small store or two, a Catholic chapel (and perhaps another, non-Catholic), and a council room for the hamlet's mayoral deputy *(alcalde auxiliar)* and assistants. Small peripheral settlements *(caseríos)* are satellite to the *aldea,* and the *aldea* itself may be subdivided into wards called *caseríos.*

Finally, the municipality is often represented in the literature as being ethnically distinct (Hinshaw 1975; McBryde 1947; Nash 1958, 1958b; Tax 1937). To some extent this is true, for the Indian residents of a municipality are often recognizably different—in dress, accent, craft skill, or occupation. But, in other respects, the Indians of one town resemble those of another, a fact notably highlighted by Robert H. Ewald (1954). Thus, in this book, the ethnic distinctiveness of communities is a problem to be discussed rather than an initial premise. But the diacritical marking of some segments of many western highland communities is real.

Municipal, Departmental, and National Linkages

One of the municipalities in each department hosts the offices of the department governor and is therefore known as the *cabezera departamental* ("departmental headquarters"). The use of the word "headquarters" rather than "capital" emphasizes the administrative, rather than the legislative, character of government. In Guatemalan culture, there is only one capital in the country, *la capital,* namely, Guatemala City.

In contrast to the department level of government, municipal government officers are elected. They can tax, spend money, legislate, and support or not support the parties and powers in the central government. As a result, the municipality per se, not the department, is the entity with which the central government must reckon. The critical and cultivated juncture of political relations in the country is between the central government and the municipalities.

This municipal priority is manifest, for example, in the symbolism of seating arrangements at political meetings. During my period of fieldwork, the president of the country came to San Marcos twice, once to dedicate a market and a road, and once to attend a political rally. On both these occasions, the president sat close to the mayor of San Marcos, while the department governor was placed a number of chairs away—out of conversational range of the president and at the extreme end of the row of dignitaries. Nor did the governor address the assembled groups at any time, although the mayor did. Similarly, when San Pedro dedicated its new market building, the most distinguished guest was the mayor of Guatemala City.[4] Again in this ceremony, the governor was to the side. The central government bureaucrats and the opposition party's national representative were close to the mayor of San Pedro and the center of the dignitaries' table. Again, the governor did not speak, but the San Pedro mayor did. These episodes indicate the essential two levels of government: central and municipal.

The two-tiered centralization of government has important cultural correspondences with the ethnic dichotomy and deep roots in Guatemalan history, as we have seen. So does the division into 325 autonomous units at the next level. The colonial history of divide—by language, village, clothing—and rule does not just linger; it grows, from time to time, with the subdivision of municipalities. The central government deals directly with the 325 municipalities, as patron to client. In this context, personal connection and interaction with the central government bureaucrats are extremely important. A personal relationship not only distinguishes one municipality from among the many competing for the limited resources administered by an overburdened and underpaid bureaucracy but also benefits the particular bureaucrat. The "favor" *(campaña)* eased through the bureaucratic operation establishes a debt that can be collected later. Out of this accrues status; power in the form of enablement, because future activities will be facilitated and needs accommodated; and, occasionally, wealth. While the favors may be carried out with utilitarian interest, the conduct of government through friendship is not. Trading political favors is a system of gift giving, in which power, a primary "good" in the Ladino economy, is the medium. Friends and favors result from the focus on interconnection and control coming out of the Ladino status ideology. But more important than any of the utilitarian benefits, personal interconnection is the essence of being Ladino, and government is a Ladino affair. The utilitarian acts take this form because they are informed by Ladino ideology.

The process of municipal funding further demonstrates the two-tiered system of government. Each municipal government identifies projects that it wishes to implement. Proposals soliciting *(solicitar, gestionar)* national aid for these projects are sent to the central government. The appropriate ministry of the central government then considers these requests and accepts, rejects, or modifies the proposals according to the ministry's political interests and financial capabilities. The approved projects are called "concessions" of the central government to the municipalities. The government "grants" the "solicitations" of municipalities.

Although the department governor has no money to grant to a municipality, the designation of a municipality as departmental headquarters is crucially important in several ways. The municipality that hosts the governorship benefits from the bulk of the services provided by the other agencies of the various ministries that are also located in the departmental headquarters, and the department center receives a better "press" as the governor supplies information to his superiors.

More importantly, the location of all these governmental agencies in a single municipal center greatly strengthens that municipality's access to the national center compared to the access enjoyed by the other municipalities in the department. For example, the mayor of the departmental headquarters can work through the governor, or he can bypass the governor by working directly with the head of a ministry. The mayors of the other municipalities must largely work through the department governor to get their requests for funding considered in central places. As a result, the departmental headquarters is not just first among equals: it is first; the others are equals. Access to and benefit from the other agencies of government strengthen both the central municipality in relation to the other municipalities in the department and the position of the mayor, making him more important than the governor. The departmental headquarters thus tends to screen off and disadvantage the other municipalities, in spite of the basically two-tiered structure of the government.

In summary, the municipal officials and the social elite of the departmental headquarters are the people who make the personal contacts to the central bureaucracy. The officials of the hinterland municipalities primarily work through the rather inefficient bureaucratic channels. Out of this flows the immense political advantage of the Ladino departmental centers and the disadvantage of the Indian municipalities.

This political structure is significantly related to the ethnic order. Political centrality is usually associated with community status as a Ladino town; in the western highlands of Guatemala, municipalities hosting the departmental headquarters are considered Ladino towns, while most of the hinterland municipalities are considered Indian.[5] Moreover, as a conceptual stereotype, Ladinos are supposed to be powerful and Indians weak. There are, however, Ladino towns that are not department centers (among them Tejutla in the San Marcos highlands and most of the coastal and coffee-producing municipalities) and Indian towns that are department centers (Quezaltenango and Totonicapán). The contradiction between their status position and their political position should make these towns particularly interesting research sites. These exceptions show that ethnicity is not a one-to-one, direct expression of political centrality. Nevertheless, power, social connections, and centrality strongly influence both personal and community ethnicity.

The Municipality of San Marcos

The municipality of San Marcos hosts a population of 15,862 persons, according to the 1973 census. Of this population, 3,839 persons, or 24 percent, are classed as Indian. However, a substantial share of these, 1,269, come from the single hamlet (*aldea*) of San Rafael Soche, which was annexed from San Pedro after considerable political dispute. If one deletes Soche from the figures, San Marcos, town and hinterland, is 17.6 percent Indian. The urban area, as defined by the census bureau, includes a few agricultural households outside the urban town center and has a population of 5,743, of which 258 people or 4.5 percent are Indian. One must be wary of ethnic figures provided by the national censuses; as John D. Early (1983) and others have shown, they are notoriously fickle regarding ethnic categorization.

The municipality of San Marcos benefits from the political advantages I have described because it is the seat for the offices of the department government. San Marcos hosts all of the regional offices of the various branches of the national bureaucracy represented in the department. These include a headquarters and staff personnel for each of the following units: the national police, the military police, an army-reserve unit, a military high school, the internal-revenue office, the only first-class post office in the department, the central telephone and telegraph office, the labor relations and claims board, the agricultural-extension agency, the forestry-management section, three national banks, two courts of initial jurisdiction, the office of the departmental attorney general, the census office, the administrative office of a national housing project, the department hospital, the nationally financed health center, the office of public

Plate 2. The urban center of San Marcos, left, and the urban center of San Pedro Sacatepéquez, Department of San Marcos. The roughly hexagonal grid between the two centers is the location of much of the disputed land. The photograph is correctly oriented to north. (Precise date unknown; ca. 1960)

sanitation, the regional offices for primary and secondary schooling, and two small libraries. Some of these deserve further analysis.

GOVERNMENT OFFICES

Several institutions charged with social control have their headquarters in San Marcos. These include the two major kinds of police in Guatemala. San Marcos hosts the department headquarters *(jefatura)* of the blue-uniformed civilian police, the *Policía Nacional*. The police staff for the department includes a lieutenant colonel, a major, a sergeant, several inspectors, and 150 patrolmen. Of these, the of-

Plate 3. The urban center of San Marcos. (Photograph taken between 1969 and 1972)

ficers, the sergeant, two inspectors, and 32 patrolmen were assigned to protect San Marcos. These police deal with disorderliness and criminal violence in the towns where they are stationed. Ordinarily, they carry only a side arm or a rifle. The *policía militar* or military police, wearing olive drab and regimented along military lines, work from a command post and barracks also in the urban center of San Marcos. The military police primarily guard banks, barracks, municipal and departmental buildings, and other governmental installations from politically motivated assault. Other military police serve as border guards, antismuggling patrols, and counterguerrilla units. The seriousness of their mission, to defend against and suppress antigovernment violence, is underscored by the shoulder-slung ma-

Plate 4. San Marcos, looking southwest from the center of town. The Catholic cathedral dominates the background. To its right is a large, rectangular residence for clergy. (1982)

chine guns all military police carry. In addition, San Marcos has a reserve army unit. While the army is not regularly concerned with civilian social control, on at least one occasion the army was called up to defend San Marcos against what was perceived to be land predation by the community of San Pedro. Because both civilian and military leaders are Ladinos and move in the same social circles, the army serves San Marcos's interests.

The two Courts of Initial Jurisdiction that serve most of the department are located in San Marcos. A third court, on the coast in Coatepeque (Department of Quezaltenango), serves the southernmost coastal municipalities of the Department of San Marcos (see Table 2). The First Court administers to all of the highland centers with a substantial Ladino population. Conversely, the Second Court serves nearly all of the predominantly Indian municipalities. In short, there is a rather close correspondence between the ethnic character of the court's jurisdictions and the numerical priority of the courts. Furthermore, the social rank of the predominant ethnic group served by each court corresponds to the court office's physical proximity to the departmental (and San Marcos municipal) government office building, the symbolic focus of power in the department. This building,

Table 2. Municipal Responsibilities of the Courts of Initial Jurisdiction Serving the Department of San Marcos

Court Location	Municipalities Under Court's Jurisdiction		
	"Ladino" *Municipios*		"Indian" Municipios
	Highland	Coastal	(All Highland)
San Marcos First Court	San Marcos San Lorenzo Rio Blanco Tejutla Tacaná*	Malacatán Catarina El Tumbador San Rafael Pié de la Cuesta	San Miguel Ixtahuacán Tajumulco
San Marcos Second Court		El Rodeo San Pablo	San Pedro Sacatepéquez San Antonio Sacatepéquez Comitancillo Ixchiguán Concepción Tutuapa San José Ojetenán Sibinal Sipacapa
Coatepeque Court		Pajapita Ayulta Ocós La Reforma El Quetzal Nuevo Progreso	

*The town center of Tacaná is Ladino, but it has a large rural Indian population.

Plate 5. San Marcos. A typical house with enclosed patio. (1973)

called the Palacio Maya on account of its facade of sculptured Mayan images, houses the First Court, the department government, the San Marcos municipal government, the state attorney general and staff, the national radio, and a formal reception hall. The second and predominantly Indian Second Court, by contrast, is located about three-quarters of a kilometer away in a dilapidated building facing the plaza of San Marcos. As both courts are in San Marcos, San Pedro Indians and all Indians of the hinterland municipalities must travel to the Ladino center to take care of wills, divorces, land disputes, or other legal matters.

Three banks, the only ones in the San Marcos highlands, and the property-tax office provide financial services to San Marcos. The banks most effectively serve the elites and the businessmen, although one,

Plate 6. The Palacio Maya. This cut-stone building houses the municipal offices of San Marcos as well as the office of the state governor and his personal staff. The building is located in the center of the main piece of territory disputed between the two towns. (1982)

the Agricultural Development Bank (Banco Nacional de Desarrollo Agrícola, or BANDESA), makes an attempt to assist the small farmers. The tax and revenue office establishes evaluations and pursues both the evaders of the government's rightful property tax and the producers of clandestine liquor. The tax office establishes property evaluations and collects the 0.3 percent levy. Thus, financial control is assigned to San Marcos, though in fact San Pedro has the more vigorous commercial economy.

San Marcos is renowned throughout the southwestern region for its educational institutions. It has the best government elementary schools and the only government daytime high school in the department. In addition, a Catholic private elementary and high school serves the rich, the middle class, and the sacrificing artisans of both San Marcos and San Pedro with the best education available in the department. Another private school operates day and evening sessions for high-school students, some of whom have had scholastic problems at other schools. The government schools and the Catholic school have the best physical facilities in the department and the best credentialed teachers. Education throughout the department is also supervised by a government-employed coordinator stationed in San Marcos. San Marcos also hosts the only university branch in the department. The preponderance of education facilities is located in San Marcos, though they are accessible to San Pedranos.

Health and social-welfare services, including a hospital, a health clinic, a child-care center, and the social-security office, are also located in San Marcos. The national hospital unit in San Marcos has facilities for some operations and postoperative care. The poor of both towns go there for obstetrical care. While lifesaving and sanitation facilities are primitive by the standards of the capital city, they are of major benefit to the poor and to the Indians of the hinterland municipalities who come in from time to time with serious problems. The health clinic, midway between the two communities on disputed land, provides free minor services, inoculations, dental care, and diagnoses that may lead to admission to the hospital. The clinic is generally quite crowded. The health-clinic building also houses the Office of Sanitation Inspection, which checks on commercial health conditions, poisons stray dogs, and develops plans for culinary water projects in the hamlets throughout the department.

The higher government officials and the business and landed elites avoid the use of both these facilities. For operations or obstetrical services, they go to Quezaltenango or Guatemala City and enter private hospitals. This latter practice, in addition to securing better health services, permits the registration of the newborn as a native of a more central Ladino city. This process is symbolically crucial to the Ladino elites resident in the Indian hinterland municipalities, for, as a result, their children are not natives of an Indian community. Rather, they are *"capitalinos"* or *"de"* somewhere else. The origin symbol of a central birthplace in a Ladino town is sought so as to correspond with and reaffirm their social status.

The day-care center in San Marcos allows single working mothers to place their preschool children. The facility is used more by San Marcos mothers than by San Pedro mothers since the San Pedro mothers generally take their young children with them to the market stalls or to other places of work.

Finally, the regional office of the Guatemalan Institute for Social Security provides accident indemnification for employees in agricultural, commercial, and industrial jobs. Arita Figueroa (1973) sharply criticized the limitations on accident insurance as discriminatory.

He reports that the majority of the highland Indians enter the cash economy through migratory labor on the coffee plantations. The pickers do not have many accidents; most of them get sick from their work and living conditions, but sickness is not covered. The social services theoretically available to the Indians miss their most urgent needs.

Several communications services operate from San Marcos, including radio stations, a small newspaper, and telegraph and telephone services. The San Marcos telephone and telegraph offices, the central offices for the department, are rated *oficinas de primera categoría* ("offices of first rank"). Calls from or to the northern municipalities of the department route through San Marcos. Making a call from San Pedro or the other municipalities can be time-consuming and frustrating since official phone calls preempt those of private citizens, and since San Marcos civilian use tends to preempt the civilian phone access of the other towns.

The assignment of phone lines on the San Marcos switchboard further suggests the overwhelming communications centrality enjoyed by San Marcos. The plug-in-pull-out switchboard links crank-the-handle phones distributed as follows: eighteen lines to national agencies in San Marcos, two lines to national agencies in San Pedro; three lines to municipal offices in San Marcos, one line to the mayorality of San Pedro; twenty-three lines to private citizens in San Marcos, and one line to a private citizen in San Pedro. Thus, San Marcos is better connected with physical communications equipment. Banking and coffee marketing require such immediate communications that the telephone and telegraph are inadequate. The banks need to communicate on exchange values of currencies and to verify account balances for check cashing. The coffee buyer must have central-office price quotes twice a day as a result of commodity-price fluctuations. Since one can quite easily spend two or more hours in the telephone office trying to call Guatemala City, these enterprises operate ham radio networks.

A station of the national radio network transmits from the *Palacio Maya* building. In addition, a private commercial radio station in San Marcos and another in San Pedro broadcast throughout the western region. In addition to radio news, three national newspapers are available in both San Marcos and San Pedro.[6] Furthermore, a government news and policy paper, the *Diario Oficial,* comes to the government offices. One San Marcos family prints a weekly community newspaper that includes social notes, upcoming events, articles by local schoolteachers or other respected individuals, and an occasional editorial or commentary on national issues.

As with other governmental agencies, the department highway offices and maintenance garages are located in San Marcos. Because of the close connection, on several occasions San Marcos has used the highway department's equipment to upgrade municipal streets with minimal cost.

SOCIAL INTERCONNECTIONS

While all these communications facilities and agencies of government assistance benefit San Marcos, the primary connections between San Marcos and the country are not physical but social. We begin to see this connection by examining the birthplace and residence of government employees and by tracing the relations of residence and career pattern among government employees.

Both the birthplace and the current residence of the government employees working in these offices are overwhelmingly focused in San Marcos. Of a total of sixty-three people working in six of the national offices in San Marcos, forty-two were born in San Marcos municipality, while twenty-one were imported from outside.[7] Of these latter, five (including the governor) were born in San Pedro, nine were from coastal *ladino* municipalities in the department, one was from a highland *ladino* municipality, and seven were from outside the department. These seven included a judge, five telegraphers, and an *oficial* secretary. Thus, San Pedro has relatively little access to the departmental offices. Even the governor proved an unexceptional exception: although he was born while his parents were residing in San Pedro, he had been raised in Quezaltenango prior to entering a highly mobile military career. Moreover, he referred to himself as *ladino;* his parents were not native to San Pedro, he lived in San Marcos, and on occasion he referred disparagingly to the residents of San Pedro as *"esos indios."*

The residential distribution of these government employees is also instructive. Fifty-eight were living in San Marcos and seven in San Pedro. One of these seven was the head of a major office but was a native of another department. He had moved into San Marcos on beginning his assignment. Later his landlord refused to paint the house to the renter's satisfaction. Rather than capitulate, the man moved to San Pedro for several months until another suitably large residence became available in San Marcos. The other employees who lived in San Pedro were native to it. They also held rather low-level jobs: a clerk, a telegrapher, a letter deliverer, and a tax-collection clerk for San Pedro. Both in birthplace and in residence, San Marcos stands in sharp contrast with San Pedro in its national, bureaucratic connections.

Moreover, a number of persons native to San Marcos and a significant number of nonnative persons resident in the community hold high regional offices in the national government. And many of the natives and residents are connected to national officeholders through kinship, marriage, godparentage, or ties of friendship arising either from participation in the same branch of government service in the same town at a particular time or from common community origin. Except for a judge, who ambiguously admitted he was from an Indian town, all the individuals in the interconnected network of local, regional, and national government officers claimed to be and were conceded to be Ladino. Indeed, to suggest otherwise would be grossly insulting.

San Marcos's linkage to central office and power does not stop with its native sons placed in high regional offices located in the department center. Nor does it stop with friendship and other ties to nonnative Ladinos who had come to San Marcos posts and were subsequently transferred. The government's policy of moving its higher officers from department to department at rather frequent intervals results in a nationwide dispersion of friendships formed during the time that the nonnatives lived and worked in San Marcos. As these men advance in age and rank within their bureaucracy, they usually finish their careers in a relatively high post in the capital city.

Just as these nonnative friends of San Marcos have gathered in Guatemala City as they rise administratively in the ministries, San Marcos natives have gone out, circulated, and risen in many branches of government. The most powerful of these is the personal secretary to the president of the country. Others include the national and western regional heads of the division of highways (construction and maintenance), a high staff member in the census bureau, several ranking military officers, a retired ambassador to Germany, and several past and present congressmen.[8] Nor is this phenomenon new. San Marcos has provided three former presidents of the country.

Thus, the municipal government leaders of San Marcos, many of its private individuals, and the temporarily resident heads of the bureaucratic agencies have many easily approachable contacts in high positions in the nation.

PATRONAGE AND PARTY

Guatemalan government is a thoroughgoing patronage bureaucracy. From the minister, through the department office supervisor, to the local employee—secretary, inspector, schoolteacher, or whatever—government employees are appointed by higher officeholders of the party in power. Patronage links San Marcos and an important share of its residents directly to the national center.

Under the patronage system, every jobholder wants his party to win. Employees of the government and hence the headquarters towns where they predominantly reside have a substantial stake in the electoral process. At election time in 1973–1974, for example, the highway workers painted the dotted line down the center of the highways in the official party's colors. Bridge railings that had been white for years turned up in the party's colors. Hundreds of advertisements, which had heretofore bid the reader to use a certain retread tire, were painted over with "Vote for Shell," the Official Party (*Partido Oficial*) candidate for president in 1974. Government offices closed when campaign figures came to town, so that employees could be present at the rallies.

Employees of the government are expected to participate enthusiastically. On one occasion, a young technical expert in charge of a minor office in San Marcos was asked to post official-party propaganda in his office. He refused, pointing out that the national constitution prohibits electoral messages in government offices. Within a few days, he was ordered to meet the vice-minister in Guatemala City and was informed that his work was substandard. A week later, the young man received transfer papers ordering him to a hinterland community in another department. Even then, he felt himself lucky, as he could have been put out of work entirely. San Marcos, then, is highly interested in and involved in the issues, relations, and activities of politics because it is the regional center of government employment and hence of patronage connection. The government supports the government.

But undergirding this utilitarian support of the party in power is a fundamental cultural emphasis that directs its residents toward

Plate 7. San Marcos. Civic and national dignitaries lead a parade honoring Justo Rufino Barrios. (1973)

political interest. San Marcos is a *ladino* town; its residents define their interests in terms of the status ideology associated with their position. Power, authority, control, and centrality are important components of the Ladino status ideology. Personal interconnection is another aspect of their ideology.

Moreover, historically, the government was not created to serve the people but to constrain and control the masses, particularly the Indians. The *españoles,* now replaced by the *ladinos,* were above the law. Thus, Ladinos today do not seek personal favors simply as a utilitarian means of circumventing an inept and uninterested bureaucracy. Rather, the use of personal ties places Ladinos higher in the status system; their behavior conforms to the ideology. Moreover, the personalistic form of the status ideology coordinates with unresponsive bureaucracy and makes the bureaucracy even more unresponsive and controlling of the masses. Thus, the governmental process itself enhances the ethnic division.

In summary, San Marcos is the most powerful municipality in the department because of its close contact to the various ministerial branches. This power is based on social-network interconnection with the central government. The power and connection of the community and its residents correspond to its ethnically identified position

Plate 8. San Marcos. Women lead a religious procession, with image of San Marcos (left). (1973)

in the status system. Power, connection, centrality, and freedom from governmental restraint are to "Ladino" as weakness, atomization, marginality, and governmental constraint are to "Indian."

The Municipality of San Pedro Sacatepéquez

San Pedro's population, urban and rural, is 31,323 persons. Of these, 17,973 persons, or 57.4 percent, are Indian. In the town center, classed as urban (though, as in San Marcos, it contains two *caseríos* that I would not class as urban), there are 10,876 inhabitants, of which 3,086, or 28.4 percent, are classified by census procedures as Indian. But these ethnic figures are almost meaningless. The census taker, according to regulations, is to "use as a base the social estimation in which the person is held in the place in which the census is taken" (Guatemala 1973:67) and is not to ask the respondent directly. Only in the case of a servant is the question "Is he/she Indian" permitted. Thus, the census takers define ethnicity according to their own agenda, whether the census taker is from San Marcos or San Pedro, without asking the persons interviewed.

San Pedro, by contrast with San Marcos, hosts only two offices of the national government: a policeman's ready room (with one inspector and ten patrolmen assigned to the town) and a combined post

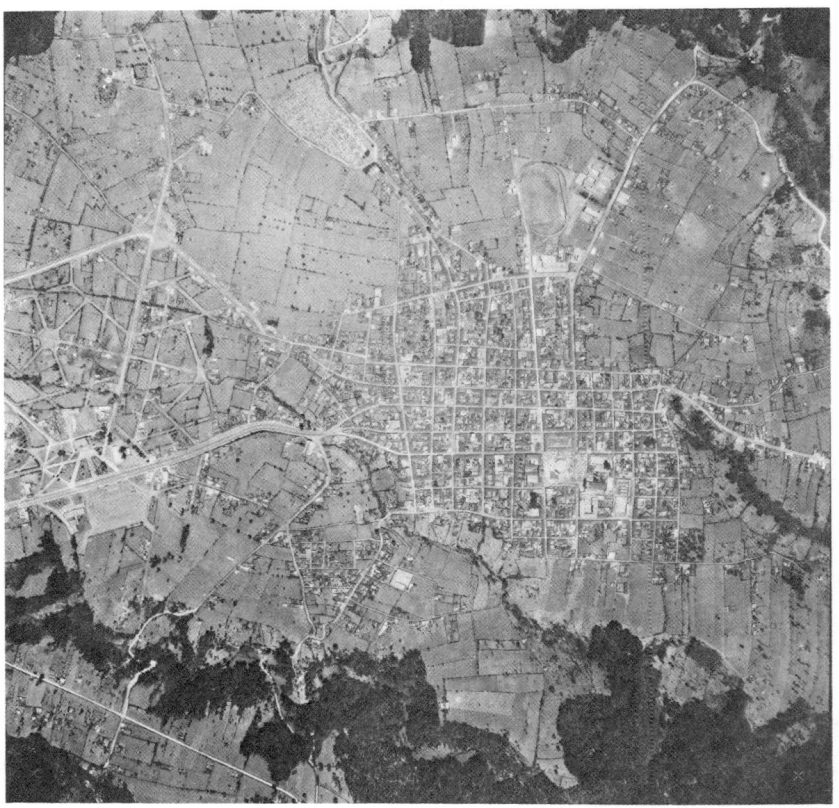

Plate 9. San Pedro Sacatepéquez on market day. The town plaza is in the lower right quadrant of the urban center. Immediately east of the plaza are the white canvas awnings that cover portable market stalls. To the north is the old market building; to the west, municipal buildings; to the south, commercial establishments. (Photograph taken between 1969 and 1972)

office-telecommunications center. These two offices, which are administered from San Marcos, are smaller, second-class appendages of the central offices in the department capital. They are of lesser official rank than those of San Marcos, and they offer commensurately fewer services. For example, the post office does not sell stamps. One goes to the post office, weighs the letter or package, marches down the block to a small store that sells stamps, and returns to the post office to drop the letter. The process is sufficiently frustrating that some San Pedro residents prefer to go to San Marcos for postal service. Again, the telephone office must work through San Marcos to get a phone line to the nation's capital or any other city. This places San Pedro in a time-consuming queue, particularly since the government offices in San Marcos as well as the customers standing in the San Marcos office take precedence. Finally, the police office in San Pedro is but a warming room directly administered by the main office in San Marcos. These services are subordinate to San Marcos and are defined as lower in status than the corresponding parent unit. These units replicate the relation of San Pedro to San Marcos and of Indian to Ladino. The structure of the status categories reverberates throughout the institutional and interaction systems like the play of images in a house of mirrors.

As a result of their institutional isolation, San Pedro residents are unable to generate many social and political contacts. The political priority of San Marcos and its Ladino ethnic status draw government officers there for residence. Although these officers come from outside, they participate in the same national status system, and they make their lives symbolically congruent by residing in San Marcos. Moreover, most San Pedranos who achieve political connection react to a decided dissonance between the social implications of their government connection and their residency in marginal San Pedro. Many such persons correct the situation by moving to San Marcos or to other cities and by making themselves (and more thoroughly, their children) Ladinos. This further isolates Indian San Pedro politically and increases the ideologically induced isolation, atomization, marginality, and powerlessness of the community.

San Pedranos do make some national-level contacts through ostensibly nonpolitical associations. For example, some San Pedranos support a *Casa de Cultura,* a cultural program bureau. Through the efforts of its directive committee, folk-dance groups, singers, musicians, poets, university lecturers, and several United States dance groups on international tour have performed in San Pedro. The national bicycle races included San Pedro on their circuit because several San Pedrano civic leaders worked in the organization's committee meetings. At least one member of the civic elite of San Pedro maintains social and intellectual contact with several members of the national university in Guatemala City.

San Pedro resident elites actively pursue these cultural and recreational programs to develop a system of contacts in the capital city that is satisfying to themselves and, symbolically, to the community. Note that these associations are of a cultural sort, using "culture" in the cultivated sense. This has positive symbolic value to San Pedranos inasmuch as the stereotype of the highland Indian is, in the Ladino's eyes, uncultured, unsophisticated, and uneducated. The Marquenses do not bring such cultural events to San Marcos and the San Pedranos taunt them with this fact whenever possible. These contacts, which some San Pedranos seek, are in part the only ones left. But they are, in addition, powerfully symbolic of the community's social aspiration and its national involvement in spite of political isolation.

In a different vein, several San Pedro businessmen have commercial contacts in the national capital. However, these contacts tend to be strictly business and do not appear to be expanded into other domains of personal favor except through occasional *compadrazgo*. In one case, a rich merchant chose his Guatemala City suppliers as godparents at his daughter's wedding. The chosen *compadres* brought a few of their own friends, and there was little social intercourse between the San Pedranos and the *capitalinos* during this evening. Thus, even in the social event itself, the San Pedranos were isolated, and after the event I saw no evidence that the *compadrazgo* link did more than morally affirm a continuing commercial relationship. Both by asking and by being from a peripheral Indian town, San Pedranos are subordinate in these relationships to the capital. The chosen compadre does the chooser a favor and establishes an asymmetrical debt.[9]

San Pedrano businessmen frequently voice an ideology of independent entrepreneurship. They say they can do without the government or political "pull" *(cuello)*. In several public ceremonies, the San Pedranos asserted that they would someday put down their arrogant Ladino neighbors through San Pedro's economic strength. Khrushchev's phrase about Russia burying the United States economically was once cited in a public meeting as a model for the way San Pedro would eventually solve its problems with San Marcos.

Nor have marriage contacts generated a significant social or political network outside the community. A number of male and female San Pedranos have married native Ladinos of San Marcos. But the potential for valuable contact is effectively defused by the fact that, while the San Pedrano brings wealth to the marriage, the Marquense is relatively poor. The Marquense's reciprocal contribution is ethnic purity or honor, that is, categorical status. Only the quite poor Ladinos move to San Pedro. The process blocks the conversion of the San Pedrano's economic assets into political assets. The same exchange of wealth for status occurs in the cases of marriage between San Pedranos and *capitalinos* or other Ladinos outside the Department of

San Marcos. For example, a wealthy San Pedrano professional married the daughter of a market vendor from Guatemala City.

The restriction of access is furthered by the fact that, when such marriages occur or when the political job and consequent opportunity for access becomes available to a San Pedrano, the San Pedrano is very likely to transfer his or her social and categorical person to Ladino status and his residence to San Marcos to express more accurately his or her new position in the social system. The reverse sometimes takes place. Of the several cases of intermarriage where the Marquense moved to San Pedro, one had redefined herself as an Indian. "Here, we are civilized Indians," she would say, reflecting at once the social separation from her natal community (only one kinsman from San Marcos regularly visited her) and her integration into a different network of relations in San Pedro. With this sole exception, those who left San Marcos to live in San Pedro were from poor households.

Let us turn now to an examination of a few cases where the ideological differences between the communities are brought into full relief in the political domain.

Case Studies of the Material and Social Implications of Inverse Status Ideologies

GETTING CEMENT

For one of the projects of municipal development, the mayor of San Marcos and his councilmen decided to pave a principal street of San Marcos with cement. The mayor cultivated his acquaintances in the capital and shortly thereafter secured for San Marcos a grant or gift of a thousand bags of cement from U.S.A.I.D. It is said that the mayor went to the president's office about the matter and to other agencies of the government. A U.S. State Department official was informed of the mayor's needs by a Guatemalan official. They were introduced, and the cement was allocated. The mayor subsequently spoke of his "good friend" in the embassy. It is not unlikely that the personal secretary to the president, a native of San Marcos, placed the mayor in contact with the embassy and thus with the aid program.

Once the paving of the road had begun, information about the grant became common knowledge. One day, after the mayor of San Pedro had helped me on another matter, he brought up the subject of the new road in San Marcos and the thousand bags of cement.

"You know we want to build a municipal auditorium. Couldn't you help us get some cement from the American government also?"

I asked him who he knew in the Guatemalan government that he could prevail upon to help him make contact with the American embassy. He could name no one; I was it. The mayor of San Pedro simply did not have a linkage to national power. In addition, he did not know, and San Pedranos in general do not know, the extent of the friends or relations of any *capitalinos* whom the San Pedranos might know. In the language of network analysis, San Pedranos do not know their second-order "star" beyond their home community.

By contrast, the San Marcos elites spend considerable time publicly discussing, identifying, and positioning the people they know or are related to. Moreover, Marquenses discuss the useful friends and relatives of those they know directly. At the frequent Ladino parties, conversations about people are the mainstay. This network cultivation is central to the ideology and behavior of Ladinos. In sharp contrast, seldom are the San Pedro elites heard discussing who they know, much less who the people they know know.[10]

LOCATING THE UNIVERSITY

On another occasion, San Pedranos organized to secure a branch of the national university (Universidad de San Carlos) in their town. Sufficient persons of reasonable academic qualification had agreed to teach, and permission had been secured from the national university. As the San Pedranos tell it, all was set. Then a delay occurred, and then, mysteriously, a branch of the national university was started in San Marcos. No one in San Pedro knew quite what had happened, although San Pedranos speculated that the officials of San Marcos first blocked and then preempted the San Pedro idea and effort. No one in San Marcos let on that they knew anything unusual had occurred, although one official did say that it was "appropriate" for a university to be in the department center, thereby implying knowledge that it might have been in San Pedro. Cynically, a San Pedro high municipal official remarked at the time that the university only mattered to San Marcos once San Pedro sought it. In any event, whenever the two communities are in competition with each other, San Marcos has the decided advantage due to the politically powerful networks of some of its residents.[11]

But the issue of appropriateness must be more carefully examined. Education is one means of access to the center. Ladino is at the center.

It is no accident that the best schools and only daytime high schools are in San Marcos. True, San Pedro has a night high school, but night study is for daytime workers and so it is not inconsistent for San Pedro to have it. Moreover, the night school can only certify graduates in business skills, a degree consistent with San Pedro's commercial Indianness. For the teaching or university high-school track, one must go to San Marcos. Had the university been placed first in San Pedro, the symbolic inconsistency would have been considerable.

BUILDING NEW MARKETS

Another example of access competition involved the construction of the new market buildings in the two communities. San Pedro has always been known as the commercial center of the department, a town full of merchants, *"comerciantes—puros comerciantes,"* as people in both towns are prone to say.

The San Pedro market, prior to 1973, was housed in a major building covering a city block next to the plaza. Like many other major markets, it had a ring of cubicle stores or *tiendas* that faced outward and were set under a covered promenade. On market days especially, the promenade was choked with wares hung out, peddlers seeking advantageous positions, shoppers haggling over prices, and youths ogling the girls. Inside, another ring of cubicles faced the covered bay. These were set back to back with the outer stores, sometimes connecting through to make large units. On market day, the inner bay was lined with rows of wooden stalls selling the goods typical of a Central American market. San Pedranos felt this building inadequate to their needs, for their market was the largest and most important in the department. Indeed, on market day, temporary stalls and stands filled the plaza in front of the central market, overflowed into three buildings, and jammed the side streets to the east and south.

In part to alleviate this crowding and in part to have a respectable building, the San Pedro municipal corporation solicited the National Office of Municipal Development (INFOM, or *Instituto Nacional de Fomento Municipal*) for aid for the construction of a market. Eventually INFOM promised San Pedro a grant of about 100,000 dollars for the construction of the market. Long-term loans made up the balance. Plans were drawn up for a modern two-story building. Shortly thereafter, San Pedro was informed that it would not be given a grant and that the town would have to finance the whole project

Plate 10. San Pedro, under the portico of the old market building on market day. Women in the center foreground are probably from surrounding hamlets, though they may be from other municipalities that have adopted the San Pedro dress as a regional style. The women in non-Indian dress may be from either San Marcos or San Pedro. The blanket seller is probably from Momostenango. (1971)

through loans. Finally, San Marcos announced that it, too, would have a new market building and that the mayor of San Marcos had secured a grant of 63,100 dollars toward the costs, the rest to be paid by loans.

Both towns eventually got their new market buildings: San Pedro financing the entire cost of a large building; San Marcos receiving a substantial grant for a much smaller building, as a result of a qualitative and quantitative difference in national access. To be fair, shifting the grant was not without justification. Indeed, the market facilities in San Marcos were abominable at that time: a dirt-floor encampment of vegetable vendors in an open courtyard, surrounded by a string of shantytown stalls housing butcher shops and eateries. The head of one government office in San Marcos phrased the issue this way: because the town of San Pedro is already commercially developed; a grant is unjustified; since San Marcos is underdeveloped commercially, a grant to spur development is appropriate. But San Pedro also merited assistance: its market was a truly regional

Plate 11. San Pedro's new market building open for business at dawn. To the northeast one can see the mountain bowl and a little of one of the rural hamlets attached to San Pedro. (1982)

market, serving the entire department. Why should San Pedranos absorb the whole cost for a center that served the whole department? Thus, both towns had valid arguments. The basis for changing the award of the grant was not the validity of the needs but the character of the social networks through which the two arguments of need were passed.

DISPUTING THE LAND

A long-term land dispute between the two communities also depends on political-access differences between the communities. Although the municipalities of San Marcos and San Pedro have been adjudicating and even warring over their land boundaries since at least 1705, I draw attention here only to recent events.

By popular election in 1966, President Julio César Méndez Montenegro, labeled as a more socialist leader, took over the government from a conservative military junta. Méndez Montenegro was perceived by many poor people as a source of mediation and alleviation of their peasant and proletarian problems. San Pedranos had seen him thus and had voted for him as a foil for the inactive, unresponsive prior government. However, as his presidency progressed,

Plate 12. San Marcos. The new market building and bus terminal. To the left are the old military barracks and headquarters (1973–74), now used as an auxiliary market and museum (1982). In the right foreground are a corner grocery store, a shoe-repair shop, and a pharmacy that was a school-supply store in 1973–74. (1982)

the San Pedranos became acutely aware that nothing had changed. Toward the end of Méndez Montenegro's administration, San Pedro sent a number of telegrams (dated 1969) and then a delegation to the capital city, urgently requesting that Méndez Montenegro support San Pedro's claims in the boundary dispute with San Marcos. The delegation and the telegrams were sent to officials of the *Partido Revolucionario,* Méndez Montenegro's party apparatus, and were apparently forwarded to the Ministry of Government. The communications contained an explicit threat that the *Partido Revolucionario* would have no chance in San Pedro without a favorable resolution of the boundary dispute. In late 1969, the central government turned the matter over to the San Marcos department governor with the request that he suggest a suitable solution.[12]

Each municipality was ordered to resubmit documents and testimony on the dispute so that these could be turned over to the National Geographic Institute for an impartial and scientific resolution. San Pedro submitted photocopies of early documents and an informal legal argument advanced by the San Pedro Workers Association

(Sociedad de Obreros de San Pedro). San Marcos apparently failed to reply until the central government ordered the governor to demand that both municipalities present their cases. San Marcos then complied. San Pedro presented its case again, and there was a flurry of telegrams and requests from the two municipalities to the central government.

With the June 1970 election approaching, the government was under pressure to resolve the issue. On October 10, 1969, the governor recommended that the state avoid controversy by nationalizing the disputed area between the two towns. In the meantime, San Marcos sought to increase its functional and de facto jurisdiction over the disputed area by providing it with potable water. San Pedro responded in two ways. On October 17, 1969, San Pedro protested this introduction of services by San Marcos. Then, on December 11, 1969, the San Pedro Workers Association again called the situation intolerable.

> The entire townspeople *(pueblo)* does not permit nor will it ever permit intervention by the national government—worse yet a [special] department district—because [the area in question] is not a crown landholding. (Land dispute documents, San Marcos mayor's office)

In April 1970, San Pedro responded competitively to the Marquenses' provision of water services to the disputed land. San Pedro began to erect street lights on the boulevard that passes through the disputed territory and connects the two towns. This event precipitated a demonstration that W. R. Smith witnessed:

> On this occasion, the San Pedranos were attempting to substantiate their claim by errecting street lights along the boulevard at their own public expense. They were vigorously opposed by the mayor of San Marcos, some of the citizens of San Marcos, and the departmental governor. The mayor of San Pedro advised them all that construction would continue and that if they interfered he would call them out his pueblo to force the issue, which he finally did. What occurred subsequently was a unique display of Indian political determination.
>
> The contested zone originated in Ladino attempts to merge the two communities into a single municipio. Reyna Barrios, president of Guatemala and native of San Marcos, made the first effort to unify the two municipios in 1893. In 1935 Ydígoras Fuentes, then

Jefe Político of San Marcos under Ubico, proclaimed another edict declaring the "public utility and necessity" of implementing Reyna Barrio's resolution by forming Ciudad la Unión, with municipal and departmental offices on the site now in dispute. This site was expropriated from San Pedro territory, and over the next six years localities in the department were taxed a total of $13,780 for public buildings. From 1941 to 1945 San Pedro Sacatepéquez and San Marcos were legally conjoined and became known as the municipio San Marcos la Unión.

This unification met instant opposition from San Pedranos. However noble the idea, they felt it was detrimental to lose their autonomy. Their feelings were well grounded. They were never compensated for the expropriated land, and they lost control over their large tax revenues. Also the municipal reorganization was not the expressed will of either community; it did not originate in local referendum but in arbitrary decrees of Ladino authorities—which are automatically suspect among Indians. Talk of unified progress was camouflage, San Pedranos feared. In reality, unification would promote the development of San Marcos at the expense of San Pedro.

Agitation against the union reached an effective level shortly after the Revolution of 1944. Attempts to suppress San Pedro opposition had been met on one occasion with violence, when the police were stoned by an angry Indian crowd. An underground party, the Partido Arevalista, was working against the union, and the revolutionary government received regular requests for separation, among them a petition of over 1000 signatures. Marquenses, too, began to favor separation when rumors spread that the Indians were on the verge of riot. Fear of bloodshed provoked the Arévalo government to dissolve the union in the famous degree of 1944.

But rather than resolving the problem, this clumsy, self-contradictory decree extend *{sic}* it. One clause clearly stated that all borders were to be returned to their pre-Unión positions (thus returning to San Pedro its territory), while another gave San Marcos jurisdiction over public works in the intervening zone. San Pedrano leaders see this as a clear violation of the national constitution: one township cannot be given authority in the territory of another.

Hence the San Pedrano street-light gambit and hence the Marquense resistance. Two lampposts had been erected, and the third was going in under the very windows of the governor's office when the brief battle was joined. A large crowd of Indians faced a much smaller one of Ladinos. Policemen and soldiers milled around ineffectively. The two groups exchanged taunts and Marquense tempers rose at the outrageous incursion into "their" territory. In a hasty conference, the governor agreed that the third post could be raised if the mayor of San Pedro would agree to a 24-hour "truce" in which the problem could be discussed. San Pedranos were delighted and hoisted the mayor to their shoulders. Marquenses, enraged, showered the Indians with rocks and fled under the return volley. One San Pedrano was hospitalized with a headwound.

That evening a town meeting was called, and the municipal auditorium filled to capacity. Leaders outlined the issues and their decision to continue the fight. Several years ago, the mayor said, San Marcos had introduced its water system into the zone, with the support of the governor. San Pedrano objections were met with appeals to reason. According to one Indian leader:

When they want to do something, they call on us to be civilized and brotherly and to favor progress. When we want to do something similar, they call us indios and accuse us of localismo *and of being uncultured.*

The doctor said the issue should have been resolved long ago, but the authorities were afraid "to touch the ember." Now, he said, it was a Supreme Court case, and legal aid could be had "at any moment." A court battle was within the social and economic reach of the community.

The microphone was opened to the audience and many individuals spoke, some denouncing the Marquenses, some ridiculing them, but all in favor of continuing the fight. "We are no longer indios and they are not going to deceive us again." "We are through," said another, "with mistreatment from those españoles with their white faces." The president of the Sociedad de Obreros declared his organization's support of the mayor's action. The next day the municipality declared the departmental governor *persona non grata* in San Pedro, and he was soon removed from office. There the matter stood when I left the field.

The San Pedranos' dedication to winning is out of proportion to the economic value of the territory in dispute. The land has become a symbol for them, and the feud is fired by all the injustices, real and assumed, that they have ever suffered at the hands of Marquenses. But their contentiousness is instructive in that it is so sustained, versatile, and organized. Traditional Indians are capable of sporadic resistance; they explode, gain nothing, and live with their frustration. San Pedranos have fought this battle for

> three decades, and can envision carrying it to the Supreme Court.
> Win or lose, they have shown their ability to fight with the
> Ladinos' own weapons. (W. R. Smith 1977:130–32)

Following this episode, the governor twice more (on April 23, 1970, and on May 18, 1970) requested nationalization of the disputed land. The last request, however, urged that the land either be nationalized or that it be definitively given to San Marcos "since it contains the municipal and departmental headquarters [of San Marcos]." The governor ordered two or three agitators in San Pedro to desist.

Then came the elections. President Carlos Arana, the leader of the party opposing Méndez Montenegro, won. This new official party had been heavily supported by San Pedro when it was the opposition party, again in expectation of a favorable resolution of the land disputes. With the election, a newly appointed governor and two newly elected mayors were installed.

Fresh faces, to be sure, but the dispute continued. The new mayor of San Pedro presented the case again, asserting to the central government that San Marcos had abandoned the upkeep of the area in question. The Ministry of Government ordered the governor to retrieve the entire folio of petitions from the mayor of San Marcos, to ascertain the original jurisdiction over the land in question, and to advise if San Pedro's assertion of abandonment was correct. The governor's reply: the land was from the jurisdiction of each city, and the area was maintained, but not in its original hexagonal layout due to an invason of San Pedranos.

The case records were then sent to the Ministry of Government and on December 22, 1970, the governor received this statement:

> In view of the report which the Honorable Department Governor of
> San Marcos rendered on this matter, this ministry resolves: that
> there is no grounds for continuing the case of petition for
> modification of the government decree of 20 July 1943, because
> the facts upon which it is based are not true. In consequence the
> case of petition is definitely [with the connotation of irrevocably or
> terminally] suspended and ordered archived. Notify. (Land dispute
> documents, San Marcos mayor's office)

In compliance with the order to notify, the governor summoned the two municipal councils. The entire town council of San Marcos as well as other citizens appeared. For San Pedro's notification, only the mayor and a single councilman appeared. And thus, supposedly, is laid to rest the land dispute.

There is a sequel, though. Sometime after the election but before June 1971, San Marcos removed the light poles installed by the San Pedranos and erected their own. A police guard station was built on the line that San Marcos claimed was the border in the dispute. The guard station has been manned twenty-four hours a day by armed police from the national civilian police unit from that date through, at last information, November 1982.[13]

San Pedro may be able to sustain an interest in a territorial matter, as W. R. Smith says. But San Pedro does not yet have the force or the connections to resolve the issues in its favor. In these regards, San Pedro remains an Indian town. Land is indeed symbolic to San Pedranos, and they are continuously interested in the disputed land (I have records of disputes over this land not just since 1935, but since 1705.) The San Pedranos can sustain interest in land because land is a necessary physical arena for enacting certain ideologies: the ideologies of isolation, subsistence, and labor. But San Pedranos did not sustain an interest in politics. They did not carefully cultivate relationships and debts during the years between elections. They couldn't. Their ideology militated against it. Those who did cultivate relationships had adopted a *ladino* ideology and they became such. Instead, San Pedranos have engaged in cycles of confrontation. In 1966, 1970, and again in 1974, they expressed their structural opposition to the prevailing order by voting for the party (or coalition) out of power.[14] Indeed, in 1978 I attended a regional mayors' conference in which the new mayor, from the official party, suggested there need be no further dispute over the contested area, that current arrangements were adequate. This pronouncement was met with cheers and a standing ovation from the governor of the department (who had been mayor of San Marcos from 1970 to 1974), San Marcos municipal officials, and others. The San Pedro representatives were quiet. No doubt the issue will heat up again; but, for the moment, San Pedro's municipal corporation had given up the struggle. In effect, San Pedro did not so much sustain its political efforts or keep them organized (as W. R. Smith has asserted), as renew them from time to time as a symbol of their structural opposition.

The central government ultimately based its decision to affirm the status quo and muzzle San Pedro on the recommendations and perceptions that the department governor passed to his superiors.[15] And in every instance the governor made recommendations favorable to the position of the San Marcos municipality. Why? A short and superficial answer is that the department governor's office is within the same building and about fifty feet away from that of the mayor of San Marcos. By contrast, the governor's office is approximately one kilometer away from the office of the mayor of San Pedro. Thus, the physical arrangement of offices facilitates a more intensive communication between the mayor of San Marcos and the governor.

More important, the spatial contiguity suggests a fundamental fusion of interests. In view of the political priority of the municipality that hosts the department government, the governor is merely the conduit of information and policy between local government and the national center. Since the Marquense elite has independent access to the center, the governor's position is precarious: he is unnecessary to the San Marcos elite as he can be flanked to the center and he is subject to the whims of the central authority. Yet his position acquires a measure of stability in three respects. First, the governor shares Ladino ethnic status with Marquenses and the central government leaders. Second, the governor interacts socially with Marquenses. Third, his future position and the need to recover favors merge his individual interests with those of San Marcos.

While such interests may constitute a partial and local interpretation, they are not a full or satisfying explanation because the interests themselves result from the cultural system. One can appreciate the cultural pressures leading to the present situation by imagining the symbolic consequences of the available alternatives. For example, one could return the disputed land to San Pedro, which would necessarily give San Pedro the building that houses the department government offices—a building constructed explicitly and elegantly for this purpose. Suppose department government stayed in the building. That would switch the departmental headquarters from San Marcos to San Pedro. Since ethnic terms, ethnic behavior, and ethnic status in life correspond structurally with centrality of political access, to thus locate department government in Indian San Pedro would seriously contradict the status order. Alternatively, department and San Marcos municipal government could be moved out of the building, thus avoiding inclusion of Indian San Pedro. However, to so evict the department government personnel and the mayoral officers from the finest building in the department—a building constructed especially for them—and to locate them in the ordinary if not ramshackle facilities available elsewhere in San Marcos would also seriously contradict the status order. Either event would be a symbolic contradiction of such magnitude as to be unthinkable among those in power. So San Marcos keeps the land and wins the dispute.

RELOCATING THE WHEAT COOPERATIVE

One can see why San Pedranos express great distrust of government in general and why they prefer to maneuver independently and in the economic domain. But the San Pedrano antigovernment, procommercial orientation applies to more than national government. The ideologies also tend to hamper locally elected leaders in the management of municipal government. Serving without pay, the elected San Pedro councilmen attend city-council meetings only irregularly. The community members show little interest in the matter and grant no sanction to force their councilmen to attend. As a result, San Pedro often goes for months—even a year or more is not unusual—without a full quorum at municipal business meetings. This ideological uninterest creates difficulties: in the absence of a quorum, San Pedro cannot transact any binding official business.

Thus, a vitiated San Pedro municipal government further erodes the community's position and benefits vis-à-vis San Marcos and the nation. One example will do. For several years prior to 1974, San Pedro had been host to the departmental offices of a quasi-public regional wheat cooperative that was quartered in a rented home. By 1973, the wheat cooperative was exceedingly cramped for space and wanted to build permanent facilities in San Pedro. To do so, the cooperative had to secure a building permit for the construction project. But a permit required municipal approval by a quorum of the town councilmen. The cooperative leaders tried repeatedly, but for more than a year San Pedro leaders had not been able to assemble a full quorum. In desperation, the cooperative decided to change its permanent location to San Marcos, which rapidly granted approval. San Marcos's leaders even backed down from their initial demand that the building sit squarely on the street edge of the property in proper Latin American style, though they were little attracted to the architect's pictures showing the building recessed from the street and diagonally oriented.

So the regional wheat cooperative shifted permanently to San Marcos. Because San Pedro could not generate local political participation, it lost the network of ties to the center through a major commercial and quasi-governmental enterprise. Thus, the consistency and coherence of the system were enhanced by cutting down on the anomalous contacts of Indian San Pedro and by increasing the appropriate contacts of Ladino San Marcos. The system as a whole was refined.

But behind this purificatory change in institutional placement and network structure, the categorical system of status and the inverse ideologies concerning connection and government remained the same. Category and ideology lay at the root of the changed location. San Pedro lost the cooperative, but in this case clearly not because it lacked the contacts to win in a competition with San Marcos. The relative strength of the interaction system was not even at issue, for the cooperative's leadership wanted to remain in San Pedro. San Pedro lost the cooperative because the Indian status ideology and categorical placement predisposed it toward political disinterest, a factor at the heart of each of these cases.

RECEIVING THE PRESIDENT

The difference in the political connections of the two communities is perhaps best exemplified in the events of the 1974 national election. As the election approached, President Arana, along with several ministers of the country, made a circuit of the departments. At each stop, they noted the past expenditures and projected the future expenditures of the national government in the departments.

President Arana, several ministers, and a retinue of aides arrived in San Marcos in helicopters and were escorted to the assembly hall of San Marcos's largest school. The president, his ministers, the mayor of San Marcos, and the department governor faced the audience from the raised stage. On the stage and to the president's left sat a minister, then the mayor of San Marcos, then other ministers and their aides, and finally, at the president's extreme left, at the end of the arc of tables sat the governor of the department. To the president's right sat other ministers and their aides and the official party's candidate for vice-president. Several of the department-level heads of the government offices, a few teachers, and the San Marcos stringers for the national papers stood behind.

Down on the floor sat the department's twenty-eight other mayors. They and their executive secretaries or other officers sat together in the main hall, off the stage, facing the seated authorities. Though they sat together in the front left (from their direction) quarter, these twenty-eight mayoral delegations were spatially equivalent to the other citizens, the government employees (whose offices had closed for the occasion), and the schoolchildren who sat in the other three quarters of the hall or found empty seats mixed in with the mayors.

The mayor of San Marcos opened the meeting. His initial greeting to the president suggested the relative importance of the municipality of San Marcos, for he welcomed the president "on behalf of the mayors of the department, the municipality of San Marcos and the townspeople of San Marcos."[16] Thereupon, beauty queens representing various social units in the municipality of San Marcos gave flowers to the president.[17]

The president gave a speech highlighting the good works of his government on behalf of the people. Then he introduced a minister who noted the past and projected efforts and accomplishments of that ministry with the municipality of San Marcos. The minister gave detailed listings of the expenses incurred and anticipated on each project or subproject within the municipality of San Marcos. When the minister finished, the mayor of San Marcos stood and thanked the government for each project, repeating in his expressions of gratitude the sum of the funds for each project. Then the mayor returned the floor to the president, who thanked the mayor and introduced the next minister. This cycle of presidential introduction, ministerial accounting, and mayoral acknowledgment was repeated for each minister (education, communications and public works, public health, and agriculture) and for the deputy director of the National Institute of Municipal Development regarding the projects each had completed in the department center.

After all the dignitaries had finished their detailed accounting of each project completed in San Marcos municipality, each minister in turn listed the total amount spent in each of the other twenty-eight municipalities and noted anticipated projects. The amounts spent in each municipality were not subdivided by project as they were for the municipality of San Marcos. Once all the ministers had finished, the president asked the body of mayors if they had any comments. At this, a few intrepid ones arose. Some of these noted in passing their thanks for past projects, but every official that stood used the occasion to complain about lack of attention or about problems with other projects. Their lack of access, by comparison with that of San Marcos, forced them to use the assembly to plead their cases rather than to give gracious thanks. President Arana concluded by emphasizing that patronage jobs were at stake in this election and that those present (who were mostly government employees) should be active in the campaign.

The relative preeminence of San Marcos among the municipalities was clearly dramatized and symbolized by the presence of its mayor on the stage, close to the president where he was spoken to as an individual and had occasion to speak frequently. This contrasts sharply with the positions allotted to the other twenty-eight mayors (including that of San Pedro) who were distanced, lowered, spoken to as a group, and allowed to speak only once if they chose to speak at all. Although the department governor sat on the stage with the central government officials, he was marginal: he sat to the extreme side and was neither asked to speak nor mentioned in any way. This symbolizes the governor's lack of importance, for he represents the central government; when the country's central leaders are present, their representative is of no consequence.

The close contact of the municipality of San Marcos to the nation by virtue of its more direct interpersonal relationships is further indicated in the following comments made during the program. First, the mayor of San Marcos said, "I wish to thank the intervention of the President, through the Minister of Agriculture, in removing the low production allotment [on price-supported coffee] on the municipal plantation." Thus, San Marcos's political networks include the president himself.

Later a minister remarked that "San Marcos requested [a tax of] ten cents per hundredweight on coffee produced in the department for [the use of] the municipality of San Marcos." That such a statement could be made without uproarious protest by the lowland municipal leaders in protecting the interests of their local coffee growers suggests the central power of San Marcos as departmental headquarters. That the Marquenses should even ask the national government to obligate the other lowland municipalities to support them seems unusual, were the Marquenses not comfortably sure of their political preeminence.

Finally, at a dinner following the rally, the president and the mayor sat together at the head table, joking sometimes, talking with each other frequently. None of the other mayors had such access at the party.[18]

It is apparent, then, that San Pedranos individually lack access and connection to the national political system. Furthermore, the municipality as a whole lacks access, both because its individuals do not connect and because there are few offices that service San Pedro. Of course, these two factors are closely related to each other. But beyond these social-network facts, Indian ideology is anticonnective and antipolitical—the opposite of Ladino ideology—within the total system. Indians are fiercely independent traders, truckers, artisans, and farmers. Virtually all San Pedranos who acquire political connections shift out of the community and become Ladinos. Locally employed teachers are the principal exception, and many of them have made the ethnic shift. There is a positive aversion to government. To many San Pedranos, government is worthless and its officers a gang of thieves. In the more remote Indian communities, the aversion is raised to fear: W. R. Smith (1977:115) reports that one Indian expressed his bravery by affirming that he was not afraid to enter any government office in San Marcos. In the hinterland Indian communities, the ideologies of anticonnection or atomization manifest themselves in subsistence isolation, in the expectation of witchcraft among brothers, in the fragmentation of the family estate, and in the community's craft specialty and distinctive Indian outfit. Inverse ideologies condition the entire social system.

I have now staked out the political positions of San Marcos and San Pedro Sacatepéquez within the nation: San Marcos, the departmental headquarters, is both de jure and de facto a more powerful community. This power differential in social relations reiterates the structural oppositions of the status system, the inversions of the ideological system, and the contrasts of the ethnic-symbol system. Power, control, authority, and centrality correspond to the points of the status system just as the ethnic symbols do. Because of the correspondences in structure, power becomes a symbol as well as a correlate of status. Thus, a shift in the political centrality of an individual may then be followed and confirmed by an adjustment in his use of ethnic symbols. Conversely, an adjustment of symbols may facilitate a move toward centrality of relations. Thus, there is no simple causality in the complex dynamic and oppositional structure of existing relations, overarching categories, activating ideologies, and mediating symbols.

Of course, the idea of the political domain is an analytical convenience; power is never pure or disconnected from other aspects of social life. And more often than not, power concerns productive resources. Property, which is the political allocation and maintenance of culturally defined resources, partakes of the characteristics of class (in the marketplace) and of party (in the domain of power and authority). In part because of its power component, land enters importantly and symbolically into the definition of Guatemalan ethnicity, even more so than money or wealth in the abstract. The large landowner and the government share in the administration of the land and in the management of the people who live on it. The more a man owns, the more he partakes of the characteristics of the central government—a focus of Ladino symbolic definition. As we have seen, occupations also have a political aspect because the prestigious jobs are in the government and are awarded by the government. Thus, it is not in fact accurate to sharply separate polity and economy. With this reservation in mind, the next chapter examines the economic relations within San Marcos and San Pedro, between the two towns, and their connections to the nation as a whole.

4
The Economic Oppositions of San Pedro Sacatepéquez and San Marcos

Like the division in political networks and ideology, an economic dualism pervades San Marcos and San Pedro, arising out of inverse production and consumption ideologies. What is the nature of this dualism, and what is its significance? I explore these questions in the light of a premise elaborated by Marshall Sahlins in *Culture and Practical Reason,* though not stated in this way: To the extent that an economy produces more than is needed for subsistence and shelter, it produces largely symbols; moreover, much of the subsistence and shelter institutions are organized to emphasize symbolic values rather than efficiency values (Sahlins 1976:178–84, 203–4, 212–15). The economy, then, is the durable language—the hard currency of communication in society; it is a self-fulfilled prophecy of the initial categories and premises of social structure. Through the economy, the people manufacture and consume the material proof of a cultural reality (Sahlins 1976:185).

The anthropological studies of Mesoamerica have noted the existence of economic differences between Ladinos and Indians, but the cultural expressions in the economy have largely been left unread. On the one hand, this occurs because of an overattentiveness to distinctive differences in economic procedure and material display. When working within this perspective, authors note the economic activities of a particular community of Indians: what they work at, how they uniquely do it, how they display and consume the products of their efforts. All this is contrasted with major or subtle differences in the economic activities of Indians of other towns and with Ladinos throughout the country. Since act and artifact are a part of culture within this genre, and since the behavioral and material productions of the groups are clearly different, one concludes that the various groups are distinct and relatively separate cultures, the bearers of which happen to rub shoulders in residence but not otherwise in substance. A difficulty with this view is that the various production activities, as well as the artifacts produced and displayed in the different communities, are ranked with regard to each other. Hoeing is less prestigious than writing, while clay pots are less prestigious than metal pans. In short, the dictionary of Guatemalan life compiles the forms of all the communities and peoples; if this is not recognized, the messages in the economy cannot be fully read.

On the other hand, the symbolic richness of the economy is often only partially read because of reservations or anxieties concerning the present morality or the future effects of the sharply different class positions of Ladinos and Indians. Thus, investigators have noted that Indians are generally poorer than Ladinos in cash income or in property ownership. Moreover, Indians are subordinate in their types of occupation and in their relationship to management. Indians generally own less land than Ladinos do. Indians concentrate in the occupations of agriculture, artisanry, and petty commerce, while Ladinos tend to control the wholesale system, the retailing of Western goods and services, and the government. Finally, Indians are frequently hired by Ladinos, usually as agricultural laborers, but Ladinos are almost never hired by Indians for such jobs. Furthermore, Ladinos hired by Ladinos are frequently placed as crew supervisors over Indians. This pervasive subordination of Indians to Ladinos is incontrovertible.

If, however, the analysis stops here, the Indians are deculturalized, subject only to the cold push and pull of economic necessity and the self-interest of one's place in the production system. Nonproduction differences are labeled traditional usages and are considered irrelevant, except as additional diacritical markers. Carried to this end, the production-relations approach also misreads the economy. For example, in the Guatemalan hierarchy, leisurely inactivity is in certain regards more important than production or control. Because of this and other uniquely cultural factors, the externally imposed Marxian analytical framework tends to misread signals sent within the economy.

The economic system of Guatemala is especially important in the life of the Indians; for in the market plaza and the marketplace fewer restrictions are placed on them. The market plaza is theirs—and in commerce generally, Indians seem to have a more vibrant freedom of movement than they do in other aspects of their lives, except perhaps religion. But even in the market arena, some authors have noted that Ladinos control commerce in the regional trade centers, buying out the Indian agricultural surplus and selling back the accoutrements of a ritual system that has been characterized as "conspicuous waste" (Siverts 1969; Stavenhagen 1975). Other authors, however, see a greater equality within the marketplace. Colby and van den Berghe (1969:130–36) note that Indians and Ladinos are both merchants and clients to each other.

Carol A. Smith (1975) sees stratified ethnic relationships as a derivative of market structure. Her presentation is complex, but, reduced to the simplest of terms, it asserts that Indians take a subordinate position in the stratification system because they have an inferior spatial position with respect to the dominant market centers.[1] She argues that the Marxian notion (though she cites Wolf) of a "'class' definition of peasantry [based] on property systems" does not apply to those "classically agrarian societies where the peasant producer owns the means of production and pays minimal if any form of tax to economic superiors" (C. A. Smith 1975:95). The Mayan Indians of Guatemala are cited as one example of this situation

However, both these assertions are partially incorrect in Guatemala. First, Indians pay taxes. Sometimes the taxes are only ten pennies as a fee for government paperwork, but that is an hour's wage or more, and paperwork is a recurring expense. Other taxes are inescapable and much higher. This is confirmed by Colby and van den Berghe (1969:121) for even the most isolated Indian regions of Guatemala. Second, since the land owned by most Indians is insufficient to meet their food subsistence needs and since Indians buy clothing, tools, utensils, transportation, and fiesta materials produced far from their homes, to say they own their own means of production exaggerates their productive capacity. Carol Smith's market-placement approach is thus a useful supplement rather than a necessary replacement for production-relations accounts of stratification in Guatemala.

All these points of view share one feature in common: they base the hierarchy of Ladinos and Indians on some kind of objective or real condition in the socioenvironmental world. The problem is that the reality arises out of a complex set of cultural propositions. Since many of the cultural propositions for economics can be arrayed in support of either capitalist or Marxist frameworks, the Guatemalan form of economic and political domination appears objectively to be the root of ethnic maintenance. However, once we consider the prop-

Plate 13. San Pedro. The home of a *patrono*. In the courtyard, hanks of thread are drying, after having been dyed in the basins along the upper left wall. Fuel storage to the lower left. Storage rooms for finished cloth at the center and right of the back wall. Entry in upper right corner, followed by kitchen, two bedrooms, and living room. At lower right, a bedroom for the married daughter and unemployed son-in-law from San Marcos. (1974)

ositions of both Ladinos and Indians as a structured set, we see that the production of materials for display is an iconic playing out of the cultural principles. Culture is not a reification, epiphenomenon, or product of production relations or economic necessity. The reverse is more nearly the case.

The Economic System of San Pedro

In the more peripheral Indian *municipios* of the Department of San Marcos, Ladinos control the major economic activities, including the sale of manufactured products, agricultural necessities, and pharmaceuticals, as well as the purchase of seasonal labor and crop surpluses.[2]

In this respect, San Pedro is quite unlike other Indian communities in the Department of San Marcos or in Huehuetenango. W. R. Smith (1977:103–9) has shown how, through price competition and consumption austerity, the San Pedro Indians forced out the Ladino wholesale and retail store owners following World War II. The regional mercantile preeminence of the San Pedro Indians seems to be a result of three factors. First, compared to Ladinos, the Indians

Plate 14. San Pedro. The work area under the awning of the left wall in Plate 13. To the left, young apprentices load bobbins for the weaver in the rear. At right, thread is prepared for dying. (1974)

have been able to operate on a lower profit margin by restricting consumption per household. Second, compared with other Indian communities, the San Pedranos have a favorable trade location. Third, compared with other Indian communities, San Pedranos readily began to adopt Spanish as the community language two generations prior to today's oldest grandparents, with the process essentially completed one generation prior to them. No doubt the San Pedranos' adoption of Spanish was partially due to their historical alliances, to their proximity to San Marcos, and to the necessities of their regional trade and manufacturing economy. Whatever the reasons, a thriving craft, commercial, and transport boom has resulted, with new monetary and managerial differences among the San Pedro Indians.

Currently, the economic strength of San Pedro centers in and radiates from cottage industry and a combination of merchandising and transport.

IMPORTANT COTTAGE INDUSTRIES

Weaving is the primary cottage industry. A few weavers, called *patronos* ("boss-sponsors"), organize much of the weaving industry. The *patronos* generally have substantial sales outlets for their prod-

Plate 15. Footloom weaving. A master weaver (arms folded) and employee in the weaving room of his house, rural San Pedro. (1982)

ucts and employ numerous other weavers. At least one *patrono* owns a pickup truck and thus controls the means of transportation of both his product and his raw materials.

A *patrono*, as capitalist, organizes production in several scattered households in a kind of putting-out system. The *patrono* purchases undyed cotton thread in bulk quantity at the mills in Cantel (Department of Quezaltenango) or in Guatemala City. He brings the bulk thread to his house site, a large patio courtyard encircled by living areas and workrooms occupying up to half a city block or more. In the patio, an employee washes the thread to remove production oils and a waxen coating. The thread is then dyed with colorfast dyes (generally German or Japanese imports) and hung in the patio to dry.

In the putting-out system, the thread is sold to the weavers for cash or in a book transaction. The sale price is often a few cents a pound under the current and readily available market price. This practice tends to keep a stable corps of workers. Nevertheless, the *patrono* makes a small profit on the sale (estimated by one informant as fifteen cents per pound of thread, or about eight cents per yard of woven cloth) on account of his bulk-price advantage from the factory.

Sometimes the *patrono* charges a few cents a pound extra for carrying the weaver on credit or for picking up and delivering materials in the rural areas.

The weaver, usually a male, takes the allotted thread to his home, strings his loom with a warp (or, more commonly, hires a specialist to do this), and weaves in the woof. When the cloth is completed, it is returned to the *patrono*. The returned cloth may be weighed to preclude diversion of materials or inadequate thread density. The yardage is then bought. If the materials were given on credit, the worker is in effect paid his per-yard wages. The *patrono* then takes the yardage and sells it to the garment makers who supply goods for the tourist market, for Guatemalans seldom buy these San Pedro cloth products. Alternatively, the *patrono* may employ other workers, usually female, to sew, tie fringe, or otherwise finish the cloth into some product: diamond-cut ponchos, capes, pants, purses, stuffed animals, tablecloths, and other items. These are then sold to the tourist market in Guatemala City or to international outlets. Several *patronos* own stores and make direct sales to Guatemala City tourists and United States wholesalers. A few weavers make cloth for the traditional native clothing of San Pedro: the silken yellow skirt *(corte)* and embroidered blouse *(huipíl)* used by some elderly San Pedro women in town and by some women of all ages in the hamlets.

The profits are layered into the process, with five to ten cents per yard added at each stage. There is little incentive to cut the price by eliminating a layer of profit since one could just as well not bother with a layer of production and sell it to someone else to finish. The *patrono* does, however, have a degree of price flexibility due to bulk production, bulk-sales position, and the profit layering. This flexibility, combined with the marketing contacts, pressures the independent small-scale weavers into clientage or into expansion as *patronos*.

How many *patronos* are there, and how big are their operations? A direct census was not possible since one would not be informed accurately. A reliable informant listed the names and number of employees of twenty-one *patronos* in just two or three minutes: four *patronos* with 150 weavers each, one with 100 to 150, one with 100, two with 75, four with 50, five with 40, one with 30, and three with 20. At around twenty employees per *patrono,* the informant paused. "There are more," he said, "especially the new ones with ten or fifteen looms." The incompleteness of this list, which is in no sense exhaustive, does indicate a large number of weavers (1,450–1,500).

Both in San Marcos and in San Pedro, the household is the unit of

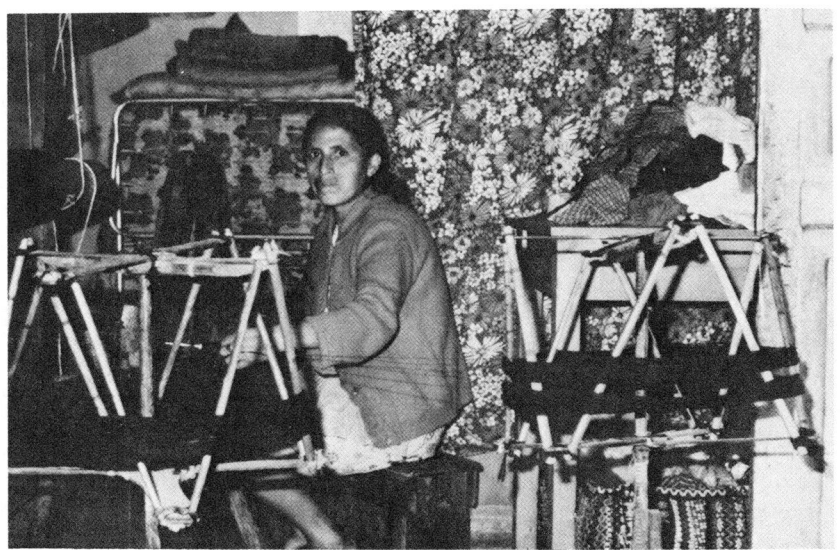

Plate 16. San Pedro. Household production in the weaving industry. The wife untangles and winds hanks of thread onto cane bobbins. The door to the right and the ropes of the loom just to the left of the folded-up cot define the available living space, with as much space behind the camera as in front. Three looms (one visible in Plate 17) line the left wall. Behind the curtain, the couple's bed; at night, the equipment is stacked behind the camera, and the cot is folded out for two children. The door opens on a patio and a kitchen beyond the back wall of this picture. (1974)

consumption.[3] But in sharp contrast to most San Marcos households, the San Pedrano household is also a unit of production in which several household members often participate. Families supported predominantly by weaving tend to involve at least the husband and wife and often an older child or two in the production organization. Typically, the labor is cooperatively divided. The husband procures the dyed thread—whether from a *patrono* at delivery or by independent purchase. The thread comes in a packet (*el paquete*) of skeins (*las madejas*). Once washed, these skeins are taken by the wife (so that the husband may continue to weave), untwisted to form a coil, and placed over a conical spinner set on an axle. Two such *madejas* are usually set up so that a pair of threads can be wound onto a bamboo bobbin (*cañizo*). This procedure is usually repeated, so that a supply of bobbins with four-stranded thread is available to the husband-weaver. Bobbin winding is the woman's usual contribution to effi-

Plate 17. San Pedro. The husband takes the bobbins and weaves the cloth. (Photographer stands in the doorway.) (1974)

cient household production. If necessary, a man will wind his own bobbins without compunction should he run out of prepared materials. The task is not restricted to women's work.

The husband takes these loaded bobbins to the loom and does the actual weaving.[4] For the most part, weaving is done by men as it is said to be heavy and fast.[5] The looms are quite large, a box frame of 10 centimeter by 10 centimeter timbers approximately 1.5 meters wide, 2.5 meters long by 2 meters high, so that with even a single loom the small houses acquire a cramped industrial aspect. Yet many small houses have two or three looms occupying most of the available space of a one-room house.[6]

Once (sometimes twice) a week the woven yardage is cut from the loom. In the independent weavers' households and in some putting-out systems, the wife then takes the material and, with the household's treadle sewing machine, sews a clothing product, usually for the tourist market. If appropriate, she may attach a fringe to it. The finished product, whether a diamond-cut poncho, a zippered cape, a quetzal-adorned shirt, a handbag, or other item, is taken to the *patrono* or sold to some buyer.

Plate 18. The wife then sews finished cloth products for delivery to a middleman or for direct sale in the markets. (1974)

The cooperative involvement of husband and wife in the productive enterprise has important social consequences; the relative equality of women in San Pedro society is in part a product of the Indian woman's substantial contribution to household production. By the same token, the fact that Indian women consistently work in manual occupations matches with and justifies the lowered place of Indians in the society as a whole, for Ladino women usually avoid such need to work and the elite Ladino women always avoid work except as schoolteachers, government clerks, or salespersons in their household shop.

The distribution of small-scale weaving is concentrated in the periphery of San Pedro. Only two households with looms in them were noted on the street that exits to Quezaltenango. The shops that line the main streets to San Marcos are entirely devoted to nonweaving commercial outlets. As one leaves the main streets toward the edges of town, one increasingly hears the rhythmic pounding of the loom combs tightening the weave, each thud punctuating the whine of unoiled bobbins in racing shuttlecocks, the continual din attesting to the importance of weaving away from the commercially valuable center streets. The number of other kinds of purely artisan operations—as contrasted with sales outlets—also increases away from the main streets. In the nearby *aldeas,* or satellite hamlets, there are a great number of households that are likewise involved in weaving, usually for an urban *patrono.* This weaving is most apparent in those *aldeas* closest to the urban center: San José Caben, La Grandeza, Chamac, and Champollap. Weaving is being introduced now to the more remote *aldeas*.

Machine knitting is a fairly new and expanding industry in many San Pedro households. Most of the machines are operated by hand. Usually one, but up to a half-dozen such machines are operated in San Pedro households devoted to knitting. When there are more than two machines in the household, paid laborers often help run them. There is one "factory" *(fábrica)* where many knitting machines are electrically driven.

One knitting machine does not require cooperation between spouses, for a wife and daughters will occupy the machine and stitch the cloth into sweaters or other products. But if the household invests in several knitting machines, the family members cooperate to keep thread in supply, workers producing, and machines repaired, and to sew material into finished products and carry them to markets for sale. For the most part, a single knitting machine in the household is the working province of the wife (at odd hours) and of a daughter or two who may have dropped out of school. Men will also run the machinery, but the ease of the rhythmic work (so they say) and the fact that the machines take little space make them a convenient source of supplemental household income for women. On the other hand, the machines' relatively high cost (two hundred to four hundred dol-

Plate 19. San Pedro. Knitting, a predominantly female cottage industry. (1982)

lars compared with eighty dollars for a loom) encourages full utilization by household members in shifts or by employed outsiders, though not all machines are fully utilized.

The spatial distribution of tailoring concentrates more to the center of the town than weaving and differs also in that there are several tailors in the community of San Marcos. Tailoring requires a lesser degree of cooperative family effort. A significant number of tailors work the local native cloth into tourist products. Some of them have stores that front on the main streets and on the plaza of San Pedro. In addition, there are many tailors who cut men's suits from imported synthetics. Seamstresses *(costureras, modistas)* make women's dresses while the tailors *(sastres)* make men's suits, slacks, sport coats, and shirts. A tailor need not split the productive tasks with his wife; occasionally a wife might press finished clothing, but usually a tailor will press his own work as needed.

Baking also requires the cooperative effort of several workers. A married couple is an efficient core for the distribution of the necessary tasks, as baking minimally involves sales by one trusted family member and either labor or laborer supervision by another.

The remaining cottage industries require little cooperative effort, but that does not mean that household members are idle. The San Pedro wife not involved in her husband's trade will very likely have

The Economic Oppositions of San Pedro Sacatepéquez and San Marcos 147

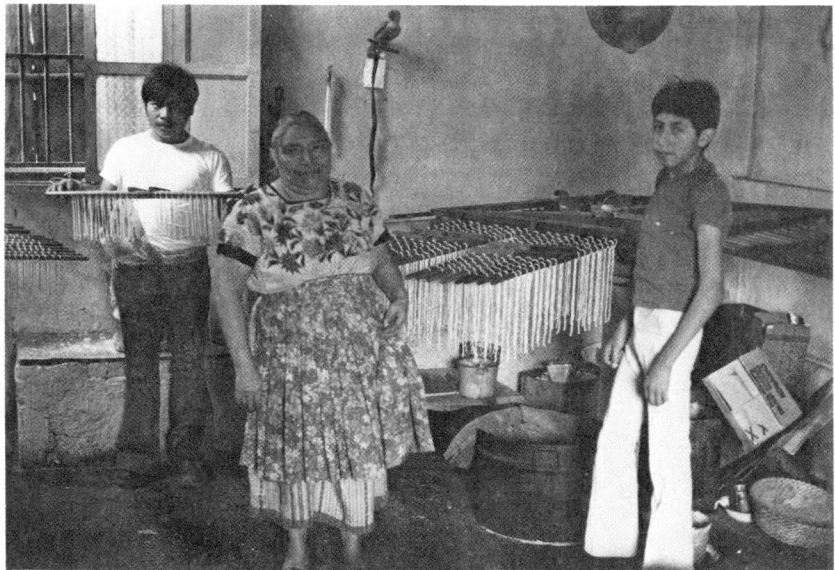

Plate 20. San Pedro cottage industry: candle making in a large kitchen. This woman also operates one of the more complete neighborhood shops, with the help of an employee to the left and a household member to the right. (1973)

her own minor industry or other form of economic contribution. She may dip candles, tend a front-door store, make soap, sew, sell in the market, cook, or attend to other enterprises. Or she may do several of these. Thus, the household is often a highly diversified production unit. Sons and daughters often drop out of school and add to the household's productive capacity until they marry and even after. If a formerly married woman is living alone or with her children, she is virtually certain to be engaged in some such productive activity.

As a consequence of this employment diversification, the occupational figures in Table 3, derived from my sample survey, should be read with some caution.[7] Table 3 is based on household heads, but there are many more weavers and knitters residing in households than there are male household heads who are weavers. The fact that a variety of household industries often coexists in a household was not elicited in this census tabulation. Thus, Table 3 underrepresents the place of weaving and other household industries in San Pedro as contrasted with San Marcos. This is especially the case for knitters, since there is a part-time female bias toward this work.

Table 3. Relative Importance of All Crafts in Urban San Pedro and San Marcos[a]

Occupation of Household Head by Frequency in S.P.	San Pedro			San Marcos	
	No. of S.P. Households	% of S.P. Household Heads Engaged in Trade	S.P.'s % of Trade	No. of S.M. Households	% of S.M. Household Heads Engaged in Trade
Tailors	21	10.8	100.0	0[b]	0.0
Shoemakers	15	7.7	59.1	6	3.3
Carpenters	13	6.7	68.4	9	4.9
Weavers	12	6.2	92.3	1[c]	0.5
Masons	11	5.6	57.8	8	4.3
Knitters	8	4.1	100.0	0[d]	0.0
Bakers	8	4.1	88.9	1	0.5
Seamstresses	4	2.1	66.7	2	1.1
Mechanics	4	2.1	57.1	3	1.6
Butchers	3	1.5	100.0	0[e]	0.0
Tile and brick makers	2	1.0	100.0	0[f]	0.0
Loom armers	1	0.5	100.0	0[f]	0.0
Soap makers	1	0.5	100.0	0[e]	0.0

Occupation of Household Head by Frequency in S.P.	San Pedro			San Marcos	
	No. of S.P. Households	% of S.P. Household Heads Engaged in Trade	S.P.'s % of Trade	No. of S.M. Households	% of S.M. Household Heads Engaged in Trade
Radio repair	0	0.0	0.0	1[g]	0.5
Watchmakers	0	0.0	0.0	1[g]	0.5
Blacksmiths	0	0.0	0.0	1[h]	0.5
Electricians	0	0.0	0.0	1[h]	0.5
Painters	0	0.0	0.0	2[h]	1.1
Total craft-based households	103 N = 195	52.8%	74.1%	36 N = 184	19.6%

Notes (interpretive comments based on qualitative knowledge of the communities):

[a] Selected occupations drawn from a 25 percent sample. See footnote 7 for definitions of urban and sampling arrangements. [See Appendix 2a for a complete listing of occupations in San Marcos-San Pedro sample.]

[b] There are a few tailors in San Marcos, but the sampling process missed them. They devote their labors almost exclusively to making professional quality suits.

[c] The weavers in San Marcos claimed to be Indians from San Pedro that had moved to San Marcos for lack of purchasable space in San Pedro. One Ladino who hired Indians for specialty weaving was not picked up in the sample.

[d] There are a very few knitters in San Marcos, none of which were picked up in the sample. This occupation involves manual operation of knitting machines and is done by the San Marcos women.

[e] Present in San Marcos but not sampled.

[f] No instances known in San Marcos.

[g] One instance present in San Pedro.

[h] Present in San Pedro but not sampled.

San Pedro is somewhat unusual in its diversity of crafts. Many agricultural Indian communities tend to specialize in a single craft. Cooper has shown how such Indian village or hamlet craft specializing isolates households from each other. Producing similar products, a community's families trade impersonally with outsiders rather than with each other (Cooper 1976).

Another action that manifests the ideology of isolation and disconnection is the degree to which the Indians (compared with the Ladinos) engage in self-employed activities. This appears to be one reason why cottage industry is the usual means by which formerly agricultural communities become nonagricultural: craft industries use manual labor in household isolation at the periphery of communities. The San Pedro behavior follows the premise of manual labor in that 52.8 percent of its household heads engage in the crafts listed in Table 3. San Pedranos largely conform to the premise of household isolation in that 43.5 percent of the household heads in San Pedro versus 19.1 percent of the household heads in San Marcos were self-employed.[8]

MERCHANDISING

The visitor to San Pedro is visually assaulted with evidences of the commercial vigor of the town. Immediately north of the central plaza stands the new two-story, block-long market building. It is filled with stalls and stores offering pharmaceuticals, herbal or prescriptive; clothing, tailored or ready-made; cloth products, native or foreign; foodstuffs, fresh or processed; and hardware and utensils of great variety. Small shops and larger stores of all kinds face the market from across the street on three sides. A dense profusion of shops, stores, warehouses, and restaurants extends westward on both sides of the outgoing and incoming streets connecting the town to San Marcos. Other stores dot both sides of the outgoing and incoming streets connecting San Pedro to the Quezaltenango highway northward from the plaza, although these streets offer a somewhat less commercial aspect as shops are interspersed among houses. Eastward from the plaza stands the Catholic church, its school and residences, a supplemental market building that was formerly a school, and the industrial junior high school. The rank of blocks behind the church houses the bus depot, more market-day buildings, and stores, craft workshops, and residences. The south face of the plaza includes a theater, a business-arts school, and several stores. Further south,

Plate 21. Interior of a household shop. San Pedranos are *comerciantes* par excellence. This woman wears a modern blouse or dress and the bib apron San Pedranos call a *gavacha*. She offers a selection of soft drinks, liquor, beer, soap, candles, snacks, fruit, juices, cigarettes, breads, broom, and medicines. (1982)

residences and household workshops predominate. The west face of the plaza houses the municipal building with the mayor's chambers and conference room, secretarial offices, treasury, police substation, utilities office, and an auditorium.

On side streets, away from the central plaza and connecting streets, the stores with employed attendants are greatly reduced in number. Instead, one finds numerous houses with a counter just inside the door, where one may purchase small or recurrent needs: a pack of matches, a single cigarette, a few candles, or a cup of sugar. And one finds the open doors of the artisan-carpenters, tinsmiths, tailors, weavers, and others—all seeking light for their tasks. Sales are made in these doorways and workrooms, it is true, but they are more a place of work than a market facility.

The merchants *(comerciantes)* of San Pedro include those whose primary income is derived from buying and reselling various products. A few sell to several communities throughout the department as wholesalers. Others are retailers focused in San Pedro and San Marcos. Some retailers maintain stores in other *municipios* of the department.

Plate 22. Heavy transport in San Pedro, looking east on the main street to San Marcos. (1982)

Great numbers of women take advantage of the market day to sell agricultural produce or craft products. Some ply this trade in the new market building throughout the week, for the new market is continuously stocked with produce and general merchandise. Neither the commercial vitality of San Pedro nor its market dominance over San Marcos appears as striking in a census as the visual comparison of the main and subsidiary streets in the two towns suggests. One reason is that many of the shops in San Pedro are outlets for household production. The owners of these shops often claim to be artisans *(artesanos)* rather than merchants. But the figures of my sample are instructive: 10.3 percent (twenty cases) of San Pedro household heads claimed to be merchants versus 4.3 percent (eight cases) in San Marcos. Thus, San Pedro provides 71.4 percent of the sampled commercial occupations. Although the reported cases are too few, the proportional distribution of commerce for the two communities is about right. If it errs, it does so by giving San Pedro too small a percentage of the total commerce.

The market importance of San Pedro is facilitated by the activities of the truckers. Municipal tax records show thirty-seven trucks owned by San Pedranos, and there may well be more. At least two of the truck owners have large wholesale warehouse outlets. Some of the other truckers have smaller sales outlets. As a result of these truckers, San Pedranos have ready access to bulk hauling facilities, a

Plate 23. San Pedro. A rural home consisting of a thatch-roofed kitchen and modified wattle-and-daub bedroom-and-craft-room on opposite sides of the work yard. The owner also sharecrops with an urban San Pedro weaver and school teacher. The man stands on the footpath leading to the road to town, surrounded by his growing corn milpa. Two daughters stand in the gateway. (1973)

fact that helps to maintain their economic importance in the highlands as well as on the coast. Indeed, highland *municipios* are rather dependent on San Pedro truckers for the export of their cash crops and labor and for the import or export of corn.

AGRICULTURE

As can be seen in Table 4, about a third of urban San Pedranos own land, usually in small parcels. Often worked by rural sharecroppers, the lands add to a household's income through crop sales or reduce a household's consumption expenses. Of the urban San Pedranos, 11.6 percent list agriculture as their occupation and, by presumption, as the primary source of their incomes. But not many San Pedranos hold extensive tracts of land. One fellow claimed to have been a plantation owner before he retired. Another individual is quite famous for being the owner of more than a thousand *cuerdas*[9] in the environs of San Pedro. These qualitative statements can be compared with my figures on landholding. The data in Table 4 are taken from my survey work and reflect reported agricultural landownership and land values both inside and outside the *mu-*

Table 4. Agricultural Land per Household in San Pedro and San Marcos

	San Pedro			San Marcos	
	Urban (N = 195)	Rural Distant *Aldea* (N = 66)		Urban (N = 184)	Rural Near *Aldea* (N = 92)
Households with no agricultural landholdings	132 (67.7%)	9 (13.6%)		103 (56.0%)	12 (13.0%)
Number and percentage of households with some agricultural landholdings	63 (32.3%)	57 (86.4%)		81 (44.0%)	80 (87.0%)
Mean land value of all households (standard error)	$1,058.4[b] (458.2)	$806.6 (258.5)		$20,250.9 (8,086.3)	$414.2 (60.2)
Mean land value of households with at least some holdings (standard error)	$3,276.0 (1,384.2)	$933.9 (296.1)		$46,002.1 (18,027.1)	$476.4 (66.6)

	San Pedro		San Marcos	
	Urban N = 195	Rural Distant *Aldea* (N = 66)	Urban (N = 184)	Rural Near *Aldea* (N = 92)
Per capita land value, all households (standard error)	$ 236.4 (109.1)	$152.5 (58.7)	$ 7,193.3 (4,965.8)	$ 97.0 (18.5)
Per capita land value, households with land (standard error)	$ 731.8 (330.8)	$176.6 (67.5)	$16,340.4 (11,237.0)	$111.6 (20.8)

[a] See note 7 for sampling details. See Appendix 2.B for a breakdown of the land values per household.
[b] Stated amounts of land owned by values of their own land as given by household informant. For those households where an informant claimed to not know the value of their land, the mean unit value for that community was imputed. One quetzal, the unit of Guatemalan currency, equaled one United States dollar throughout the fieldwork period (1973-1974).

Note on the reliability of the figures: To check against informant unreliability due to variations in the values some natives assigned to their lands, I checked all statistical inferences in the text with an assigned land-value calculation based on Q200 per *cuerda* for flatland and Q40 per *cuerda* for hillside. All statistical inferences based on land value given by a native were also confirmed using assigned land values controlled by the author.

nicipio.[10] A histogram breakdown of landownership is given in Appendix 2.B.

EDUCATION AND THE PROFESSIONS

The economic prosperity of San Pedro and its proximity to the high-school system in San Marcos have permitted educational advancement *(superación)*. As a result, there are a considerable number of professionals and schoolteachers among the present parental generation and in a few instances in the grandparental generation as well. Many of these teachers now work in other communities.

In a little booklet boosting the community, Consuegra (1969) gives some interesting information on the professional occupational successes of San Pedro residents. He lists fourteen medical doctors, fourteen lawyers, four pharmacists, four miscellaneous university degrees, thirty-two accountants (high-school degree), and more than five hundred teachers (a position also requiring only a high-school degree and sometimes less) "since the first of the century." The last number may be patriotically high, but it is possible. Even if it is true, the figures on other professionals are somewhat misleading: the doctors and lawyers Consuegra listed, with only three exceptions, were either members of families tied socially to San Marcos or were members of Ladino families that had moved to San Pedro and departed for Guatemala City after a generation or two of commercial exploitation or medical service.

It is easier to describe the present situation. One doctor and two lawyers, born of San Pedrano families, reside and practice in San Pedro. Two other doctors live and work in the town but are outsiders and are socially connected to San Marcos. Another lawyer, nonnative but married to a San Pedrano, lives and works there and identifies substantially with the community. San Pedro also enjoys the services of a very competent and very busy dentist. (These data are summarized in Table 7, where they are compared with the data on professionals in San Marcos.)

All these professionals are self-employed in that they derive their primary income from services provided to and paid for by private citizens. However, one native doctor and the dentist earn a monthly stipend of four hundred dollars (approximately one-third of their incomes) for practicing half-time in a government health center. One native San Pedrano is a university-educated businessman who splits his work and his residence between San Pedro and Guatemala City.

Regarding schoolteachers, my survey identified 3.1 percent of San Pedro household heads as schoolteachers, 6 instances out of 196 households. Teachers, then, are not numerically prominent, but they are certainly not inconsequential. For the municipality of San Pedro, teachers and professionals are symbols of the progress *(progreso)* and civilization *(civilización)* that distinguish San Pedro from other Indian *municipios*. In summary, the economy of San Pedro is predominantly based on household industry and commerce; it is privately capitalized, Indian-owned, and only marginally connected to civil service through its schoolteachers.

The Economic System of San Marcos

San Marcos has an entirely different cross section of occupations. By native appraisal, the center of the San Marcos economy lies in government employees' salaries. San Marcos is a community of *empleados del gobierno y finqueros* (government employees and large landowners)—as townsmen of either community assert.

LANDOWNERSHIP

Finqueros are primarily lowland plantation landlords. There are thirty-two San Marcos residents with lowland coffee landholdings that they administer by occasional visits. Thus, with respect to their plantations, they may be termed absentee landlords. According to a knowledgeable informant, there are not more than two or three additional cattle and cotton producers in San Marcos.

In addition to these absentee landlords, several San Marcos residents own substantial tracts of land in the highlands and are occasionally called *finqueros*. Holdings of persons so termed generally exceed five hundred *cuerdas* and are devoted to corn production. The owners of these highland estates sharecrop with or rent to Indian or rural Ladino residents.

Usually, civil-service employment or other occupations are intertwined with landholding. Such individuals live in San Marcos and visit their lands to supervise coffee production or to collect rents or shares of the harvest. These absentee landlords usually state their occupation by identifying their government employment or business in San Marcos. Examples of this include a government administrator, a hotel owner, a busline owner, and a coffee buyer.

The native perception in both towns that there is a major property-ownership distinction between them corresponds to statistical indices of landownership in the two communities. The figures in Table 4 show that San Marcos has more than nineteen times the mean household land value and more than thirty times the mean per capita land value as San Pedro does. In terms of these figures, San Marcos is indeed a center for substantial property ownership.[11] However, such summary statistics need to be complemented by a fuller description. In the histogram presentation of land-value distribution (Appendix 2.B), one sees notable similarities between the two towns over the middle range of household land values. They differ primarily in the highest and lowest values. Not only does San Marcos have more people in the wealthiest category (15 versus 6 in San Pedro), but the San Marcos mean land value ($212,830) in the highest category is eight times higher than the mean ($25,024) of the wealthy San Pedranos. Moreover, San Marcos has fewer people who do not own land. It is principally these extremes of ownership and nonownership that distinguish San Marcos from San Pedro and give San Marcos such extraordinary means. Nevertheless, the difference between San Marcos and San Pedro is statistically significant even if the extreme values are deleted.[12]

However, the majority of the members of the two communities are not radically distinguished by the amount of land owned. Rather, the distinction is in where the land is (coastal for San Marcos, local for San Pedro) and in the existence of a few individuals in San Marcos with extraordinary wealth in property. This leads to the conclusion that it is not the total wealth difference between the communities that defines their ethnic distinction. Rather, it is the social linkage to the categorically opposed kinds of wealth. Large landholdings are opposed to small plots, lowland is opposed to highland, rental income from land is opposed to subsistence labor, and export produce (coffee) is opposed to household consumption (corn)—as high status is opposed to low, and as Ladino is opposed to Indian. The associations between these symbols and concepts—of status, of origins, and of lowland export estates—have led Ladinos through time to acquire plantations where possible. Then the socially distributed ownership of the plantations feeds back on and confirms the validity of the conceptual oppositions.

GOVERNMENT EMPLOYMENT

All persons paid by the bureaucratic agencies of the government, including public-school teachers, are national government employees, *empleados del gobierno*. Over one-third of San Marcos households depend

Table 5. Relative Importance of Government Employment and Professional Jobs in Urban San Marcos and San Pedro[a]

	San Marcos			San Pedro	
	No. of Cases	% of Household Heads Engaged in Occupation	San Marcos's % of Occupation	No. of Cases	% of Household Heads Engaged in Occupation
Persons claiming national or municipal government employment	65	35.5	84.2	23	12.0
Persons claiming employment as					
Teachers	26	14.1	83.9	5	2.6
Police	4	2.2	80.0	1	0.5
Military officers	3	1.6	100.0	0	0.0
Plantation owners	2[b]	1.1	100.0	0	0.0
Agricultural advisers	2	1.1	66.7	1	0.5
Judges	1	0.5	100.0	0	0.0
Court employees	2	1.1	66.7	1	0.5
Health inspectors	1	0.5	100.0	0	0.0
Total	41 (N = 184)	22.3	82.0	9 (N = 196)	4.6

[a]See note 7 for sampling details and definitions. See Appendix 2.A for complete occupational listings.
[b]Since most plantation owners report their civil-service or other work as their occupation, this percentage is not as representative of the place of absentee agriculture in San Marcos as are the landownership figures given here and in Table 4.

primarily on government employment (see Table 5). The majority of the government workers are men; the few female employees tend to be single or divorced women or wives of men employed elsewhere in the government.[13]

The government jobs available in the community total about five hundred. If these jobs were filled only by household heads, they would support nearly half the heads in the urban community. But many of these jobs—particularly those of secretaries, clerks, and teachers—are parceled out to single people and to a few wives who are not household heads. The 35 percent figure for government-employed household heads drawn from my sample survey is, then, very close to correct for the population as a whole.

Government salaries are quite varied. The governor and the judges, for example, earned 500 to 600 dollars per month. In addition, the governor has some perquisites of office, particularly his chauffeured vehicle. Other major office heads reported 150 to 250 dollars per month income. Schoolteachers, office administrative assistants, and responsible clerk-secretary *oficiales* earned 90 to 150 dollars per month depending on service, time, and position. Skilled workers (telegraphers, for example) made 80 to 100 dollars per month. Ordinary typists earned around 60 dollars per month while unskilled workers other than day laborers and janitors earned 40 to 50 dollars.

In the municipal offices, the typists and office administrators earned 50 to 65 dollars, and the unskilled laborers were paid 25 to 30 dollars per month. In both towns, the mayor, secretary, and treasurer reported the offically set monthly salaries of 90, 100, and 125 dollars, respectively.

COMMERCIAL ACTIVITIES

Commerce in San Marcos, though not as important as it is in San Pedro, may be divided into three categories. First and most obvious are the stores selling status products. There are a number of such outlets: two auto accessories, parts, and tire stores—the only ones in the department; one gift shop selling watches, jewelry, clocks, and fine European or North American clothing accessories; one electrical-appliance store; one household and kitchen furnishings store; the only exclusively school-supplies store in the region; and an expensive, well-styled restaurant. The second category of commerce consists of a sprinkling of food and *primera necesidad* (basic essentials) stores, three of which are fairly sizable, the rest being but counters in scattered households. These small shops provide convenience items to nearby homes. The third category is market merchandising. On San Marcos's market day especially, and to a much lesser extent throughout the week, men and women of San Pedro travel to San Marcos to provide the bulk of San Marcos's available selection of produce and market products, usually at a slightly higher price than that given at the San Pedro market.

The smaller San Marcos market differs from the San Pedro market in another respect: San Marcos is better stocked in melons and other products from the coast. The greater selection of coastal products reflects San Marcos's close social and symbolic ties to the coast. To be sure, gifts of fruit from coastal kin and ownership of coastal land by some Marquenses facilitate their learning to eat the tropical foodstuffs. But not all Marquenses have coastal kin or land. More significantly, the lowland:highland–Ladino:Indian correspondence makes the consumption of lowland coastal products especially valuable for the anomalously highland Marquense Ladinos, whether they have direct coastal ties or not.

In summary, merchandising is not so strongly represented in San Marcos as it is in San Pedro.[14] The bulk of San Marcos's commerce is either largely status oriented or provided by San Pedro residents.

COTTAGE INDUSTRY

Another peripheral aspect of San Marcos's economic base consists of a variety of small artisans—tailors and carpenters mostly, and a sprinkling of electricians, plumbers, blacksmiths, and others. Table 3 shows how relatively insignificant artisanry is in the San Marcos economy. Competition from San Pedro artisanry has driven down prices, making it difficult for San Marcos artisans to either afford apprentices or to retain their interest. As a result, the artisan shops appear to be dying out in San Marcos.

The construction artisans are more likely to ply their trades outside their home *municipio* than are the equivalent tradesmen in San Pedro. Many of the artisans have a shop or stall away from their house. However, most of the finish carpenters as well as the community's two bakers and two blacksmiths perform their occupations in their household compounds. Plumbers, electricians, masons, carpenters, and others in the building trades obviously work wherever there is work to be done.

Only two households of weavers were noticed in San Marcos. One of these was a household of immigrants from the community of San Pedro who had chosen San Marcos simply because of the lack of space in San Pedro. The other, a Ladino family who owned a bar-restaurant that provided their primary source of income, had bought a loom and hired a San Pedrano to weave tablecloths. There are also a few immigrant Indian families in the Ladino *aldeas* who engage in weaving.

TRANSPORTATION

By contrast with the thirty-seven San Pedro trucks, only nine trucks are registered to San Marcos owners. On the other hand, two coalitions of San Marcos kin and other outside Ladinos provide the overwhelming bulk of the passenger bus services in the department. Marquense families have been able to assemble the necessary network of trusted ticket sales agents and drivers, and so they have succeeded in largely monopolizing the transportation of people while San Pedranos largely monopolize the transportation of goods.[15] This general division is not surprising: because of the ideology of interconnection, Marquenses can more easily organize the networks of relations necessary to maintain a bus system. Moreover, the transport of people is part of the communication system as well as an important contribution to the construction of networks. Thus, it is not only socially easier for Ladinos to organize a bus system; it is also more appropriate symbolically for them to do so. It is a relatively small symbolic inconsistency that the trucks these Indians own are the most expensive mechanical instruments in the region. Something else is far more important in the local context of San Marcos and San Pedro: Indians still carry the loads.[16]

THE PROFESSIONS

Professional persons show a residential preference for San Marcos. The government brings at least two doctors and three lawyers to the community to fill the positions of hospital head, director of the health center, judges for both courts, and attorney general. One or two medical students are also imported from the capital to do their rural residencies. Since legal matters must be cared for in the department center's court buildings, more legal offices are found in San Marcos than in San Pedro. This slightly affects the residence pattern, since a lawyer usually uses two or three rooms on the street edge of his home for offices. Though the total is quite small, two of the three law-

Table 6. Professional Services in San Marcos and San Pedro

Professional Persons	Practice in		Residence in		Born in			
	SM	SP	SM	SP	SM	SP	Other	Not Known
Doctors and Dentists								
A	X		X		X			
B	X		X		X			
C	X		X		X			
D	X		X		X			
E	X		X					
F	X		X				X	
G		X		X			X	
H		X		X			X	
I		X		X		X		
J		X		X			X	
Subtotal	6	4	6	4	4	1	5	
Lawyers								
A	X		X		X			
B	X		X		X			
C	X		X				X	
D	X		X				X	
E	X		X					X
F		X		X	X			
G		X		X	X			
H		X		X			X	
Subtotal	5	3	5	3	2	2	3	1
Total	11	7	11	7	6	3	8	1

yers born outside these communities have chosen to reside and practice in San Marcos.

Medical practices are also found in either city, although there is some imbalance in favor of San Marcos. While San Marcos is the more prestigious residential location, there are some advantages to a San Pedro location in that people from all over the department come to San Pedro, especially on market day, to buy products and services, including medical attention. The doctors born outside the community have almost evenly split their decision on residence and practice between the two communities, slightly favoring San Pedro. It would appear that the pull of business opportunity quite evenly balances the attraction of ethnic identification. The comparative distribution of professional practice and residence is summarized in Table 6. These figures constitute a total count, unrelated to the sample survey.

The Household Division of Labor and Ethnic Symbolism

Ladino children work relatively little. Whatever work they might be able to do is both manually degrading and, except among the urban poor and the rural Ladinos, very low-paying in relation to the parent's job. The future value of their educated occupations discourages early work. But more important, except for the very poor, young men do not work because work is incongruent with their Ladino status. And even among the poor, the young boys who do work are transient and underemployed, favoring the shining of shoes or the selling of lottery tickets. This, too, is in keeping with the ideological system, for freedom, rather than submission and restriction, is achieved. Again in opposition to San Pedro, the San Marcos plaza where the shoeshine boys operate is a focus of communication and leisure, never a place for petty Indian commerce.

In San Pedro, family cooperation of husband and wife in the productive enterprise is both common and expected; in San Marcos, by contrast, there is much less production cooperation among the spouses. The ideal Ladino occupations—*finca* ownership and government employment—do not lend themselves to a household division of production tasks: the *finca* is handed over to an administrator; the government employs a single person for a specific office. However, the distinctive difference in household cooperation is more than just a matter of convenience or the product of the job's demands for labor. Work is to leisure as Indian is to Ladino. Indian women and children tend to work regardless of whether they have to. Indian women work along with their husbands. Ladino women and children, provided they have a husband/father to support them, prefer not to work— again, regardless of need. There are exceptions to this in San Marcos, but the exceptions are largely confined to the wives of middle-level civil servants; these women may manage a store or teach in the primary or secondary schools. It would appear that a prestigious form of government employment plus the increased income available for consumption overbalances the value of leisure display by Ladino women.

Among both Ladinos and Indians, men provide the occupational and political ties on which a household's social status within the broad ethnic category is based. Women provide a subtle symbolic confirmation of that status. Perhaps because they are the symbolic source of ethnic-group purity and continuity, women and children are the sign-vehicles by which these work-ethic oppositions can be expressed. The careful display of the well-groomed Ladino woman shows at once freedom from economic distress and the ideal sociality of the Ladino sector. Moreover, the consumption of time and the purchase and display of status symbols by women conjoin status, wealth, family purity, and leisure in each interaction setting. Domestic ceremonies, such as birthday parties, confirmations, and marriages, as well as public ceremonies, such as fiesta dances, nighttime school events, the military ball, and Lion's Club socials, provide occasions for such display. And all such events are opportunities when elite men gather to communicate, to arrange favors, and to cultivate networks. In the party setting, men can casually do this without engendering the social debts that would arise out of a meeting specifically arranged for a particular need.

Married Ladino women, then, at all class levels are preferentially withdrawn from the labor market. One young Marquense, a Ladino, recently returned from studies in Spain and sufficiently marginalized to be quite perceptive, put it this way: "In Spain, the women expect to help provide. In Guatemala, they expect to be provided help."

Here the symbolic value of servants emerges. Servants are chosen largely from among the Indians. Though low-class Ladino women whose marriages (or unions) have failed may work as domestics, they are usually classified occupationally as cooks *(cocineras)* or washer women *(lavanderas),* not as servants *(servientas).* To some extent, they are treated as professionals and allowed to go about their principal task without interference. Servants, on the other hand, are ordered about from task to task as needed. These Indian servants are seen even in some of the poorest Ladino households. They free the woman of the house from labor and make her a master over others in a limited domain. Indian servants thus provide a symbolic confirmation of Ladino status at every turn. Indeed, perhaps the symbolism of Indian servitude is most valuable in the household, the source point of ethnic-origin symbolism.

The symbolic behavior of Indian women is a part of this same system. In those highland Indian communities where the oppositions of economic wealth, political access, network dispersion, and status evaluation are unambiguously congruent and superimposed, ethnic symbolism is crisply expressed. The woman's distinctive costume, the *corte* and *huipil,* as well as her daily involvement in the productive enterprises of the household confirm the household's place in the status system. In towns like San Pedro, on the other hand, only the social and political marginality and the occupations are congruent with the ethnic categorization of the community. But the economic system has shifted so that the exceptional wealth of San Pedro is incongruent with its status categorization as Indian, and the occupations of San Pedranos in the town center, though different from those of San Marcos, have shifted away from the agricultural bases of the traditional Indian communities. So in San Pedro, women work preferentially and thereby symbolize Indian status and ideology at the household level. They freely wear the *gavacha* (a bib or smock apron) or the *delantal* (a waist apron) outside the household. Indeed, many San Pedro women do not feel adequately dressed without a *gavacha,* for work is their lot in life. By contrast, if a Ladino woman has to wear an apron for lack of servants, she removes it before leaving the house. This symbolizes her distance from work and her involvement in social display. Only in one event does the San Pedro traditional outfit appear without the *delantal* or *gavacha:* when it is worn for specific social display at the annual festival beauty pageant.

But most (106 of 150 or 70.6 percent) urban San Pedro women do not now wear the traditional Indian clothing of the community, and those that do tend to be older parents or grandparents. The various domains of the social and cultural system are no longer completely congruent, and to so symbolize the state of affairs would be inappropriate. The phenomenon of the "traditional" versus the "generalized" (Tax's terminology) or "modified" (R. N. Adams's terminology) Indian is not a matter of acculturation, as has been asserted. Rather, it is an expression of congruence, incongruence, and variations in the articulation of the social and cultural domains of the total system.

Class Identity and Status Difference

Does the Weberian notion of class fare any better? Weber "decomposed" Marx's notion of class into orders of class, status, and power (Bendix 1962:286; Cooper 1976:6). Though he further subdivided

Table 7. Household and Per Capita Monthly Incomes in Urban San Marcos and San Pedro[a]

	San Marcos	San Pedro
Total household income per month		
Mean	$173.1[b]	$ 92.4
Number of cases	184	190
Per capita income per month		
Mean	$ 49.2	$ 22.8
Number of cases	184	190

[a]See note 7 for sampling details and definitions. See Appendix 2.C for a more descriptive histogram comparison.
[b]One quetzal equaled one United States dollar throughout the fieldwork period (1973-1974).

the concept of class, Weber's most general formulation was that class consisted in the life chances of individuals, derived from their relation to the market (Weber 1968:1:302–5). One way to partially summarize the class or "market chances" of persons in the two communities is to compare their household and per capita incomes.[17] (See Table 7.) In income, San Marcos is favored, and the statistical test figures are unequivocal.[18]

Nevertheless, incomes are sufficiently high in San Pedro that its citizens can purchase and display the manufactured indices of high social status. Except for elderly women, urban San Pedranos do in fact dress in the Ladino style, and many live in comparably furnished houses. Indeed, no one in San Marcos had a home as elegantly furnished as one ardently "Indian" San Pedro professional.[19] San Pedranos can acquire dark glasses, a radio, a watch, or if wealthy, a car or even a trip to Spain. Though San Pedranos do in general spend less on personal consumption, ethnic distinctiveness from the marketplace has become blurred. The loss of store-bought consumption differences, however, is not crucial.

Time display through vacations, elaborate and longlasting social occasions, political meetings, social visits at midday, coffee interludes, and other activities are more important indices of ethnicity, and time display is not easily imitable. Indians who use time for noneconomic purposes do so at the expense of their incomes as independent artisans or traders. Ladinos who use time for noneconomic purposes announce their favorable governmental employment at regular hours, or their wealth derived from land. For the elite, time display and social connections, rather than consumption, reflect the crucial relationships in the total system.

Thus, the epitome of Ladino symbology is to do nothing, "to live by your rents," as they say. Extensive landownership is the most appropriate way to achieve this leisure because landownership combines a colonial control over resources and people with time and sufficient income for social purposes. The plantation, then, is a focal symbol of Ladino status. *Finca* ownership is the goal and dream of everyone with a chance for wealth, and even of a few peasants who have no chance at all. The *finca* has high value because it generates many symbols that clearly reveal the person's position in the status system that underlies ethnicity: with a *finca,* a person's life-style derives from the fact that others work for him; he is in a position of control, authority, power, and paternal supremacy. Without working, income flows to the *finquero.* Time is at his disposal for whatever purposes he may choose. His status is further oriented by the symbols of lowland location of his land, export involvement, coffee production, and the large size of his holding. The ownership of land ties him to the social circles of the economic and political elite. The behavioral life-style is relevant because it symbolizes status placement and a structure of access to occupations, prime land, laborers, lawyers, and political power. The elite life-style apportions the time necessary to cultivate and maintain this social, political, and economic access through interaction. But life-style is not the culture, Rather, life-style is the symbol of and product of one's mental participation in a culture, that system of ideas that, through our acceptance of it, orders the nature and tempo of our existence.

Moreover, it is not necessary that a *finquero*'s properties be efficiently run. The money to purchase other status indices is secondary to the structural information conveyed by socially oriented leisure. The attractiveness of absentee landownership derives from its capacity to produce symbols, but the symbols work against a goal of maximum productivity. This relation of the *finca* to the symbolic system accounts for the phenomenally inefficient management of much of Guatemala's *latifundia* economy.[20]

The symbolic value of leisure also helps to explain why the sons of the poor Ladinos, unable to finish school and thus secure a *puesto* or "position," pride themselves in and joke about their calculated shiftlessness. *"Andando vago"* or *"vagando"* ("on the loose," "hanging around,") and *"vacilando"* ("horsing around" and "cutting up"), as these youths describe what they do, are behavioral symbols that closely approximate the social freedom of the Ladino elite.[21] In the mornings, the plaza of San Marcos is awash with young men and shoeshine boys "messing around." In San Pedro, the plaza on nonmarket days is relatively empty of all but serious buyers and sellers—and taxi drivers awaiting a fare. The San Pedranos, both male and female, try more obviously to be at work.

Does this mean that Ladinos and Indians are indeed separate cultures, on the basis of the demonstrable difference in the meaning and value of the symbol work? Certainly not. Differences in the work ethic are structurally congruent with the oppositions in status category, political access, and occupational contrast. The differences are meaningless except in their structure of opposition. The distinctive economies and life-styles of Indians and Ladinos cannot be separately examined; they must be dealt with in contradistinction as symbols. Otherwise, the Ladino weavers in Salcajá, Department of Quezaltenango, would have to be as Indian as the San Pedrano weavers. Or the San Pedro owner of several large trucks or a large store would have to be Ladino. Rather, the issue is one of a reiterated structure of oppositions. In the case of Salcajá, the weaving by Ladinos no doubt contrasts with the agricultural or craft aspect of the nearby people thought to be distinctively Indian.[22] Only the oppositional structure is stable; the sign-vehicle content may be greatly varied. Seen as a national system, the actualities of the relations to the means of production are less important than the fact that oppositions can be expressed in them. In Guatemala, the Marxian notion of class opposition seems fully correct at any given local level, because the economic relations seem objectively opposed in the microcontext. But actually, economic relations are symbolically opposed, a fact that emerges in the broader perspective because the same objective conditions have variant ethnic meanings in different oppositions.

San Pedro is indeed a remarkable Indian community. For, in spite of its economic vigor and market centrality in the department; in spite of its three-story buildings, its paved streets, lamp posts, and traffic lights; in spite of its cars and trucks, market building, and radio station; in spite of tiled floors and cultural events, Spanish language and predominantly Western dress; in spite of the educational advancement of its youth; its doctors, lawyers, and teachers; San Pedro is still Indian. None of these objective conditions has changed that fact. The changes in wealth, occupation, dress, and language that San Pedro has experienced in the last forty-five years have not made it Ladino.

But San Pedro is not without change. Viewed as a local system, San Pedro is Indian in relation to San Marcos and the political center of Guatemala. However, taken as a regional and national system that includes the subsistence-agricultural hinterland, San Pedro is economically and symbolically distinct. When comparing themselves against the agriculturally dependent Indian communities, some San Pedranos call themselves and their town *mestizo* (a term that we explore in considerable depth in the next two chapters), for San Pedro does not fit the ideal linkage of Indian to subsistence agriculture and seasonal migration. Thus, the Ladino symbolism of San Pedro's clothing and language is consistent with its structural placement, both as the dominant market center of other Indian communities and as a nonsubsistence economy. But by comparison to Marquenses and the national center, San Pedranos are still independent rather than employed by and connected to government, and they are given to labor rather than to leisure. Thus, the San Pedranos achieve a consistency between the Indian character of their social orientation and their anomalous economic placement by being both Indian as a community and Ladino in appearance. In this regard, San Pedro is unusual, though not unique: it is an Indian town with largely Ladino markings for both males and females. The town and its residents are thus sociological *mestizos,* and they not infrequently call themselves such. San Pedro's outward visual peculiarity results from symbolizing its social-relations placement in the total system, given the oppositions of cultural category. But the ideology, the dominating viewpoint of its people, is still Indian, and whatever qualifications they may make, they so consider themselves.

In the final analysis, San Pedro remains an Indian community because, since the conquest, it has been placed inescapably in a system of oppositions. As a community, it is in opposition to San Marcos. As an Indian ethnic category, it is in opposition to Ladinos. Its mythical native origins contrast with mythical European origins. Its low status is structured against high status elsewhere. Its independent occupational structure contrasts with salaried government employment. Its sustenance by labor and commerce is opposed to the sustenance of rent and salary. Its compulsive marginality is opposed to the centrality and access of San Marcos. Its ideology of independence, atomization, and isolation takes meaning from the interdependence and connectivity of Ladinos. In short, San Pedro is not an Indian community with peculiar characteristics per se, the center of a local culture. Rather, it is an Indian community with peculiar characteristics per systematem, a social entity whose significance appears only in the widest context of Guatemalan culture and society.

5
The Conceptual Organization of Status and Ethnicity

My analysis of politicoeconomic dualism and opposition ignores some of the complexities of the current ethnic-category system. But the complexities of the categories raise important issues with which I must now deal. First, are the ethnic labels arbitrary descriptors, tags of a simple and self-evident reality of origin, or race, or place in the social system? Or do the labels subtly permute and combine with fleeting circumstances to connote shifting debates about one's being, one's social position, or one's intent? And, second, do the ethnic labels denote a material reality? Or do they bring to mind ideas that mimic the shapes of something more subtle still: the structure of cultural concepts, the ordering of ideas common to these people? In this chapter and the next, I aim for the more complex and symbolic perspective on the use of ethnic labels.

Ethnic Categories: Ideal Types and Institutional Continua

In native use, the terms *indígena* and *ladino* often represent ideal types, concepts whose special nature is often explicitly marked by the use of the word "pure." Thus, to call someone "pure Indian" does not mean that he or she is a biological Indian, a condition of which no one can be sure. Rather, "pure Indian" means "ideal Indian," or, at least, more ideal than something else under discussion. Ideal types, of course, perform an essential function. They cut the real world into tidy categories, forcing one to ignore rough variations and focus on specified similarities. This simplification process is the essence of discrete categorization and naming, and the simplicity introduced lies at the heart of a manageable social and cultural world. But the terms *indígena* or *ladino* do not just attach individually to an ideal-type category. Rather, the two terms exist as a structured set of oppositions, and they connect to real groups of people who play out their lives in social institutions derived from the colonial past.

In the context of these institutions, the categorical opposition of Ladino to Indian is set alongside the oppositions of high status to low status, power to powerlessness, centrality to marginality, education to illiteracy, and the occupational complex of government employment and *latifundia* management to petty commerce, manual crafts, and agricultural *minifundia* subsistence. While each of these institutional oppositions are polar opposites, they are poles of a continuum; thus, the cut between high and low status or between political centrality and marginality is not at all obvious. However, by bringing the ideal-type opposition of Ladino-Indian into parallel with the continuous institutions of relative status, relative wealth, relative class, relative centrality, relative education, or other institutional rankings, the former can be used to talk about any of the latter. Thus, the relatively dichotomous structure inherent in the ideal-type ethnic terms divides the continuum of status evaluation into the quanta of ranked groups, a gross but useful simplification.

Conversely, the continuum of evaluation underlying education, wealth, or political access gives the ideal-type ethnic terms a scalar notion: one is more or less Ladino, or more or less Indian than someone else. Moreover, given the several associated scales for evaluation—education, wealth, power, social skill (the etiquette of body language), social connection—the ideal-type ethnic terms can be manipulated so that an individual is Indian in one context or conversation but Ladino in another, or more Indian versus less Indian according to circumstances of interaction.

Of course, the middle ground implied between high and low on any of the scales of evaluation invites a discrete categorization. The Guatemalan idiom of ethnicity handles the middle range by speaking of miscegenation. The purely Hispanic Ladino and the purely autochthonous Indian, when crossbred symbolically, produce the *mestizo*. *Mestizo* represents a conceptual middle ground, a discrete packaging of the non-Ladino and non-Indian, a tag for the people whose life chances and institutional placement have not left all of the evaluative scales congruent, or whose institutional placement is congruent but not ideal-typical in either the positive sense of Ladino or the negative sense of Indian. But *mestizo* attribution is not just a matter of a person's existence in the middle institutional sector, where low placement is Indian and high placement is Ladino. Rather, the *mestizo* of San Pedro shares the ideology of his Indian townsmen but has substantially achieved some institutional attributes of Ladinos. Conversely, the *mestizo* of San Marcos shares the Ladino ideology but has a low institutional placement, thereby acquiring Indian attributes. While *mestizo* no doubt accompanies incongruent placement in the many institutions (for example, between town of birth and formal education), the primary reference is to incongruence between ideology held and placement in one or more institutions.

Historically, the term *mestizo* referred to the service population of neither elite nor enslaved that arose from biological miscegenation, for the Spaniards brought few women. But the term quickly acquired a sociosymbolic reference: the nonelite, nonenslaved who could or had to ply the social middle ground, regardless of their color, build, or blood.

There is some indication that in the 1930s the multifaceted divisions of high and low status and of Ladino and Indian were fairly congruent, at least in the countryside. Indian and Ladino were recognized legal statuses with sharply different rights, duties, privileges, and obligations. Labor laws impinged coercively on the Indian only. The economy was less diversified in the rural areas, formal education was more urban, transportation and communication access to the center were less available. Given the congruence of the various institutions and the gulf between center and periphery, there was little opportunity for the rise of a middle category in the provinces. Indeed, the early anthropological literature of the undeveloped Guatemalan hinterland seldom refers to the *mestizo*. Tax, for example, affirms that *mestizo* was not in socially acceptable usage. No doubt this was then true.

But the legally defined and socially real congruence of ethnic categories and social institutions was shattered by the social revolution of 1944–1954. This decade ended the Indian's inferior legal status and terminated the predatory labor laws. Subsequent labor-union movements, industrial development, road improvement, and increased educational access added complexity to the formerly polarized, bifurcate, and congruent social structure of the hinterland. For the country as a whole, the day of the *mestizo* began again.

Precisely within this revolutionary period, San Pedro changed most rapidly (W. R. Smith 1977), though Smith does not give this as the reason. First the economy shifted ground, moving from agriculture to craft sales. Then its trade base increased with mechanized transportation. Finally, its educational quotient lifted. Yet the political reality remained: San Pedro was and is isolated, powerless, socially disconnected, and the ideology remained an anchor. To see how this complex social reality is represented in ethnic terms, we must listen closely to the natives.

Ethnic Concepts in San Pedro and San Marcos

First, I present a conversation with some San Marcos high-school students who had on other occasions clearly identified themselves as Ladino. (A = anthropologist; I = informant, of which several participated)

    A: What is an *indígena?*

(1) I: An inhabitant of Guatemala. The native race *(raza natural)* from here in Guatemala, and other countries which were conquered by the Spaniards *(españoles)*.

(2) I: On account of being of another race *(otra raza)*.

(3) I: *Criollo.*[1]

    A: What is a *ladino?*

(4) I: It is a person who is different from the Indians *(indígenas)*.

    A: In what sense?

(5) I: Because the Indians are put[2] to daily work at a lower daily wage than the Ladinos, isn't that so?

(6) I: On account of their being of another race *(otra raza)*.

(7) I: Indians have Indian parents. Ladinos are of various foreign nationalities.

(8) I: Ladinos have mixed blood *(sangre mixta)* but not from natives from here.

    A: In what way are they distinguished now in Guatemala?[3]

(9) I: The Indian race *(raza indígena)* always is poorer *(más pobre)*, it has less intellectual knowledge *(conocimientos intelectuales)*, and it is the race which cultivates, eh, the earth.[4] On the other hand, the Ladino has more knowledge because he has more money. His socioeconomic and

political position is always distinguishable because the Indian lacks the basic knowledge *(conocimientos básicos)* to be able to be even with the Ladino.[5]

(10) *I:* The Indian is the type that labors in the field *(es él que hace los trabajos del campo).* The Ladino is the intellectual, the one from the more purified race *(él de raza más purificada).*

(11) *I:* They wear distinctive costumes *(trajes típicos).*

(12) *I:* They have ancient customs. The Ladinos no longer have those customs.

A: How are they different as to race? Is there a difference of race today?

(13) *I:* Today, there is no difference of race.

(14) *I:* I say yes, there is a difference in race. The Indian race is one. The Mestizo race *(raza mestiza),* the one that we are [that is, our race] is another.

A: What kind of town is San Marcos?

(15) *I:* It is purely Ladino. On the other hand, San Pedro Sacatepéquez is Indian.

(16) *I:* The San Pedranos *(los de San Pedro),* how they love business (literally "commerce, *el comercio")!* They come and put their business establishments here and that is how Indians get here. Those of San Marcos—they only like to study and to do office work, and that is how they are different.

A: Is there a biological difference?

(17) *I:* To me, yes, biologically there is also a difference because, let's say, the Ladino race *(raza)* and the Indian race differ by the degree *(el grado)* of culture *(cultura)*[6] each individual may have.

(18) *I:* Of course, there are white Indians *(indios blancos),* and there are Ladinos that are brown *(morenos).*

A: Then can it be biological?

(19) I: It is something biological.

   A: But on what is the difference based?

(20) I: It is social.

   A: Why do you say this?

(21) I: Because they have the same rights.

   A: Then why Ladino and Indian?

(22) I: Because of the type of blood *(tipo de sangre)*.

   A: But we already decided that there is no difference in blood.

(23) I: (Everyone laughs.)

(24) I: The Indians do not have the culture *(la cultura)* which the Ladinos have.

(25) I: (Contradicting the former vigorously) But there are San Pedranos who are doctors, et cetera, yet who are Indians!

(26) I: They differ in language *(lenguaje)*.

   A: In San Pedro they speak a tongue *(en lengua)?*

(27) I: They used to (literally, "before—*antes*").

After the recording session had ended, they pressed me about my opinions, and I offered the thought that the only difference between San Marcos and San Pedro was in work habits, with some distinction in dress in the other townships. They resisted this but came to agree, though somewhat reluctantly. They thereupon returned to the racial theme and pointed out, with special interest, that (28) one can tell an Indian by the Mongolian spot on his back when he is born and by the slant of his eyes (not an exact quote).[7]

A comparable response was elicited from several high-school students struggling to improve themselves by attending school at San Pedro. One informant was born and raised in a nearby hamlet of San Pedro, two were born and raised in the town center of San Pedro, and one was born in Guatemala City, though raised in San Pedro by his San Pedrano mother. All the students claimed to be *raza mestiza* and, thus, not exactly Indian. But they did identify themselves as Indian if the context was in contrast to San Marcos.

	A:	What is a Ladino?
(29)	I:	One who descends from[8] the other continents.
(30)	I:	It is in the anatomy or, in other words, it's physical.
(31)	I:	One who is developed *(se desenvuelve)* in science, who is more adequate than the Indian *(indígena)*.
	A:	What is an Indian?
(32)	I:	Indian could be from the physical aspect, for example, short stature, dark color, protruding cheekbones, and the eaglelike nose.[9]
(33)	I:	People who still wear costume *(traje)*.[10] Those who speak in idiom *(idioma)*, although not all of them speak one. Those who work in the fields *(trabajan en campo)*, [who work] in something which is not a profession *(que no tiene profesión)*.[11] Peasant people *(gente campesina)*.
(34)	I:	*Indígena* [applies to] those who belong to[12] a country.
(35)	I:	Indians are different, like those of Comitancillo who have another way of living.
	A:	What kind of town is San Pedro?
(36)	I:	It is an Indian town *(pueblo indígena)*.
	A:	The residents of San Pedro are Indians?
(37)	I:	Right now they are Mestizos *(mestizos)*, because they now have mixed with others.
	A:	Do any Indians live in San Pedro?
(38)	I:	Some. But now they are quite rare. Now they are more of the mixed type *(Ya son más de mestizos)*.
	A:	How does one recognize an Indian?
(39)	I:	By the physical aspect, their growth, they are small in stature, their language *(el idioma)*.
	A:	What kind of town is San Marcos?
(40)	I:	It is a Ladino town *(pueblo ladino)*. Because now there are various university graduates residing there.

(41) I: Well, they are not exactly Ladino *(ladino propiamente no)*, but they are said to be because they are better schooled *(son mejor estudiado)*, they have better professions, they are dedicated to studies and not to work in the fields.

(42) I: Yes, San Marcos is a Ladino town; all of them work in professions, because they do not dedicate themselves to working with cloth, such as weaving, tailoring, in short all those kinds of work which they do here. Over there they all have a profession.

(43) I: That's a town [San Marcos] just like this one [San Pedro]. It's just that over there everyone believes that they are Ladinos because they are not inclined to work in the fields, but they do this because they think that work denigrates *(trabajo denigra)*.

A: Work?

(44) I: Field work *(trabajo del campo)*, or tailoring, or weaving, but this is not so. All work is honorable to man if it earns well. Over there, they dedicate themselves to office work. Others study.

A: What kind of people are there in San Pedro?

(45) I: In San Pedro there is more the class of . . . of course, they say that they are Indians, but they are not exactly Indians.

A: Who says they are Indians?

(46) I: The San Pedranos say so. On account of dressing in costume *(traje)*, but only because they do not speak the Indian language *(el idioma)*.

A: Then would you say that it is or is not an Indian town?

(47) I: By virtue of the costume *(el traje)* we would say it is. But, frankly, it is not an Indian town, but a Mestizo town *(pueblo mestizo)*.

(48) I: It is Indian because it existed before the conquest.

A: What kind of a town is Comitancillo?

(49) I: Over there, there arrived very little of the Spanish race *(raza espanola)*. Yes, it has more Indianness *(mas de indígena)*, it is recognized as more Indian.

(50) I: It is Indian because they do not understand Spanish very well.

(51) I: They have the same customs as the ancestors *(Tienen los mismos usos que los antepasados)*.

A: What kind of work do they do in Comitancillo?

(52) I: Agriculture. And commerce in peaches.

A: What do the people of San Marcos say that the San Pedranos are?

(53) I: Well, those in San Marcos treat us as Indians.

(54) I: San Marcos says that the town of San Pedro is very Indian and that they are Ladinos, but actually they are not Ladinos, they are Mestizos. We are all Mestizos.

A: If I say that I agree with you that we are all Mestizos, in what way are the towns distinguished? Why do they say that one is Ladino and the other is Indian? Better said, why does the distinction continue today?

(55) I: By virtue of the costume *(traje)*.

(56) I: The distinction between San Pedro and San Marcos is simply in studies. They dedicate themselves more to studying. By contrast, those of San Pedro dedicate themselves, in the majority, to trades *(artes)*, or agriculture.

(57) I: There is no difference. The only thing is, over there, there is one kind of job *(otro oficio)* and here there is a different one. Over there, well, the majority work in offices, although they earn very little. They disparage work in the fields although they may have lands *(terrenos)*. Here, no work denigrates. Over there they think that to work in the fields *(trabajar en el campo)* or weaving or something like that is only for ill-mannered people *(gente inculta)*[13] or those who do not think.

(58) I: In San Pedro and San Marcos there is no distinction at all except that perhaps here there is. . . . In San Pedro they dedicate themselves more to commerce. By contrast, in San Marcos they dedicate themselves more, . . . they orient themselves *(se dirigen)* toward the government, asking for help. By contrast, San Pedro achieves *(supera)* by itself *(por sí mismo)*.

(59) (The conversation became animated [and hence untranscribable] but the general consensus was that San Pedro is a poorer town than San Marcos. One student pointed out that at least in San Pedro everyone works and has something, but in San Marcos there are many indigents who do not work and are probably poorer than the poor of San Pedro.)

A: Why do they [the Ladinos] think that work denigrates?

(60) I: Because they think themselves superior and they think that if some of their other companions from there in San Marcos saw them, upon seeing them working, well, they would think that they are now Indians, or something like that. For that reason, they do not like to work (pause), for example, in the fields. Instead of sweeping their houses, sometimes they pay others to sweep so that no one will see that they sweep, or something like that.

Two characteristics permeate these native statements concerning the significance of "Indian" and "Ladino" in the two towns. First, there is a multifaceted system of opposed categories that parallels the opposition of Ladino and Indian (an opposition early seen in passage 15). Within the general notion of origins, "Ladino" is associated with Europe, foreign lands, and the nonlocal context, as opposed to "Indian," which is associated with particular towns and the local context (compare passages 1, 7, 8, 29, 34). The languages are distinct, with Spanish *(español)* opposed to the Indian tongues *(idioma, lengua, dialectos)* (see passages 26, 27, 33, 39, 46). The character and style of clothing are distinct. Ladino clothing *(de vestido)* approximates the Euroamerican styles, in opposition to Indian clothing, which is perceived to be a "distinctive" *(típico)* form of costume *(traje)* (passages 11, 33, 46, 47, 55). Custom or way of life in general is thought to be different within the two groups (passages 12, 17, 24,

35, 51, and perhaps 16, 20, 33, 42-44). The term "race" *(raza)* features as an important origin symbol (passages 1, 2, 6, 10, 13, 14, 17, 18, 19, 28, 29, 30, 32, 37, 38, 39, 47, 49, 54). Allied with race, as well as with kinship origins, is the notion of distinctive blood *(sangre)* (passages 8, 22). Finally, a matter closely linked to race is one's ancestry (mentioned in passages 7 and 51).

The overarching concept that joins Indian and Ladino in these usages is the notion of distinctive origins. Language, clothing, race, parentage, and locality are intimately linked to the domestic context, to a general locus of origins. Things foreign, distant, western, and Spanish contrast with things nearby, autochthonous, and uniquely local to form the symbol set. To speak Spanish, to dress in the national style of clothing, to be from an urban center or simply not from "here," to claim European parentage—each of these is a symbolic link to a particular origin. It is a link to the national center in Guatemala City or to the intellectual center in Spain. By contrast, to speak an Indian language, to dress in clothing peculiar to a given community (especially when that community, in the process of the conquest, was subjected to taxation and slavery), to have localized ancestry or parentage, or to depend on a plot of ancestral land is to link oneself to the symbolic margins that are labeled Indian. The oppositions in these symbols of origin are homologous to the oppositions in the concept of center and periphery as well as of Ladino and Indian.

The second characteristic that informs these passages is the idea that Indians and Ladinos are linked rather than separated. This is the case both socially and conceptually. Nor is the notion of linkage contradictory to opposition. The opposition exists within paired or linked sets. Furthermore, the pairs are oriented by the idea of hierarchy. Thus, one element of the pair is esteemed, preferred, superior, while the other element is the inverse of these.

There are multiple evidences of this ranking. First, the respective jobs of Ladinos and Indians are scaled (passages 5, 9, 10, 33, 41, 42, 43, 44, 57, 60). In a few passages, the occupations are not scaled against each other but are merely declared different (passages 16, 56, 58). Nevertheless, such statements must be interpreted in the context of the temporarily unspoken hierarchy. Indeed, evaluation is inescapable, for the occupations always conform to the wider hierarchy expressed in center versus periphery, educated versus uneducated, skilled versus unskilled, or nonmanual versus manual. Thus, the hamlet agriculturalist (and agricultural work in general) is low status in all four of these oppositions: he is rural, uneducated, unskilled, and manual. Agricultural knowledge does not count as a skill since it is learned in the domestic context. The hamlet artisan is higher status by virtue of being skilled. The urban artisan is even more central and hence higher in status than his equally skilled rural counterpart; and higher still if the rural artisan occasionally works his own fields. Thus, the ranking of occupations need not be overtly expressed. Occupations always are ranked by virtue of the way their attributes become meaningful within the total system of opposed yet hierarchic elements in the symbol sets. Passage 25 is particularly interesting in that it sharply confirms the appropriateness of pairing high-status jobs with Ladinos and low-status jobs with Indians. Unless the conceptual congruence is expected and implicit, the contradiction by means of noting empirical conditions would be meaningless. Second, Indians and Ladinos are distinguished by the degree of their education (passages 9, 10, 16, 17, 24, 31, 40, 41, 44, 56). Third, relative wealth difference is affirmed (passages 9, 44, 59). Fourth, there is a differential evaluation of the nobility of labor: nonmanual and manual labor are opposed as high and low status, respectively (passages 5, 16, 25, 41, 42, 43, 44, 57, 58, 59, 60), with Ladinos disdaining manual labor and Indians affirming its appropriateness. Fifth, differential access to power and government is also mentioned (passage 58).

Thus, Indian and Ladino are categories that are ranked with respect to each other. The terms mark the principal structural opposition in cultural ideology and social relations. Rank and opposition are communicated because the sets of origin symbols and indices arising from institutional placement bear the same structure and are activated in the course of ordinary institutionalized performances. Those on the subordinate side of a social relation are perceived as Indian or as more Indian. Because the ethnic categories are suitable for describing one's institutional placement, the conceptual hierarchy of Ladino versus Indian penetrates and permeates the lives of all Guatemalans (passages 9, 31, 41, 49, 54, 57, 60).

But the categories are not just dichotomous. Ladino and Indian can also merge and blur on a continuum of "more or less" (passages 12, 14, 17, 24, 31, 49, 54, 60); the positions in the hierarchy are accorded shaded degrees of honor or prestige (passages 10, 17, 57, 60). Such continua appear when all the symbolic oppositions are not congruent (passages 18, 25, 27, 33, 41, 45, 46, 47, 59). This is especially the case in those passages referring to "Mestizo" in its several forms. Mestizo is neither clearly Indian nor clearly Ladino. It is interstitial by virtue of incongruities in the symbolic linkages of conceptual oppositions and by one's actual circumstances in more than one institution (passages 14, 37, 38, 47, 54).

Thus, the overarching concept that joins Indian and Ladino is the notion of social status. Indian and Ladino are the end points of relative honor. The terms are linked by the concept of status hierarchy as well as by always being opposed and contrastive; neither term would be meaningful without the other. But the conceptual system is not free-floating, shorn of contact with the real world. Rather, the idea system is connected to the institutional setting by systems of symbols, among them language, dress, race, color, labor, urbanity, and occupation. As sign vehicles, these symbols complete a round trip, bearing meaning and thus connecting the cultural domain and the interaction domain. In one direction, they are mediators through which the regnant categories of culture (Schneider 1976:204) are called down to define and order the interaction context. By reverse mediation, every interaction evokes and thus raises up the validity of the categories, because each performance, intentionally or not, passes through the grid of symbols to thereby evoke meaning.

For example, the ideology of independence leads the successful San Pedro artisan to invest his excess capital in an additional form of self-reliance, the subsistence parcel. Where is the connecting symbol? In the small plot of land itself and in the personal work expended to farm it. This then marks the individual for subsequent categorization vis-à-vis the owners of larger units who hire others. Thus, to anyone born into the system and learning the meaning of the categories at first by observation, the divisions of the land and the differences in people's willingness to work it confirm the existence of the categories and ideologies that generated the behavior in any given context. Circular, to be sure; and because the system is circular it is an efficiently self-fulfilling prophecy.

Indígena and *ladino* are the primary categories in the concept of origins. They are the initial categories of discussion when native thought turns to sources, to genealogy, to family, or to town of birth. Unfortunately, that fact is not unambiguously native in the passages I have presented, because I used the terms *indígena* and *ladino* in the initial questions. While "Indian" did emerge in contrast to "Ladino" in San Pedro (passage 31), other passages must be cited to establish the fact in San Marcos.

One San Marcos male established the system in the following way:

            A: How do Guatemalans divide themselves?

(61) *I:* Here they divide themselves as Indians and Ladinos. Every Guatemalan can be divided thus.

            A: What is the difference?

(62) *I:* The difference: (pause) Indian is by dress *(vestido)*. If he progresses he can be a lawyer or an accountant, and thus ceases being an Indian, but he always. . . . Over there [pointing to a school] they identify the Indian by his surname, because if a student has a known surname, Orozco, Navarro, Quiquivish—these are Indian surnames. And by the physical aspect.

            A: How do the Ladinos divide themselves up?

(63) *I:* No. Here, everyone is just Ladino *(todo parejo es ladino)*.

            A: Do they not distinguish "working Ladinos" from "teaching Ladinos" or anything like that?

(64) *I:* No. Only as poor, of limited resources, but it always is Ladino.

On another occasion, and using a different approach, I asked a San Marcos tailor what were the various things he considered himself to be.

(65) *I:* I am a Marquense, which is to say, from the Department of San Marcos. I am a worker *(obrero)*, for I dedicate myself to the trade *(arte)* of tailoring, I am a father of a family[14] but a responsible father of a family. I am a lover of work.[15]

I then asked him how Guatemalans were divided up *(dividirse):*

(66) *I:* Ladino and Indian. Every Guatemalan is divided up thus.

Both the Marquenses and San Pedranos affirm this distinction without prompting in ordinary speech.

Nevertheless, these two divisions do not exhaust the taxonomy.

One of the definitions of "Ladino" offered by natives is "foreigner *(extranjero).*" Thus, the "European," and "North American," and other foreign nationalities are subdivisions of Ladino. The more common of these are *español, francés, alemán* (German), *libanés, turco, chino,* and occasionally *judío* (Jew). The Indian sector of the population also subdivides, again in terms of origins. But the Indians see themselves as the autochthonous people and subdivide themselves by municipality. Persons from this town identify themselves as *San Pedranos,* persons from that town as *Comitecos* (from Comitancillo), and so forth. The contrast between external foreign origins and internal local origins corresponds precisely with the distinction between Ladino and Indian.

The passages so far cited manifest a native tendency to quickly shift from one set of expressions that define ethnicity to another. This phenomenon is manifest even more sharply in one section of an exploratory survey I conducted in 1971.[16] In this early sample survey, my assistants and I acquired a considerable number of relatively short answers to a series of questions on primary social categories. We asked the natives in both towns the following four open-ended questions and recorded their answers verbatim. The questions were:

1. In your way of thinking, what is an Indian?
2. And what is a Ladino?
3. Do you consider yourself Ladino, Indian, or what?
4. Why?

The answers are recorded in Appendix 3, using somewhat abbreviated direct quotes.[17] Of course, there are many shortcomings to data gathered in the census context, but they do show the pervasiveness of a particular coding system among both Ladino and Indian: the rapid change of symbolic idioms used to define ethnic categories.

In more than 300 sets of answers (of which only 124 are given in Appendix 3), one is struck by the fact that very few people define Indian, Ladino, and self (questions 1, 2, and 4) by consistently using just one symbolic opposition concerning origins. Only three San Pedrano responses exemplify such consistency (Appendix 3:P1–P3). Similarly, only four Marquenses' responses held to one origin symbol (Appendix 3:M1–M4). It seems noteworthy that so few informants consistently stuck to a single set of origin symbols for their definitions of ethnicity.

By contrast, a great many sets of answers make use of origin symbols only but use different origin-linked oppositions for two and often all three of the open responses requested. Ten San Pedro sets shift between different origin symbols (Appendix 3:P4–P13). Similarly, nineteen San Marcos sets shift through different origin symbols (Appendix 3:M5–M23). These responses show the manifold combinations of race, language, clothing, parentage, and locality oppositions within the general focus of origins. Given the number of responses from each town that I have listed, the Marquense Ladinos see the system as more ethnically fixed in terms of their dependence on origin symbols. The combinations draw our attention to the easy shifting between the several origin oppositions. The three cases that shift through three different idioms of origin (for example, race, clothing, and parentage) dramatize the fluid interchangeability of the origin symbols (Appendix 3:P4, P6, M21, M22). The other responses use just two origin symbols (Appendix 3:P5, P7–P13, M5–M20, M23). Although attributions of racial differences are made more frequently by Marquenses, both towns exhibit considerable thematic similarity.

In both communities, race, blood, parentage, community or nation of origin, color, language, surnames, general customs, and clothing are set up as oppositions that parallel the opposition between Ladino and Indian. While some of the oppositions are given categorically (P9–P11), others are quite relative, ranking Ladinos and Indians on scales of more or less, and better or worse (P12, P13).[18] Thus, hierarchy exists among the terms and is confirmed by the presence of "Mestizo." We have here origin symbols of hierarchical placement; in short, ethnic symbols.

Why should there be such switching between different origin symbols? Only in a few sets are Ladinos and Indians related or defined by the opposed elements of a single origin concept. In most sets, they are defined by different pairs of oppositions. Are the natives inconsistent? Or are Ladinos and Indians so different that they must be defined in different frames of reference? The latter possibility is untenable, because some people do define Indians and Ladinos in terms of one set of origin symbols. Moreover, all the origin symbols are applied to each ethnic segment. It would appear that Indians and Ladinos are comparable in the same idiom. This leaves inconsistency. However, the possibility of inconsistency disappears if one assumes the symbols, idioms, or indices of origin are equivalent and, hence, interchangeable codes. Under this assumption, the format of the Marquense and Pedrano responses is not inconsistent but redundant. And redundancy is essentially a matter of multiple code equivalence. Thus, Spanish language is to a Mayan dialect as national *vestuario* is to a municipal *traje*, as white is to brown, as foreign is to local. The structure of the code—the opposition between paired origin elements—is equivalent in each case. The pairs are thus interchangeable. The natives are hardly inconsistent in the passages given in this chapter and in Appendix 3. Rather, they redundantly use the common structure of interchangeable origin codes.

Lévi-Strauss is especially instructive on the significance of code interchangeability, though he had different problems in mind than the ethnic symbolism of status hierarchy. For the Australian aborigines, he suggested that "each tribe possesses two codes to express its social structure." One code consisted of the "kinship system and rules of marriage," while the other consisted of the "organization into sections or subsections." But the two codes do not "transmit different messages." Rather, "the message remains the same; only the circumstances and the recipients differ" (Lévi-Strauss 1963c:50). In short, distinct codes can bear the same message.

Much of Lévi-Strauss's work develops the proposition that conceptual opposition—like Durkheim's division of labor—integrates. This idea supports the contention that Ladino and Indian cultures are analytically inseparable precisely because they are conceptually opposed as categories, in symbols, and through ideologies. In this regard, Lévi-Strauss's view that totems stand as a "code," operating on "a principle consisting of the union of opposites . . . the union of which results in an organized totality" is instructive. Lévi-Strauss concludes that the problem of totemism and other modes of symbolizing either the interactions of groups or the relations among categories is "a general problem, viz., how to make opposition, instead of being an obstacle to integration, serve rather to produce it" (Lévi-Strauss 1963c:88–89). Elsewhere, Lévi-Strauss emphasizes the idea that one social system can be an inverse transformation of another. If, he asserts, the social structure of one group of islands had been historically derived from another group, then only the "remains or survivals" of the source islands "should be found in" the colony islands. But "what is striking, however, is that the two systems are exact counterparts of each other," the island structures being "symmetrically the reverse of each other, as if [each] system represented a transformation of the same group" (Lévi-Strauss 1966:79 [my correction of the translation, by comparison with Lévi-Strauss 1962:105]). A similar idea appears in "The Bear and the Barber" (1963a), where Lévi-Strauss observes an inverse relationship between Australian totemic systems and Indian caste. The central issue is that one system can be the reverse or inverse transformation of another system, or that they both can be transformed elements of a set.[19] The structure of Guatemalan culture differs from Lévi-Strauss's presentation only in that the Guatemalan Indian component of society is viewed as an inverse of another component *within* a system rather than a reversal or transformation of some other *entire* system.

As Malinowski has long ago shown us, codes for discussing social groups can be represented through origins as well as in totems. But the totemic form is instructive to our thinking about origins. Man "extracts" "the differences between animals" and "transfer[s]" the differences as "opposites and contrasts" into culture. The animal attributes are "adopted as emblems by groups of men in order to do away with their own resemblances" (Lévi-Strauss 1966:107). Emblematic opposition is crucial to group differentiation. The emblems may be presented in natural totems or mythical origins. Or, as is frequently affirmed in this part of Guatemala, people are descended of Pedro Alvarado and Tecún Uman, an attribution of social race which combines the character of both totem and origin.

Thus far, I have presented only the census responses that switch between the several available themes and indices of origin. But origins are not the only media of definition nor the only elements that may be interchanged in the code-switching phenomenon. In both towns, origin codes not only are interchangeable with each other, but they are both substituted for and mixed with representations of relative institutional hierarchy especially through such words as "more," "less," "little," "much," "better," or "worse," "high class," and their cousins. Given that the origin codes freely mix with descriptions of institutional hierarchy, one concludes that the interchangeable origin codes are indeed interchangeable symbols for hierarchy and institutional placement.

Thus, while the definition of "Indian," for example, may be entirely origin-linked (with or without direct hierarchical expression), the other answers to the parallel questions may be explicitly hierarchical and oriented toward institutional placement.

When the references to origin symbols and institutional place-

Table 8. Kinds of Symbolism Used to Define Indian, Ladino, and Self

Control:	San Marcos					San Pedro					S.M. and S.P. Combined		
	Indian Defined By					Indian Defined By					Indian Defined By		
Self Defined in Origin Symbols	Origin Symbols	Institutional Placement	Subtotals			Origin Symbols	Institutional Placement	Subtotals			Origin Symbols	Institutional Placement	Subtotals
Origin Symbols	23 cases[a] 53.4% of T	1 case[b] 2.3% of T	24 cases 55.8%			13 cases[e] 28.3% of T	3 cases[f] 6.5% of T	16 cases 34.8%			36 cases 40.4% of T	4 cases 4.5% of T	40 cases 44.9%
Ladino Defined by Institutional Placement	10 cases[c] 23.3% of T	9 cases[d] 20.9% of T	19 cases 44.2%			17 cases[g] 36.9% of T	13 cases[h] 28.3% of T	30 cases 65.2%			27 cases 30.3% of T	22 cases 24.7% of T	49 cases 55.1%
Subtotals	33 cases 76.7%	10 cases 23.3%	43 cases 87.7% of S.M.			30 cases 65.2%	16 cases 34.8%	46 cases 61.3% of S.P.			63 cases 70.8%	26 cases 29.2%	89 cases 100%
Self Defined by Institutional Placement													
Origin Symbols	—	—	—			—	—	—			—	—	—
Ladino Defined by Institutional Placement	1 case[i] 16.7% of T	5 cases[j] 83.3% of T	6 cases 100%			15 cases[k] 51.7% of T	14 cases[l] 48.3% of T	29 cases 100%			16 cases 45.7% of T	19 cases 54.3% of T	35 cases 100%
Subtotals	1 case 16.7%	5 cases 83.3%	6 cases 12.3% of S.M.			15 cases 51.7%	14 cases 48.3%	29 cases 38.7% of S.P.			16 cases 45.7%	19 cases 54.3%	35 cases 100%

Table 8. (continued)

Control:	San Marcos					San Pedro					S.M. and S.P. Combined			
	Indian Defined By						Indian Defined By					Indian Defined By		
Self Defined in Origin Symbols	Origin Symbols	Institutional Placement	Subtotals			Origin Symbols	Institutional Placement	Subtotals			Origin Symbols	Institutional Placement	Subtotals	
Self-Symbolism														
Irrelevant (Total of above)														
Origin Symbols	23 cases 46.9% of T	1 case 2.0% of T	24 cases 49.0%			13 cases 17.3% of T	3 cases 4.0% of T	16 cases 21.3%			36 cases 29.0% of T	4 cases 3.2% of T	40 cases 32.2%	
Ladino Defined by Institutional Placement	11 cases 22.4% of T	14 cases 28.6% of T	25 cases 51.0%			32 cases 42.7% of T	27 cases 36.0% of T	59 cases 78.6%			43 cases 34.7% of T	41 cases 33.0% of T	84 cases	
Subtotals	34 cases 69.4%	15 cases 30.6%	49 cases 100% of S.M.			45 cases 60.0%	30 cases 40.0%	75 cases 100% of S.P.			29 cases 63.7%	45 cases 36.3%	124 cases 100% of S.M. and S.P.	

Key: X percent of T refers to that cell's percentage of the 2-by-2 table controlling for both town and type of ethnic definition.

Notes:

a: M1-M23
b: M41
c: M23-M33
d: M34-M40, M44, M45
e: P1-P13
f: P38, P39, P60
g: P14-P27, P54, P55, P61
h: P28-P37, P51-P53
i: M42
j: M43, M46-M49
k: P40-P50, P56-P59
l: P62-P75

ment (contained in Appendix 3) are numerically summarized, as in Table 8, one can see the various combinations of origin versus institutional-placement definitions for Indians and Ladinos, and the reasons for attributing ethnicity to one or another. Several interesting numerical characteristics emerge. First, Marquenses define themselves by origin symbols more consistently (87.7 percent) than San Pedranos (61.3 percent). Second, with the self defined in origin symbols or the self-attribution ignored, a much higher percentage of Marquenses define both Indians and Ladinos in origin terms than do San Pedranos. Conversely, a generally higher percentage of San Pedranos make some (86.7 percent for San Pedro, 53.1 percent for San Marcos) or all (36 percent for San Pedro, 28.6 percent for San Marcos) of their definitions in institutional symbols. Finally, the rarest combination in either San Pedro or San Marcos is to define the Indian in institutional terms and the Ladino at the same time in origin symbols. Indeed, origin symbols are only used to define ethnic terms if the informant also uses them to define the household head; that is, if the household head is defined in terms of institutional placement, then origins are not used to define either Indian or Ladino. These observations suggest images of greater mobility among San Pedranos and greater rigidity among Marquenses. Indeed, ethnic mobility is greater in San Pedro, for Marquenses do not become Indians.

Moreover, in the construction of Table 8 and in Appendix 3, I deleted those definition sets where the respondent either denied a difference or could not define one. Such expressions of uncertainty were much more common from San Pedranos, again indicating greater perceptions of individual mobility across the ethnic boundary. However, these matters of mobility must be deferred until the next chapter.

One can also see from Table 8 and Appendix 3 that all but one of the logical permutations of the coding system are present: consistent origin symbolism, shifting multiple-origin symbolism, origin symbolism and relative institutional placement, origins and status honor, and institutional placement according to just one criterion or shifting through two or three.[20] The only exception: if the people of either town define themselves by institutional placement, they never defined Ladinos with origin symbols. Why this is so is not so clear to me except that those who see themselves as mobile could hardly ossify the Ladino domain to which or within which they might move. Nevertheless, the many native variations in the answers to a simple set of questions make logically consistent sense when the origin and institutional definitions are viewed as equivalence codes.

This mixing of origin symbolism and notions of institutional centrality occurs not only in these passages taken from a census but also in many discussion settings. In the high-school interviews discussed earlier, such conflations occur in passages 9, 10, 17, 19–20, 33, and 39–40. The interchangeability of origin concepts and status concepts linked to institutional centrality manifests itself in many other interview situations.

For example, one afternoon I was talking to a San Pedro *aldea* resident who said of himself, "to us peasants *(para nosotros los campesinos)*, the machete is the most important thing." Our conversation ranged over agriculture, kinship, and other topics, and I carefully made no mention of ethnic terms or categories. The topic came up like this:

    A: Let's make a list of your *compadres*.

(66) *I:* There are two kinds! There are the *compadres* who sought me out, and there are the *compadres* that are the godparents of my children.

    A: Which is more important?

(67) *I:* Those of my children, that I went to seek out: [two names are given]. They are the godparents of my children. The person searches out his equal, someone of the same status *(categoría)*. One cannot carry on with someone who is greater *(más grande)*.

    A: Doesn't one look for some advantage?

(68) *I:* I don't. Some seek a *padrino* in the city *(la ciudad)* or rather, a *ladino*. FOR GAIN! They give clothing, things, gifts. In my way of thinking this is bad. One ought to work to provide this by oneself.

    A: What does Ladino mean?

(69) *I:* It's a matter of dress, and that they have more money. They are civilized.

    A: Are there people who are not civilized?

(70) *I:* There are. In the hamlets. They can't talk very well.

    A: You said other clothing?

(71) *I:* They dress well, they have money, and they do not work in the fields (countryside, *el campo*).

A: What is the opposite?

(72) *I:* The poor countryside people *(la gente pobre campesina)*.

A: What does Indian mean?

(73) *I:* Native people in the countryside *(el campo)*. Indians are now disappearing. The true Indian is [one of] the people from long ago who do not understand. Every town had Ladino people and Indian people.

A: What are you?

(74) *I:* Indian. Since my woman *(mujer)* dresses native *(viste de natural)*.

A: Why does she dress native?

(75) *I:* It is the style and custom of the town.

One can see in these passages that language, dress, work, status, and money are combined interchangeably. In passage 68, the urban *padrino* is quickly redefined as a *ladino*. This follows the discussion of status (67), although I intervened with an unfortunately utilitarian question. In passages 69–71, the rapid recodification of the Indian social category is particularly apparent. Again, the issue must be raised: is this evidence of inconsistency on the part of the natives? Do these passages mean different things although they are closely grouped together? The answer suggested here is no. The rapid shifting between sets of symbols is best seen as evidence of a code equivalence between the sets.

Categories of Institutional Placement

Just as origin categories may be used alone as symbols of status, categories of institutional placement may also be used alone to fix status. Here is a San Marcos example:

A: What are the social classes *(clases sociales)*?[21]

(76) *I:* Employees, lawyers, workers, and peasants. The first class *(la primera clase,* the upper class) includes lawyers and

doctors. After that, the second class, includes employees *(empleados)*. [The informant's son, a student at the local extension branch of the university, added the clarification "government bureaucrats," to which the father nodded in agreement.] And after that, the workers *(obreros)*. Then peasants *(campesinos)*.

A: What does the word *agricultores* mean?

(77) I: *Agricultores* are those who are owners of coffee or cotton estates *(son duenos de finca de cafe o algodon)*. They are among [high] society *(son entre la social)*, the first, by virtue of money.

The informant in this case was a San Marcos tailor. His representation of society, divided into professionals, government employees, workers, and peasants was repeated over and over again by all levels of society in both San Marcos and San Pedro. To be sure, sometimes the categories most distant from that of the particular speaker were collapsed. Thus, sometimes the poor would represent the system in the following way:

(78) I: The classes are the social people who have much money *(gente social)*, the working people, and the poor humble peasant people who have less means or options.

While this is from a San Marcos informant, similar conflations were made by San Pedranos. On another occasion, in discussing families, and without prompting toward the subject of social status, a Marquense said:

(79) I: That family belongs to the middle class. They have the means, money, with which to live. This [other] family does not come up to the middle class *(no llega a la clase media)*. They live by their work, they have no lands.

Asked about the kinds of people that live in this department, a well-to-do San Marcos landowner offered:

(80) I: From bottom to top: Peasants *(campesinos)*. They earn very little, are illiterate, perhaps up to a third grade [education].

> From there: Tailors, masons, blacksmiths, those who have a trade (*un oficio*), and they earn more than a peasant.
>
> Then bureaucrats (*oficinistas*), and teachers. These are more or less the same. And the smaller agriculturalists, who might earn 150 quetzals per month with perhaps two hundred or three hundred *cuerdas*.
>
> Finally, the university-trained professionals, such as doctors, lawyers, and engineers. Or the *finca* owner with two or three *caballerías* [one *caballería* equals one thousand *cuerdas*], although this depends upon the products from his *finca*. However, at this size you earn a lot. The *finquero* is high because of his wealth.

While occupations are a principal means of subdividing the categories of social status, it may also be done simply in terms of money. One hears, in the words of one informant who immediately uses code equivalence, that there are two kinds of people, "the rich and the poor, or in other words, those of high society."

The structural equivalence of rich/poor to Ladino/Indian is manifest in various ways. As a guest at a San Pedro wedding, I was told the following by the rather drunken father of a bride:

(81) I: It is an honor to have a North American in my home. I am humble (pause), poor (pause), Indian.

On another occasion, a certain San Pedrano store owner became quite excited (according to the informant, his business neighbor) when a Marquense Ladino talked to him as an "equal." It was the first time a Ladino had ever treated him as such. My informant noted, in describing the scene to me, that the assets of the Ladino would be generously estimated at five thousand dollars, while those of the San Pedro "Indian" would be conservatively estimated at three hundred thousand dollars. Unfortunately, my informant did not press on to interpret the event, though the interpretation is perhaps quite simple: the Ladinoizing symbol of the San Pedrano's huge wealth had begun to override the Indianizing symbols of his commercial occupation and his town of birth and residence.

The expected congruence of ethnic category and institutional placement is manifest in other ways in the hamlets. There are poor subsistence agriculturalists in the hamlets of San Marcos who are said to be Ladinos. But when one asks what they consider themselves to be, the rural Ladino's answer is frequently accompanied by a rather nervous laugh, or a tense laugh follows no answer at all. For these villagers, poverty, agricultural occupation, and hamlet marginality are symbolically discordant vis-à-vis their public claims to Ladino status by virtue of language, clothing, descent, and municipal origin. Even with these indices of Ladino status, the rural agricultural-plot owner or laborer is strongly Indianized by the structure of the symbolic system since the oppositions of urban/rural, central/peripheral, nonmanual/manual, and employed/independent parallel the structure of Ladino/Indian. Thus, a San Marcos woman offered this:

(82) *I:* Nowadays there are three classes. It is no longer a matter of race but of money. An Indian family can be high class *(de clase alta)*. For example, Lic. _____ . Almost as soon as they get money, they can be high society *(alta sociedad)*. Those of status *(los de categoría)*, of high society, sometimes maintain themselves not by money but with marriages. The middle class are those that work. Then the poorest people, the peasants *(campesinos)*, the Indian people, the rural element.

In this region, peasants and Indians are kept distinct only with considerable effort.[22]

Granted that there are nameable exceptions, the cultural expectation unites the Indian with poverty and peasant life. This unity derives from the structure of the interchangeable symbolic codes, though the natives can identify empirical exceptions at every turn. The exceptions, it turns out, are people whose behavioral circumstances generate incongruent symbols bearing dissonant messages; but their ideologies are decidedly Indian regarding the work ethic and their interest in cultivating social connections.

Such individuals may apply the term *mestizo* to themselves or be so designated by others. The natives invoke *mestizo* most often when the several aspects of one's social position or ideology are inconsistent. The term's use is on the rise, but not because there is more biological crossbreeding, for throughout this century Guatemalans have been pretty well-mixed and not much changed. But social institutions have been changing rapidly since 1944, so that for many individuals, one's hierarchical placement in the several institutions is not concordant. Because biological symbolism is fundamentally a reexpression of social placement, with increasing institutional complexity and incongruency there is an increasing phenomenon of discordant sociological mestizos.

I reemphasize, however, that the categories Ladino and Indian are always ranked with respect to each other. Those who dispute the difference between Indians and Ladinos do so by emphasizing the biological or racial connotations of the terms and interpreting them within an intrusive Protestant ideology. Ladinos and Indians are the same biologically, the *evangelicos,* especially, will assert. They then suggest that the categories refer to distinctions that arise from the "pretensions" that exist among men. Thus, biological difference may be denied, but the existence of status differences among Guatemalans is seldom disputed. And even those who radically contest the existence of status differences grant the implicit hierarchy of the terms when they assert that the terms are "invalid" and need no definition because "all are equal *(Todos son iguales)."* Of course, if the ethnic terms were not fundamentally hierarchical, they couldn't be rejected as "invalid" due to a protestant premise of equality.

Two important consequences follow from this linkage between status and origins. First, origin symbols tie the domestic domain, in which origin symbols are produced, to the public domain, in which status considerations are paramount. The valued position of the status system is high honor. The valued position of origins is Spain, urbanity, the white race, and European custom. High honor and Spanish urbanity are thus linked. Because of these correspondences, personal placement in the Guatemalan institutions can be read out in terms of ethnic origins. We must therefore consider how an individual manipulates ethnic symbolism in relation to indices of his status. This we take up in the next chapter. More important, the linkage of status and origin symbolism requires a consideration of kinship and family, the topic of Part 3, for kinship and family are the major sources of origins and their symbolism and hence enter importantly into the public domain of status considerations.

Second, while origin symbols link groups in terms of status, they preserve the appearance of group separation. It is this appearance of separation that has led to the proliferation of separate anthropological studies of either Indians or Ladinos, and the appearance of separation has also led to the genre of plural-society studies in which the distinctive groups are linked together not by culture but by the force of political institutions or by the mutual benefits of marketing arrangements.

However, the appearance of separation between Ladinos and Indians is a deceptive Guatemalan "native model." It is deceptive precisely because it is close to the surface, especially in expressions of language, clothing, and town of origin. As a native model, this appearance of separation is subject to the limitations voiced by Lévi-Strauss:

> A structural model may be conscious or unconscious without this difference affecting its nature. It can only be said that when the structure of a certain type of phenomena does not lie at a great depth, it is more likely that some kind of model, standing as a screen to hide it, will exist in the collective consciousness. For conscious models, which are usually known as "norms," are by definition very poor ones, since they are not intended to explain the phenomena but to perpetuate them. Therefore, structural analysis is confronted with a strange paradox well known to the linguist, that is: the more obvious structural organization is, the more difficult it becomes to reach it because of the inaccurate conscious models lying across the path which leads to it.
> (Lévi-Strauss 1963b:273–74)

To be sure, unity, through hierarchy and inversion, does not lie at great depth. Linkage through inversion and hierarchy appears repeatedly in ideas and at times savagely in interaction. But ethnic-origin symbolism is the surface structure: the exuberant, colorful, noisy, distinctive screen that hides the union implicit in the hierarchy and in the inversions. Yet hiding linkage with the appearance of separation perpetuates hierarchy. The deeper structure that the system cannot raise to consciousness and the fundamental model on which Guatemalan life is ordered for both Indians and Ladinos is the cultural linkage by opposed categories in status hierarchy.

6
Institutional Congruence, the Individual, and Ethnic Change

As we have seen, the ethnic categories *ladino* and *indígena* are ranked, joined by their opposition, and mediated by one or more variants of the interstitial *mestizo*. This sets up the categorical ability to express both polar opposition and a gradient of relative placement. Likewise, each aspect of the society—such as education, occupation, wealth, or power—has a culturally identified center and periphery with regard to prestige. To be sure, the boundaries between center, middle, and periphery are not at all precise. But the system allows institutional placement vis-à-vis others to be spoken of by reference to either a polar opposition or a gradient of relative placement.

The categorical series and the institutional structures are brought together and made parallel by a rich symbolic medium. On the one hand, *ladino, mestizo,* and *indígena* are linked through the idea of racial or descent transmission to the origin context. Thus, relative skin color, canonical body features (Mayar nose, straight hair), the ethnic category of one's parents, the language of the household and the way that it interferes with or is the same as the language of the state, the rank of one's town of birth, and perhaps even one's choice of clothing are acquired in the origin context of the home. On the other hand, all these productions of the household context rise to the level of symbols because of the cultural emphasis on their central-peripheral connotations, an emphasis maintained since the conquest. The origin symbols thereby parallel the central-peripheral hierarchy of institutional involvement in education, in government, in control over land or over people, the relative manual involvement and educational prerequisites of one's occupation, and the connecting or isolating nature of one's personal or community social network. Because of the structural parallels, origin symbols may substitute for institutional placement and thereby symbolize social position. This ethnic overlap gives the institutions the appearance of a fixed, natural, even god-ordained, and stable social system. Given the degree of social continuity from the conquest to the present, one can suppose that the ethnic-origins idiom was effective in pacifying the Indians and in obscuring from them their common class position—and at salving the conscience of the benefiting elites.

But if origins may substitute for institutional placement, the reverse is also true. Especially since the liberal reforms of 1944, the congruence of one's placement in the various institutions has shifted. Advancement in education or a government-paid job nowadays frequently contradicts one's Indian ethnic placement, pressuring toward recategorization as Mestizo or Ladino.[1] For example, in discussing the land conflict between San Marcos and San Pedro, a high municipal official of San Marcos referred to an important family of professionals in San Pedro and said, "Those *indios*[2] are more Ladino than we are." The community-level symbolization of ethnicity by race-family-birthright linkage to a particular community here shifted to symbolization by individual access to the central institutions. The symbol "Indian" placed the family in question in low status vis-à-vis the Marquense speaker by virtue of community affiliation. The symbol "Ladino" placed them on a par, at least by virtue of an undefined mélange of institutional centers, with education and profession chief among them.

On another occasion, I interviewed a San Marcos high-school teacher who was studying nights to complete a university degree. As the questions proceeded, he offered considerable personal data—birthplace, birth date, family composition, employment, education, and other items—as well as his opinions on a range of topics. The discussion turned to a consideration of social categories (A = anthropologist, I = informant):

A: In your own way of thinking, what is an Indian?

I: It is a sociocultural group (pause) that speaks its own language, wears a distinctive costume *(traje típico)*, and has primitive customs.

A: And what is a Ladino?

I: The opposite. A sociocultural group that speaks Spanish, dresses European, with Western customs.

A: Which do you consider yourself?

I: Ladino.

By this point, my friend had become noticeably uncomfortable. He squirmed in his chair and looked around.

A: Why?

He froze. Then he parted the curtain separating the living room *(sala)* from the next room. Finding no one listening, he leaned forward and whispered:

I: I suppose you already know since I told you I'm from San Jerónimo:[3] On account of having passed in speech and dress *(Por haber pasado de hablar y vestir)*.

At the beginning of this conversation, "Ladino" category and behavioral customs were used as appropriate symbols of the informant's growing access to the central institutions. After all, he was highly educated, improving thereon, and employed by the government in a prestigious position. But when I asked "Why?," my friend shifted to his race-family-birthright connection to a particular community, which he had already identified. Thus, the community's positional status became the basis for his self-definition. This forced him to account for his present Ladino status by a change of speech and dress.

A single example from San Pedro will suffice. At Christmas, parents gather their sons and daughters for a festive dinner. One family, proprietors of a thriving store, had several sons and daughters in the national university who had returned home for the holiday. During the dinner, we discussed the relations of San Marcos to San Pedro. Members of the family presented the San Pedro version of the history of the Ladino founding of San Marcos and the Indian background of San Pedro. In the context of identifying themselves as San Pedranos and contrasting their town with San Marcos, the family members had identified themselves as being Indian. Yet, a little while later, I asked each member of the family what he or she considered himself to be. The illiterate grandfather (mother's side) asserted that he was a "true native *(mero natural)* of San Pedro." The father and store proprietor, a man of sixth-grade education, claimed he was *"indígena"* and a "pure San Pedrano." His wife (having completed third grade only) retorted, "We are not feathered Indians *(indios)* but San Pedro *indios."* Their children, who were all university students nearing completion of professional degrees, spoke for themselves. One son opted for *mestizo*. Another agreed, adding that that was so "in the racial sense. But in the cultural sense I am Ladino on account of not being a traditionalist." The oldest daughter claimed to be *"ladina* because

I do not practice *(no llevo)* the Indian customs *(costumbre)*." Thus, without rancor, dispute, or identity crisis, the members of a single family claimed distinctive ethnic categories by virtue of origin symbolization and of their relative access to the center through education, occupation, and communication skill. Yet there was an undertone of ambiguity. They spoke disparagingly of Ladinos, in that the latter, the Marquenses, thought themselves superior to San Pedranos. In this context, the family members thought of themselves as Indian, by virtue of their community of origin. .

In these examples, the informants are categorizing and recategorizing themselves on several different institutional axes. On the one hand, they may place themselves in the system through affiliation to the community of their birthplace. On the other, they may place themselves in terms of individual access and placement in other institutional frameworks such as education, occupation, wealth, political ties, place of work, current residence, or social skills and speech. Each of these institutional frameworks has a center and periphery, or some other polarity, that structurally corresponds to high status and low. The status of one's placement in any of these institutions can be communicated by using the high- or low-status ethnic terminology or in the symbols derived from the oppositions of origin. That is why one Ladino can call another Ladino an *indio* if he is being ignorant, incompetent, uncouth, or malicious. Furthermore, since some individuals, especially San Pedranos, may find status placement at different levels in the several institutions or frames of reference, they may call themselves *mestizos,* or they may oscillate, manipulate, or "commute"[4] in their personal ethnic claims by selectively appealing to one or another of the symbolic sets. Marquenses, on the other hand, tend to assume permanently a Ladino classification.

To call such behavior an ethnic shift or ethnic change obscures the relationship between the individual and the system perspectives of the social process. Ethnicity does not refer to *what* one is in the social and cultural orders but rather to *where* one is within them by virtue of a symbolic claim. The terms *indígena, mestizo,* and *ladino* and the variations of ethnic behavior are communication symbols with which natives order and thereby socialize the interaction system. Given the different institutions in which one may use ethnicity to communicate placement, it is not surprising that individuals "shift" their ethnicity. But there is really no "shifting," "manipulating," or "commuting" of what one is. There is only a continuing symbolization of one's context and goals in a complex system of ideas, ideologies, and ongoing relationships.

Similarly, at the system level, ethnicity is applied to communities to represent their relative access to the central institutions. Such representations are rather more rigid because the system-level political structure is relatively more rigid. However, there is contextual flexibility even here: San Pedro is Indian, compared to San Marcos, and San Pedranos see San Marcos as closer to the center. But San Pedro is Mestizo, compared to most other highland towns, and San Pedranos see these other towns as further toward the periphery.

Herein lies the dynamic as well as the stability of the Guatemalan sociocultural system. Most Indians who construct atypical social networks relabel and realign themselves ethnically because a wide-ranging network is symbolically contrary to the Indian feature of marginal isolation. Further, because the atypical Indian individuals do disconnect themselves, their communities retain a consistency between the structure of their actual interaction system, the overarching ethnic categories, and the ideologies of prestige centrality, on the one hand, and Indian disconnected marginality, on the other. As a result, the highest level of the cultural taxonomy and the political-group level of the interaction system are congruent and bifurcate: Indian and Ladino. But the lower levels of the cultural taxonomy and the individual's positions in the interaction system are more complex. Nevertheless, culture and interaction are interlocked at both levels through the mediation of symbols.

The complexities of the individual's context in the total system are revealed in terms interstitial to the basic Ladino-Indian dichotomy. As previously noted, a substantial number of the residents of both communities label themselves neither Indian nor Ladino, asserting that such do not exist. In San Pedro, one often meets with individuals who reject the implication that they are Indians. They do not consider themselves Ladinos either, though only a few dispute the real existence of the two groups. The most common alternatives are "I am *mestizo,*" and "I am *guatemalteco.*" Occasionally, one hears "I am *clase media.*"

The following San Pedranos speak for themselves. One woman was a *"mestizo,* on account of being civilized." Another woman asserted that she and those around her were *"mestizos* because we carry the two bloods." Yet another woman: "[We are] Mestizos because we are neither Indians *(índios)* [n]or Ladinos." A man, asked if he considered himself to be Indian, Ladino, or what?, replied, "A human being, [because] we are all the same." A woman said that she and her husband were "Ladinos, because of favorable circumstances." And a man, after defining Indians and Ladinos, termed himself *clase media*. It appears that in San Pedro such alternatives to the primary ethnic division are used by economically better-off individuals whose household industry has prospered or by individuals who, through education, have entered into the government salariat as teachers. Individually they had "overcome *(superado)*" some of the institutional constraints usual among San Pedranos and expected among Indians. But they had not yet developed fully favorable social networks, nor had they (I suspect) deviated from the individualist ideology. Note that "being civilized," being "all the same," and enjoying "favorable circumstances" are comparative terms. The inapplicability of the primary ethnic symbols derives from individual deviations from the culturally expected antipodal circumstances. But even though San Pedranos are a class above the neighboring Indian *municipios,* as we have already seen and will see again in Part 3, they still retain the fundamental elements of ideology in opposition to Ladino ideology.

In San Marcos, on the other hand, one encounters the *mestizo* alternative among some nonnatives who are middle- or lower-level civil servants and among some artisans whether they are native or not. A teacher, who had been born in San Pedro but had moved to San Marcos, was referred to by a cousin as *mestizo*. A tailor, born and raised in San Marcos and having paternal and maternal surnames of the aristocratic elite of the town, likewise termed himself *mestizo,* justifying this "on account of being a Guatemalan." A male taxi driver, also native of San Marcos, so adjudged himself "because there is not a single difference [between Indians and Ladinos]." Another native male, a watch repairer, was *"mestizo* on account of originating from two races." A female teacher, native of San Marcos and married to an electrician from a coastal municipality, styled herself *"mestizo,* because of not knowing whether I'm Indian or Ladino." A taxi driver born in Guatemala City and his wife, a teacher born on the coast, termed themselves "mixed *(mixtos)* or *mestizos."*

In these and other instances of San Marcos *mestizo* identification, the individuals concerned are marginal in some sense. Mestizos are often not natives of San Marcos, and they are usually of the low-prestige artisan-laborer class. If government-employed, the San Marcos *mestizos* are distinctly marginal to the community in some sense,

Table 9. Household and Per Capita Monthly Incomes and Land Values for Each Ethnic Sector of Urban San Marcos and San Pedro[a]

	San Marcos			San Pedro		
	Ethnic Status Claimed			Ethnic Status Claimed		
	Indian	Disclaiming Applicability[b]	Ladino	Indian	Disclaiming Applicability[b]	Ladino
Total household income per month						
Mean	$ 63.2[c]	$ 140.3	$ 195.8	$ 81.1	$ 96.0	$ 116.0
Number of cases	18	32	134	88	71	31
(standard error)	(12.0)	(22.5)	(11.6)	(17.5)	(14.6)	(14.3)
Per capita income per month						
Mean	$ 11.9	$ 25.3	$ 59.9	$ 17.4	$ 27.7	$ 27.4
Number of cases	18	32	134	88	71	31
(standard error)	(2.3)	(5.0)	(5.2)	(3.4)	(6.4)	(6.3)

Table 9. (continued)

	San Marcos Ethnic Status Claimed				San Pedro Ethnic Status Claimed		
	Indian	Disclaiming Applicability[b]	Ladino	Indian	Disclaiming Applicability[b]	Ladino
Total value of lands per household							
Mean	$330.9	$2,526.1	$27,159.5	$640.9	$1,434.6	$1,376.2
Number of cases	18	32	134	90	72	33
(standard error)	(143.6)	(1,414.2)	(11,050.3)	(340.1)	(1,138.3)	(586.2)
Per capita value of lands per household							
Mean	$ 59.8	$ 340.1	$ 9,788.0	$129.0	$ 366.6	$ 245.3
Number of cases	18	32	134	90	72	33
(standard error)	(26.5)	(178.7)	(6,811.9)	(52.4)	(285.3)	(92.8)

[a]See Chapter 4, note 7, for sampling details and definitions.
[b]The column "disclaiming applicability" includes those households in which the surveyed informant declined either Ladino or Indian as appropriate. See Chapter 6, p. 205 and Chapter 6, note 7, for discussions of alternatives frequently given.
[c]One quetzal equaled one United States dollar throughout the fieldwork period (1973-1974).

working, for example, in Guatemala City or in a hinterland *municipio*. Whether native or not, none of those claiming to be *mestizo* is important in the political power system of national and regional government.[5] Thus, for them individually, ethnic categorization in the polar extremes of Ladino and Indian would be inappropriate.

In part to bring more comprehensive economic and social data to bear on these open-ended responses, I also explored ethnicity in the 1974 sample survey. In one part of this second survey, the respondents were asked to indicate whether they considered the household head to be (1) Ladino, (2) Indian, or (3) neither Ladino nor Indian; they could also say (4) that they did not know. For computational purposes, the latter two responses are grouped together on the assumption that not being able to specify is perhaps only slightly less a disputation of ethnic categorization than plain rejection of it.[6]

In Table 9, a neutral term—"disclaiming applicability"—is used for those persons choosing not to be termed Indian or Ladino in the survey.[7] Table 9 shows that those who call themselves Ladinos have more income and land assets than do Indians in either town. However, the Ladinos of San Pedro do not differ nearly as significantly from the Indians as do the Ladinos of San Marcos.[8] The greatest differences between the Ladinos of San Marcos and the others are in household and per capita land value.[9]

Those disclaiming polar ethnicity in San Marcos fell between the Ladinos of San Marcos and the Indians of either town, being rather closer to the Ladinos in income (slightly more per household but rather less per capita) but vastly separated in landholdings. The San Marcos disclaimants are higher than the San Pedro disclaimants in both household income and land value, but they are slightly lower in per capita land value.

Interestingly, 44 percent of the San Marcos disclaimants work for the state versus 36.2 percent of the San Marcos Ladinos. This difference seems contradictory to the ideal of government employment by Ladinos. Perhaps it reflects the wide circulation of petty bureaucrats and low-level government workers who term themselves *mestizo* because they are temporarily in San Marcos but are isolated from the social aspect of San Marcos power relations. It may also include some who are from Indian communities and who are correcting their ethnic category to match their new position as petty government-service employees. Superficially, a most surprising figure is that 46.7 percent (seven individuals) of the San Marcos Indians work for the state.

However, four of these are menial laborers in roadwork and gardening, which renders the figure less surprising. Overall, lower landholding figures and higher percentage of government employment with good income are mild (but statistically inadequate) supports for the medial social circumstances earlier suggested for persons in the disclaimant category in San Marcos.

The San Pedrano disclaimants who disavowed the extreme ethnic terminology exceed San Pedro Ladinos in property value, though not by much. This seems contradictory, for the supposition of congruence between the categorical structure and the social and material orders of life would suggest that disputants (largely *mestizos*) should be in between Ladinos and Indians. Clearly, the disclaimants are not like Indians in these economic characteristics. Perhaps their disputation is a symbolic representation of relatively great capital wealth with very little change in the Indian pattern of multiple producers in each household. In this perspective, the positive claim of Ladino status by San Pedranos may represent the full appropriation of the Ladino work ideology and its symbolic ordering of relations. Adopting time consumption and social display on the San Marcos and national Ladino model would tend to reduce the San Pedro Ladino's household per capita income, by comparison with the productive involvement of the family members among the other San Pedranos.

Thus, *mestizo* is a representation of one's economic deviation from one's community ethnic stereotype and of one's medial relationship to individuals in both communities. But the term *mestizo* can only be understood as part of a system that includes "Indian," "Ladino," and the other terms and disclaimers listed earlier. It is a "racial" term that has closely attached to it an ethnic connotation arising out of origin stories highlighting the miscegenation aspects of the conquest. *Mestizo* does not appear to have a set of behavioral indices, such as dress or language, that makes it distinctive from "Ladino." Yet categorically and symbolically (as blood), it is interstitial. Used in opposition to "Ladino," it means lower-status non-Indian. In opposition to "Indian," it means higher-status non-Ladino. This medial term *mestizo* is further evidence that ethnic symbols link to status honor and to centrality of placement in the Guatemalan institutions.

In summary, ethnicity has elasticity and fluidity that accommodate the varied and changing social circumstances as well as the ideological and categorical orientations of individuals. At the same time, the symbolic oppositions of origin imagery impose categorical rigidity over the political relations of the *municipios* by the primary division of status into Ladino and Indian. Thus, in spite of the variety of individual circumstance, there is a rough correspondence between the conceptual, ideological, and symbolic opposition of the two communities and their predominant ethnic sectors and the existence of actual relational differences between them.

The income and land-value figures in Table 9 may be viewed as indices that crudely summarize and point toward the existence of actual differences in position and interaction.

Statistically, the Mann-Whitney/Wilcoxon and Kolmogorov-Smirnov tests on land value and income differentiate the towns taken as wholes.[10] Curiously, the tests do not significantly discriminate the three ethnic sectors from each other within each town for landholdings, though they do discriminate for household income. While the Indians of San Pedro are poorer than the Indians of San Marcos in both income and land values, and the Ladinos of San Pedro are poorer than the Ladinos of San Marcos, neither of these are sufficiently different to warrant a claim of statistically significant difference.[11] By contrast, the medial groups "disclaiming applicability" are statistically quite distinct.[12] This would suggest that, indeed, most of the "Mestizos" in each of the towns are in fact tuning their lives by different processes. Moreover, within either town, the disputants can be classed with either Indians or Ladinos with no major effect on the statistical-separations probability that mean incomes of the resulting groups are not ranked as expected, though either merging ends the statistically probable ranking by land value. But the combination of ethnic sectors that yields the strongest land value and income separations—as occurs when the towns are contrasted—is to class the Indians and disclaimants of San Pedro together in contrast to the disclaimants and Ladinos of San Marcos. The disputants and Ladinos of San Pedro, for example, do not separate statistically from the Indians and disputants of San Marcos. Thus, although Indians are statistically different from the disputants in terms of income (but not agricultural capital) within the San Pedro milieu, as a group they contrast with the disputants and Ladinos of San Marcos in all regards.[13] We are brought back to the conclusion that there is a correspondence between the native conceptual order and the actual system of social relations. To be sure, no native observes the interaction system with a precisely statistical eye. Nor is the statistical eye precise. But it is interesting that gross tests of crude indices suggest sharp differences in position. These results support the idea that the interaction system, in spite of its variety, generates symbols that daily reconfirm the validity of the conceptual order and its ideological oppositions. Both in concept and interaction position, San Pedranos are distinctively Indian and Marquenses are distinctively Ladino with respect to each other and to the nation as a whole, regardless of the internal differentiation among the inhabitants of either community.

So Indians and Ladinos are empirically different and categorically distinct, and Indians are subordinated to Ladinos by the overarching government. Anthropologists have maintained these views for some years, but there is more. The matching structures of categorical and symbolic opposition, and the patterns of inverse ideology evidence a closer connection between Indians and Ladinos than is suggested by the model of the plural society, for the plural-society model asserts that the society is held together only by force and economic need. Clearly, though, the repetitive and pervasive structures of opposition and inversion imply that a single though complex culture bonds the two ethnic sectors.

But the single-culture model, if appropriate, has certain ramifications that can be examined. The several inverse ideologies of the cultural system should consistently penetrate the domestic domain, thereby shaping, informing, and suffusing domestic life with the inverse characters of the status ideologies. Thus, if this single-culture theory appropriately models the social system, then the domestic institutions of both Indians and Ladinos should be consistent with and functionally linked to the larger political and economic structures that encompass domestic life. Moreover, the consistency will be marked by repeated inversions.

By contrast, if the plural-society model is more appropriate, then the domestic domains of the two ethnic sectors should be autonomously and quite arbitrarily distinct from each other. Informed by the heritage of ancient Maya tradition, Indian family institutions should appear arbitrary and inexplicable in relation to the overarching, colonially imposed political economy. Thus, the nature of the domestic domain sharply tests the relative merits of these two views of the fundamental nature of Guatemalan society. To that task I now turn.

Part 3

The Domestic Domains in San Marcos and San Pedro: The Impact of Inverse Ideologies

7
The Kinship System

The recent trend toward using the plural-society model for interpreting Indian and national culture has overcome some of the problems inherent in separating Ladinos from Indians. Even so, the plural-society approach retains a behavioral definition of culture and encourages a theoretical separation of Indian and Ladino family and kinship institutions that is not justified by the data of this study. While the plural-society model as it is applied to Guatemala appropriately views the nation as a single polity and economy, it maintains that there are fundamentally different cultures[1] in the domestic and ritual domains of most plural societies. Colby and van den Berghe, for example, define a plural society as follows:

> Societies are pluralistic insofar as they exhibit, to a greater or lesser degree, the conjunction of two basic features: segmentation into functionally similar corporate groups (whose members frequently, though not necessarily, use different cultures or subcultures); and a social structure compartmentalized into analogous, duplicatory, parallel, noncomplementary, but distinguishable sets of institutions. (1969:7)

The authors go on to say that these distinguishable characteristics of the institutions must not be merely a result of differing functional place or contribution in the system. As they put it, there must be differentiation "into groups and sets of institutions on a basis other than functional differentiation or pure duplication of culturally identical, undifferentiated units (such as lineages or clans)" (Colby and van den Berghe 1969:9). Thus, they distinguish a plural society from the functionally organic industrial societies, revealing that in the plural society the differentiated institutions are functionally equivalent but unrelated to each other in form and that the differences in form of an institution such as the family are not a product of class placement in the society.

The plural-society model postulates a society in which a single political apparatus holds together diverse cultural and economic elements. In Furnival's formulation (1944), each of the distinctive cultures under the polity (usually a colonial government) had its own culturally specific economic needs. Such needs were not necessarily met by production outside each cultural group. Therefore, the cultural groups might be economically separate or not bound together by important economic reciprocities.

In Guatemala, however, Colby and van den Berghe demonstrate that the ethnic segments are linked not only by political force but also by economic reciprocities and Catholic institutions. Thus, the plural nature of Guatemalan society comes from other aspects of social life, most notably from domestic relations and from certain ritual practices.

The feature in each cultural segment that makes the society plural may be a difference in some institution (such as postmarital residence) or in the form of a certain kind of group (such as the household). This appears to be the meaning of such terms as "functionally similar, . . . analogous, duplicatory, [and] parallel." Presumably, two rules of residence are functionally equivalent because they solve the same problem—say, the need for household reorganization at marriage.[2] The key is that these differentiated aspects must be "noncomplementary"; they must not contribute reciprocally to the symbiotic functioning of each other. Moreover, the differences in the parallel aspects of each plural segment must not be molded by or functionally maintain the structure of the political economy. Thus, for example, differences in family organization cannot be a product of or contribute to the cultural group's class, status, or political position in the larger society for the pluralism to exist "on a basis other than functional differentiation."

Most plural-society analysts would probably agree that the domestic institutions of family and kinship are one of the most frequent areas of such noncomplementary differentiation. For example, M. G. Smith, who largely introduced the plural-society model into the literature of anthropology, asserted that cultural pluralism depends on "diversity of the basic institutional system" (1974:82, 85) and that the basic institutions include "marriage," "the family," "kinship," "mating," "family organization," "property rights," "value systems," and other elements (1974:14, 82, 112). Since domestic life is a key domain that makes Guatemala plural and since the central argument of pluralism is that the differences are not linked to social place in the political economy, one way to invalidate the use of the plural-society model in Guatemala would be to show that the differing domestic norms and behavioral manifestations of the plurally viewed ethnic cultures result from status differences at work on the same basic culture. Such is the intent of Part 3 of this book, and it parallels the considerable literature asserting that the domestic domain is always conditioned by the structural pressures of the politico-jural domain (Fortes 1949); shaped by the confluence of jural, economic, and social-status factors (R.T. Smith 1956); bent to the form of economic and governmental requirement (Stack 1974); and infused with the character of the overarching culture and social order (Schneider and Smith 1973).

Domestic life differs between San Marcos and San Pedro as a result of their distinctive positions in the political economy and as a result of the penetration of the inverse, status-linked ideologies into the domestic domain. Thus, the domestic-system variants will be shown to be both systematically consistent with the status system and its ideologies and appropriate to the specific economic and social constraints of each ethnic sector in particular communities.[3] In other words, the domestic-system differences between Indians and Ladinos are related transformations in which status ideologies are the logical multiplier, domestic culture the common constant, and differentiated norms and behavior the transformational product.[4] Such being the case, Indians and Ladinos cannot be different or distinctive cultures, let alone separate societies. They are bound together as transformations within a single sociocultural system. To detail how this is so, we begin with an examination of kinship in San Pedro.

The Kinship System in San Pedro Sacatepéquez

CATEGORIES OF KIN

The key words in any discussion of the social relations within the domestic domain are *familia* and *familiares*. Although both words have a variable semantic range, *familia* displays the richest multivocality. When one asks for the meaning of the word *familia*, a frequent answer in San Pedro is *"padre, madre, e hijos*—father, mother, and children." This response is ambiguous in a certain respect. On the one hand, it may refer to the ideal of a nuclear unit. On the other, it may also refer to an actual household group of that composition. A young man, married and yet living in his father's household, will make the distinction between the nuclear unit and the household by distinguishing *mi familia* from *la familia* or *los de la casa*. Such a contrast isolates his social responsibility for a nuclear cluster—potentially and ideally a household group—from the actual household group of which he is presently a part. Thus, at one level, *familia* is contrasted with a household, and yet, at another level, *familia* is the unmarked encompassing term that means "household."[5] In some cases, there is more than one cooking group sharing a common entrance to a house compound. When used contrastively, *la familia* would then separate the cooking group from the whole compound, which is often inclusively referred to as *los de la casa*.

A further contrast is made between *familia* and *familiares*. This is apparent in one response to a question of what *familia* means: "That which inhabits *(compone)* a house. Now *familiar,* this is outside of the house." On another occasion, I was seeking a genealogical listing and gave no prompting as to terms. After listing the members of his household group, the male informant said, "This is the *familia* of the house. Now, for the *familiarismo* of outside," whereupon the person began to list uncles and aunts. *Familiares,* then, are relatives beyond the household. Actually, they are relatives beyond the household linked by once having been members of the same household of procreation. This is made abundantly clear in those references of parents and children to each other after they have separated to independent households. They term each other *familia* and not *familiares*. One instance of this will suffice (*A* = anthropologist; *I* = informant):

A: What would you call Paco?

I: He is my son.

A: Is he a *familiar* ("relative")?

I: He is my *familia* ("family").

A: But is he a *familiar* ("relative")?

I: No. *Familiar* is used for uncle, cousin, or nephew. *Familia* is used for the two dads *(papás),* the two moms *(mamás).*

A: And a daughter-in-law?

The Kinship System

I: She is *familia*, but she is not a *familiar*.

Thus, the daughter-in-law discriminates the crucial boundary, for she is in the family but not a relative.

Yet, at a higher level, all *familiares* are *familia*. At marriage ceremonies, especially, one hears the word *familia* used in this way. There is talk of a union of the *familias* of the bride, the groom, and the *compadres*. But in ordinary conversation, this level of inclusion is rarely expressed in San Pedro. Except for my notes on marriages, I have no explicit usages or definitions of *familia* at this highest level of generality. As we shall see after comparing the usages of San Marcos, there are pressing structural and ideological reasons why "household" is the primary meaning of *familia* among San Pedranos, though the larger meaning is known and available.

One also hears the term *pariente*. This term has a distinct connotation of social distance. It is used for the fringes of the field one would consider *familiares*, for *parientes* is often defined as *familiares lejanos* ("distant relatives"). A final level of contrast ends the domain of kin. *Familia*, in its most general sense of "kin," is contrasted with *particulares* or "non-kin," the rest of the citizenry in the community and nation.

Thus, a hierarchy of contrast and encompassment exists that is in part responsible for the rich multivocality or polysemy (Turner 1969:41) of the term *familia*. The hierarchy of terms may be expressed graphically in the following way:[6]

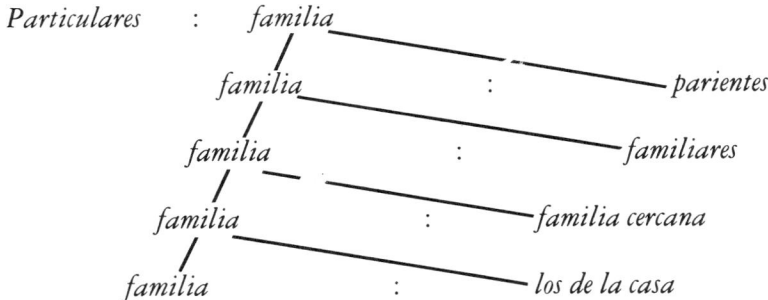

Within the range of *familia* and *familiares*, relatives are designated by whether they are lineal or collateral, senior or junior, and male or female. The San Pedro kinship system is precisely bilateral. Its character is not fully apparent until compared with kinship in San Marcos, and so, after discussing kinship in San Marcos, we will return to a discussion of the kin terms and give a graphic comparison. For now, it is sufficient to note that collaterals are limited to siblings of parents and their descendants. The focus of the terminological system is essentially lineal.

THE NORMS OF KINSHIP

Whether rich or poor, urban or rural, San Pedranos all assert that a recognized kinship connection implies a moral obligation to kindly help one another. The obligation is general and ideally a product of devotion rather than duty. This is summarized in the native expression *cariño*—tenderness, appreciation, and self-sacrificing care. In a word, *cariño* is nonsexual or cognatic love.[7] Examples of this meaning abound. The mother of a bride invited a very dear friend (*amiga pero muy íntima*) to her daughter's wedding because the mother felt for her friend "a special appreciation (*cariño*) like one of the family (*como parte de familia*)."

In weddings, as in other ceremonial contexts, drinks are served in rounds by the various kin groups brought together in the ceremony. Hard candies are passed out after each round of drinks. The sweetness of the candy and the reciprocal exchange of drinks "signifies recompense and the tender feelings (*cariño*) of *familia*." People talk of doing things *por cariño* for relatives but often *por interés* and *amorosamente* for wives, mistresses, or girl friends.

The principle of general helpfulness and trust among kin is exemplified by the natives with statements about what one might do for kin under unusual conditions. San Pedranos speak about helping one another when sick, with visits and gifts of food; of helping another to find work if necessary and possible; or of providing a temporary or even permanent place of residence. Whenever kinsmen are in difficult circumstances, help is expected.

The open-endedness of this principle is well illustrated by a segment of the speeches at a particular wedding, which I shall presently refer to again. The guests and other relatives stood to the edges of the principal room, with the couple, their parents, and their *padrinos* forming a small circle in the middle of the room. First, the father of the groom spoke of the moral obligations of helping one another. He exemplified this by saying, "Perchance when something happens to you, I come and help. And if something happens to me, there you are." To this, the brother of the bride replied that kinship is friendship, not just now but forever. "Let our doors be open to each other. We have created family ties *(familiarismo)* today, [among] all of us."

While the moral obligation of helpfulness, symbolized in *cariño*, is diffusely incumbent on all kinsmen, in any given instance of need, the closer the kin, the greater the obligation. Responsibility *(responsabilidad)* rests primarily with the household group. In emergencies, it is usually extended by seeking or receiving aid of first-degree relatives of the head of the household or his spouse, that is, to his or her parents, siblings, or children. In most cases, these near kin are sufficient to ameliorate any misfortune or need. This narrowed focus of kinship responsibility was expressed by one San Pedro informant who affirmed that "Cousins have a bit *(rasgo)* of relationship *(familiarismo)*, but they do not have [any] responsibility."

Specific responsibilities or obligations are limited to the family: between husband and wife, between parents and children, and between siblings in the same household. (The obligations of spouses are not a matter of kinship and are discussed in the next chapter.) The obligation of a father to his children is to work to provide such food, clothing, shelter, and formal education as he can afford, in addition to informal education *(buena formación,* "good upbringing") through discipline. A mother should see to adequate household functioning, which includes preparing meals, cleaning clothing, and cleaning the house site. In addition, she cares for her children by working for additional cash where practical, by tending household animals in the rural areas, and by teaching good character enforced by verbal upbraiding when occasionally necessary.

Children are expected to abide by their parents' wishes with quiet dignity *(respetarlos)*. The children are expected to better themselves through school. When not in school, the daughters are expected to help their mothers with household chores and, especially, to care for younger brothers and sisters. Older sons not in school should apprentice a trade, work at a profitable occupation, or help their fathers in agricultural or family business tasks.

Children also have an obligation to care for their aging parents and see to the parents' needs. This responsibility is formally built into the role of the lastborn son, in return for which he inherits the house site.[8] Sometimes the brothers will rotate the responsibility for feeding and caring for one or both aging parents, taking them into their respective houses for a month or so in turn.[9] Specific responsi-

Plate 24. San Marcos. A church wedding. (1973)

bilities between kinsmen do not stop with death. Although the details of funerary obligations are described in Chapter 11, San Pedro parents, in spite of shared *cariño*, often fear that their children will not properly care for them or see to their burial needs.

Of course, the mutual obligations of kinship can be nullified by grossly deviant behavior. This is illustrated by other events at the wedding I referred to earlier. By custom, before dawn of the morning after the church ceremony and the celebration at the groom's house, the bride's relatives deliver her trousseau, ideally consisting of a wooden wardrobe containing her clothing, possessions, and some kitchen utensils. On this occasion, the bride's relatives rented a truck and delivered the trousseau. To their surprise, the bride's real (and in this sense, social) father *(mero padre)* had come to the groom's house for the event. Her father had not been present for the previous ceremonies. Worse yet, he had abandoned his wife and children several years earlier, after having lived with them in common-law union, leaving the bride's mother with the task of raising and supporting the children. Because of the abandonment, the bride's older brother had served as ceremonial father and household representative during the wedding. And so the brother also delivered the trousseau to the groom's parents. The groom's father, however, was standing arm in arm with the bride's (and brother's) *mero padre*. Here is the conversation among the principals:

Brother of bride to father of groom:	I come here to deliver you a thing which is very simple but significant. I give you these keys (to the wardrobe, which they had hefted into the parlor *{sala}*), in the name of my mother.
Father of groom to brother of bride:	In the name of her *mother?*
Brother of bride:	Yes.
Father of groom:	*Only* of her mother? Not of her father? Why? Didn't she have a father?
Brother of bride:	(Mumbled something)
Father of groom:	Only of her?
Brother of bride:	Yes.
Aunt of bride:	That's all! (emphatically, *"Solo!"*)
Father of groom:	Only of her? You disparage (*lo tengas despreciado*) your father?
Brother of bride:	My father is my father, but he is only my father. The person who is responsible is my mother, and precisely in her name I came to deliver these (points to keys).
Father of groom:	Not of him? Not of the father? You repudiate (*desconocer*) the father? You repudiate him?
Brother of bride:	No. My father is mine.
Father of groom:	But it is not good that you disparage him. How can that be?

At this point members of the groom's kin group entered the conversation, giving support to the brother of the bride, pleading forgiveness for the bride's and groom's fathers' drunkenness. Other kin of the bride hustled away the bride's father. But before leaving, the father of the groom and the perhaps repudiated father of the bride hugged each other.

> *Father of groom
> to
> father of bride:*
>
> But as a man and as father of his children, they ought to esteem him *(apreciar)*. The father is the father. I esteem the father. To not esteem the father is to not esteem me. I do not want you to depreciate me. The father is the father and you shouldn't depreciate him. That means that men are worthless. That's foolishness.

Perhaps needless to say, the rest of the visit was somewhat tense and the bride's kin went home rather sooner than customary.

These statements recognize fatherhood and its continuity. However, the source of the man's position as *mero* or real father is not a known genetic connection but his former open cohabitation with and economic support of the mother.[10] Thus, the other relatives made their comments about the man being the father but stated that he had abandoned the children and the wife. Although the man's categorical kinship did not terminate, it ought not to have been corrupted by his behavior. And as illustrated in this conversation, reciprocal kinship roles may be placed in abeyance if major offenses are committed.

THE STRUCTURE OF SAN PEDRO KINSHIP FIELDS

In addition to contrasting levels of *familia,* San Pedranos can express social distance with degrees *(grados)* of relatedness. Marriage prohibitions are commonly expressed in this way. For example, with one informant the conversation drifted into kinship and marriage; he expressed the view that marriage is prohibited

> *I:* . . . until the fifth degree of blood relationship *(consanguinidad)*. Until close relationship *(familiarismo cercano)* has completely disappeared.
>
> *A:* Fifth degree?
>
> *I:* These are the children *(hijos)* of great-great-grandchildren *(taranietos)*.

Five links from ego equals five *grados* or degrees. So fourth cousins (children of *taranietos*) might circumspectly marry; third cousins may not. Other San Pedro informants expressed the matter more directly, saying that third cousins *(primos terceros)* should not marry.

Interestingly, neither these informants nor anyone else I met in San Pedro could name third or fourth cousins. The determination of eligibility, to the degree it is abided, is made on a rather different basis. The apical ancestor of a third cousin is the grandparent of a grandparent. If the grandparent of one prospective spouse knew himself or herself to be a cousin of the grandparent of the other prospective partner, then the marriage or union might be discouraged.[11] Since beyond grandparents there is no recollection of connection, the prospective couple is either distantly related because one of the bride's senior living relatives knows he or she is related to a grandparent of the groom, or the marriage can occur. While a courtship is not circumspect if the oldest living lineal relation knows of a connection, the patterns of secrecy in courtship and elopement (discussed in the next chapter) sometimes override this prohibition of marriage.

This is not to say, however, that genealogies are remembered for five generations above ego or that third or fourth cousins are known. Quite the contrary. Genealogies are remembered two generations above one's own position or generation level, whatever that may be. This is a consequence of the household interactions—when a couple takes their children, or family of procreation, to see the couple's parents, or family of orientation. Given the age spans generally, children may frequently interact with grandparents; they are known. But there is no evidence in San Pedro of keeping genealogies beyond the two, or at most three, senior generations alive when one was a youth.

Moreover, a number of San Pedranos only recognized a much narrower field of kinship. Some informants felt that kinship descended of grandparents only—that brothers of grandparents and their descendants were not kin. This greatly reduced vision of kinship was offered by both rural and urban San Pedranos.[12] By comparison with the focus of the relatively wider kinship field that we shall see in San Marcos, the ideology of restrictedness and of atomization has infused Indian kinship and given it a limited character.

In this regard, compare the composite San Pedro genealogy in Figure 1 with the composite San Marcos genealogy in Figure 2. Both of these were constructed using five genealogies that university students in each town did for me in a course on field methods. The

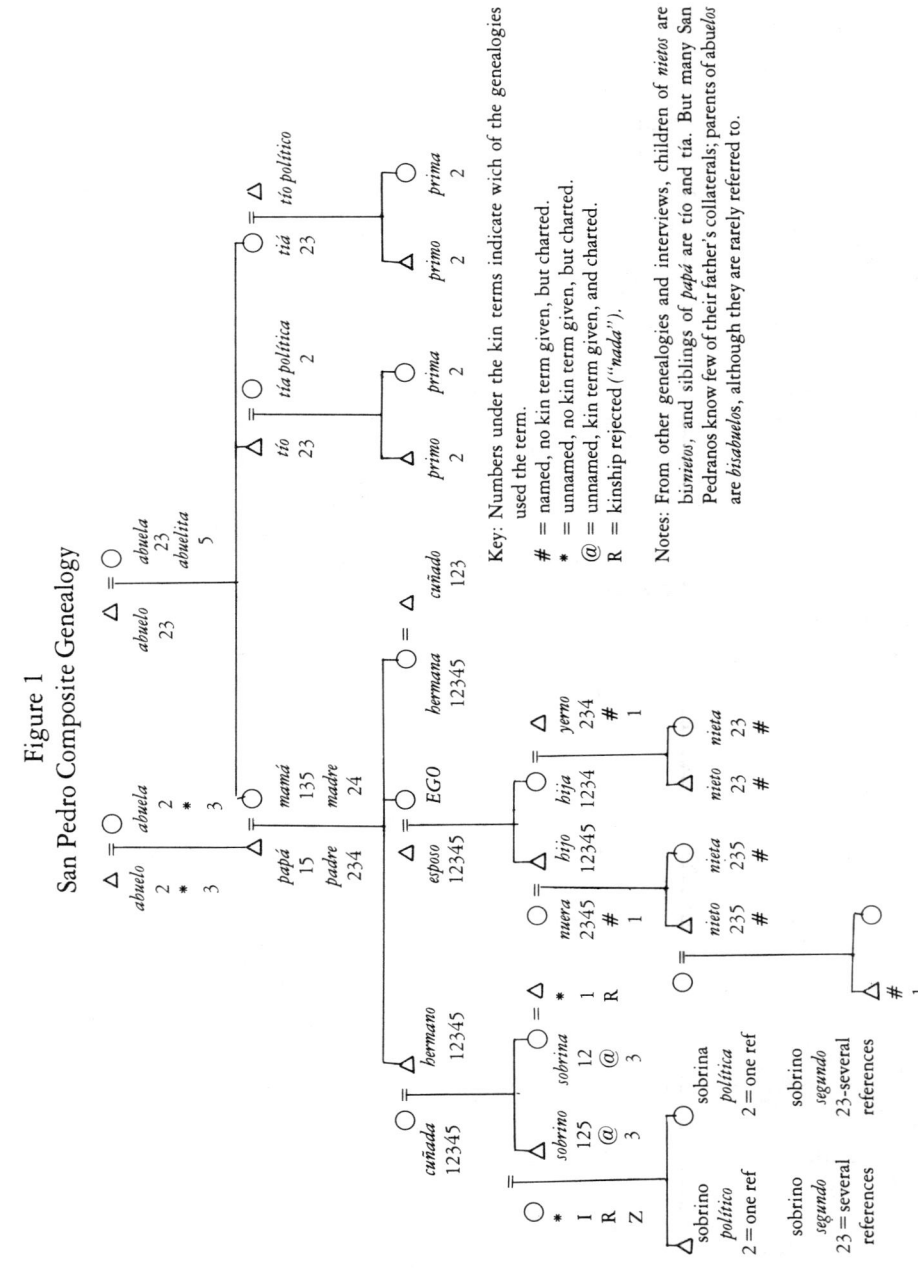

Figure 1
San Pedro Composite Genealogy

Figure 2
San Marcos Composite Genealogy

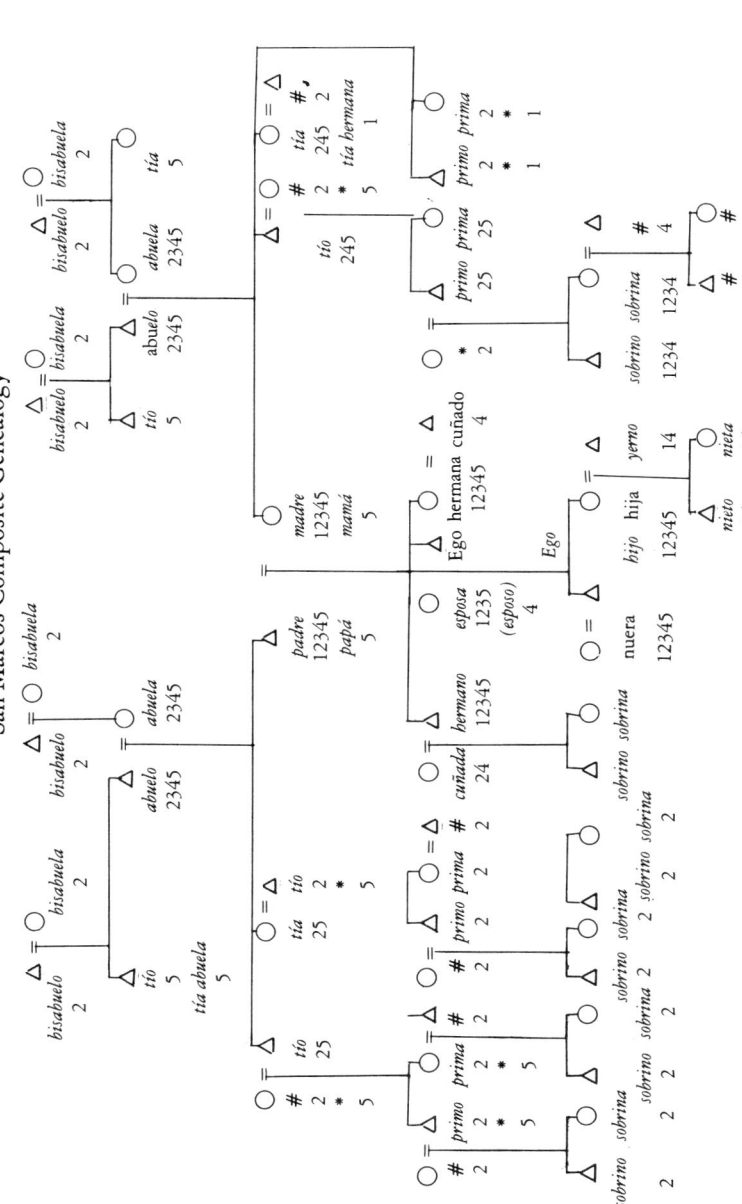

Key: Numbers under the kin terms indicate which of the five genealogies used the terms.
\# = Named, no kin term given, but recorded on chart by native.
* =' Unnamed, no kin term given, but recorded on chart by native.

Note: From other genealogies and interviews, children of *nietos* are *bisnietos*, children of *tío abuelo* are called *tíos*, sibling's grandchildren are called *sobrinos nietos*, and grandchildren of cousins are called *sobrinos en segundo*.

227

genealogies reflect the differences in the degree of genealogical interest when not pushed by an anthropologist to artificial limits. The San Pedro composite is interesting because it skews matrifocally above ego and patrifocally among the descendants of ego's siblings. Furthermore, compared to the San Marcos composite, it is considerably truncated.

The on-the-ground kinship network of an urban San Pedrano concentrates in the *municipio*. For some, a substantial portion of the field of kin lives in the urban center. However, the genealogies of typical urban residents extend at many points into the surrounding *aldeas*, especially if they have recently settled in town. But even persons whose families have lived for generations in the town center will have ties that trace out into these hamlets as a result of marriages between rural and urban persons.

Kinsmen beyond the *municipio* tend to be concentrated in Guatemala City and Quezaltenango. San Pedranos have moved to Guatemala City to go to school, to expand their businesses, to pursue careers, to hide their ethnic background, to take up politics, and to avoid the condemnation of their fellow townspeople for locally rumored excesses in political or social behavior. Although San Pedranos seem to be scattered throughout the city, there is a section of Guatemala City known as *El Gallito*, "The Little Rooster," which is reputed to have a sizable population of San Pedranos, many of them weavers. According to one informant, this zone was largely founded by San Pedranos who named it after the rooster that is always attached to San Pedro's patron-saint icon.[13] A number of expatriate San Pedranos are active supporters of the *Club Shecana*, named for the distinctive wheat loaves called *shecas*, which are made "only" in San Pedro.[14] Another *Club Shecana* is active in Guatemala's "second city," Quezaltenango. These individuals and the respective clubs are important symbolic linkages between San Pedro and the urban centers. As we have seen, urban centers are central to the symbolic order and relational networks of the Guatemalan social system. Representatives of these clubs return to San Pedro for civic occasions and for religious festivals, and they are often invited to speak at public meetings. Unfortunately, I neglected to inquire about San Pedrano kinship interactions with these club members. However, in ordinary genealogical discussions, interaction of urban San Pedranos with their kin in the capital was infrequent except for parents and children visiting each other.

This formulation of kinship interest and behavior appears to be consistent with the main tenets of the Indian status ideology. An ideology of atomization and isolation, imposed on the Indians in the colonial process, continues to define their status. This ideology is manifest in the municipal rather than national political orientations, in the distinctive municipal rather than uniform national styles of clothing, in the self-contained subsistence production and subsistence value of the land, and in the relative freedom of action that the Indians have in what is perhaps the most atomized of all institutions in Mesoamerica, the Indian marketplace. This same ethnic ideology informs the kinship system. In the structuring of relationshps and in the performances expected, the San Pedro system turns inward, focusing on the household, highlighting the nuclear family, concentrating kinship responsibility, narrowly defining the range of kin, and limiting the generational depth. But to see this structure most clearly, we must view it in relation to that of the San Marcos Ladinos.

The Kinship System in San Marcos
CATEGORIES OF KIN

As in San Pedro, the key terms that refer to social relations in the San Marcos domestic domain are *familia* and *familiares*. Again, as in San Pedro, the term *familia* stands at each level of a hierarchy of contrastive oppositions, each usage of *familia* encompassing a contrast below. But there is a difference: the native-born Marquenses who classified themselves as Ladinos and the nonnative Ladinos in San Marcos both tend to focus on the opposite end of the semantic range of *familia*. Whereas for San Pedranos *familia* predominantly means "household" or "nuclear family," for Marquenses *familia* focuses much more often on the wider kin field.[15] To show this, first I establish the parallel hierarchial structure with native quotes. Then I show the wide-field semantic focus of Marquenses.

The contrast between the nuclear family, which is always a potential household form, and the household cooking group is made clear in a quote taken from a family of rather poor residents in San Marcos. I had been exploring the meaning of the word *familia* with a mother, and I asked her of whom it ought to consist. She replied, "The children, the father, and the mother." A few questions later in the interview I returned to the topic of *familia* and asked how many "families" there were in this household. To this she replied,

> There are two *familias*. Well, now there are three. There is me with my two [young children]. There is my mom *(mamá)*. There is my aunt, her husband, and her granddaughter.

She had already taken me on a tour of the household and had pointed out the kitchen, fixed with two hearths and their respective wood and food supplies. I turned the questioning to the issue of the two hearths and the two expense accounts (A = anthropologist, I = informant):

> A: In this house there are separate expenses *(gastos apartes);* how does one talk about this?
>
> I: The two *familias* have their two different expenses *{gastos diferentes*—she corrected me to the more common term}. We are two families here.

At the lowest level, the nuclear family is identified as a potentially independent group nestled in the larger cooking unit. The phrase "two families. Well, now there are three" shows the contrast between the nuclear family seen individually and its context within a cooking group.

If there is more than one cooking group in a compound, then the cooking group, termed *la familia,* can be contrasted with the compound group termed *los de la casa*—"those of the house." But *los de la casa,* as well as *nosotros aquí,* may also mean the cooking group, especially when there is only one in the house compound. These terms may be used for "household," in opposition to *familia,* in which case the latter refers to a "nuclear family" or a dependent nuclear group within the household.[16]

Moving up the hierarchy of terms, *familia* in the household sense may be contrasted with *familia más cerca* or "close family" (technically, "closest family"). "Close family" may be used to refer to the compound group in the more complex households whose cooking-group family heads are siblings rather than parent and child. But more often, *familia más cerca* refers to the persons in the kinship network who once inhabited the same household that the speaking person was raised in. Thus, "close family" includes households headed by parents or siblings of the speaking person.

Los de la casa as well as *familia más cerca* are merged when *familia* is used in contraposition to *familiares* or "relatives." *Familiares* are persons from beyond the households of procreation and orientation who are related "because they have the same blood." In other words, "they come *(vienen)* from" or "they descend from the same family" *(descienden de la misma familia).* As in San Pedro, Marquenses order *familiares* in terms of a social genealogy of distance and degrees, with the socially distant occasionally called *parientes*. *Parientes*, however, is a rare word, much more so than in San Pedro. Finally, *parientes* can be merged under *familia* at the highest level of inclusiveness, when *familia* contrasts with *particulares*. These contrasting and encompassing Marquense usages may be displayed in the same hierarchical form diagrammed earlier for San Pedro.

In contrast to San Pedranos, Marquenses are more likely to use the term *familia* for the entire field of kin. This statement applies with even more force among the elites than among the artisans or "working people." Two examples of the usage will be illuminating. Using the interview model of David Schneider's kinship project, I asked the informants to list their relations *(parentesco)*. One, whose husband was a schoolteacher who worked the weekdays in a hinterland Indian town and returned weekends, responded thus:

> First the children: [first names given]. Now my folks *(papás)*: [name given], my mom; [name given], my dad. My siblings (hermanos): [first names of both sexes given]. Cousins too, right? [No answer offered.] [First names given.] There are so many that I don't remember a lot of them. [More names given.] There are a lot—*mucha familia*. [More names given.] Now nephews and nieces *(sobrinos)*. [More first names given. She stalled a bit, and a six-year-old daughter helped her out. More names.] That's a lot of family *(bastante la familia)*. A whole lot. Now uncles and aunts *(tíos)*? I have a lot of them, but many are dead.

This passage shows the broad focus of the Ladino *familia*.

In another household, the husband *(H)*, a professional-level person, and his wife *(W)* responded together. I *(A)* cued in with *parentesco*:

A: What does *parentesco* mean?

H: All those who are united in the *familia*, who comprise a *familia*.

A: What does the word *familia* mean?

The next two statements were given simultaneously:

H: The group of persons who have bonds *(nexos)* or relations on account of origin.

W: The group made up of (*que tiene*) dad (*papá*), mom (*mamá*), and children.

The husband then spoke to his wife to correct her and buttress his statement.

H: Those who are of the same origin! *Familia* we feel includes my dad, my mom, the children, wife ["or husband," interjected the wife], uncles, cousins—the consanguineal family (*la familia consanguínea*). Now the in-laws (*familia política*): mother-in-law, father-in-law, brothers- and sisters-in-law [i.e., *cuñados*]; that is, siblings (*hermanos*) of each other. And we call the children of a brother-in-law or a sister-in-law *sobrinos políticos*. This is not consanguineal but rather on account of relation to the wife. They call me uncle (*tío*). I call them nephews/nieces (*sobrinos*). This is no longer direct family.

The latter part of the quote refers to descendants of a sibling of a spouse:

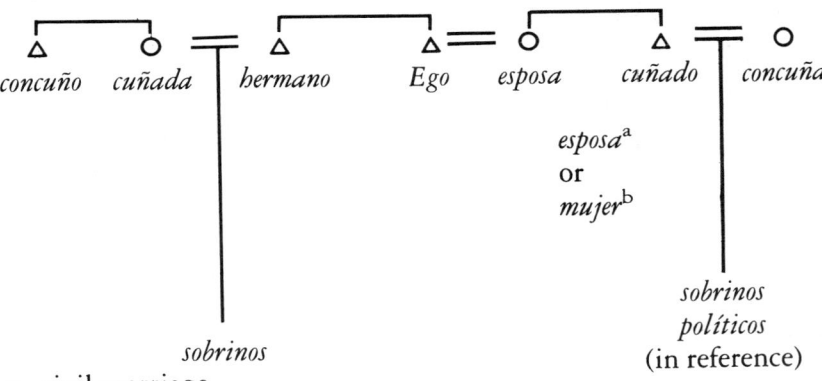

a. civil marriage
b. consensual union (In the case of a female ego, the terms are *esposo* and *marido*.)

While this distinction and social distancing are made in terms of analytical reference, they are never made in ordinary speech, where both spouses refer to their partner's nephews as *sobrinos*. More importantly, the conversation highlights the preferentially inclusive nature of *familia* among elite Ladinos as well as the hierarchically latent nuclear usage.

This "kin-field" orientation for *familia* in San Marcos is manifest in my field notes about twice as often as in San Pedro. More significantly, in San Marcos, wide-field reference is not always connected to formal occasions, as it is in San Pedro. While the figure of two times greater frequency is no doubt a product of pure happenstance, the relatively greater frequency of *familia* as kin-field and the nonceremonial use of this meaning need to be accounted for. Again, the focus on kin-field versus household as the dominant interpretation of *familia* in San Marcos relates to the inverse status ideologies. Ladinos as a status group are ideologically oriented toward the maintenance of wide-ranging relationships generally. This status-linked ideology gives the Ladino kinship, compared with the Indian system, a characteristic spread and breadth. Cultural focus on the most inclusive meaning of *familia* is a domestic manifestation of the Ladino ideology of unity through social interconnectedness. By contrast, the narrowing and atomized Indian ideology places the primary emphasis of *familia* in the household. Because of this difference, Ladino access to political power tends to be enhanced. Furthermore, the broad-field perspective widens kinship access to economic assistance and favors. Thus, these differences in kinship are precisely complementary, for they derive from and are consistent with the system of status ideologies. Moreover, these kinship distinctions are directly and functionally related to the overarching political economy, serving as they do to enhance the political and economic disparities between Indian and Ladino. This, however, is directly contrary to the requirement of noncomplementarity, necessary for a plural-society model.

The inclusive social orientation of Ladino ideology has also affected the system of dyadic kin terms and, as we have seen, the degree to which any particular kin term is viewed as applying to near kin (*familia*) or to more distant kin (*familiares*).

Figure 2 gives San Marcos usages, which form a bilateral system as in San Pedro. But the San Marcos terminology is quite distinctive from San Pedro in several other respects. First, Marquenses use more collateral terms than San Pedranos; for Marquenses the term *familiares* specifically includes *tío abuelo* and *sobrino nieto,* whereas in San Pedro there is no term for these relatives, and such persons are considered *parientes* or distant relatives at best. Moreover, a comparison of Figure 2 with Figure 1 shows that the San Marcos genealogy is more precisely bilateral in the inclusion, for example, of both *primos* and *sobrinos* that are descendants through female links.

THE NORMS OF KINSHIP

As in San Pedro, proper kinship behavior in San Marcos is predicated on the idea of rendering help and is represented in the term *cariño*. San Marcos residents of all social levels and circumstances will give a general statement to this effect or mention a variety of circumstances when various kinds of help ought to be given. But help is also rendered when not urgent, as a social amenity. These native statements manifest the flavor of this general principle among Ladinos (*A* = anthropologist; *I* = informant):

A: What are the duties of kinship?

I: First of all, *cariño*. To try to be united. To protect them and help them. *Mutual* help.

A: Protect them?

I: Moral and economic help.

A: Moral and economic help?

I: To give advice, set examples. Should a cousin's father die, let him feel the support *(respaldo)* of *la familia*, so that he does not feel alone. If a brother dies, one can act as *(representar)* father to the nephews *(sobrinos)* on occasion. When a woman marries, she is accompanied by her dad. If he is missing, an uncle or brother goes [with her].

On another occasion the wife of a rather poor tailor said, "One ought to treat neighbors like relatives: with *cariño*, trust *(confianza)*, lend aid and help." Help, cooperation, visiting, asking, and offering all derive from this axiom of amity. All kin relations bear the imprint of this most general principle of kinship behavior.

The specific obligations of Marquense fathers, mothers, and children to each other are closely similar to the obligations expressed in San Pedro. The main difference is in the degree to which a Marquense woman is expected to contribute to the household economy.

A man is morally and jurally responsible for the nurture and socialization of his socially recognized offspring. Both in the citizen's concept and in the body of law, a father should provide his children with food, clothing, and shelter, and after these, such education as he can afford. The legal adequacy of his provision is perceived and judged in relation to his income. A poor man is not legally delinquent for providing poorly. It is the father's responsibility, in consultation with his wife, to determine how best to allocate their resources toward these ends.

Parents and children are responsible for one another in times of need throughout the life cycle. Sons or daughters, once independent, may rejoin the parental household in San Marcos if their economic position worsens. Or a woman may rejoin her parents if a husband is often absent due to his work or his efforts to finish an education. Similarly, a parent or parents may join a child's household if income or health fails.

These norms are jural; a man who does not so provide for his children or a child who does not provide for his needy parents can be legally sanctioned. A case may be brought up in court; often a deserted wife will sue on behalf of her children if there is sufficient material wealth or income at stake to warrant the effort. Among the very poor that will not be done, as there is insufficient benefit to be gained by court action. Nonetheless, a negligent person is censured in community gossip and will be the object of demeaning remarks by the spouse.

A mother is responsible for the nurture of her children. This includes economic support in the absence of a father, but usually her responsibility is limited to running the domestic household. Her domestic responsibilities include purchasing food and clothing, cooking, cleaning, and washing. In middle- or upper-class households, and often even in the poorest households, the wife will manage one or more servants in these tasks. If the family is quite poor, the wife will perform the tasks and will see to it that the female children learn to do them. Of course, she expects help and geriatric care from her children at the appropriate points in her life cycle.

There is a less passionate concern on the part of Marquense parents for the demonstration of deference by their children than is the case in San Pedro. Respect *(respeto)* is required, though not in the submissive bowing-and-greeting behavior called *mostrando respeto* or "showing respect" that San Pedro children render to adults. While both ethnic sectors subscribe to the idea of male dominance or authority, the relationships where an Indian is dominant are limited by the ideology of public-domain submission, restrictedness, and household orientation. Thus, an Indian exercises control within the household domain over the children. The Ladino, on the other hand, by virtue of the implications of his ideology, exercises control not so much over his domestic children in the household as over the public children—the Indians—in the wider society.[17]

THE STRUCTURE OF SAN MARCOS KINSHIP FIELDS

Compared with San Pedranos, Ladinos' kinship networks are relatively widely dispersed geographically. Marriages are performed that link individuals and families from various parts of the country. This connects in-laws *(consuegros)* to each other at one generation and widens the dispersion of kinsmen for the children of such a marriage. Furthermore, in the life span of many civil servants there is considerable residential mobility, tending toward the capital. Brothers and sisters who inherit a large estate often move to different parts of the country and administer their holdings as absentee landlords without partitioning.

The elite natives of San Marcos will trace their heritage *(herencia)* back to notable old *(de abolengo)* families. This interconnects the descendants of the older families and provides them with ethnically pure, noble ancestors. In San Marcos, the most notable such ancestor is Justo Rufino Barrios, a past president of the country and leader of the reform movement and national modernization of the 1870s. Barrios was born of a wealthy family in what was then a hamlet of San Marcos, and he spent some time in the municipal center of San Marcos. He epitomizes the elite of both San Marcos and of other regions of the country.

Mobility does not affect the Ladino field of kin in quite the same way as it does the Indian. In San Pedro, a move out of the *municipio,* even to the capital, increases the likelihood of genealogical amnesia. For a Marquense this is not the case. Sometimes a move increases a Ladino's importance to the field of kin. This is particularly the case if the individual who has moved is an official with any control over or connection to jobs. Ladino genealogies are not truncated by mobility. Rather, Ladinos maintain a dispersed bilateral geneaology and espouse a status-linked ideology that focuses on interconnectedness and dominance and the maintenance of actual social relations to persons in power. By contrast, Indians are localized, focused on the household and *municipo,* and isolated from usable personal relations to office and power.

Comparisons

KIN TERMS AND STATUS IDEOLOGY

In both communities, the kinship terminology is bilateral and based in the same Spanish lexicon. For lineal relatives, the terms of reference and address are the same in the two communities. However, differences exist in the coverage of the terms, as can be seen by comparing Figures 1 and 2. Ladinos cover more collateral and affinal relatives in their basic terminology. This appears to be a correlate of the Indian premises of restrictedness and atomization and the Ladino inverses of extension, inclusion, and connection.

Beginning with ego's siblings, the urban San Pedrano informant often (and the rural San Pedrano always) distinguishes older from younger siblings (*hermano* versus. *hermanito*). The Marquense seems to make this distinction less frequently unless the context demands such an emphasis for a specific purpose.

Siblings of ego's parents are treated the same in both communities. Parents' brothers are *tío* and sisters are *tía*. The spouse of a *tío* is addressed as *tía* (and vice versa) and may be referred to as *tía* or a *tía política* (or *tío político*, if male). Interestingly, in San Pedro a *político* is not considered a *familiar*, but in San Marcos most spouses of consanguineals are considered *familiares* although they are not consanguineals (*de consanguinidad*). Here the inclusion of affines as *familiares* corresponds with the Ladino ideology of inclusiveness and connection in social relations.

Parents' siblings' children (or first cousins) are called *primos* in both towns. However, in the rural area of San Pedro, such are often called *primos hermanos*. More distant collateral relatives of ego's generation are termed *primo* by both townspeoples. In the San Pedro hamlets, first cousins are often the limit of terminological concern and genealogical remembrance.

Siblings of a grandparent are termed *tíos abuelos* by the Marquenses. That term is not used by the San Pedranos, and they appear to have no alternative for it. Among Marquenses, the children of a *tío abuelo* are *primos tíos* or just *tíos,* and their children are *primos*. If precision is necessary, the latter can be called *primos segundos*. The San Pedranos do not use the terms *tío abuelo* or *primo tío,* but they do recognize *primos* and can specify their degrees beyond first cousin.

Children of ego's siblings are *sobrinos* in both communities. In San

Marcos, the child of a *sobrino* is a *sobrino nieto,* and the child of a *primo* is a *sobrino en segundo.* These two terms were never offered in San Pedro, although I neglected to check if they would be rejected. But their absence or diminished usage corresponds again to the ideological restrictedness and lack of connection among Indians as against the inverse ideology among Ladinos.

Thus, the Ladinos and Indians of the San Marcos–San Pedro region share the same bilateral or categorical structure of kin terms, but the extent to which the system is extended out or pulled in corresponds to their respective status ideologies.

COURTS AND KINSHIP

The Guatemalan legal system regarding the family conforms quite closely to San Marcos and San Pedro precept and belief about kinship responsibility. The close correspondence of native precept and legal prescriptions is due in part to the updating of the family legal codes in 1964.[18] The 1964 revision also made free legal services relatively accessible to people of all classes.

In Guatemalan law, kinship[19] is established in the following way. A child's legal mother is the woman who bears it, unless legal documents override birth and provide another individual through adoption. Either the natural mother or the legally defined one is subject to certain liabilities that are discussed later. A child's father is whichever man established householding relationships with the child's mother 180 or more days prior to the child's birth, or terminated householding less than 300 days prior to a child's birth. A child born to a female in a household having a male associated with it according to these specifications will have a judicially protected claim on that man.[20]

Immunity from this claim can be gained only if the man on whom the claim is made can prove that he was biologically incapable of fertilization or geographically incapable of access during the first 120 of the 300 days prior to the birth of the claimant (Guatemala 1972: 43). The geographical claim is very difficult to make, but a judge told me of cases where paternity was successfully contested by proof of army duty without absence or leave. Biological infertility must be medically substantiated. Interestingly, the legal proof of an adulterous relationship does not nullify paternal responsibility for the issue of the adulterous wife.[21] In effect, both in law and native precept, co-residence symbolizes coitus and presupposes paternity unless the man can prove himself incapable of procreation.

Thus, four premises interact to require careful vigilance, supervision, and control over women. First, the law establishes paternity through mutual householding of unrelated persons. Second, "pure blood" is a crucial symbol of high status, and women must be supervised so as to insure continued symbolic unity. Third, the culture admonishes women to submit to men; hence, women are susceptible to a man's suggestions. Fourth, men are expected to be sexually diverse because sex denotes dominance. Thus, any self-respecting Ladino must control his wife carefully and chaperon his female children—sharply limiting their contacts with other men to safeguard the social status of an elite household's presumed blood purity. Moreover, the control thus exercised affirms the ideal of Ladino dominance. The Indian woman, already of low status, is somewhat more free in public markets and elsewhere but would generally not admit a man to her household without someone to vouchsafe the occasion.

As noted earlier, a man is responsible by law for the protection of his offspring—the offspring of his household. This responsibility is defined legally; he must provide food, clothing, shelter, and education. Claims may be made on a father for the provision of these children's rights. If no man is forthcoming out of moral or legal suasion, a mother may make claims on other relatives after she has exhausted her own capacities for supporting the children. She could even get a legal decision obligating other kin for monthly support or a place of residence. In practice, this is not done because the living arrangements would be too strained. In any event, both in San Marcos and in San Pedro, relatives share what housing they have or take in others' children if needed out of moral obligation.

The legal order of responsibility for providing support and assistance to a person is (1) the person's spouse, (2) the person's children (if adult), (3) the person's parents, and finally (4) the person's siblings. All these except the spouse are relations of first degree. If none of these relations can fulfill the claims that a person might needfully make, then the claims can be extended successively to the fourth degree of kinship.[22] This establishes the institutionalized primacy of jural claims. In practice, the order is different and depends on perception of financial ability and the requisite kinship sentiments. A potentially valid claim often is not made if the claimant judges the economic circumstances of the potentially responsible person too marginal to merit the effort.

With rare exceptions, the only enforced obligations are those economic responsibilities of a man toward his wife or ex-wife (by legal marriage) and toward his children by marriage, common-law residence, or visiting union. When a wife with a nominally ongoing relationship seeks a court decision to remedy her spouse's economic deficiencies, she has effectively terminated the relationship except for its economic aspects. The obligations of a man toward his children are enjoined on the husband after a marriage or common-law union has been terminated. The obligations are translated by the court into monetary demands consistent with his economic level.

A woman is rarely coerced legally to fulfill her domestic obligations. Problems in this area simply result in divorce or separation. If a woman abandons her children, the parents of either spouse will likely take care of them. Equally rarely would a grandparent be enjoined legally for support, but it is possible and it has been done.

Status Inequalities and the Permutations of Kinship

We have seen that these Indians and Ladinos are the same in concepts and symbols of kinship, in terminological relations of nuclear family to household and to field of kin, and in generalized bilaterality. Yet the inverse ideologies of the status system combine with this common culture to generate a number of differences. The focus on the household among Indians versus the focus on the kin-field among Ladinos as a principal meaning of *familia,* the comparative reduction of collateral terms among Indians, and the shallow, truncated Indian genealogies derive from their status-linked ideologies—the Indian atomistic, the Ladino interconnective.

This ideological complex of restrictedness and atomism is not limited to the San Pedro Indian. Rather, it is general to the Indian and is manifest in differing degrees in the kinship systems of other towns and language regions. For example, Ruth Bunzel reports that, in Chichicastenango, there are simple kin terms for bilateral antecedents, siblings, and descendants (Bunzel 1952:410–11) but not for collaterals. True, these Indians can refer to collaterals by compound constructions. But the tenor of Bunzel's book suggests an insignificance of interest in and interaction with relatives other than parents, brothers, and children. Collateral relatives are virtually unmentioned.

The restrictive tendency is quantitatively confirmed in Tax's report of Chichicastenango genealogies. In the numerous genealogies given in his notes, the minimum size was 11 persons, the maximum was 50, and the mean was 28.5 persons (Tax 1947:576). By contrast, Marquense Ladinos subsume even the parents-in-law of one's children under the term *familia* and present the investigator with extensive genealogies. It would appear that the urban San Pedranos play out their medial position—individualistic but nonagricultural—not only by wearing Hispanic clothing and speaking Spanish while claiming to be Indian (or Mestizo), but also by paying more attention to nonhousehold collateral kin and genealogical matters than the Maxeño (Chichicastenango) Indians but less than Marquense Ladinos.

The key to the system of differences lies in the culture of status. Although Nutini (1976:3) accuses anthropologists of intolerably neglecting the study of kinship among Mesoamerican Indians, the suggestion offered here is that the anthropological neglect is a culturally correct reflection of the general Indian disinterest in interconnections. The fact that these differences in kinship focus are status-linked permutations undercuts the common view that Guatemala is a plural society with noncomplementary or distinctive but unrelated domestic domain cultures.

8
Courtship and Marriage

The institutions of courtship and marriage bring men and women of different kin-fields together as the starting point, at least potentially, of new households. The logic of courtship and marriage in San Marcos and San Pedro is an intrinsically interesting cultural system. Beyond this, however, an analysis of the ideological basis for differences in marriage duties further tests the adequacy of the plural-society model and supports the single-culture approach. To accomplish such an analysis, however, one must be careful with the term marriage, for these people recognize several kinds of sociosexual union and call only one of them *matrimonio*. One needs, therefore, a neutral analytic term. In this book I use domestic alliance or conjugal union interchangeably to refer to any institutionalized relationship that links a man and a woman in socially expected rights and duties concerning sexual liaison, responsibility for children, co-residence, economic support, and domestic service. In Guatemala, such domestic alliances can be established through either legal documentation or common-law symbolism. This chapter also treats the equally institutionalized but sometimes less enduring relationships that eliminate co-residence from the package of rights and duties. In all these aspects of their lives, San Pedranos and Marquenses have a common categorical culture, which I now present.

San Pedro Sacatepéquez

CATEGORIES OF DOMESTIC ALLIANCE

The highest status and most "formal *(formal)*" type of domestic alliance is called *matrimonio* and is translated here as "marriage." According to national law, a *matrimonio* "is a social institution by means of which a man and a woman are legally united, with intent of permanence as to the purpose of living together, procreating, sustaining and educating their children and helping each other" (Guatemala 1972:19).[1] In the social scheme of San Pedro, as well as in San Marcos and the rest of Guatemala, there are two varieties of *matrimonio*. The first is a simple legal or civil marriage called *matrimonio civil*. In essence, the civil documentation fixes until divorce the legal status of the partners with respect to each other, their descendants, their kin, their properties, and the state. Moreover, a marriage once instituted engenders responsibilities for children even after a couple divorces. The legal specifications of this relationship are set forth in the family law section of the *Código Civil*, a substantial portion of which is read to the couple and to all witnesses at each marriage ceremony. The second type of marriage begins with a preliminary civil marriage and is followed by an ecclesiastical ceremony in either the Catholic church or one of the Protestant chapels. This is called *matrimonio eclesiástico* or, more commonly, *matrimonio religioso*.

Following their marriage, whether civil or religious, a couple will say of themselves " *Estamos casados*—We are married." A nominal reference to the state of matrimony *(el matrimonio* or *nuestro matrimonio)* is also commonly heard. The flavor of this terminology is embodied in a statement made during a family reconciliation meeting that occurred after a young man, the son of a modestly well-to-do San Pedrano merchant family, had eloped with a poor San Marcos girl and entered common-law union. The participants included the young man, his father, and the father's brother. After entering the San Marcos household, the boy's uncle, speaking on behalf of his brother and nephew, said to the relatives of the girl:

> Pardon us for having to inform you that the [that is, our] youth indeed eloped *(se llevó)* with the girl . . . We came [here] to fulfill *(acordar)* the responsibility of parents—which is to marry *(casar a)* their children, because marriage *(el matrimonio)* is the woman's protection.

The other category of socially legitimate domestic alliance does not have the protection (or the limitation as the people variously see it) of government legalization. San Pedranos (as well as Marquenses) refer to a public but unlegalized co-residence as *unión* or *unión de hecho*. I translate this as common-law or consensual union. Since the status is consensual and has no external legal definition beyond its enactment, people not surprisingly refer to such a relationship in the progressive tenses—"We are *united (Estamos unidos)*"—rather than referring nominally to their *unión* as a possessed thing.

But an *unión de hecho* is not illegitimate in any sense. It is merely less "formal" than a marriage. Based on open co-residence, common-law union is public, but not assertively so. It is acceptable and not demeaning, but it does not enhance one's social evaluation in the community.

After a common-law union of three years' duration, a couple may take neighborhood witnesses to the municipal registry and record their union as a legal marriage. However, most people legalize a common-law union by going through a complete civil marriage ceremony rather than by the legally permissible but unceremonious registration of proof of socially open co-habitation for three or more years.[2]

A married person (civil or religious) refers to his or her partner as *mi esposo* (my husband) or *mi esposa* (my wife). By contrast, the partners in a common-law union refer to each other as *mi marido* (my [male] mate) and *mi mujer* (my woman). This distinction is violated when married people joke with each other or among close friends, or when some common-law couples choose to hide their conjugal status from acquaintances who will not know them long or well.[3]

THE SYMBOLIC BACKGROUND OF COURTSHIP

The pattern of courtship behavior in San Pedro can best be understood against the background of the symbols used to mark the initiation of marriage, consensual union, and formal engagement (*noviazgo oficial*).

In civil marriage the couple walks in a procession of kin and friends to the mayor's chambers, where the mayor or his deputy pronounce the ceremony while others witness. The ceremony entails reading relevant portions of the legal code to the couple and to all present. The parts of the code selected detail obligations assumed with respect to each other. The groom and bride then sign the marriage document, followed by the *padrinos* ("sponsors," that is, "godparents"), the parents, witnesses, and any others present who wish to mark their involvement and consent.[4]

Ecclesiastical confirmation consists of a marriage mass for Catholics or a church ceremony for Protestants. For the religious confirmation, the couple walks from the mayor's chambers to the church where the rites are performed. On one occasion there was a delay of several days between a civil and the religious ceremony, supposedly because the civil offices had been booked by other couples on the day that the church was available.[5] If the parents of the couple are interested in the social benefits of a festive celebration, and if they have enough money, the church ceremony will then be performed, for it connotes social status within the community. The young people seem less concerned; no one said they would not get married if they couldn't do it in church.

Consensual union is distinguished sharply from illicit or transitory sex liaisons by a public assertion that a responsible relationship exists. Thus, when a youth and a girl in the process of their courtship decide to live together, they determine that on a certain date the girl will slip out of her household and meet the boy at a particular spot. From there, they walk to the boy's home. Ideally, he leaves the girl outside and enters to announce to his father the decision to live with a woman, the one he has brought with him. The father then steps outside and asks the girl if she comes of her own accord. This confirmed, the girl steps across the threshold, and arrangements are made for them to have sleeping quarters that are as private as the household facilities permit. Alternatively, the boy may bring the girl inside where the girl is interviewed by the father or by some other responsible relative. In either event, the interview with the father begins to establish the public nature of the union-to-be as well as the intended social responsibility for the girl. Regardless of where the interview is conducted, stepping across the threshold of the boy's parents' house is a momentous occasion, for it indicates submission to the young man and his parents. In short, crossing the threshold symbolizes common-law union.

Subsequently, the father and other relatives and, nowadays, the young man will go the girl's parents to announce as *fait accompli* the disposition of their daughter.[6] It would appear that the essential symbolic effect of having relatives other than the father or the youth make these announcements (as well as enter into premarital negotiations) is that the union is thereby made more public, open, and socially responsible. This is also the case with the initiation of a consensual union by entry into the father's household; the intent of social responsibility is openly established through parental involvement in consent at the threshold.

These steps apply ideally to the first union. Subsequent unions, or unions formed after a death, divorce, or abandonment, are more casually entered into. But the essential fact is that a girl who steps across the threshold of the house of a non-kinsman—except at a public fiesta, or when chaperoned or accompanied by a group of friends—symbolically communicates consensual union. And if that is not the case, the girl may be subjected to severe gossip.

For somewhat parallel reasons, a youth cannot enter the household of his girl friend (*novia* or *traida*). If the parents are not there, immorality is presumed. If the parents are home, then parental consent to the boy is implied. Unless one has the good fortune to attend a party or family ceremony, the only proper occasion to enter the girl's house is with one's relatives, to make a formal request for betrothal. Young men do not go into their girl friends' houses alone because, as one San Pedro youth put it, "It is too much commitment (*compromiso*)."

Nevertheless, on one occasion I did see a girl of high-school age in the home of the son of a San Pedro professional, but it was in midafternoon, the parents were home, and the meeting was ostensibly concerned with completing a school assignment. It would appear that the clear expectation of a civil-ecclesiastical marriage among upper-class families makes it less necessary for upper-class young people to strictly avoid entry in one another's households.

For the most part, however, the symbolic value of the threshold forces the young male San Pedranos to court "in the streets." *Andando en la calle,* they and their parents call it (though this may also refer to associations and activities other than courtship). As dusk approaches and gives way to the night, groups of fellows stand on the corners of the streets, conversing and joking with each other but always keeping an eye open in the direction of the front entry to the house of their established or hoped-for girl friend. As soon as she appears, the interested fellow abandons his friends and moves to further his acquaintance with the maiden.

The girl, for her part, must extricate herself from her own household. This is done by arranging an errand for some minor supply for the household—a trip to the bakery or to the corner penny grocery, a visit to a relative's house to borrow something or to learn a crochet stitch. This errand is called "the pretext (*el pretexto*)." Both the parents and the girls know that this is so, but for the parents to consent to a *salida* ("excursion") without an announced *pretexto* is to consent to a liaison with the young man. In theory, the parents say they would give a beating (and most girls say they would get a beating) if their child's meetings under pretext were discovered. Again, for the parents to suggest otherwise would be to imply consent. So the couple keeps to the shadows for the brief time that they can extend the errand. In fact, however, the parents seriously seek to thwart the meetings only if the girl is too young or if, through the gossip of others, they discover both who the boy is (as they well might) and that he is in some way undesirable.

While girls have less overt freedom than the boys "in the streets," they do manage to make themselves visible to the fellows. They may, for example, sit on the front stoop knitting by the light from inside the house. (Pretext: It is too hot inside.) Or they may join a group of girls for a Sunday afternoon promenade on the plaza. Finally, on major fiesta nights, they may attend the dances with their mothers, aunts, or spinster relatives. The spinster is known to the young men as *la señorona* ("the Big Mrs.") or as *la roca* ("the rock").[7]

CONJUGAL BEHAVIOR AND INDIVIDUAL CIRCUMSTANCE

Mainly, adult San Pedranos live in legalized domestic alliances. For example, from my sample survey the household head's most recent domestic alliance is reported to be legalized in 71 percent of the cases. Marriage, however, is dynamic. Sixteen percent of the total population (or 36 percent of all who began in common union) had subsequently legalized their initially common-law union. The full data are presented in the left half of Table 10.

The left half of Table 10 includes both currently co-resident couples and those who have separated for one of several reasons. A few (7 cases = 3.6 percent) are separated by their current work conditions. Some are widows (18 cases = 9.2 percent). Some are divorced or legally separated (10 cases = 5.1 percent). Some separated de facto (5 cases = 2.6 percent), while others never entered domiciled alliance (6 cases, with 1 case = 0.5 percent having children, and 5 cases = 2.6 percent having no issue). The right half of Table 10 eliminates single household heads and shows the percentages of each type of domestic alliance among the currently co-resident couples. One notes that the percentages for the various legal statuses of alliances among the currently co-resident couples are not markedly different from those of the present or most recent alliance of all household heads.

To see what impact money has upon the category of conjugal union, let us look now at the relationship between wealth and the

Table 10. Legal Status of Household Head's Domestic Alliance in Urban San Pedro Sacatepéquez[a]

	Most Recent or Current Alliance		Currently Co-resident Alliances	
	Number of Households	%	Number of Households[b]	%
Consensual union of less than 3 years	5	2.6	5	3.3
Consensual union of 3 years or more duration	46	23.5	35	23.3
Civil marriage only (including legally recorded conversions of common law unions)	54	27.6	41	27.3
Ecclesiastical marriage (including a civil ceremony)	85	43.4	69	46.0
Never entered an alliance (that is, single household heads)	6	3.1		
Totals	196	100.2	150	99.9

[a]See Chapter 4, note 7 for sampling details and a definition of "urban."
[b]Forty-six household heads were without a spouse and, therefore, do not appear in the right half of the table.

legal status of currently co-resident domestic alliances. This is presented in Table 11. Table 11 suggests consensual union, especially recent consensual union, is indeed a poor-people's phenomenon, though I must note that the San Pedro mean of $92.40 is within this lowest category. Above $200 income per month there is a decided favoring of ecclesiastical marriage. However, the considerable percentage of ecclesiastical marriages in the lowest incomes reflects some detachment from strictly wealth considerations. Nor do the standard statistical tests imply that wealth is a major differentiating factor in type of union.[8] In San Pedro, total household income is not a sharply significant factor in determining the social and legal status of conjugal unions. Regarding the value of lands owned, the statisti-

Table 11. Relation of Current Household Income to the Legal Status of Coresident Domestic Alliances of Household Heads in Urban San Pedro[a]

	Household Income in Dollars per Month															Row Total and CC's
	0-100			101-200			201-300			301-400			400 or More			
	#[b]	%IG[c]	%CC[d]	#	%IG	%CC	#	%IG	%CC	#	%IG	%CC	#	%IG	%CC	% of Total
Consensual union of less than 3 years duration	5	4.2	100.0	—	—	—	—	—	—	—	—	—	—	—	—	5 3.3%
Consensual union of 3 years or more duration	30	25.2	85.7	4	26.7	11.4	—	—	—	1	25.0	2.9	—	—	—	35 23.3%
Civil marriage only	34	28.6	82.9	4	26.7	9.8	2	25.0	4.9	—	—	—	1	25.0	2.4	41 27.3%
Ecclesiastical marriage (including civil ceremony)	50	42.0	72.5	7	46.7	10.1	6	75.0	8.7	3	75.0	4.3	3	75.0	4.3	69 46.0%
Column total and IG's % of total	119	79.3%		15	10.0%		8	5.3%		4	2.7%		4	2.7%		N = 150 100.0%

[a] See Chapter 4, note 7 for sampling details and a definition of "urban."
[b] # = Number of cases
[c] %IG = Percentage of income group
[d] %CC = Percentage of the conjugal category

cal measures showed no relationship of land wealth to conjugal status.[9] Consequently, the tabular material is not reproduced here.

In summary, individual circumstance, insofar as this is represented by reported income or land assets, does not sharply correlate with the kind of domestic alliance within which a San Pedrano chooses to live.

THE NORMATIVE CONTENT OF THE MARITAL RELATIONSHIP

A husband is expected to work and earn money to contribute to his household. Interestingly, I encountered no instance in San Pedro where husbandly duty is expressed solely in terms of money—though this is almost exclusively the case in San Marcos, as we shall see. Indeed, the San Pedro expectation of both men and women is that the husband will not have *vicios* ("vices"). Vices are defined as laziness, careless expenditure through drunkenness or betting, and womanizing *(mujereando* [verb] *mujeriego* [adjective or noun]). Ranking men by expectations that focus not on variations in money but on differences in industriousness and the acquisition of a trade is another domestic-domain manifestation of the Indian work ethic and the relatively equalitarian Indian ideology, which ranks people morally according to their performances rather than according to their assets and social connections.[10]

For the woman, the expectation is that she will be moral (that is, sexually confined to her spouse as manifest through the observance of circumspect behavior); that she will provide the domestic amenities by preparing food, maintaining clothing, and keeping an orderly house for her spouse and children; and that she will work wherever possible to the direct economic benefit of the household. Said one gentleman from San Pedro,

> The young man ought to have a trade, his funds *(centavitos)* for living separately. And the wife *(esposa)* has to work to help her husband. [Problems come] when there isn't any understanding *(comprensión)* or when women *(mujeres)* are very demanding of money and the husband doesn't have any.

Notice, however, that the excessive expectation of money is labeled more a fault than the absence of funds.

NOTES ON ILLICIT RELATIONSHIPS

If a man contributes money to a second household regularly, and is known in gossip to have exclusive access, I call it a *sub-rosa union*. Several instances of concurrent sub-rosa unions came to my attention.

The married wife of a man engaged in a sub-rosa union refers to the other household by saying that her husband "supports *(mantiene)* another woman *(mujer)."* The second woman in such an arrangement is commonly called a *casera* (a term perhaps best rendered as "kept woman"), and the socially defined wife *(esposa)* will refer to her as her husband's *mujer por allá* ("woman on the side"). The male supports the second household in return, purportedly, for sexual and commensal rights. But a man will usually spend considerably more time with his socially recognized wife *(esposa)* than he will with his ostensibly sub-rosa *casera*. Particularly, he will sleep the nights with his wife and visit the *casera* much more briefly and even very irregularly. There is more than one instance, however, of San Pedrano men with extensive business dealings in the capital or in other major cities who maintain consensual unions in towns where they reside during their business trips.

I did not conduct a vigorous inquiry into these relatively covert relations. However, some of them were brought to my attention repeatedly. Thus the following comments on frequency may be made, although quite guardedly. The professional-level elite (referring to the native-born) and the wealthy businessmen and transporters are the only ones who can easily support secondary households. In each of the instances for which I have information, the secondary partner also contributes to her own support, usually through a petty household industry or sale outlet but in one instance through salaried employment. My best estimate is that between a third and a half of the professional or wealthy male household heads continuously maintain a subsidiary household. One man is reported to maintain four households and another ten, although the legally espoused wife of the latter is now divorced from him.

More casual visiting unions also exist, but it was impossible for me to ascertain their prevalence. In the one visiting union that I did come to know fairly well, the man visited a woman whose common-law husband had abandoned her. Her children told me he was a *padrastro* ("stepfather"). I had thought, having seen the man there repeatedly, that he was a common-law partner. Not until much later was I informed that he just comes, not sleeping there too often, and that he was not considered a *marido* (common-law spouse) or a source of support. Such a relationship might be viewed as somewhere toward the middle of a continuum between a common-law union, with continual residence and relatively exclusive mutual support, and the temporary illicit relationship with only furtive interaction. As to the frequency of such casual visiting unions in San Pedro, I cannot even hazard a guess. In male verbal lore, and in the instance I became familiar with, visiting unions are associated with widowed or abandoned women.

San Marcos

CATEGORIES OF DOMESTIC ALLIANCE

As in San Pedro, the Marquenses also distinguish between socially acceptable and socially unacceptable unions, also dividing them by using the same terms. As one Ladino, born in an eastern department but for fourteen years a resident in San Marcos, stated, "Marriage *(el matrimonio)* and consensual union *(unión de hecho)* are the two preferred and socially recognized." He went on to say that the ones which are not preferred include "carnal union *(unión carnal),*" which is "just for sex," and "concubinage *(concubinato),*" which is "having a woman *(mujer)* on the side *(por allá)* without fulfilling *(reconocer)* one's duties of [that is, entailed by] lovemaking *(deberes amorosos)*." Thus the same terms for marriage (civil or ecclesiastical) and consensual union, as well as the same terms for spouses under marriage or union, apply in San Marcos as in San Pedro and the meanings of these terms in the two towns are identical.

THE SYMBOLIC BACKGROUND OF COURTSHIP

The symbol of crossing the threshold is also the same in San Marcos as in San Pedro: it means that a consensual union has begun. Thus, girls must not and do not enter into a boyfriend's house unless chaperoned. Similarly, a great deal is read into the relationship if the young man enters the girl friend's household. A woman, whose husband is the chief of staff for the head of one of the largest bureaucratic offices in San Marcos and an important member of the Lions Club, had this to say about the events of her daughter's courtship while the daughter was still in school:

> [The boyfriend] asked permission to enter our house. Her father [that is, my husband] prohibited this in order to avoid the possibility of her dropping her studies. . . . If one grants permission [for a boy] to enter, it is all right. But if they [subsequently] fight and separate, the people would say, "They

gave permission [for him] to enter, and now he left her." That is how the honor of the girlfriend is destroyed by gossip. [They say] "now he [has] entered, now he is the fiancé *(novio oficial)*." That is how people think and thus it is much more difficult to break off *(dejar)*. Around here there is this meaning of "fiancé" because now [a boy] has obtained permission from the family.

As in San Pedro, the presumption of ecclesiastical marriage among the elite Ladinos reduces somewhat the significance of a girl entering a young man's home or the boy entering the girl's house. In San Marcos, also, I only once saw a young man in a girl's home without a companion, or party to justify the visit. In this instance, a visiting male university student (of a well-to-do professional family formerly of San Marcos) repeatedly entered the home of a professional-level family. Because the parents wanted their daughter to marry the young man, the courtship was exceptional only in its lack of chaperoning. This courtship did not endure, however, and the girl extricated herself, apparently without a blemished reputation. I suspect that, as in San Pedro, the social importance among the elite of a religious marriage makes less compelling the threshold symbol for consensual union. But few youths of opposite sex enter each other's homes unless committed, if for no other reason than the possible ambiguity of interpretation.

In San Marcos, too, for the most part the youngsters must court one another "in the street *(en la calle)*". However, for many Marquenses the high schools provide a more open place to meet to pursue a friendship. Most middle-class and all upper-class Marquenses, as well as the aspiring wealthy of San Pedro, send their children to a private, expensive high school, thus enhancing the marriage market and the social closure of the relatively well-to-do. If the youths courting here wish to see each other after school, a meeting must usually be arranged "in the street," on the basis of a "pretext," and at an appointed time. For the children of Marquense artisans and occasional workers, as for those in San Pedro, it is strictly courtship "in the street" unless the family makes an effort to sacrifice for the education of their children (which many do). In San Marcos, too, clusters of young men watch the appointed doors for the hoped for *salida* (exit) while here and there couples talk and sometimes even embrace in the shadows of an unused doorway, behind a utility pole, or in some other place partially protected from view. And as in San Pedro, they often try to hide their interest in each other should the

Table 12. Legal Status of Household Head's Domestic Alliance in Urban San Marcos[a]

	Most Recent or Current Alliance		Currently Co-Resident Alliances	
	Number of Households	%	Number of Households[b]	%
Consensual union of less than 3 years	4	2.2	3	2.4
Consensual union of 3 years or more duration	63	34.2	43	35.0
Civil marriage only	37	20.1	25	20.3
Ecclesiastical marriage (including a civil ceremony)	69	37.5	52	42.3
Never entered an alliance (that is, single household heads)	11	6.0		
Totals	184	100.0	123	100.0

[a]See Chapter 4, note 7 for sampling details and a definition of "urban."
[b]Sixty-one household heads were witout a spouse and, therefore, do not appear in the right half of the table.

headlights of a taxi or of a wandering anthropologist's van perchance flash upon them.

The ethnic division between San Pedranos and Marquenses has been sufficient to prevent courtship associations in the private school from generating a single elite group that bridges the two communities. There is some distance among the students, due to ethnic prejudice. And the San Pedranos who successfully connect into the Marquense elite sever their social ties with San Pedro and claim Ladino status.[11] As we have seen, this practice maintains the isolated political and social network of San Pedro and thus it remains an Indian community, even though its members become Ladino in their persons.

CONJUGAL BEHAVIOR AND INDIVIDUAL CIRCUMSTANCES

The frequencies of the types of domestic alliance in San Marcos differ somewhat from those of San Pedro. In San Marcos, too, the legal unions predominate, although in the rather lesser degree of

57.6 percent (versus 71 percent for San Pedro). Slightly less than 11 percent of the total population had legalized an initially common-law union, as indicated in Table 12.

Paralleling Table 10 for San Pedro, Table 12 regarding San Marcos is presented in two halves. The left column gives data using the current or most recent domestic alliance of all the household heads. Among Marquenses, 6.5 percent (12 cases) of the couples are separated by their work arrangements, although they consider themselves to be viable couples. Other household heads who do not have a co-resident spouse include the widowed (23 cases = 12.5 percent), the divorced and legally separated (2 cases = 1.1 percent), couples who separated without legal sanction or abandoned each other (14 cases = 7.6 percent), and heads of households who were never married (9 cases, with 6 cases [3.3 percent] having children and 3 cases [1.6 percent] claiming none).

As in Table 10, the right half of Table 12 presents the statistics only for those unions which are currently co-residential. San Marcos (Table 12) mirrors San Pedro (Table 10) in that the right column (current co-resident unions) is not significantly different from the left column (most recent unions) except for a slight increase in the percentage of ecclesiastical marriages.

WEALTH AND CONJUGAL UNIONS

Is there any relation between household income and the category of one's conjugal union in San Marcos? The answer to this question is yes—and rather more clearly so in San Marcos than in San Pedro, as a comparison of Tables 11 (San Pedro) and 13 (San Marcos) shows. In Table 13 we see a sharper rank correlation of legal status with household income. Ecclesiastical marriages take a progressively larger percentage of each income group, starting lower (28.1 percent versus 42.0 percent) in the lowest category and ending higher (100.0 percent versus 75.0 percent) in the highest category. Statistical tests show that the distribution is not likely a matter of chance; Table 13 shows a significantly (though not too closely) ranked correlation between income and type of union, and the means and distributions of the common-law compared to the legal and ecclesiastical unions are significantly different.[12] The rank correlations, however, are not overwhelming because the system is complex, but in San Marcos income is a rather more important variable than in San Pedro.

While there is a strong tendency in San Marcos for the elite to

Table 13. Relation of Current Household Income to the Legal Status of Co-Resident Domestic Alliances of Household Heads in Urban San Marcos[a]

	Household Income in Dollars per Month															Row Total and CC's
	0-100			101-200			201-300			301-400			400 or More			
	#[b]	%IG[c]	%CC[d]	#	%IG	%CC	#	%IG	%CC	#	%IG	%CC	#	%IG	%CC	% of Total
Consensual union of less than 3 years duration	2	3.1	66.7	1	3.3	33.0	—	—	—	—	—	—	—	—	—	3 2.4%
Consensual union of 3 years or more duration	27	2.2	62.8	2	40.0	7.9	3	21.4	7.0	1	12.5	2.3	—	—	—	43 35.0%
Civil marriage only	17	6.6	68.0	5	16.7	20.0	2	14.3	8.0	1	12.5	4.0	—	—	—	25 20.3%
Ecclesiastical marriage (including civil ceremony)	18	8.1	34.6	12	40.0	23.1	9	64.3	17.3	6	75.0	11.5	7	100.0	13.5	52 42.3%
Column total and IG's % of total	64	52.0%		30	24.4%		14	11.4%		8	6.5%		7	5.7%		N = 123 100.0%

[a] See Chapter 4, note 7 or sampling details and a definition of "urban."
[b] # = Number of cases
[c] %IG = Percentage of income group
[d] %CC = Percentage of conjugal category

mark their social alliances ceremoniously and expensively by means of a church marriage, this is not invariably the case. One man, descending from a family of longstanding cultural-elite status who had begun a consensual union while he was away from San Marcos pursuing his university education, said this:

> We are thinking about marrying *(casarse)* civilly, in order to fix up the papers [that is, acquire civil documentation for their children.] But it doesn't matter, really. The two surnames are [socially] recognized. Our union is enduring and that is what matters.

Thus, it would appear that the social ceremony is not as important if one has temporarily moved out of the social network in which one's hierarchical position is determined.

In San Marcos there is some tendency for conjugal status to correlate with the value of one's landholdings.[13] Here, the social milieu has a great deal to do with the legal status of the marriage. However, the ecclesiastical ceremony does not make a legitimate domestic alliance out of an inappropriate consensual union. Rather, it communicates the highest social ranking of the series of legitimate and enduring domestic alliances, including consensual union, civil marriage, and church ceremony. This does not mean that the series (church, civil, or common-law) correlates directly with the ranked ethnic groups or with the class divisions in each ethnic group. Ecclesiastical marriage does not mean that the participants are of elite status; rather, it means that, whatever the social milieu of the participants may be, they are attempting to enhance the social significance of their action. However, the economic and social elite of San Marcos are more usually concerned with such status communications. I am not sure why such a high percentage of the Indians in the lowest income group sustain the cost of a church wedding, but I suspect a combination of factors. First, religious activity is appropriately Indian, regardless of one's wealth. Second, a church ceremony is essential for participation in the ecclesiastical fiesta system, which is mentioned little in this book but treated at length in W. R. Smith's *Fiesta System and Economic Change* (1977). Third, San Pedro is more thoroughly Protestant, and the Protestant *evangélicos* require a church wedding.[14]

NORMATIVE CONTENT OF THE MARITAL RELATIONSHIP

Among all levels of the San Marcos non-Indian population, the primary expression of the male partner's role in the marriage is that he should provide money for the household's expenses. One hears both men and women state that so long as the expenses of the household are provided women have no further claim and should not complain about their conjugal partner's behavior.

Women, in return, are to be sexually exclusive, circumspect in their social contacts, tidy in the house, and servile *(servicial)* regarding meals, clothing preparation, and other maintenance duties performed for their spouses. Said one young woman,

> Problems often come when [the husband] has many friends. Or if he insists on having [another] woman. There is argument. Then the husband leaves ["splits" would be the best colloquial translation]. It is better to keep quiet. Sometimes the woman errs *(hace mal)* by disrespecting him *(hacerle desprecios)* through not working, cooking, or attending to him.

We see here that the women are not indifferent to their spouses' escapades, but they sense themselves unable to take corrective action. Thus, women claim they "suffer a great deal *(sufren mucho)*." Yet, while both sexes assert that sexual relations peripheral to a conjugal union are morally improper, both sexes also affirm that men have a "right" to such "liberty *(libertad)*."

In contrast to San Pedro, San Marcos women are not expected to work. They may work if they wish, as in the case of a number of middle-class female teachers and a few shopkeepers whose husbands also work. Or they may have to work, as in the case of abandoned women, the widows, and the very poor. As noted earlier, *ladina* women expect and prefer to have servant help in the household, and even some relatively poor families have a live-in Indian *muchacha*. Thus both communities function within a single communication system, where wives are additional symbols of the men's social status, and work versus leisure and display are crucial signs of ethnic status.

NOTES ON ILLICIT RELATIONSHIPS

At the professional level, one of the professional men lived with a woman *(mujer)* in consensual union and was purported to have other *mujeres* and a wife *(esposa)* in other towns. A department-level official in one of the government offices gave considerable support to the household of a local divorcée in return for access to a daughter. But this official was not the sole source of support, for the mother was married to and living with another divorcé. Rumors of liaisons circulated about several other professional men. The wives of these men were quite fastidious in accompanying them whenever possible, but the men did not seem to maintain dual households in the local communities of San Marcos and San Pedro (or elsewhere that I know of). In the town scandal, a doctor was seeing the daughter of another professional.[15]

Among the artisans and poorer Ladinos, men spoke of occasional sexual liaisons, but these relationships did not develop into concurrent households. For financial reasons, they couldn't. At this economic level, a frequent visiting union or a secondary household would rupture the primary domestic alliance, since it would drain the finances of the spouse's household. But if a liaison does not strain the finances of the household, the wives suggest that it be overlooked as a passing *ilusión,* best forgotten if discovered.

It is interesting to compare the views of husbands and wives on the nature of illicit unions. In San Marcos, the lower- or lower-middle class men would refer to an illicit relationship beyond marriage as an *aventura.* (The ready English cognate would be "adventure," but it also implies "daring" as well as "chance occurrence.") The discussion of such escapades is carried on with a chuckle, a brightened eye, and a quickened interest. It is considered good fun, inconsequentially immoral but risky; something in which one engages willingly but with care and discretion insofar as possible. Those married males who do not exercise some care and camouflage are considered to have gone a little bit *loco* ("crazy").

The woman's point of view is rather different about this kind of behavior. For the woman such activities on the man's part are labeled *ilusiones*. (Here the obvious English cognate is "illusions," and that word pretty well sums up the woman's viewpoint of her husband's wandering interest.) As long as a man's illusions do not interfere with the economic support of the woman who considers herself the legitimate social wife, whether consensual or legal, she will tend to tolerate or to overlook his activities and not confront him. However, when the man's outside behavior begins to affect the economic foundations of the home, as it often does, then the socially legitimate spouse will respond rather vigorously by quarreling and by withholding domestic services. If proper financing is not restored, this often brings about a rupture of their marriage or union. Only occasionally will it bring about the rupture of the outside relationship.

Why should this be so? Why would the marriage break up? Is it because the desired physical attributes of the wife (as defined by Marquenses) have worn out, to be replaced by those of a paramour?

A number of residents remarked how homely a few of the consorts were, by comparison with the legitimate wives. In such cases physical beauty would not be the motivation. (Others, however, were younger and more beautiful than the wife.) Is it because the wife's sanctions come too late? Early or late, the wife's complaints usually tend more to sever the relationship than to repair it.

Rather, I suspect that the primary impulse for the breakup of a marriage lies in the symbolic and cultural system of male priority. Politics, economics, and dominance are essentially male domains, and since the conquest, non-Indian men have had much license and freedom, especially over women. Thus, many men pursue women to symbolize their dominance. Yet remonstrations by a wife are at odds with a husband's ideological freedom and dominance as a male, especially if he is a Ladino male. Thus, if she doesn't complain she runs the risk of being edged out economically, then residentially, and finally socially. And if she does complain, she speeds the process by further alienating the man who culturally must be dominant. So the wife remains quiet; she "suffers," hoping it is indeed an *"ilusión"*; and the quality of the marriage relationship deteriorates. Here we begin to account for the greater "right" of men to have illicit relationships and for the fragility of Ladino domestic unions, especially those in which a woman presses for her dues.[16] The colonially derived dominance of non-Indian men over women demands the general acquiescense of women regardless of their spouses' behavior, especially if they are married to men of means.

Comparisons
PREMARITAL SEX IN THE TWO TOWNS

Sexual intercourse prior to the symbolically appropriate beginning of a common-law union or marriage is discouraged. However, although I have limited data on this, interviews with a number of people in both towns suggest that sexual liaison prior to the beginning of a common-law union or marriage is frequent. Eligible young men suggested that approximately "90 percent" of the young women enter into common-law union or marriage without virginity. This figure should be discounted and attributed to male bragging, no doubt, for young men thus affirm their masculine dominance over women through the conquest-symbolism of sex. But given the degree to which the Ladinos and Indians chaperon and care for their daughters, the 90 percent image indicates a conflict over the highly sensitive symbolism of sex, whatever the reality. One doctor, resident in San Pedro but ethnically Ladino, indicated the extreme vulnerability of women to the social and sexual advances of high-status men. He repeatedly emphasized the availability of the middle- and lower-class Ladino girls to a male of greater occupational, financial, or social status. Indian girls, particularly servants in Ladino homes, are said by young Marquenses to be especially susceptible to economic inducements. The picture is balanced by noting that several Ladino girls possess, by local standards, scandalous reputations. The young men, taxi drivers, shoeshine boys, and cynical adults are quick to point out girls who are the easy marks. Coupled with the institutionalized chaperoning, the parental anxieties over young girls in both communities, and the wives' assertions of male liberty, the degree to which women are said to be susceptible to male sexual advances provides further evidence of a general ideology of female submission to male prerogative.

Nor is the matter trivial, for the procreative capacity of the women is one source of ethnic symbolism—race. Thus the control of women affirms both masculine dominance and ethnic division, issues that lie at the core of Guatemalan society.

CONJUGAL UNION AND SOCIETY

The people of San Marcos and San Pedro, regardless of their individual ethnic assertions, share identical categories and symbols of marriage and common-law union. The cultural domain of the marriage relationship is the same in both status groups. There are two differences in the normative expectations of spouses, and both center in the Indian work ethic. First, Indian wives should contribute economically to their household. The Ladino expectation is the contrary: women, if possible, do not work. Second, Indian men are expected to be good *workers,* with relatively little emphasis on how much they make. By contrast, Ladino men are expected by their wives to bring home money, regardless of whether they are good workers or not. In both cases, the status ideologies of the total system have penetrated the marriage relationships of the two ethnic groups in a manner that is highly complementary. Although these norms are different for the ethnic groups, the differences are precisely linked to the overarching status system, thus contradicting the assumptions of plural-society analysis.

NOTES FROM THE WIDER ETHNOGRAPHIC FIELD

Persons familiar with the region under study might well object to the assertion of the cultural identity of Ladinos and Indians. After all, San Pedro is Spanish-speaking and has been for some time. And San Pedranos support themselves by craft industry and commerce rather than by peasant or proletarian agriculture. The San Pedranos certainly look Ladinoized. Would it not be better to view the San Pedranos as Ladinos who mark their class inferiority with the term "Indian"?

The answer is no, among other reasons because the San Pedrano ideology of work and isolation is closer to that of Mayan-speaking communities than it is to the ideology of the Ladinos. To understand this with regard to marriage, we must now look beyond San Pedro and consider other communities in which Spanish is not the domestic language or even the preferred language of public intercourse among Indians.

Atchalán[17] is one such community for which there are adequate details on courtship and marriage. Alexander Moore (1973) presents us with a fine account of a community formed of a Ladino town center surrounded by Cakchiquel-speaking Indian homesteads and nearby coffee plantations.

Atchalán shows a similar pattern of courtship "in the streets" (Moore 1973:48). Moore does not indicate with quotation marks that the phrase is native, and the passage is thus ambiguous. Is it a straightforward description of where young people court, or is it a native term incorporated into the text? I suspect it is both. Moore says of the older boys, "their afternoons from about 4:00 to 6:00 are spent on the street corners"; and of the older girls, "Nubile girls go out every day into the streets alone to do countless errands at their mothers' biddings" (1973:46, 48). It is in the afternoons that the young men press their suit with the young women, and if successful they do indeed find a "private street" to further their courtship (1973:49).

The couple formalize their intentions when the boy arranges for a "go-between *(pedidor)*" to ask the girl's father for the marriage of his daughter. The request is denied on two occasions but usually accepted on the third visit, in part because the couple might elope (Moore 1973:50–53). Concerning the categories of domestic alliance, two-thirds of the Atchaleño Indians live in free union (Moore gives no native term), while civil marriage is rarely sufficient but is followed by the ecclesiastical ceremony (1973:55–63).

Moore's apparent dependence upon Spanish as the field language weakens his study. When the native terms are used in the text to substantiate translations, they are given in Spanish. It may be that Spanish is supplanting Cakchiquel as the domestic language among these Indians, although the book suggests that Cakchiquel is in vigorous home use. It is more likely that Moore did not use Cakchiquel during his investigation.

Benjamin and Lois Paul provide data on another town. In about 1940, they studied the village of San Pedro la Laguna, a Mayan-speaking *municipio* not then accessible by road but nonetheless connected to the surrounding world by culture and position (Paul 1950). Here, we find the young men trying to interest their intended girl friends by accosting them on the path as they carry water home from the lake. Once a couple decides to form a union, which is done in considerable secrecy, family members as well as an unrelated "honored outsider" negotiate the arrangements. We are told that "seldom are marriages recorded in the civil registry or sanctified by a priest. However, it can be seen that the participation of the honored outsider is the social and moral equivalent both of a legal act and a holy sacrament" (1950:489). Again, the process is carried out against the background of a potential elopement, the results of which cannot be rescinded (1950:491–92).

While it may sound contradictory, it would appear that the extensive formalized negotiations needed to link households in marriage and the frequency of elopement to establish a union are both indications of the atomization of or isolation of Indian households. There is no middle ground, where households already linked in some fields of relations, such as private school attendance and Lions Club membership, might move less precipitously toward a domestic alliance as a furtherance of the initial linkage. Unfortunately, Paul does not give us native terms; and it is not convincing to assert cultural similarity, a matter of categories, solely on the basis of the behavior which he describes.

In order to get at native terms, I turn to a dissertation by Joseph Gross on the neighboring lake town of Santiago Atitlán. This town is of Tutujil linguistic background. Gross provides us with Tutujil terms for "house marriage," civil union, and ecclesiastical linkage, which match the categorical divisions for San Pedro and San Marcos. But the dissertation attends to other topics, and thus we are not given comparable behavioral and symbolic data on the courtship pattern or on the frequency of each category of alliance (Gross 1974).

Zinacantán provides data from a more distant, though still Mayan, area. Jane Fishburne Collier has issued her bachelor's thesis, based on a summer of work in the *municipio* of Zinacantán, under the title "Courtship and Marriage in Zinacantán, Chiapas, Mexico" (1968).

Here, too, the courting partners select each other and may effect their wishes by elopement in spite of parental opposition. The arena of courtship is likewise in the streets, or on the paths, but we are not given native terminology:

> young girls are often sent alone to the stores on errands for their mothers. Young men know this and stand around the stores to watch for the girls . . . A boy chooses his future wife from among the girls he sees along the paths, at fiestas, or in the homes of relatives and friends, but at no time may he talk to them alone. (Collier 1968:149)

Having decided to marry, the boy presents his father with a gift, the acceptance of which obligates the father to select a party of "petitioners" (or *h-hak'oletic*, in the Tzotzil terms given by Collier) who proceed to "the asking" *(hak'ol)*. Only some of the petitioners are kin; at least one must be a respected man of influence.

Again, the atomization and social distance between the households is highlighted in several ways. The use of the go-between, rather than a direct request from the parents, is one evidence of social distance.[18] More to the point, the petitioners are not informed beforehand of the intended girl's name but are only told that they will petition a marriage. This is done so that word does not leak and enable the girl or her whole household to escape. On the night of the asking, the petitioners gather at dusk to avoid suspicion, and only then are they given the girl's name. After dining, the party of petitioners sets out. Having surrounded the house so as to apprehend escapees, the petitioners trick their way through the front door and burst in upon the selected household (Collier 1968:150–51).

After the petition, "a year or more usually elapses before the *ochel ta na* (the entering of the house)" (Collier 1968:156). This year is an extended gift-giving period, which may be interpreted in part as an amelioration of the structural distance between households as well as a reciprocal exchange for the pending transfer of rights over the bride-to-be.

Although the boy may have physically entered the girl's father's house during the gift-giving period, he apparently has not done so symbolically. For this purpose, there is a "house-entering ceremony" (Collier 1968: 162–66). In the due course of ceremonial drinking, "the boy enters, [and] the petitioners tell the girl's father that the boy is now his son" (1968:164).[19] The boy stays and works from two to four weeks, a period of increased acquaintance. The youths may also on occasion sleep together. Further preparations lead to a marriage mass and the associated feast.[20]

Collier informs us that the ecclesiastical marriage is the preferred form of conjugal union, with its disadvantage being its high cost. An alternative is elopement followed by consensual residence. Civil marriage without fanfare is perhaps another alternative, but Collier does not discuss it (1968:172). Since common-law union is acceptable, marriage must be seen as an event in the status system, necessary for participation in the religious cargo hierarchy, as Cancian (1965) and others have noted, rather than as a necessary initiation to a socially legitimate domestic alliance.

The main variant appears to be uxorilocal residence following the house-entering ceremony, with no further effort made at transference of the bride. This uxorilocal consensual union is socially acceptable, if somewhat undesired. Again, the symbol of crossing the threshold begins the process of development cycle differentiation within the respective households.

Compared with San Pedro, Zinacantán is more agricultural and marginal. Corresponding with this, the marriage-arrangement institutions display more atomization and isolation in the greater resistance to marriage negotiation and betrothal. But the agricultural and marginal conditions themselves have not caused the marriage system to be as it is. Rather, the total system of categories has made small-plot agricultural life and Indian identity significant for a kind of rigidity in establishing new social connections. Given this continuum of linkages between ethnic status, economy, and family life, the plural society model again appears inapplicable to the domestic domain.

The institutions of courtship and marriage or common-law union bring men and women of different kin-fields together to form the embryos of potentially new households. The question of when the couples move away to found new households depends on the rules and tactics of postmarital residence and, ultimately, on the ethnic ideologies which back them. To this topic I now turn.

9
Postmarital Residence

Perhaps the sharpest test of the plural-society versus the single-culture model emerges when one compares the postmarital-residence beliefs and practices of San Marcos with those of San Pedro.[1] Essentially, postmarital residence rules are nonspecific and nonrestrictive among Ladinos but specific and restrictive among Indians. The differences in the status ideologies of the two groups explain the basic dichotomy: the Ladino ideology of license and freedom from restriction penetrates the residence-rule component of domestic social life, giving its residence rules a more optative, open character. By contrast, the inverse Indian ideology of restrictedness penetrates and infuses the Indian domestic system with a tightly bounded character in specific rules. Within this major dichotomy, there are residence rule variations between Indian communities, though all are restrictive in some degree. For example, some communities maintain household continuity by requiring the married firstborn son to remain with his parents until they die. Other communities hold the lastborn son to the same obligation. It is possible that such rule differences are functionally compatible with each municipality's Indian social economy. More likely (or perhaps just in addition), the variations in domestic rules serve the same function as variations in clothing style: to mark and separate the Indians of each community. Nur Yalman's (1967) analysis of structural changes among the Sri Lankans fits well here: from a common or base culture, the kinship structure of each community manifests a minor transformation achieved by emphasizing a different principle of the common core. Similarly, the Guatemalan Indian variations are members of a related set and are equally within the common culture of restrictedness.

A subsidiary conclusion of this chapter emerges upon examining not the norms but the actual patterns of postmarital-residence behavior. Census tabulations demonstrate there are performance variations, though the most frequent behavior tends to correspond to the rules. However, since following the rules is not so much the pursuit of blind tradition as it is the construction of meaningful and consistent statements about who one is or hopes to be, we of course expect variation from the community ideal. Our task, then, is first to tease out the ways in which the status ideologies penetrate and shape the postmarital-residence rules that characterize each ethnic group and, second, to explore the ways in which actual behavior communicates the complex realities of individual or family social position.

San Pedro Sacatepéquez

The San Pedranos say that at marriage a young woman ought to move out of her natal household and into a household with her husband. The young man at marriage ought to move out of his natal household and found a new residence unit. However, this rule does not apply to the youngest son. It is felt that the youngest son ought to remain with his parents and bring his wife permanently into his parents' household. Thus, ideally, the household unit is replicated and dispersed by forming nuclear units when female children and elder male children marry, while it is developed, by incorporating a daughter-in-law and by bearing children, when the youngest male marries.[2]

The San Pedranos consider a lack of money the primary factor inhibiting compliance with the norm of nuclear family residence. Phrases such as "I have no options *(posibilidades)*" or "I have no means *(facilidades)*" are interchangeable with "I have no money *(dinero, pisto)*."

San Pedranos vigorously assert that any young man who cannot establish a separate household at marriage ought to remain with his own parents; the bride should be the newcomer. Indeed, San Pedranos joke about a man who moves in with his parents-in-law, disparagingly referring to him as a *nuero*. The use of *nuero* emphasizes a social and residential abnormality with a play on grammatical and sexual abnormality. Spanish gender usually applies "-o" to the masculine classes of nouns and "-a" to the feminine. *Yerno* may thus be translated "son-in-law," and *nuera* "daughter-in-law." A *nuero*, then, is a "male daughter-in-law," the term being applied only to a husband who moves into the wife's parents' household.

Both Indians and Ladinos share the notion that independence connotes higher status and that dependence or subordination connotes lower status. But in the public domain Indians are the status inferiors of Ladinos and are supposed to subordinate themselves.[3] With matters thus relatively fixed in the domain of politics and economics, Indians play out their status movements in the local arenas of religion[4] and kinship.[5] Thus, nuclear residence is not just a step to independence and adulthood. It is a step up in the local prestige hierarchy that, along with religion, operates among those who are in the lowest ethnic stratum. The ideal of the independent nuclear family is relevant in this context because it manifests the condition of economic separation, subsistence independence, minimal parental control, and hence minimal domestic subordination. Thus, household independence connotes social adulthood and the higher status of jural responsibility.

The San Pedrano residence rules also have a practical functionality. For example, nuclear dispersion allows for occupational diversity, since expanded household space is often necessary for the implements and work area of an additional cottage industry. Indeed, San Pedranos encourage craft diversity among their children, for it is seen as a hedge against economic risk in one's old age. But the matter is not purely practical, for craft diversity is now a symbol of San Pedro's distinctiveness in the region. Also practical, the rule requiring the youngest son to remain in his father's household provides a base of social security for the father as the elder's physical abilities in handicrafts, trading, or farming decline. Moreover, the youngest son is the least hampered by this expectation because his achievement of adulthood most closely coincides with parental death. Along with these practical consequences, the residence rule maintains the father's position of status through the symbol of control over others within the domestic context. Finally, many an elder son that cannot viably establish a separate household economy finds himself dependent on his father. By continuing to reside with his father, he can labor in the marginal cottage industry and thus increase the household's profits, or he can reduce his personal expenses in preparation for building a home and separating. Nevertheless, the structural correspondences between inadequate subsistence base for independence and increased domestic dependence are quite symbolic and cannot be ignored. Thus, while all rules have a practical outcome, and while practical life is attended to, the practice of life is a symbolic art, where every act sends messages—desirable or undesirable, appropriate or inappropriate—of dominance or submission, of Ladinoness or Indianness, and of proximity or distance from the primary values of the society.

In this light uxorilocal residence[6] is unacceptable to the San Pedrano because it establishes the young man in yet another set of dependence relationships under the father-in-law. This sharply contradicts the Indian ideology of independence and atomization. Worse yet, uxorilocality connotes a dependence on the female side of relations that contradicts masculine control. The wife, through her familial connections and her own estate, is somewhat protected from the necessity to obey the new husband. In this reasoning, virilocality adds some authority and responsibility over a wife,[7] although it maintains the initially given pattern of dependence and subordination under a father. By contrast, uxorilocality adds a voluntary tie of dependence under a father-in-law, and it gives precious little arena to exercise authority over a wife. Rather, it is thought to entail the subjugation of the in-marrying male to his wife. Uxorilocality thus sharply contradicts the cultural assumption of masculine dominance, and from this derives the power and the derision of calling the in-marrying male a *nuero*. Should one need to live with someone, virilocality is the lesser of the two symbolic evils from the maturing son's viewpoint. In this way, the rules provide optimal compromise solutions for the competing interests of family members, and they do so in a manner consistent with the overarching status ideologies that apply to the Indians.[8]

One might expect, then, that the rules are followed by a fair percentage of the people, especially those people whose social circumstances conform quite closely to those of the ideal San Pedrano Indian: the self-employed peasant, artisan, or merchant.

But the differing social and economic circumstance of each San Pedrano is a potential cause of minor variation from the residence norms. In the face of social variety, the strict application of the rules does not always enhance the culturally provided goals of the people. For example, once the oldest sons and daughters are grown and married, a rural or poor San Pedro family may finally have enough money to send their youngest son further in school than they could send their other children. However, the rule that the last son remain, which in an agricultural community guarantees the protection of the parent, now obstructs the family's opportunity for later dependence on a richer and more securely employed youngest son, who has gone away to school. In such an event, an older brother may help care for the parents while the youngest son goes to school. In such ways, San Pedranos may disregard the specifics of the rules in favor of other arrangements, for it is not the rules that are paramount but the cultural premises. The cultural premises provide the goals. The rules in most circumstances supply the goals or provide a back-up or guarantee for their provision. In other cases, individuals may be so attracted by the idea of status change that they disregard the constraining obligations embodied in residence rules. Thus, a young man may effectively sever his kinship ties in the attempt to achieve Ladino status in some other urban center. Whether complying with the norms or the underlying cultural premises or by violating them entirely, the system allows for considerable behavioral diversity. We may therefore ask: To what extent are these norms acted out?

In San Pedro, 28 out of 196 households (14.3 percent) were three-generation stem-type households declaring a single economy. However, given the San Pedranos' strictly stated preference for a son to reside with his parents rather than with his wife's parents (as a *"nuero"*), the fact that only 12 of the 28 three-generation houses (that is, 42.8 percent) are connected around an in-resident son while 15 (or 53.6 percent) are connected through a daughter seems incongruous. One additional case (3.6 percent) is a household with two married in-resident children, the oldest a daughter and the youngest a son, who may be added to either category.[9]

In order to determine if this is an anomaly, however, one must examine the reasons for permissible deviations. In the first place, San Pedranos believe that a man stays in his father's house upon marriage if he is poor, while a youngest son should stay regardless. This would suggest that the firstborn and intermediate sons should reside in houses markedly poorer than the community average. My survey data bear this out: the mean household monthly income for all San Pedro households is about $92.40 (190 cases, standard error [s.e.] = 10.1). For all non-three-generation households the sample mean is $99.40 (153 cases, s.e. = 12.3). For all male-headed nuclear houses with the spouse present, the sample mean is $100.30 (95 cases of 190, s.e. = 16.5). For all practical purposes, these are equivalent.

But the sample mean for all three-generation households (35 cases) is $64.20; for those three-generation households where at least one stem child is present (that is, if one excludes the three-generation households where the parents of the third generation are absent), the mean for the 25 cases is $72.60. If one takes only the virilocal stem households (12 cases), the mean income is $64.60—a substantially lower figure than the community mean and the mean income of $85.90 for the 15 wholly uxorilocal households.[10] Moreover, the mean household income of the older son stem households is hardly higher ($66.30 for 8 cases) than that of the lastborn son stem households ($61.20 for 4 cases). This renders tenuous the supposition that these older sons are poorer and, as a result, deviate from the ideal of independence due to poverty, whereas lastborn sons conform regardless of wealth. Rather, all the virilocal three-generation stem families are poorer than average.

Interestingly, the seven senior couples whose children have all moved away have a much higher than average household income ($164.60), two and one-half times the virilocal stem family average and 1.8 times the town average. And since they are now just two-person households they also have a much higher than average per capita income ($82.30). This would suggest that in San Pedro the lastborn-son rule operates to protect parents in the poorest Indian households and to provide for the economic necessity of the poorest lastborn sons. But when a household is significantly better off than average, the lastborn residence requirement is easily and perhaps preferentially ignored in favor of other values such as independence, educational advancement, and occupational diversity.

Recalling that San Pedranos assert a poor man may reside uxorilocally with a family that is better off, one notes that the mean household income of uxorilocal families is $85.90. While this is somewhat higher than for households with a male stem ($64.60), there is not a statistically significant separation between virilocal and uxorilocal stem families regarding income.

If the household types are compared by ethnic category, as in Tables 14 and 15, the results are more equivocal. While Indian uxorilocal families are marginally better off than Indian virilocal families, they are both poorer than the nonstem families. The biggest difference lies in the higher incomes claimed by those families shifted toward Ladino. In land value, the Indian stem families are also poorer, especially the uxorilocal stem families. Unfortunately, my numeric data do not directly bear on the San Pedro idea that only a desperately poor man would live uxorilocally with a well-off spouse's family, for I do not have data on incomes prior to marriage. However, if

Table 14. San Pedro: Urban Stem Household Monthly Income

	Claimed Ethnic Status											
	Indian			Non-Indian/Non-Ladino			Ladino			Total		
		Mean in $			Mean in $			Mean in $			Mean in $	
	No.	House	Per capita	No.	House	Per capita	No.	House	Per capita	No.	House	Per capita
All non-three-generation households	68	145.8	20.3	61	101.3	30.6	26	112.8	29.2	155	98.6	25.9
All three-generation households												
Married son present												
NLB[a] son	6	52.2	8.2	1	98.0	16.3	1	119.0	9.9	8	66.3	—
LB[b] son	3	40.0	4.3	—	—	—	1	125.0	17.9	4	61.2	5.7
Married daughter present												
NLB daughter	3	71.3	8.3	3	79.3	7.9	2	118.5	18.1	9	78.4	10.4
LB daughter	3	54.0	8.6	—	—	—	1	180.0	25.7	4	85.5	12.8

Table 14. (continued)

	Claimed Ethnic Status											
	Indian			Non-Indian/Non-Ladino			Ladino			Total		
		Mean in $			Mean in $			Mean in $			Mean in $	
	No.	House	Per capita	No.	House	Per capita	No.	House	Per capita	No.	House	Per capita
Married daughter and married son	1	80.0	8.0	—	—	—	—	—	—	1	80.0	8.0
Male absent from empty middle generation	1	25.0	12.5	2	32.5	8.5	—	—	—	3	30.0	9.8
Female absent from empty middle generation	1	12.0	1.5	3	67.7	12.4	—	—	—	4	53.8	9.6
Sex unknown, absent from empty middle generation	2	15.0	5.8	1	32.0	5.3	—	—	—	3	20.7	5.7
Total: All households	88	81.1	17.4	71	96.0	27.7	31	115.9	27.4	190	92.4	22.9

[a]NLB = non-lastborn
[b]LB = lastborn

Table 15. San Pedro: Urban Stem Household Land Values

				Claimed Ethnic Status								
	Indian			Non-Indian/Non-Ladino			Ladino			Total		
		Mean in $			Mean in $			Mean in $			Mean in $	
	No.	House	Per capita	No.	House	Per capita	No.	House	Per capita	No.	House	Per capita
All non-three-generation households	68	670.0	14.8	61	1,671.9	429.1	27	1,121.7	236.9	156	1,153.1	272.4
All three-generation households												
Married son present												
NLB[a] son	6	100.0	11.6	1	800.0	133.3	1	0.0	0.0	8	175.0	25.4
LB[b] son	3	1,661.6	164.3	—	—	—	1	0.0	0.0	4	1,246.2	123.3
Married daughter present												
NLB daughter	4	400.0	52.6	3	0.0	0.0	3	5,041.7	566.5	10	1,672.5	191.0
LB daughter	4	0.0	0.0	—	—	—	1	0.0	0.0	5	0.0	0.0

Table 15. (continued)

	Claimed Ethnic Status												
	Indian			Non-Indian/Non-Ladino			Ladino			Total			
		Mean in $			Mean in $			Mean in $			Mean in $		
	No.	House	Per capita	No.	House	Per capita	No.	House	Per capita	No.	House	Per capita
Married daughter and married son	1	400.00	40.0	—	—	—	—	—	—	1	400.0	40.0
Male absent from empty middle generation	1	0.0	0.0	2	0.0	0.0	—	—	—	3	0.0	0.0
Female absent from empty middle generation	1	0.0	0.0	3	166.7	27.8	—	—	—	4	125.0	20.8
Sex unknown, absent from empty middle generation	2	1,250.0	441.7	2	0.0	0.0	—	—	—	4	625.0	0.0
Total: All households	90	640.9	129.0	72	1,434.6	377.0	33	1,376.2	245.3	195	1,058.4	236.4

[a]NLB = non-lastborn
[b]LB = lastborn

these men come from families substantially poorer than their uxorilocal spouses, then they are destitute indeed.

Obviously, factors other than money also play a role in delaying the desired fission of households. Some occupations may encourage a closer cooperation between a man and his sons or daughters, either because the resources necessary for pursuing the income are not easily partible for managerial or ecological reasons (a small busline, several store outlets) or because the pursuit of the trade requires additional, trustworthy, and cooperative labor (store clerking and management). For example, among store owners and market vendors stem households represented 3 out of 9 instances, or 33.3 percent; among farmers, 4 out of 15, or 26.7 percent; among common laborers, 2 out of 7, or 28.6 percent; among truckers, 1 out of 3, or 33.3 percent; among mechanics, 1 out of 4, or 25 percent; among tailors, 7 out of 21, or 33.3 percent; among masons, 4 out of 11, or 36.4 percent; and among butchers 1 out of 3, or 33.3 percent. These figures are sharply above the community average of 14.3 percent. On the other hand, those occupations that require a few tangible resources and little cooperation seem to have a more rapid fission, though the laborers and tailors noted above are an obvious exception. For example, soap makers (2 cases), bakers (8 cases), carpenters (13 cases), and seamstresses (4 cases) had no cases of stem households. Shoemakers (1 of 15, or 6.6 percent), weavers (1 of 12, or 8.3 percent), and knitters (1 of 8, or 12.5 percent) had stem families below or slightly below the San Pedro average rate. Among the professions, only one ministerial family and one accountant, or 9.5 percent of the 21 noncommercial and nonlaboring types of occupations, had three-generation stem families.[11] However, the simplicity of these statements is inadequate to the social complexity of San Pedro. For example, a number of San Pedro's successful businessmen now convert or transfer those profits available for business expansion into secondary and university educations for their children. Thus, they effectively invest in their children a portion of the estate and thereby give them an independent economic base. As a result, the children may reside and work independently even though the parents could use the children's labor to expand the size of the business.

San Pedro shows a close correspondence between the rules for postmarital behavior and the overarching conceptual system as well as with the local social and economic conditions. San Pedro is defined as "Indian." Indians are the restricted category, and, as a result, so are their residence rules. Deep cultural premises suffuse and color all the Indian institutions, but San Pedranos and their premises are only part of the system, an inverse image in a larger dichotomy. San Marcos provides the opposed position in the dichotomy.

San Marcos

In urban San Marcos there are no clear-cut rules about residential arrangements after marriage.[12] There is an adage that any couple will want a residence separate from either pair of parents (*"Al casado, casa quiere"*), but this is not insisted upon and is apparently quite unsanctioned. There is no expressed feeling that an individual ought to move out upon marrying, only that most would want to move out. However, there is no loss of esteem if one does not move. If one does not establish a new household at marriage, residence with the parents of either the groom or the bride is equally acceptable and unstigmatized. Normatively, then, there is no specific expression of either compelling duty or of negatively sanctioned behavior with regard to postmarital residence. The nuclear household is suggested as desirable because it is either less abrasive or more conducive to social adulthood through separation from the parents. Nevertheless, alternative possibilities such as virilocal or uxorilocal residence are not ill-viewed, nor are particular conditions specified for such behavioral alternatives. Ladino statements suggest flexibility and openness: a common response to questions on where to live after marriage is "well, it depends."

This last phrase provides the key to understanding the "fit" between these "nonrules" and the cultural matrix of Ladinos. I have shown (in Chapters 3 and 6) that an essential difference between Ladinos and Indians lies in the manner in which Ladino status ideologies of connectedness and control generate social networks that encompass the utmost possible power and authority and usually (though not necessarily) property and income. Whereas the Indian pursues social position through household cooperation in work, the Ladino pursues position through social connection. The oppositions of work and of connection are at once indices of social position and symbols of cultural ideology and status category. Deduced from this cultural logic, the central pursuits in Ladino life are not principally productive or pecuniary. Rather, the central pursuit is interconnection: the construction of social networks that give one access to the central values of power and office.

Residence choice is one mode of enhancing social interconnection. Judiciously used, some residential options can give a couple greater social and symbolic centrality than others. Thus an openness to behavioral variety at marriage or consensual union allows the couple maximum latitude for the construction of social networks. At the same time, it is maximally consistent with the Ladino ideology of openness or lack of restriction. The "open" rule institutionalizes both cultural principles. To be sure, Ladino flexibility also results in increased economic opportunity or in ease of educational advancement, and such processes keep the social relational system relatively consistent with the cultural hierarchy. However, these relatively utilitarian results are not the reason for the rule's flexibility. Flexibility is utilitarian because it is symbolic; Ladinos are above the law and unrestricted. Likewise, interconnectedness per se is both symbolic and practical: Ladinos connect. While this ideology of flexibility principally accrues to the advantage of the Ladino elite, it does not hamper the nonelite, who deliberately connect where they can to each other and to the elite. Even when they have no *good* connections, the mere possession of the ideology of interconnectedness gives nonelite Ladinos the basis for their ethnic status when by other "objective" indices they are not very different from the Indians.

Let us turn now to behavioral data on the residence of urban San Marcos and examine how the data are related to the rather nonspecific statements concerning postmarital residence.[13]

In San Marcos, 41 out of 184 households (or 22.3 percent) were three-generation stem families, with the stem-child present in the household. Of these 41, 13 (or 31.7 percent) were connected through an in-resident son, while 23 (or 56.1 percent) were connected through an in-resident daughter. Five other households had two stem marriages: two with an older male and younger female (4.9 percent), and three with two females (7.3 percent).[14] Thus, uxorilocality is a more prevalent phenomenon in San Marcos than in San Pedro. While the San Pedro households with any uxorilocality comprised 57.1 percent of the stem households and 8.2 percent of all households, uxorilocal or partially uxorilocal households in San Marcos comprise 68.3 percent of the stem households and 15.2 percent of all households. As in the San Pedro figures, these numbers for San Marcos do not include the eight three-generation households where the middle generation is either wholly absent or consists of unmarried siblings of a departed parent (as detailed in note 16).

In San Marcos, two premises of the culture system interrelate to determine the formation of three-generation families. On the one hand, people pursue advantageous interconnections. On the other hand, poor men are suspected of being bad residence risks, leaning the choice of women among the poor and the uneducated toward uxorilocality. Thus, for the town as a whole, the 75 nuclear male-headed households had a mean income of $146.60 per month. The mean income for all 133 nonstem families is $160.18, while the mean income for all 184 households including three-generation stem households is $173.10.[15] By comparison, the 13 virilocal three-generation stem families had a mean income of $377.10[16] while the 23 uxorilocal households with only one stem marriage had a mean of $170.60 or slightly below the community average.[17]

This same pattern of income distribution is reflected in the more complex two-stem households. The two households bearing older-son and younger-daughter stems—structurally half-male, half-female—had a mean income of $260.00, almost exactly midway between the all-male mean of $377.10 and the all-female (one stem-child) mean of $175.30. The three households with two female stems—ultra matrifocal if you will—had an even lower mean of $138.30.

When the San Marcos economic figures are broken down by ethnic category (Tables 16 and 17), several patterns emerge, and also several complications arise. Among the patterns, one notes that Indians in San Marcos are the poorest of the poor; moreover, as in San Pedro, the Indian stem households are poorer than the Indian nonstem households.

Second, the Ladinos show considerable land wealth in the complex households. Moreover, Ladinos are consistently wealthier than the non-Ladino/non-Indian "disclaimants" for any category of stem or nonstem households except in the instance of married lastborn-daughter stem households.

Here the complications begin. I doubt that one should place much significance in this anomaly to the pattern. The case numbers are small and therefore subject to distortion by a single unusual case. This reservation is manifestly needed in two categories. First, in the female-female category of double-stem household, there is one exceedingly wealthy household, with a land value of $813,500.00 (Table 17) and an income of $300.00 per month or $42.86 per capita (Table 16). This, however, understates the probable agricultural income. When imputed agricultural-income figures are used, this household has an income of $1,085 per month, or $157 per capita. The other two female-female double-stem households have no land, and incomes

Table 16. San Marcos: Urban Stem Household Monthly Income

	Claimed Ethnic Status												
	Indian			Non-Indian/Non-Ladino			Ladino			Total			
		Mean in $			Mean in $			Mean in $			Mean in $		
	No.	House	Per capita	No.	House	Per capita	No.	House	Per capita	No.	House	Per capita
All non-three-generation households	14	66.8	12.5	20	120.8	24.1	101	179.1	66.9	135	158.9	55.0
All three-generation households												
Married son present												
NLB[a] son	2	81.0	9.9	3	170.7	33.0	4	886.5	139.2	9	468.9	75.1
LB[b] son	0	—	—	1	220.0	55.0	3	154.0	25.3	4	170.5	32.7
Married daughter present												
NLB daughter	2	20.0	3.0	2	155.0	27.5	12	161.6	26.4	16	143.1	23.6
LB daughter	0	—	—	2	253.5	30.6	5	226.0	34.1	7	233.8	33.1

Table 16. (continued)

	Claimed Ethnic Status											
	Indian			Non-Indian/Non-Ladino			Ladino			Total		
		Mean in $			Mean in $			Mean in $			Mean in $	
	No.	House	Per capita	No.	House	Per capita	No.	House	Per capita	No.	House	Per capita
Multiple												
Male-Female	0	—	—	1	250.0	22.7	1	270.0	14.2	2	260.0	18.5
Female-Female	0	—	—	0	—	—	3	138.3	18.0	3	138.3	18.0
Male absent from empty middle generation	0	—	—	2	82.0	10.4	0	—	—	2	82.0	10.4
Female absent from empty middle generation	0	—	—	1	111.0	15.9	4	50.8	13.9	5	62.8	14.4
Grandchildren by three children who are sex unknown, absent from empty middle generation	0	—	—	0	—	—	1	172.0	21.5	1	172.0	21.5
Total: All households	18	63.2	11.9	32	140.3	25.3	134	195.7	59.9	184	173.1	49.2

[a]NLB = non-lastborn
[b]LB = lastborn

Table 17. San Marcos: Urban Stem Household Land Values

	Claimed Ethnic Status													
	Indian			Non-Indian/Non-Ladino			Ladino			Total		
		Mean in $			Mean in $			Mean in $			Mean in $	
	No.	House	Per capita	No.	House	Per capita	No.	House	Per capita	No.	House	Per capita
All non-three-generation households	14	379.0	69.8	20	1,094.8	181.2	101	23,449.4	11,100.4	135	17,745.1	8,338.8
All three-generation households												
Married son present												
NLB[a] son	2	75.0	10.7	3	223.3	46.6	4	3,062.5	457.8	9	1,455.6	221.4
LB[b] son	0	—	—	1	600.0	150.0	3	67,900.0	11,308.3	4	51,075.0	8,518.8
Married daughter present												
NLB daughter	2	250.0	39.3	2	0.0	0.0	12	17,122.1	2,853.4	16	12,872.8	2,145.0
LB daughter	0	—	—	2	25,475.0	3,134.4	5	1,745.0	428.0	7	8,525.0	1,201.3

Table 17. (continued)

	Claimed Ethnic Status												
	Indian			Non-Indian/Non-Ladino			Ladino			Total			
		Mean in $			Mean in $			Mean in $			Mean in $		
	No.	House	Per capita	No.	House	Per capita	No.	House	Per capita	No.	House	Per capita	
Multiple													
Male-Female	0	—	—	1	4,000.0	363.6	1	25,000.0	1,315.8	2	14,500.0	839.7	
Female-Female	0	—	—	0	—	—	3	271,166.7	38,738.1	3	271,166.7	38,738.1	
Male absent from empty middle generation	—	—	—	2	1,344.0	168.0	—	—	—	2	1,344.0	168.0	
Female absent from empty middle generation	—	—	—	1	0.0	0.0	4	587.5	200.0	5	470.0	160.0	
Grandchildren by three children who are sex unknown, absent from empty middle generation	—	—	—	—	—	—	1	0.0	0.0	1	0.0	0.0	
Total: All households	18	330.9	—	32	2,526.1	—	134	27,159.5	—	184	—	—	

[a]NLB = non-lastborn
[b]LB = lastborn

of $80.00 and $35.00 per month, which gives per capita incomes of $6.15 and $5.00 respectively. Thus, two processes are at work in the formation of these households: the rich ones tend to hold together because of the estate; while the poor ones tend to slough off husbands and live uxorilocally with broken conjugal bonds, thus forming a decidedly matrifocal household.

A second difficulty arises from two nonstem households in San Marcos that have high land values. One of these, $900,000.00 in total, is a one-person household; as a result, this inflates the Ladino land-value figure by $8,437.00 and the per capita land-value figure by $8,551.10. The other case has a land value of $700,000 and a per capita land-value of $100,000. Again, these cases inflate land value and per capita land value. When these two cases are subtracted, nonstem land values are still high but not so distorted now, totalling $7,484.10 in land value and $1,184.00 per capita land value, respectively.

The relationship of these behavioral data to their social and cultural context is thus rather complex. Some of these stem couples are present due to economic hardship, with their behavior resembling that of the Indians and for comparable reasons of potential savings and economic marginality, though skewed toward uxorilocality. Others are pursuing a closer residence in order to participate more fully in the parental household's high symbolic status or wealth.

We would not want to conclude that such utilitarian intentions and benefits cause rule flexibility; rather, they are permissible within it. Both the behavioral variety and the "rule" openness are consistent with Ladino ideology. Flexible postmarital residential behavior is one manifestation of the culturally induced social thrust to construct diverse networks of kinship, marriage, or friendship and, wherever possible, to connect with greater power, office, or other opportunities. The object is to interconnect.

In summary, residential norms of each community are correlated with the historically derived political and occupational structure of the community and with the status-group ideology that is indexed by ethnicity. The norms are intelligible to us since we see that they are consistent with—indeed, suffused with—the Indian premises of resrictedness and the Ladino premises of flexibility and their existence above the law. The variability of behavior with respect to a given norm also relates to the symbolic schema, for it is symbolic of the variety of individual social circumstances. The range of wealth and other exceptions to the general symbolic structure within each town guarantee variability of behavior, but it is symbolic variability—a meaningful deviation from a meaningful community norm.

Since San Pedro is an unusual Indian community, the general validity of this cultural and symbolic analysis will be enhanced by examining residential rules and residential behavior in another Mayan community, one in which Mam is the predominant household language and non-Western dress a principal diacritical index of social status.

Comitancillo[18]

SOCIAL CIRCUMSCRIPTION IN AN AGRICULTURAL INDIAN COMMUNITY

Guatemalan Indians are often stereotyped both in native statements and in anthropological literature as uneducated, poor, isolated, apolitical, Mayan-speaking agriculturists. The San Pedranos clearly do not conform to this stereotype, although the residents of San Marcos usually talk and act as though they do. Perhaps because of this deviation from the ideal type, a group of San Pedro youth (referred to here in Chapter 5, passages 35–38) on one occasion denied that there were any Indians at all in their town, insisting that the only true Indians live in the mountainous townships to the north. We shall now discuss one of these "true" Indian communities. However, the material below is based on limited field observation and interviews.[19] It is an impressionistic account which needs confirming research, and it is therefore advanced tentatively.

Comitancillo is a township of 18,619 residents, of whom 627 live in the town center (Dirección General de Estadística 1975). Located about fifteen kilometers north and slightly east of San Marcos, Comitancillo is accessible by a dirt road that, in the course of its thirty-four kilometers, rises sharply as it snakes northward and drops precipitously just before entering the town center. The road is categorized officially as all-weather but it is in fact frequently unserviceable during the rainy season.

Two bus companies run daily round trips, leaving Comitancillo in the morning and returning in the afternoon. This service offers the Comitancillo residents (Comitecos) reasonably convenient access to the administrative and commercial facilities of San Marcos and

Plate 25. Mam-speaking Indians of Comitancillo wait for a bus in the plaza of San Lorenzo. (1973)

San Pedro. However, the bus schedule inhibits convenient access to Comitancillo by outsiders, for they must remain overnight in rather spartan guest facilities.

Like other remote townships, Comitancillo's municipal government suffers from benign neglect in the political sphere. The state governor visits the *municipio* to inaugurate the annual county fair. Department health officers visit to inspect wells or water systems and to vaccinate children. I could not locate a newspaper to buy or borrow, though I would be surprised if none reached the town. The community is politically and communicationally isolated from the national pulse. However, Comitancillo is not isolated from the national culture of social-status categories or the cultural ideologies of the ethnic-status dichotomy. Indeed, its physical isolation is a symbolic factor that defines more precisely, redundantly, and forcefully the community and the majority of its residents as Indian.

The population of Comitancillo, like that of all Guatemalan communities, is divided into the two status categories of Indian and Ladino. One municipal official estimated the number of Ladino families at about ten, and this number was confirmed by the resident Catholic priest as well as by Indian informants.

The ethnic category of the Indians is visibly and unambiguously manifest in their dress. The Comiteco Indian men wear cheaply manufactured cotton shirts and pants. Patches are common; a few sport more patches than original garment material. Their shoes range from cheap rubber boots and old leather castoffs to tire-tread sandals. Some use no footgear at all. Indian women wear mostly a traditional community costume, which is distinctly nonmodern. The home-woven, wraparound, ankle-length blue skirt, a bright red blouse, a multicolored ribbon braided into the hair, and an absence of shoes announce from afar that these women consider themselves Indians. As in other communities, the Westernization of clothing styles and the ability to speak even rudimentary Spanish is concentrated among the men. This marks their relatively greater participation in the national system as heads of family and representatives of the household in most outside dealings. It also suggests the male participation in the mainline and national occupational framework of status symbolism. The few Ladinos in the community try to emulate, though sometimes rather maladroitly, the urban mercantile styles.

Compared with San Pedro Sacatepéquez, the Comitecos sharply and visibly distinguish between Indians and Ladinos. One reason for this sharper cleavage is that the Ladinos in Comitancillo are all (so far as I could determine) persons in positions of control. They are labor contractors, large landowners (and therefore labor employers), municipal officers, schoolteachers, the priest, the innkeeper, and the pharmacist-shopkeeper. The Comiteco Indians lack San Pedro's economic range, occupational variety, and educational access. Therefore, all these components of their social persons are consistent and low status. They are Indians, and Indians with little chance of mobilization at that.

Indeed, the Indians in Comitancillo are mostly small-plot agriculturalists who usually supplement their incomes with migrant labor on the coastal plantations. In this regard, the priest thought that 80 to 90 percent of the men migrated to the coastal coffee harvest, taking their households with them. The area's isolation is an impediment to the development of artisanry and trade. Thus, the institutionalized structure has limited symbolic production to such an extent that "individual status mobility *in situ* is virtually impossible" for these Indians.[20] Since the Comiteco cannot produce the symbols of a category change *in situ,* in order to change categorically he must move physically so that he can restructure symbolically.

The only choice, then, is to move out of the community if one is to move up in status. Colby and van den Berghe have discussed the process at length, though not from a symbolic viewpoint, in *Ixil Country* (1969). They identify the social relations and expectations that maintain a person's Indian status in his home community. If such a person is to Ladinoize, he must move out of this social system and into an urban area where he is unknown. In order to pass for Ladino in this new community, he must be able to speak fairly good Spanish and buy the necessary Ladino clothing symbols. At minimum, this presupposes some means of support in the outside world. But beyond this, movement per se alters one's placement in the system of meanings inherent in the culturally evaluated geography. Usually one moves to a *municipio* of higher rank and of more central location. This move in itself adds Ladino features to the once symbolically consistent Indian, and thereby automatically initiates the first steps in the symbolic process of becoming Ladino.

The Comitancillo Indian is hard pressed to meet the minimum requirements for abandoning one's community successfully. For one thing, educational facilities in Comitancillo are limited to the first six grades. This is hardly enough to acquire a secure position in the Ladino urban centers. The six grades teach one how to read, write, and speak some Spanish, but they give little hint about how to live in any of the communities where one might hope to become a Ladino. Not only is available primary schooling inadequate, it is very difficult to complete. As a first obstacle, more than 96 percent of the people live in satellite hamlets that have no more than third- or fourth-grade facilities. Thus, the children in the *aldeas* must walk from one to four hours over rough terrain to get to or from the town center's upper elementary classes. As a second obstacle, most families lack enough agricultural land for family food and minimum purchases. Consequently, most of the Indian residents of Comitancillo are forced to migrate annually to the coastal plantations in order to work for the cash necessary to buy food and other items. This migratory pattern conflicts with the educational process, for final examinations are scheduled nationwide during the peak migratory labor season. Since the whole family unit migrates, they annually interrupt the school year and miss the required grade-completion examinations. Hence, very few Indian children complete the six grades. Parents recognize this and assert that once the school has taught the rudiments of reading and writing there is no further need to lose the children's labor capacity. Therefore, the children are pulled out of school between the second and fourth grades.

These liabilities could be overcome if it were possible to gain access to the large cities through some kind of protected residential arrangement. Such access does not appear to be available to the Indians. Brian Roberts's report on urban migration to Guatemala City (1973, chap. 2) suggests that 95 percent of the migrants are Ladinos. Roberts did not explore the symbolic aspects of getting strangers organized in the cities. The initial lack of connections faced by the newly arrived slumdwellers appears to be consistent with the problems that would be faced by an Indian with few connections who is attempting to become a Ladino capable of cultivating many connections. Nor did Roberts trace deeply the ethnic histories of the migrants. We may surmise, however, that many Ladino migrants have made an ethnic shift at an earlier stop in their migration career and are still struggling to build the networks that validate their relatively new status. Because status is symbolized by origins, the symbolic transition to Ladino requires the obscuring of one's "Indian" community origins and the severing of one's social ties. Such ethnic changes would suppress the development of an Indian community's connections to the center and would limit the kin-sponsored and regional club-sponsored flow of natives into the urban centers that William Mangin has reported in Peru (1959). Unfortunately, the relationship between Guatemalan urbanization and ethnic change has not been adequately studied, and the three previous sentences here are speculative only.

In addition to the social isolation induced by hiding one's ethnic background, the pattern of village endogamy reported throughout the highland region inhibits the establishment of kinship connections in strategically located educational or occupational centers. Indian endogamy closes and isolates the low-status communities in the inverse of the Ladino model, which leaves marriage choice open. The rules for marriage, as the rules for residence, are consistent with the Indian status ideologies of restrictedness and atomization.[21]

Thus, there is no easy way to leave the *municipio* permanently.

One can join the army. Or one can become a permanent resident laborer on a coastal plantation, a choice that is felt to be both unhealthy and degrading. How often Comitancillo natives choose to leave or are forced to leave is not known. Two Comitecos questioned about this process named some acquaintances who had made such a choice.

By contrast, the Ladinos living in Comitancillo and other such hinterland Indian communities have kinship connections beyond the villages. An elderly couple will often turn over the family commercial interests to their children and then move to an educational center such as San Marcos. There they provide housing and care for their grandchildren, who move from the hinterland municipality to a larger center where they are able then to continue their educations through high school. Such children insure their respectable Ladino status by obtaining higher occupational and cultural credentials.

Since these Ladinos are seldom born in the remote community where they reside as adults and since they often marry outside their residential community, they have relatively widespread kinship connections that favor the placement of their children in commercial or governmental positions through the "pull" *(cuello)* of these influential relatives. In addition, Ladino occupational patterns in the predominantly Indian towns never compete with schooling. Finally, the Ladino who moves from the educational and cultural center of the country to the remote villages brings with him a control over Spanish and Ladino culture that is passed on to his children, who may then freely leave the remote community confident that they have the symbolic skills and the ideology necessary to cultivate further Ladino relationships in the national society.

POSTMARITAL RESIDENCE

The primary norm for postmarital residence among Comitancillo Indians is that a young man should remain in his father's house to render service after his marriage.[22] His bride's arrival adds to the services which are accorded to the parents. As one of my informants put it, "Here, as a custom that exists, parents want their sons to give service, as well as with their wives, to the parents, so that thus they may be more contented. . . ." Service means "to take care of the parents and help them in their needs." It is clearly spoken of as a form of old-age security.

Failure to render such service is grounds for disinheritance. To the Indian resident of the remote village, disinheritance is a powerful sanction. How could one otherwise eke out a living? Disinheritance insures a life of desperation by Indian standards. One would have to work on someone else's land and enter ever more deeply or even permanently into the hated coastal labor market. Thus, disinheritance would thwart the crucial Indian goal of independence through subsistence isolation.

This dependence on one's parents' land is highlighted in a conversation I had with a Comitancillo Indian about alternative forms of land inheritance that might relieve the tendency to fragment the land plots. First, he drew a square in the dirt of his courtyard, telling me that it represented the land of a man. Then he divided the square into four equal strips, saying that each strip represented the inheritance of a child. Then he subdivided one strip into four patches, pointing to each patch as the land of a grandchild. Finally, he subdivided one patch by four and indicated that such was the portion for the children of the grandchildren. He explained that this was how the plots became too small to support a family and that only a few people could buy more land.[23] I then asked him (A = anthropologist; I = informant):

A: Why don't they abandon the land?

I: Some do, but what can they do? Perhaps they can go to the plantations.

A: Why not leave it all to the eldest son in order not to divide the plots?

I: Because there isn't any education and what can the rest [of the children] do?

A: Why not divide it only among the sons?

I: There are fathers who have already thought of this, but the law [Guatemalan national law] dictates that an equal portion be left to each child, and the parents have to divide the land or the daughters seek [judgment] with the law.

National law does in fact stipulate an equal inheritance among the children, regardless of sex, but only when land is intestate. To change this situation requires the considerable effort of leaving a will, which would entail an association with bureaucracy that most Comiteco Indians, I suspect, would prefer to avoid.[24] Such behavior would contradict the Indian ideology of disconnection from government and depersonalization of social ties.

The norm that each non-lastborn son should remain in his father's household after marriage, at least until a younger son marries, is the principal difference between the residential rules of Comitancillo and San Pedro Sacatepéquez, where the rule is to move out as fast as possible. Why does this difference exist? First, we have shown that the Comitancillo youth is forced to abide the wishes of his father because his father controls the only viable mode of livelihood as well as the basic symbol of independence, land.[25] By contrast, the San Pedro youth can arrange a craft apprenticeship even without the help of his father, thereby making the son more independent. Second, we noted that a middle-aged[26] Indian peasant in Comitancillo is in an extremely precarious position because, while his social responsibility is growing larger, his land base stays the same and his ability to work it is diminished steadily by the inevitable fact of aging. It is only by intensive, backbreaking labor that this life can be sustained. Therefore, every parental couple needs the cooperative contribution of maturing adults, and the logic of the system insists that a married son stay in the home. The norm identifies a standardized solution to this recurring problem, providing at once for the parents' care, the child's inheritance, and an ultimate independence. In urban San Pedro, however, the majority of the people relegate their agricultural income to a minor contribution through their artisanry or some other activity. It is to their symbolic advantage to encourage sons to diversify by taking advantage of the various craft opportunities that are available. Labor control is not needed, and geriatric care derives from a wider base. The norm is, therefore, for the first sons to leave. Moreover, this greater San Pedro flexibility, a Ladinolike aspect, is consistent withh San Pedro's occupational and wealth deviations from the ideal Indian agricultural community.

The implication of the paragraph above is that the economic organization or system has certain implications for the structuring of domestic relations. On the surface, this explanation violates the cultural and symbolic framework of this book. It presents the Comitancillo rule differences as the institutionalized and crystallized recommendation for patently practical action: to provide for labor and geriatric care. But the contradiction of the functional approach to the cultural viewpoint is only a superficial one and exists only if it is not realized that functional variation as an explanation is subordinate to the cultural categories and ideological premises (Sahlins 1976:4–18, 206). In this particular case, the cultural limitations include restrictedness, household orientation extending into production, household atomization, and municipal atomization through diacritical transformations of Indian symbols and institutions. Since the wealth and nonagricultural economic base of San Pedro produces symbols which are discordant with the fundamentally Indian symbol of small-plot subsistence isolation, San Pedro is to this extent less Indian than Comitancillo. Thus, the more flexible residence rule is in the first place compatible with the less Indian symbolic productions of its institutionalized economic base. Only in the second place is it a functional response to the productive predicament. Similarly, the tighter Comitancillo rule that the older sons remain satisfies first the symbolic requirement of greater rigidity in the ideal-typical Indian community. Only second does it satisfy the functional needs of the parents. After all, the parents' needs could have been satisfied with a wage-labor system or with a requirement that sons who have moved out will continue to labor for their fathers. But these rule possibilities would be too interconnective between households. Thus, functional consistency and economic utility may fine-tune the system, but they are subordinate to and constrained by the cultural order.

Though I lack any statistical corroboration, the developmental cycle of the Comitancillo Indian family seems to be primarily a sequence of household extension, with new units being founded by older married sons and their wives and children as they move out of the parental compound, usually to a nearby plot, when their younger brothers marry. Finally, the youngest son stays and inherits the house buildings and surrounding plot.[27] Aside from his equal division in the lands, the youngest son receives the house as compensation for his contribution to his father's final comfort and funeral. This rule, like its counterpart in San Pedro, is expressed as a prescriptive norm.

In short, the Comitancillo Indian's social circumstances and hence his symbolic productivity are more homogeneous and restricted than those of San Pedranos. Socially, Comitancillo is more marginal to the political and status centers of the nation. The ideology of constraint or restrictedness applies even more thoroughly to these Indians than to the San Pedranos. Both in category and in the symbols of circumstances, Comitecos are more Indian. There are correspondingly more restrictive residence rules which correlate with this more restricted social and cultural position, at the same time that they provide for the mutual care of the family members.

Insofar as I was able to ascertain, the amount of residential-behavior variation is also quite limited. Since there are few exceptions to the system of small-plot land dependence and hence very little symbolic contradiction of the Indian status of the community, the norms apply more evenly to all. A greater regularity of domestic behavior would indeed symbolize this restricted circumstance by a close correspondence to the norms.[28]

Notes on the Wider Ethnography

While most Guatemalan Indian communities include the lastborn son or child (Gross 1974) in their residence rules, there is variation. Ruth Bunzel (1952) and Sol Tax (1947) report that in Chichicastenango the first son always remains with his father's house. The younger sons (and daughters, unless wealthy) must move out when they marry or shortly afterwards. This and other variations may be simply free transformations of emphasis on certain principles, comparable to Nur Yalman's analysis of the transformations of kinship in Sri Lanka and South India (Yalman 1967). Nevertheless, such transformations are not completely "free." They are always compatible with the general context of rule-defined restrictedness among Indians. Viewed as transformations, these variations enhance the atomization of the Indian communities by making them distinctive not just in language, clothing, and other "surface" customs. Indian communities become further atomized by differences in the rules and structure of domestic relations.

It is possible to imagine a functional explanation that may account for the Chichicastenango variation within the overarching ideology of restrictedness. Chichicastenango has a large population as well as a considerable land base. From the accounts of Bunzel (1952) and Tax (1947) it is apparent that agricultural landholdings are a significant aspect of Chichicastenango's subsistence. At the same time, one of the distinctive characteristics of the community is its major involvement in regional trade. This characteristic is incorporated in the distinctive symbolism and community ideology of the Maxeño (person of Chichicastenango) just as much as craftsmanship and trade are incorporated in the San Pedrano's symbolism and ideology. It is possible that the rule requiring the oldest son to stay in his father's home may allow the land to be cared for as well as the trade routes to be serviced at the earliest possible stage in the developmental cycle of the household. Unfortunately, it is not possible to determine from the available notes and monograph whether there exists a related division of labor between father and son or if there exists an explicit justification for this rule (Tax 1947; Bunzel 1952). The answer to whether such domestic-rule transformations are distinctive, atomizing, *and* functional to particular microeconomies or if they are just distinctively atomizing must await further research.

Functional Explanations: Marriage, Inheritance, and Lastborn Residence

The strict implementation of the rule that the lastborn son reside with his parents would result in the creation of an extended-household group of the sort that Frederic LePlay has called the stem family. One of the reasons he suggests for the stem family is that it maintains the continuity of personnel in a household enterprise based on agriculture or cottage industry (LePlay 1871, 1872:40). Obviously, if an estate is to remain intact there must be restrictions on inheritance. It must either be restricted to one heir or held without partition as (or as if it were) a corporate estate. Cole and Wolf (1974) provide an interesting contrast between a Germanic tradition of restricting succession to nonpartible peasant estates and an Italian tradition of dividing the estate equally. Both systems are carried on within the confines of a single Alpine valley.

The Guatemalan cases conform more in structure and appearance to the Italian example, for in San Pedro and San Marcos, as well as in most towns in Guatemala, inheritance is bilateral. There are a few Mayan areas, such as some towns of the Tzotzil-Tzeltal language groups in Chiapas, where the agricultural lands are inherited by a division among the sons only (Vogt 1969; Collier 1975). But even this restriction to sons only does not prevent excessive fragmentation of the Indian household estates.

In the presence of estates fragmenting under bilateral inheritance, there is a certain social functionality to endogamous marriage. The wife also brings an inheritance that is passed and divided to the children. Thus, there is not only a fragmentation but also a great dispersion of the plots as husband and wife combine their eventual assets. Under such conditions there is clear sociological merit in the expectation and practice among Indians of municipal and even hamlet endogamy. Even marrying beyond the hamlet could create some problems of access to one's fields, although this might well be compensated by the widely reported insurance value of some ecological dispersion of one's holdings. However, such arguments are neither necessary nor sufficient to account for endogamous marriage. First, there are endogamous Mayan villages in which there is negligible inheritance by the women (Collier 1975). Second, there are divisive inheritance systems with village exogamy, as in Lebanon (Friedl 1959). It would appear that the understanding of both village endogamy and the partitioning of estates lies not so much with their functional contribution as with their relational consistency to the Indian ideology of atomization.

In a similar vein, a functional explanation of partition of estates among all the children of a household does not appear fully adequate. The Comitancillo native's response as to why the inheritance of land was not restricted shows considerable functional insight: "What could the noninheriting children do?" Yet even without education, the Indians could look more to the city than they do. The functional argument has difficulty in explaining why certain possibilities are excluded; there is room for further analysis. In the Cole and Wolf study, the citizens of the German town clearly depend upon the more central towns and cities for the economic and social placement of the noninheriting children. This is also the case for the Irish countrymen (Arensberg 1937). Indeed, a relationship of peasant dependence on the city has long been unquestioned. While Indian dependence on the city is built into the system through their subordinate political and economic positions, dependence is, nevertheless, contrary to Indian status ideology. Ideologically, Indians are alien to the city. But a restriction of inheritance to one child would seem to force dependence on the city into the kinship network. One surmises that the noninheriting children would necessarily look to the city and probably to their kin in the city for jobs and placement. Such orientations, both to the city and to the kin-field, would be essentially Ladinoizing and inconsistent with the status and ideology of being Indian. To be sure, the lands of many *municipios* are insufficient, and further partition of the plots can only make an almost untenable situation worse (W. R. Smith 1977). Functionally, the rules should change. Yet the equal inheritance to men or to both men and women orients all Indians to the land, to miniscule plots, and to seasonal plantation labor rather than pointing many toward the Ladino city. The point of the rule is not so much economic rationality as symbolic consistency.

However, the lastborn residence rules are not unrelated to the nature of the productive enterprise. The most successful household enterprises and those that do not demand a hard-labor input seem quite relaxed about the issue of postmarital residence. Yet for most Indians it is a significant social concern. In the absence of access to external institutions, security depends on kin. With the focus away from the wider field of kin, security depends on the household. Thus, control of at least one of the children is necessary for a secure old age. This is particularly the case in an agricultural context that demands heavy physical labor and in the face of an ideology that tends toward fission of the households into independence and isolation.

Many San Pedranos, by contrast with the Comitecos, can relax both the rigidity with which they express the lastborn rule as well as the rigor with which they observe it, precisely because many of their occupations are secure and do not tax the labor capacities of an older person. Elderly shopkeepers are less dependent on the labor of a son than are elderly peasant farmers. Yet both would need someone to care for them in their final infirmity, and the inheritance of the house site, above and beyond the equal division of the productive enterprise, is seen as an enticement to and a reward for final service. The lastborn residence rule, with all its variability in implementation and even in expression, appears to be more of an expression of the issue of parental security than of the continuity of viable estates.

The difference between Indian rule-bound restrictedness and Ladino open flexibility should not be viewed as separate derivatives of a pre-Columbian Indian versus European-Hispanic cultural heritage. This view, following from a plural-society model, is inappropriate. Rather, there is a structural relation among the rules from all the communities, whether Ladino or Indian, and among the ethnic ideologies, also taken as a system. The residence rules exist as a set with meaningful relations to each other. They are not just an item or element in a particular culture, whether Indian or Ladino. On the contrary, the rules take a particular form within the Indian status ideology and in symbolic opposition to the open residential pronouncements deriving from the Ladino ideology of flexibility and connectivity. The rule variations between the ethnically symbolized status groups are the result of the intersection of the common categorical culture of the domestic domain with differing status group ideologies. Ladino norms make sense when compared to Indian norms, provided one understands the linked but hierarchic social contexts and the linked but opposite ideologies of the two ethnic sectors. The sense of each ethnic ideology, being derived from its relation to the other, underscores the cultural unity of Guatemalan society.

10
Divorce, Separation, and Abandonment

When marriages or common-law unions dissolve, the process highlights certain stresses and contradictions that arise where conjugal expectations, social institutions, and cultural premises intersect.[1] One source of conflict centers on work and income. The work and income that are expected in an alliance, the degree to which these are available in the institutions of society, and the way in which work and income are evaluated and therefore pursued or avoided differs for each ethnic segment and generates distinctive domestic conflicts. Another source of conflict centers on sexual dominance. Again, the sexual dominance that is expected in the marriage relationship, and the effect of economics and social hierarchy on gender hierarchy colors the character of each ethnic sector's household disputes. There are other conflicts, of course, but to begin to penetrate these matters we must understand the native categories of conjugal failure as fully as we have come to know the native categories of alliance. Since these categories are the same among the townspeople of San Marcos and San Pedro, I will consider both communities together.

Categories of Alliance Termination

The people of both San Marcos and San Pedro refer casually to any end to a marriage or common-law union by saying *"nos separamos*—we separated" or, less formally, *"nos apartamos*—we split up." This primary focus on being "separated" as an index of conjugal failure reconfirms the importance of living together. Co-residence is a critical symbol of a socially acceptable conjugal union and of parental responsibility.[2]

Separations can be either de jure or de facto, and it is thus reasonable for a native to inquire, *"Legalmente?"* If the answer is *"Sí"* or *"Sí, nos divorciamos,"* the native then knows the couple was legally married, for a de jure separation only occurs within a de jure alliance. Thus a *divorcio* (divorce) is a court-ordered termination of the sexual, residential, commercial, and service rights pertaining to a *matrimonio*. However, a divorce leaves intact some economic obligation on the part of the husband to the former spouse: alimony payments until the remarriage of a wife are usual. Moreover, a divorce document invariably specifies an ex-husband's economic responsibility to children born within the alliance. In this regard, divorce defines a continuing but attenuated set of social relationships.

A minor category of de jure separation is *separación legal* (legal separation). Legal separation does not terminate a woman's responsibilities in a marriage relationship; rather, it places a woman's co-residential, sexual, and service obligations in a temporary court-ordered abeyance. But the male makes support payments in spite of the woman's termination of domestic services.[3] Legal separation differs from divorce in two ways. First, the family estate has not been partitioned. Second, both parties retain exclusive sexual, domestic, and residential rights over each other, even though these rights have been declared as nonfunctioning. Furthermore, since these obligations have been inactivated legally, the failure to perform them does not constitute symbolic de facto termination. The man and woman are, then, married but not performing. But given the symbolic value of co-residence, a *separación legal* is an exceedingly liminal situation for the natives of both towns; ending co-residence, sexuality, and service obligations has already terminated the alliance as far as the daily culture is concerned. Thus, most legal separations proceed either to divorce or to abandonment.

The main categorical alternative to divorce, then, is *"separación de hecho"* ("de facto separation"). This is the usual meaning of *"nos separamos"* ("we separated"). In this case the native replies to the question *"Legalmente?"* with *"Así no más"* ("We just did it"). A de facto separation provides no guarantees for the wife or the children. But a woman formerly in a common-law union can sue for child support. This is especially easy if the common-law husband had "recognized" (*"reconocer"*) the children by "registering their birth—*sentar el partido"* in the municipal records. The woman then hires a lawyer or asks the court clerk to certify the existence of the birth registry, which the clerk does without charge. The judge passes pro forma in her behalf, setting a child-support payment in accordance with the man's salary or wages, after his income has been determined by an interview with a court-appointed social worker. If the man had not registered the births of her children—a rather unlikely event if they were living together continuously—she can sue to establish his paternity. Paternity is legally imputed on the testimony of neighborhood witnesses, who would only need to affirm the couple had been living in the same house. However, a common-law wife can not claim alimony—just child support.

Occasionally a legally married couple will separate *"así no más."* But such circumstances are unusual. Usually the man abandons the woman, and she just lets the situation stand. For some, divorce would be too expensive and child support or alimony nonexistent due either to the husband's disappearance or to his low or intermittent salary. In a similar vein, a woman whose common-law union has ended will sometimes not sue for child support or will not legally pursue a former spouse who does not pay a court-established sum. Such women explain: If he can pay at all, the amount would not be worth the effort; and what good does it do to put him in jail?

The category of "abandonment—*abandono"* does not have a rigid denotation. It indicates a de facto separation under prejudicial conditions. *"Me abandonó"* is the usual description if a man disappears from a legal marriage and makes no legal provisions for wife or children. Even if he is found and a divorce is subsequently arranged, the wife will likely describe the events to confidants as *abandono*. Likewise, a man who disappears from a common-law union—presumably to avoid child support—is usually said to have abandoned his common-law wife. In either case, the man will probably describe his behavior with the less prejudicial form *"nos separamos."*[4] But if child support is paid willingly, a woman usually will not claim that she was abandoned; she will probably say that they "separated." When a woman walks out on a man, taking the children, he may call it abandonment or separation. If, however, she leaves him the children—a rare but known phenomenon—it can only be called abandonment. Thus, the language of conjugal failure rather clearly confirms the primary responsibilities that people acquire during and after a marriage or common-law union: for a man, the prejudicial category is applied if he fails to make appropriate support payments, and for a woman, if she fails in custodial care of the children.

The law states quite clearly the justifiable causes for a divorce suit, which include:

1. Infidelity by either partner
2. Mistreatment, continuous disputes and bickering, bodily injury and offenses of honor and, in general, conduct which renders communal life insufferable
3. Attempted murder
4. Unmotivated absence [absence due to work or some other common goal is motivated] from the *casa conyugal* [conjugal house] for more than a year
5. Giving birth to a child conceived before matrimony if the husband did not know of the pregnancy before the marriage
6. An attempt by the husband to give his wife into prostitution or to corrupt his children
7. An unjustified refusal by either partner to fulfill the duties of service or feeding that is legally required
8. Squandering the family estate
9. Habitual gambling, drunkenness, or drug use when these threaten the ruin of the family or constitute a continual source of marital discord
10. Slanderous or criminal accusation of one spouse by the other
11. Criminal indictment with a sentence of more than five years
12. Serious, incurable, contagious disease harmful to the spouse or descendants
13. Incurable infertility arising after marriage, or
14. Incurable mental illness (Guatemala 1972:34–35)

One notes several peculiarities in this list. Item 6 specifically prohibits a husband from selling or giving his wife sexually to others. That such behavior is not counted under immorality implies a husband has latent rights over a woman (which she does not have over him) that must be restrained specifically by law. Moreover, the law specifically states that infidelity, once known to the partner, is not a cause for divorce if the partners continue to live together. Finally, whatever the grounds, a divorce request must be filed within six months of the date that one becomes aware of the grounds. Thus, the law, like the culture, introduces a statute of limitations, so that a person who tries to tolerate offensive behavior loses the fact of that behavior as a ground for divorce and effectively comes to condone—or at least resign oneself to—the behavior. While a new act of infidelity may legally become a new ground for divorce, the pattern is cast culturally and the behavior has become admissible. Ladino women are most throttled by this statute of limitations because they have the fewest alternatives outside a marriage and they have the most to lose if their husbands possess prestigious employment or a significant estate.

A divorce may take place without having to establish cause if the husband and wife are in mutual agreement. In such cases, the reasons for the divorce will not enter the record, except, perhaps, for a statement that the couple agreed they were "mutually incompatible." Here again, a social worker will determine the husband's salary and assets, after which the judge will set alimony and child support.

Of course, the law concerns itself with the causes of separation or divorce only if a legal marriage is at issue. As far as the law is concerned a consensual union may end for no reason at all; the law's only concern is to guarantee a father's financial obligations to his children by the union.

The actual figures on abandonment, de facto separation, legal separation, and divorce are intriguing, though perhaps tricky to interpret.

The high percentage of abandonments in San Marcos indicates a greater sense of betrayal and male unreliability than in San Pedro. If abandonment and de facto separation are grouped together to remove the emotional judgment from the figures, San Marcos still exceeds San Pedro in nonlegal separations as a percentage of all alliance failures, 93.6 percent to 82.7 percent. Table 18, however, gives the figures for the most recent failure, whether or not the couple is still separated. Another way to compare the two towns is to show that 7.6 percent of the San Marcos household heads versus 2.6 percent of San Pedro heads are *currently* in a state of de facto separation or abandonment. San Marcos domestic alliances seem more brittle.

The Causes of Conjugal Breakdown among San Marcos Non-Indians

Essentially, conjugal alliances break up in San Marcos when one or both parties fail to adequately fulfill the duties or obligations understood to arise out of marriage or common-law union. Court cases often label the problem *"incompatibilidad*—incompatibility," one of the grounds for divorce (see Item 2, p. 304). But personality differences per se rarely seem to be a cause of stress, for Ladino men and women live semi-separate lives except when brought together by the specified obligations. Rather, some cultural expectation was offended that, when dwelt upon, made the couples incompatible. In one court clerk's opinion, *incompatabilidad* is usually an ex post facto cover term designed to hide particular social failings and subsequent manipulations among the partners.

A lower-class Marquense woman explained a woman's duties in

Table 18. Reported Types of Most Recent Conjugal Failure

Type of Separation Reported	San Marcos			San Pedro		
	Number	Type as % of Total Failures (N = 31)	Type as % of All Cases (N = 184)	Number	Type as % of Total Failures (N = 29)	Type as % of All Cases (N = 196)
Abandonment	26	83.9	14.1	13	44.8	6.6
De facto separation	3	9.7	1.6	11	37.9	5.6
Legal separation	—	—	—	3	10.3	1.5
Divorce	2	6.5	1.1	2	6.9	1.0
Total	31	100.1	16.8	29	99.9	14.7

the home as "preparing meals and cleaning the house." I asked what would happen if the woman refused to do this. Her reply was:

> It is a duty to do it. There are difficulties if she doesn't fulfill it. They will mistreat each other. . . . Sometimes there are divorces if the man doesn't work or if the woman doesn't know how to serve [that is, perform for his benefit—*servir*] well.

The man's chief expectation is to provide an income to the household. Therefore, the chief fault and cause of conjugal partition is failure to provide the expenses of the household. Unless one can "live by his rents," an income depends on a job. Often one hears of liquor, or another woman, or laziness cited as the cause of domestic breakdown. But these factors, as I shall demonstrate shortly, are usually related to failure to provide household expenses.

CONJUGAL FAILURE AND JOB TRANSFERS

One fine but poor San Marcos Ladino woman:

> There are three reasons for separation. He works far away, or he doesn't work [that is, can't find work], or he accustoms himself to not working at all.[5]

These three problems—and the women seem to see them as problems more than the men do—are endemic to the Ladino subsistence system in the urban milieu.

The first problem is working outside the home municipality. This is the lot of many Ladino construction artisans, day laborers, and salaried government workers. Their jobs force them to move from one *muncipio* to another. Whereas government workers get transferred, construction workers must move on after completing a project. My qualitative impression was that couples with one partner living away from home in order to work were more common and certainly more problematic in San Marcos than in San Pedro. My survey, however, showed that the percentage of couples temporarily separated by their work requirements was identical in both towns. Nevertheless, working away from home was indeed more of a problem in San Marcos. Sixteen percent (five of thirty-one) of the San Marcos conjugal failures volunteered the husband working away from home as a major cause of the conjugal failure, while only 3.4 percent (one of twenty-nine) San Pedro cases volunteered work away from home as the reason. San Marcos women see a job in another town as a disruption of the home: children's educations are interrupted, and housing arrangements are difficult and expensive. More critically, important supportive ties to kin and to friends must be made less active. Because Ladino wives value such society, they are inclined not to move about, at least not for a few months after each transfer. If the work looks temporary, or if the husband's social status and implied reliability are low, a wife is not inclined to move at all. Yet their husbands must move to work.

When a man moves to another job and leaves his wife, however, he is rather incapacitated because he lacks the support services provided by a woman. One alternative to this handicap is to reside in a hotel or rooming house and pay for laundry and other services. Another alternative is to begin a consensual union in the new place of residence. Both options are common. The precise mechanics of how a new alliance is initiated are no doubt varied. In one case, a Ladino government employee who had moved to San Marcos described to me what happened when he was transferred there. After a few days in the local hotel, he made cheaper arrangements in a boarding house, where the landlady also did his laundry. Soon my friend was sleeping with the landlady. He was frankly at a loss to explain how or why the boarding house agreement had changed to a consensual union. The episode can easily be understood, however. Economic provision from male to female, domestic service from female to male, and co-residence are the core symbols of a marriage or common-law union. The sexual liaison was almost inherent in this situation because the working contract differed so little in appearance and convenience from the highly symbolic and reciprocal prestations of marriage or consensual union.[6]

In time, the man became a father in San Marcos. Of course, he was already a father by his legal wife, who still lived in the town of his former post. Before long his government salary would not support both households adequately. The reduced sums that the man sent home to his legal wife soon signaled the problem, and she began to arrange a court-ordered lien on his salary. My friend countered by registering his paternity of the children by the landlady. Since in Guatemalan law a man is responsible for all of his children, regardless of the legality of the domestic alliance, the paternity registration made it impossible for the legal wife to take most of the man's income. Now she could only get a share. Had she been awarded the whole of the disposable income, the legal wife would have squeezed out the second woman in San Marcos, because the man would have lost the income needed to maintain his economic part in a consensual union's reciprocities. By registering his children the man guaranteed his ability to fulfill a continuing obligation to the consensual spouse. He thereby insured her and kept the rights to his place of residence as well as to the domestic and sexual services convenient for pursuing his San Marcos job. In addition to showing the powers of economic and domestic reciprocities, the episode shows how *"algotra* [that is *alguna otra} mujer*—some other woman" is both an impending economic problem and the frequent result of Ladino work mobility.

CONJUGAL FAILURE AND THE POOR LADINO

The second source of failure offered in the previous quotation (see p. 307) is the inability to find work. To the degree of 35 percent of its household heads, San Marcos is a residential center for civil servants whose jobs are reasonably secure. Other employment, however, is limited to a few service crafts, which are tenuous. In San Marcos there is no industrial base for jobs. Commerce is largely transferred to San Pedro, Quezaltenango, and Guatemala City. Moreover, manual and unskilled jobs are highly Indianizing, and there are plenty of Indians who compete for them. Thus, it is somewhat difficult for an uneducated Ladino to find employment at all, and such work as may be found is quite tenuous. Unfortunately, my sample survey figures do not support this interpretation whatsoever, for San Marcos shows a low rate of unemployment among male household heads (1.5 percent). But I am persuaded that this discrepancy is an artifact of survey procedure. On the one hand, an additional 4.5 percent of the male heads in San Marcos report that they are employed in domestic chores without pay. This implies a total of 6.0 percent male unemployment in San Marcos compared to a 3.1 percent unemployment figure in San Pedro. On the other hand, San Marcos household heads who cannot find work (or cannot live by their rents) are pushed from the household. They drift out of town or go back to their parents or to other relatives. As a result, my survey does not capture the character of the problem.

But Marquense natives clearly understand male employment marginality. For the poor and the uneducated, many jobs are temporary and tenuous sources of protection and subsistence, and they are, in any event, undesirable. This situation has repercussions in the domestic alliance. Lower-class women, particularly, expect problems in the employment of their spouses. The lower-class Ladino woman dislikes leaving her mother and natal household at marriage because of a culturally ingrained recognition of the lower-class Ladino male's uncertain ability to provide as a spouse. Men are irresponsible, these women say. If a man's work does terminate, he is likely to leave home to find work, thus increasing the risk to the union. Or the woman may force him out of the house due to his failure in the primary male obligation to provide economically. Moreover, if the woman, due to her expectations, does not leave her mother's house, the man and his mother-in-law then come in conflict, for the mother-in-law is often head of the household by virtue of widowhood or abandonment. These conflicts revolve around right to headship by virtue of masculinity versus right by virtue of ownership. In either case, the parties make conflicting claims on the wife-daughter. These social stresses exacerbate the economic tenuousness of the domestic alliance and increase the probability that the man will abandon the tightly knit and self-protective matrifocal group.

The third source of failure—because men "accustom themselves to not working"—is even more subtle. As we have seen, the claim to Ladino status, particularly in the urban milieu, is a claim to social status that is focused on and modeled after the elite network of individuals who centrally define Ladino as a meaningful national category. This claim to status would be contradicted by work that would point to peripherality and, therefore, Indianness. "Manual" labor, by which is meant physical labor needing no education, is one symbolic focus of Indianness and peripheral status. Thus, some Ladinos prefer not to work rather than to engage in activities that would contradict or undermine their claim to Ladino status.[7]

If they can, such persons live off the income of a female consort—perhaps she is a school teacher, or she runs a corn mill, or she cooks. Although this situation directly contradicts the norm of a male providing for the female, it mirrors, albeit poorly, the ideal of "living by your rents" emanating from the elite center. Thus, the claim to Ladino status increases the occupational precariousness of lower-class persons, namely, the uneducated, the unconnected, and the poor. One avoids work to appear Ladino, but the loss of income disrupts the domestic alliance.[8] Therefore, lower-class Ladino marriages are made relatively unstable by the nature of the work ethic, by the limited possibilities for work, and by the matrifocal arrangements that women make to protect themselves against the possibility of conjugal abandonment, a possibility which is sensed by men and women to be inherent in the total system.

CONJUGAL FAILURE AND THE WELL-TO-DO LADINO

The impact of status on the rich Marquenses is even more obvious. Since high status reduces divorce, I shall only briefly review here matters that were discussed at more length in Chapter 8. As a general proposition, the higher the social status of the male, the more stable the marital system. The female's position in society is largely fixed through attachment to males, either to a father before marriage or to a husband afterward.[9]

Thus, attachment to a high-status male through marriage is of considerable social value. As a corollary, the Ladino woman has a weak status outside marriage; she essentially steps out of the prestigious level if she detaches herself from a male. Moreover, in such a case she may not be prepared to support herself. Except for personal dignity, a woman's threat of separation is a bit silly: she loses much, while the man can get the services he needs elsewhere.

I surmise that men, in perceiving the structural and cultural dependence of the female position, are in certain respects able to exploit the weak positions of their legal wives. The women say to one another, "She is crazy to stay with him, but what can she do?" They describe their rich husbands as maintaining and often even flaunting a secondary union or visiting relationship.

In Chapter 8, I have already alluded to several secondary relationships in San Marcos. The issue at hand is that this behavior is offensive to the wife. "How the women suffer here!" was a common sentiment expressed to my wife. Yet the elite San Marcos wife cannot resolve the situation to her satisfaction. If she places too much pressure on the male, he may leave her. If she places no pressure on him, she is resentful. And the shift of his allegiance may ultimately entail an economic impairment to and consequent collapse of the legal union. If she leaves him, she loses her position and wealth advantage in the community. While she may return to her natal household, such a move effectively severs her from social intercourse in the community. This is not just an idle possibility. One wealthy young divorced woman is a virtual shut-in in her parents' household.[10] So women, for the most part, look the other way. *"Hay que aguantarlo—*one has to put up with it." They expect that their prestigious husbands will have such a relationship, and they suffer. *"Sufrimos mucho,"* they say.

The bothersome part is not the second woman, for she can be tolerated. What bothers the wife is that the *casera* (mistress) may come to her and insult her. First, the *casera* coming into the legal wife's presence is an affront; it suggests a social recognition of an offensive competitor. Worse, however, from the viewpoint of the legal wives, is that they believe the mistress will insult them verbally. Wives' conversations are riven with examples of such incidents happening to others, and indeed they occasionally do occur. Furthermore, wives are perturbed by the flagrance with which a professional-status male may visit and even escort his mistress. Finally, they are afraid that the husband might abandon them residentially and live permanently with the younger and, in some cases, sexually more attractive mistress.[11]

In summary, power and centrality are critical needs in Ladino ideology, the defining values throughout the social system. One way to highlight a privileged access to these values is to make manifest the dependence of others upon oneself and, especially, their inability to be other than dependent. One acquires dependents in the political domain through the structures of patronage: a well-connected man who places people in the government bureaucracy or secures them other employment makes them his dependent debtors. One acquires dependents in the economic domain through the preferred symbol of plantation ownership: the *colono* tenants are also a man's faithful and responsive dependents. One acquires dependents in the domestic domain through the maintenance of multiple households: the wife who cannot get away from a man and the *casera* who finds mistressing a better choice than a lower-class exclusive union feed the power and centrality symbolism of their shared man. He is in control.[12] For Ladino women, conjugal unions, whether legal or not, are inherently unstable in the lower class, while they are inherently uncomfortable in the upper class.

We see, in addition, that the pressures toward conjugal failure among the Ladinos arise from the larger system. This observation again contradicts the plural-society hypothesis that the domestic domain is culturally independent of the larger system. The contradiction becomes telling when we see, next, how the San Pedro Indian alliances respond to the status-induced pressures of the larger system.

The Causes of Marital Dissolution in San Pedro

Though the urban Ladino may systematically exclude himself from opportunities for manual labor, such is not the case for the native San Pedrano, whether Indian or Mestizo. Quite to the contrary, the Indian San Pedrano work ethic suggests that any job that pays is acceptable. The more it pays, the more acceptable it is. Nor are jobs in particularly short supply. Thriving craft industry, expanding construction, basic agriculture, and a vibrant and far-reaching commercial and transportation network combine to leave the area with perhaps even a labor shortage.

One manifestation of both the basic work ethic and the availability of jobs is an aphorism expressed by a forty-year-old San Pedrano agricultural laborer, Indian by self-designation. He had just been informed he was fired. I was mortified and fearful for his prospects. He calmly said, "A day's wages can be found anywhere."[13] That, it seems, encapsulates the Indians' occupational situation. I doubt that many San Pedranos of any ethnic self-ascription would refuse work of any sort if it paid as well or better than the work for which they had prepared in school. And if there were no work available for which they had prepared, they would most likely do other work even though it paid less. Work is both good and appropriate for Indians; it is the hallmark of the San Pedrano. *"Estamos luchando*—we are fighting"; *"Estamos chambeando*—we keep hopping." Diligent and continuous effort, even in the face of adversity, is their watchword. As one Marquense put it, "Those San Pedro *indios* work *hard!"* And they do. Around the clock there is activity in the town, a matter that has been described eloquently by Waldemar Smith in his dissertation (1973) and book (1977) comparing San Pedro and San Miguel Ixtahuacán fiesta practices and processes.

We find, then, that the San Pedrano's income is relatively secure even though his employer may shift. This is so provided he acquires no *vicios,* the habitual vices that corrupt an Indian man's culturally inherent ability to work. We have seen that the expectation of income is a problem in the Ladino sector of San Marcos, yet it is the man's principal obligation in an alliance. But in the Indian sector—for San Pedro, as we have seen, is categorically Indian—income is inherent because work is inherent. The work may not earn much, but some work is available. The problem lies in avoiding economically debili-

Table 19. Economics of Separation

	San Marcos		San Pedro	
	Current Unions	Failed Unions (At Time of Failure)	Current Unions	Failed Unions (At Time of Failure)
Number of cases	124	31	142	29
Mean household size	5.96	4.1[a]	5.76	4.2[a]
Mean household heads' monthly income	138.9	24.1[b]	70.3	43.1[b]
Mean per capita divison of heads' monthly income	23.9	6.6[c]	12.2	11.2[c]

[a] Number of children plus two adults. If other relatives were present, this figure would increase.
[b] Relatively less accurate, by qualitative field judgment.
[c] Or less, if other relatives were present.

Table 20. Mean Male and Female Incomes at Time of Conjugal Dissolution[a]

		San Pedro	San Marcos
Mean income at time of separation	Male partner's	39.2	18.2
	Female partner's	51.7	18.0
Mean income at time of separation for those declaring these incomes to be above zero	Male partner's	39.2	21.5
	Female partner's	77.5	26.0

[a] Note that these incomes are unlikely to be accurate as to absolute monthly incomes. Rather, they portray relative advantage between the towns.

tating habits or vices—whether girls, gambling, or grog. So, as we have seen in Chapter 8, work without vices is the normative expectation in San Pedro marriages.

Of what consequence is this income stability to the domestic alliances? It would appear that the work ethic and work availability accounts, in part, for the slightly greater stability of the San Pedrano marriage system. As indicated previously, 14.8 percent of San Pedranos have had a failure sometime, compared to 16.8 percent of Marquenses. The difference, however, is not sufficient to dwell upon.

A slightly smaller sample size results from taking cases for which I also have income data. These cases are presented in Table 19.

Should San Pedranos not have a higher divorce rate due to their lower income? Unfortunately, my answer is both complex and speculative. In part, as I have demonstrated, the San Pedranos do not focus culturally on income. Beyond this, one can examine the figures more closely. In the first place, in both communities, the male head's income just prior to conjugal failure is lower than the mean for households that have never separated. By dividing the head's income at separation by the number of children and their two parents (in the case of failed unions), one can roughly compute the head's per capita income at the point of conjugal dissolution. By dividing the income of current heads of ongoing (that is, never separated in any form) conjugal unions by the number of persons, one can arrive at a figure for extant unions. (The comparison of these data in Table 19 with Table 10 is interesting.)

In the case of failed conjugal unions, the San Pedro male's income prior to a conjugal failure is much nearer to the San Pedro mean and higher in absolute value than that of a Marquense male. It would appear that since the poor Indian male is culturally able to do *anything* and get *something* he is less marginal to the household than the poor Ladino male.

A class-status factor also affects the conjugal failure rate. The Indian class expectation is less than that of the Ladino in two senses. First, the mean household income in San Pedro is lower than that in San Marcos. Second, the lower ethnic status presumably implies lower expectations in the class sphere. Both Marquenses and San Pedranos remark on the fact that the San Pedrano gets along with less conspicuous consumption and lower basic-living costs. With the class expectations lower in the lower status group, we might surmise low income on the part of a male is less of an offense in San Pedro than in San Marcos and yields a lower rate of failure for the same income.

But the possibility of lower demands on the San Pedro male is counter-balanced by the greater economic security of the San Pedro female. In Chapter 4, I described how the artisan and commercial families involve women and, indeed, the whole family in the productive enterprise. This gives the woman direct economic value to the male partner. This importance, I submit, gives her bargaining leverage in relation to the potential infringement of her rights by the husband. He can have a relatively high income and yet she can still leave him because her income and occupational experience give her something to live on. Since she can support herself to some degree, the loss of a husband's income is less traumatic. Furthermore, the loss of status is nil; both partners are low-status San Pedranos.

Table 20 presents both male and female incomes just prior to the most recent separation. Both male and female incomes of couples about to separate were much higher in San Pedro than in San Marcos. The implication is that a man's income failure is not so large an issue in San Pedro as in San Marcos, especially in view of the difference between these figures and the lower reported mean income of San Pedranos generally.

However, I do not trust these figures for income at the time of a separation. I think it is unreasonable to expect memories of income to be very accurate. However, the relative differences are probably correct, and the point is obvious. The San Pedro woman is less of a hostage farther up the income scale than is her San Marcos counterpart. Moreover, one would suspect that there would be relative ease in establishing a subsequent union since the earnings and labor capacity of a wife, and perhaps of her older children, make her less of a liability. Finally, the San Pedro husband is of low status. He is an Indian by self-claim, or through presumption based on community of origin and family even if he chooses to call himself *mestizo*. Hence, he is of little status-fixing value to the wife. This independent economic viability of the female and low-status contribution of the Indian male mirrors the situation among the Guyanese Negroes reported by Raymond Smith in *The Negro Family in British Guiana* (1956).

One might think that the Indian woman's enhanced paramarital status would increase the conjugal failure rate; but such is not the case. The daily round of field experiences impressed upon me that in the middle- and lower-income levels, and often among the wealthiest cooperating couples, San Pedro men are more appreciative of their wives and of the female contribution to the household in both cash and essential, trusted labor. In addition, the cooperative enterprise requires daytime togetherness. Thus, extramarital affairs or other *vicios,* and the economic problems these bring, are much less easy to arrange. The respect for the woman's labor power and the value of

Table 21. Notes of Serial Reunion (All Conjugal Types)

Male Household Heads
Number of Domestic Alliances Previous to the Present or Last Alliance

Prior Alliances	San Pedro		San Marcos	
	N	%	N	%
0	168	86.2	139	76.0
1	25	12.8	39	21.3
2	2	1.0	5	2.7
	195	100.0	183	100.0

Female Spouses or Female Household Heads
Number of Domestic Alliances Previous to the Present or Last Alliance

Prior Alliances	San Pedro		San Marcos	
	N	%	N	%
0	183	93.8	164	89.1
1	12	6.2	20	10.9
	195	100.0	184	100.0

her income counterbalances the centrifugal force of her ability to be independent. Apparently, as a result, the conjugal failure rate balances out at about the same level as that of San Marcos. Rather than less divorce or separation, the San Pedrano woman gets more respect.

Although the evidence suggests that San Marcos women have only a marginally higher current failure rate than San Pedro women, Table 21 indicates that San Marcos women circulate more through a series of failures. Indeed, this is so for both men and women. The probability of concluding that San Marcos males have a higher mean prior union failure rate than San Pedro males, if in fact they were the same, is 0.0057. The probability of concluding that San Marcos females have a higher mean prior-union failure rate than San Pedro females, if in fact they were the same, is 0.0496. Both probabilities derive from the Mann-Whitney calculation. However, if the San Marcos Indians and the San Pedro Ladinos are deleted from the calculations, then only the men show the above pattern of difference at a statistically significant level. Furthermore, the San Marcos women spend more time being single between unions then is the case with San

Table 22. Divorce or Separation Timing since Conjugal Union

Years from Union or Marriage to Separation	San Marcos			San Pedro		
	N	%	Cumulative %	N	%	Cumulative %
Less than 1	11	36.7	36.7	5	17.2	17.2
1				4	13.8	31.0
2	2	6.7	43.3	2	6.9	37.9
3	1	3.3	46.7	2	6.9	44.8
4	4	13.3	60.0	1	3.4	48.3
5	2	6.7	66.7	2	6.9	55.2
6	1	3.3	70.0	1	3.4	58.6
7				2	6.9	65.5
8				1	3.4	69.0

Years from Union or Marriage to Separation	San Marcos			San Pedro		
	N	%	Cumulative %	N	%	Cumulative %
9	1	3.3	73.3	1	3.4	72.4
10				1	3.4	75.9
12				3	10.3	86.2
13				1	3.4	89.7
14	1	3.3	76.7	1	3.4	93.1
15	1	3.3	80.0			
17				1	3.4	96.6
20	3	10.0	90.0			
22	1	3.3	93.3	1	3.4	100.0
28	1	3.3	96.7			
30	1	3.3	100.0			

Table 23. Volunteered Reasons for Conjugal Failure

Reasons Given	San Marcos (31 failures)					
	Number giving this as 1st reason	% of 1st reason	Number giving this as 2d reason	% of 2d reason	Sum of 1st and 2d reasons	% of 1st and 2d reasons
1. Incompatibility (*incompatibilidad*)	3	10.0			3	7.5
2. Husband drank liquor	6	20.0			6	15.0
3. Husband had lover	13	43.3	1	12.5	14	35.0
4. Wife had lover	1	3.3	1	12.5	2	5.0
5. Husband failed in expenses						
6. Husband absent			1	12.5	1	2.5
7. Wife absent	1	3.3			1	2.5
8. Physical mistreatment by husband	2	6.5	2	25.0	4	10.0
9. Verbal mistreatment by both						
10. Husband worked away from home	2	6.7	3	37.5	5	12.5
11. Gossip, jealousy (*chismes, celos*)	2	6.7			2	5.0
12. Work demanded by parents-in-law	1	3.3			1	2.5
13. Bad conduct						
14. Mother intervened	1	3.3			1	2.5
Totals	32		8		40	

		San Pedro (29 failures)			
Number giving this as 1st reason	% of 1st reason	Number giving this as 2d reason	% of 2d reason	Sum of 1st and 2d reasons	% of 1st and 2d reasons
10	37.0			10	30.3
6	22.2	1	16.6	7	21.2
5	18.5	1	16.6	6	18.1
1	3.7			1	3.0
		1	16.6	1	3.0
		1	16.6	1	3.0
		2	33.3	2	6.1
2	7.4			2	6.1
1	3.7			1	3.0
1	3.7			1	3.0
1	3.7			1	3.0
27		6		33	

Pedro women. The mean time between unions for women is 50.0 months in San Marcos and 43.4 in San Pedro. For men, it is 32.4 months in San Marcos and 32.7 in San Pedro. However, neither difference is significant statistically.

Raymond Smith, in *The Negro Family in British Guiana* (1956), found that the increasing income of the children and their mother, coupled with the racially fixed low status of the male, led to a pattern of brittle unions and matrifocality. A similar pattern of brittle unions and matrifocal residence holds for the poor Ladino.[14] He is low class, but high status. The crucial variable is not status, then, but the impact of status on the ability to make a valued and stable economic contribution to the household. In Guatemala, the work premise of high ethnic status pushes the Ladinos away from manual work, which, for many of the poor and uneducated, is to deprive them of work entirely. With no estate and little income, the Marquense male has little to contribute, and for his wife, if Marquense, acquires her ethnic status independently. By contrast, the San Pedrano male has both income, though modest, and a family enterprise that he manages and in which his wife may participate. While unions fail at a nearly equal rate in both towns, there is less tendency toward matrifocality in San Pedro.

The two towns manifest distinctive patterns in the timing of conjugal failures. Table 22 shows that, in the first year especially, and throughout the first four years, domestic alliances (unions or marriages) in San Marcos are more likely to rupture than during the same years in San Pedro. Then, between the seventh and thirteenth years the rate of failure in San Pedro exceeds that in San Marcos. From the twentieth year on, San Marcos exceeds San Pedro again. In both towns, the highest percentages of failures occur in the first years. Just why San Marcos is relatively more brittle in the earliest and latest years and San Pedro relatively more unstable in the middle years remains as yet a mystery.[15]

Having surveyed the cultural and structural factors that enter into the patterns of conjugal failure, I return to the crude figures of the expressed causes of conjugal failure. In my survey, I allowed respondents who had experienced divorce, separation, or abandonment first to volunteer the reasons for the failure and then to give "yes/no" answers to a checklist of questions concerning troublesome issues for each sex. In Table 23, which shows the volunteered reasons for conjugal failure, there are a few notable differences. San Pedranos offer

Table 24. Elicited Causes of Conjugal Breakdown

Cause	San Marcos (N = 31)		San Pedro (N = 29)	
	N	% of Failures	N	% of Failures
Alcohol used by X	11	35.5	13	44.8
X = Male	10	32.3	12	41.4
X = Female	1	3.2	1	3.4
X had lover	16	51.6	10	34.5
X = Male	15	48.4	8	27.6
X = Female	1	3.2	2	6.9
X failed to provide expenses	5	16.1	7	24.1
X = Male	5	16.1	7	24.1
X = Female	0	0.0	0	0.0
X failed to serve spouse	4	12.9	3	10.3
X = Male	3	9.7	2	6.9
X = Female	1	3.2	1	3.4
X abandoned household	10	32.3	10	34.5
X = Male	9	29.0	8	27.6
X = Female	1	3.2	2	6.9
X physically abused spouse	6	19.4	9	31.0
X = Male	5	16.1	9	31.0
X = Female	0	0.0	0	0.0
X = Each other	1	3.2	0	0.0
X verbally abused spouse	8	25.8	11	37.9
X = Male	5	16.1	8	27.6
X = Female	0	0.0	3	10.3
X = Each other	3	9.6	0	0.0
Person demanding separation				
X = Male	7	22.6	7	24.1
X = Female	19	61.3	15	50.7
X = Both	2	6.5	6	20.7
X = Not applicable	3	9.7	1	3.4

"incompatibility" (Item 1) as the major reason for failure considerably more often than do Marquenses; this conforms to my suggestion that the power structure of domestic alliances is more balanced in San Pedro than in San Marcos. Men are blamed for taking lovers (Item 3) about twice as often in San Marcos as in San Pedro; this again confirms the dominance patterns described above. In concert with this, problems with gossip and jealousies (Item 11)—suggesting the expectation of a husband's problems with another woman—are almost twice as frequent in San Marcos as in San Pedro. Finally, as noted above, the husband's work away from home (Item 10) is volunteered as a cause of conjugal failure about four times as often in San Marcos as in San Pedro.

When confronted with my checklist (to which they gave verbal responses as summarized in Table 24), alcohol figured more disruptively in San Pedro, while the husband taking a lover proved considerably more disruptive in San Marcos. Contrary to the volunteered causes, San Pedranos report more reaction to physical and verbal abuse. Whether this means that more of such abuses were present, or that, given the San Pedro woman's stronger position in the household, less abuse would be tolerated, I do not know.

Conclusion

The interconnectedness of divorce, separation, and abandonment with status ideology and economics is apparent for both Ladinos and Indians. These are not functionally parallel autonomous domestic domains for which the plural-society model would be appropriate. Rather, this is a single system, a portion of which is labeled Indian and a portion, Ladino.

The singleness is, of course, quite complex. At the cultural level, the categories of domestic dissolution are the same. In addition, the symbolic forms by which dissolution is announced are likewise the same: nonresidence, nonservice, and economic partition. And the behavior affixed as appropriate for a male after divorce (supporting wife and children at a reduced rate) and after a separation (supporting payments of children on account of kinship obligations) is the same.

On the other hand, the normative system is split as to similarities and differences. There is a considerable difference between ethnic sectors in the expectations (or, rather, "suspectations") as to the behavioral probability of a dissolution. The women of San Marcos, especially the poor women, refer often to this probability and they take steps to protect against the eventuality through uxorilocal residence. By contrast, among the rich Ladinos, a divorce is sometimes desirable morally, but socially it is too costly. We have here countervailing pressures adding to and subtracting from the crude rate of conjugal failure.

The San Pedranos, on the other hand, are much less likely to make spontaneous reference to the issues of separation. Structurally there is much less pressure for separation to occur. Indeed, there is a positive economic inducement to keep a relationship intact and to keep the reciprocity of prestations. On the other hand, the economic contribution that makes a woman more appreciated also allows her to be less tolerant of offenses. Again, we have countervailing pressures. As a result, San Marcos and San Pedro do not differ significantly in their crude rates of conjugal failure. But the processes that lead to the numerical similarity are remarkably different.

We are reminded of the importance of a conceptual rather than a behavioral definition of culture. We are directly confronted with the weaknesses of the survey approach. Indeed, the figures in this chapter are the weakest in this book, since remembrances of former unions are those most subject to distortion by time. And we are again reminded to be skeptical of the plural-society or separate-cultures approaches to understanding the domestic domain. The institutional pressures toward both alliance continuity and dissolution come from outside the domestic domain; the cultural assumptions that guide ethnic behavior in each sector are linked by their systematic opposition and mutual ranking.

11
Death and Inheritance

Catholics mark the transition from life to death with a funeral mass, a ritual considered essential for the salvation of the soul. Funeral services are available to Catholics for the appropriate fee, regardless of their prior ecclesiastical participation or their state of grace.

In the section that follows, I recount a single description of the funeral that will suffice for both San Marcos and San Pedro. Except where noted in the description, I was unable to ascertain significant differences.[1]

The Funeral

Guatemalan law requires that a body be buried within twenty-four hours of death. As there are no facilities for preserving a corpse, it is essential for health reasons to bury the body quickly. This requirement puts some pressure on the deceased person's relatives, who must quickly make final arrangements, assemble kin, carry out a mass, and bury the corpse.

If a person dies sufficiently early in the day, the family will provide an evening ceremony called *velación*, to be followed by mass and interment the next morning. For a *velación* I observed in the town of San Marcos, the bedroom was cleared of furniture except for chairs around the outside of the room. The bed on which the body lay had been moved so as to jut out diagonally from the corner of the room. A canopy of white and purple crepe papers and cloth arched over the head of the bed, with flowers, generally of the same colors, set about. The women—kin and neighbors—occupied the room throughout the night, offering chanted prayers to the Virgin Mary for the benefit of the deceased. Most of the men sat in the adjoining salon, drinking and talking. A few young men and young women used the occasion to socialize. Sometimes men would enter the room where the corpse lay, but only the females in the room would kneel now and then to chant the *novena* under the guidance of a female cantor.

In a San Pedro *velación,* the body was in a casket in the *sala,* for there was only one room and a kitchen in the house. Male and female relatives and neighbors chanted the *velación* with this poor Indian family. However, I was told that elite, educated San Pedro men did not usually attend the *velación* chants, and such was the case at the one elite funeral I attended in San Pedro.

On the following morning of an evening death, close relatives—usually brothers or brothers-in-law—make arrangements for the burial.[2] A well-to-do family commissions a mason to open the brick facing of a slot in the already prepared family mausoleum. In San Pedro a poor family commissions the digging of a grave plot, or they dig it themselves; I neglected to ascertain if a poor Marquense family might dig their own. Casket and burial clothing are purchased if needed. Often the poorer rural or urban Indians prepurchase their caskets and funeral clothing, storing them in the attic or hanging them from the rafters. With these arrangements made and the mass commissioned and scheduled, the relatives reassemble in the home of the deceased. There, the friends and relatives bolt the casket to the carrying rack and exit from the house. Close kin carry the coffin outside and down the middle of the street; the remaining *familia* and *familiares* follow in a bunch closely behind, also walking in the center of the street. More distant relatives, neighbors, and others form single-file columns that walk on the narrow sidewalks or at the edges of the street, one sex on each side. They walk slowly to the church, taking turns carrying the coffin, with the closest relatives generally taking the first turn out of the house.

For funerals, the Catholic churches in both towns are hung with the black draperies of mourning that are accented with flowers emphasizing the white of purity, the purple of mourning and pain, and mixed with other flowers and colors as may be in season at the time. As in all Catholic masses and other ritual occasions within the church, men sit to the left of the center aisle and women sit to the right as they face the altar. Once the mass has been completed, the closest relatives of the deceased pick up the casket and carry it down the center aisle, between two lines formed by the men from the left pews and the women from the right pews. The family members carrying the casket and the two lines of guests move slowly out of the church and down the street, with women to the left sidewalk, men to the

Plate 26. A funeral procession in San Pedro. (1974)

right, and the casket in the center followed by the *familiares* walking bunched.[3] As when they left the house, the closest relatives take the first shift out of the church, with the near relatives taking subsequent turns and neighbors and friends taking the later shifts. The casket is returned to the closest relatives, however, for the final entry into the cemetery. Throughout the procession, church bells along the way toll a distinctive death knell.

If the family is poor, the deceased's relatives, neighbors, and friends lower the casket into the grave by ropes strung under the casket. Then they fill and tamp the grave and perhaps set a headstone cross or nameplate. If the family is more well-to-do, a close relative of the deceased slides the casket the final few inches into the vault, and a mason then bricks over the slot and sets a plaque containing name and dates. In either case, the deceased person's relatives then receive and greet the other persons in the procession, who offer the family their condolences *(pésame)*. At this time relatives, close neighbors, and close friends are invited to a meal in the home of a family member.

For nine succeeding evenings women offer chanted prayers *(novena)* in the home of the deceased. During the next year, the family offers an additional *velación* once a month, on the numerical date of the person's death. I do not know how faithfully this monthly ritual is adhered to, or to what degree the poor excuse themselves from the ceremony, but informants talked about it as the appropriate procedure. A final ceremony, called the *cabo de año,* occurs on the one-year anniversary of the person's death. For the *cabo de año* a *velación* is minimal, with a mass highly preferred. Both in San Pedro and in San Marcos, some wealthy families commission memorial masses on succeeding annual anniversaries of a relative's death.

Funeral Expenses versus Inheritance

SAN PEDRO SACATEPÉQUEZ

Providing for the funeral and allocating the inheritance are points of tension in San Pedro society. A proper funeral is essential for a deceased person's well-being, and minimal estimates for a poor person's funeral, without ostentation, range between 150 and 200 dollars. On a wage system where an Indian laborer makes roughly one dollar for an eight-hour day, this is a sizable sum and may be a considerable strain. The essential tension, however, is not due to the cost, but to the ideology of independence.

Only when faced with the prospect of a funeral is a San Pedrano utterly dependent on others for an element crucial to his continued well-being. The matter was never stated quite so analytically, but San Pedranos would note that the funeral was essential and that children could not necessarily be trusted to carry it off for and in one's behalf. Thus, some people took the precaution of prepurchasing needed funeral items; it was not uncommon, especially in the hamlets, to visit a home where a casket wrapped in plastic would be hung in view from the ceiling. Within the casket, I was told, were the funeral clothes *(mortaja)* in which the person would be dressed upon death. All this was considered partial insurance against the children failing to perform the necessary ritual.

More importantly, a man or woman would often draw up a legal document that would specify not only the division of the person's estate to his or her heirs but would also state which lands were to be sold specifically to cover funeral expenses. Thus, one old San Pedro woman, who owned two *cuerdas,* had a lawyer specify that one *cuerda* went to one of her three daughters, while the other *cuerda* was to be sold for the funeral. In other cases, a specific plot was designated to go to the heir or heirs un-named that did, in fact, cover the funeral costs.

In the absence of other legal arrangements, rural San Pedranos expect the lastborn son to cover the cost of the funeral. In compensation, this son expects to inherit the parental house and yard and perhaps an additional piece of land over and above the otherwise equal division of the land inheritance among the male and female siblings. Thus, inheritance and the rule of lastborn residence are partially tied together. One San Pedro informant suggested that a lastborn son was economically favored by such a transaction, for, the informant said, a house of modest rural size might be worth two thousand dollars while the expenses incurred in both a funeral and in caring for parents during their final sickness might cost roughly six hundred dollars.

There are, nevertheless, variations from the cultural expectation. Informants have described legal documents in which the house is allocated not to the lastborn son but to whomever in fact defrays the costs. Such a provision is legalized and notarized in a manner calculated to insure enforcement of the parents' wishes by an external legal sanction. Anxiety with regard to death and inheritance is clearly manifest in a statement by one San Pedrano, who observed:

> A father, when he sees himself in a grave state, gives inheritance. If he gives it when he is well, the son tries to kick the father into the street. For this reason he does not give inheritance until he sees himself near to death. Then a father looks for a lawyer in order to deliver the inheritance to the children.

This anxiety over the provision of a funeral seems to be consistent with the Indian ideology of independence and, consequently, their lesser ability to form and depend upon social networks.

SAN MARCOS

By contrast, Ladinos seemed to suffer no anxiety over funeral expenses. The Ladinos did not bring up the issue of documents allocating specific responsibility for funeral expenses, nor did I see the occasional casket hanging from the ceiling in Ladino households.[4] The Ladino's relative lack of concern over the prospect of his funeral is also consistent, for the inverse Ladino ideology provides the people with a system of interconnection that makes dependence on social networks appear more reasonable. A Ladino is culturally able to trust his kin to perform for him a necessary ceremony.

Even though the most inexpensive funeral is quite costly for the poor San Pedranos, the anxiety over funerals does seem predominantly due to the nature of social ideologies rather than to the cost, for even the poorest families could divide up the costs, sell an animal or two, and at worst take on a debt to cover adequately the cost of a funeral. The children of a deceased Ladino, even if poor, seemed to have a sense of cooperative obligation to cover the funeral costs. Given their ideology of social involvement and interconnection, Ladinos seem to show little stress on this issue, whereas Indians, faced with an ideology of atomization and independence, find the obligatory funeral a trying and hazardous prospect indeed.

Inheritance

I have already alluded to inheritance immediately above and in Chapter 9, but it is appropriate to summarize here. People inherit from the mother's property when the mother dies and from the father's property when the father dies, although some of a man's property will pass to his wife for her sustenance, and this property, upon her death, will be passed on to the children, who consider it as having come from the father. Thus, in both San Marcos and San Pedro, inheritance is essentially bilateral.

Within the general framework of bilateral inheritance, which the government applies rigorously when an Indian or Ladino dies intestate, there is a tendency in San Pedro for women to be shorted in their equal share of the estate. Some informants offered that San Pedro women, not knowing exactly what was available, took somewhat smaller or less desirable shares. In one specific instance of inheritance in San Pedro, each of the sons received two *cuerdas* of flat and fertile agricultural land, while each of the daughters received ten *cuerdas* of more rugged and infertile mountainside land. The informant suggested that while the monetary values of the inheritances were about the same the men got an obviously better deal. In another instance in San Pedro, the sons received houses near the center of town, while the daughters received houses on the perimeter. In this case, the brothers inherited "much larger, proportionately, than that which my sisters received." The whole arrangement was made four years prior to the father's death, with the wife receiving about one-half of the estate for her subsistence during the remainder of her life. However, the husband had legally allocated the precise division of these lands among his children upon her death. In another instance, a San Pedro businessman was building two identical houses for his sons. They were set face to face and shared a common courtyard, but had separate exits to the street. His daughters would live with their husbands, and while they would probably receive an inheritance it was as yet unplanned. Reasonably well-to-do San Pedro parents have often expressed the idea that they would like to set up one house for each of their children, whether male or female: "This is something any family head (*jefe de familia*) struggles to achieve."

Nevertheless, the ideal of equality conficts with the cultural thrust toward male priority and toward the idiosyncrasies of personal closeness. Thus, said a San Pedrano, although

> there is always a preference among one or another child, every father must satisfy his obligation to give something, even though it be just a little, and that he divide his land because they have here a form of thought which says that a person who dies, and who has land or has money or has goods, and doesn't leave it divided—these people say that such cannot enter into the Kingdom of God.

Other San Pedro informants tend to emphasize greater equality in the division. And one informant, a lastborn son, felt so uncomfortable receiving the entire but undividable inheritance of a tiny house that he subsequently made cash payments to his siblings.

In San Marcos, women might similarly be shorted in their share of the smaller pieces of an estate. But where shares are maintained in a large unit of the family estate, such as a *finca,* it would appear on the surface that women are treated to a precisely equal share. In practice, since men are more involved in supervising the *finca* manager and in accounting for the estate financially it would be easy for them to take a relatively larger share of the annual proceeds. But the thrust toward equality is clear. As one Marquense put it: "If the father is of proper heart, he gives equally to sons and daughters. If he is not of good heart, then he gives less to the daughters. There are some who give nothing to their daughters." But while San Pedro and San Marcos share these similarities, there are differences.

The key difference is that San Pedranos always parcel out the inherited lands, partitioning them among the sons and daughters. Each heir holds his inheritance in full and separate ownership and can dispose of it as he or she sees fit. The inherited land plot, the small corner business, the truck, or whatever the legacy is then worked or put to productive use by the individual. As noted above, the inheritance is often completed before the death of the parent. For example, one San Pedrano described how his father gave each child, male and female, a small piece of land.

> Now the house and six cuerdas of land, these were not divided up. These were kept pending because [my father] said that once one of the persons cared for him and buried him and performed the nine days *velación* and the *cabo de año,* to this one would be left the house and land.

By contrast, the Marquenses tend to hold their estates intact, especially their larger coastal plantation estates. The inheriting siblings will employ a manager to operate the estate and each inheritor will take equal shares out of the annual profits of the operating estate. This takes place "often" in San Marcos, said one of the court clerks, "provided all the children are agreed." This key difference in partition is consistent with the Indian ideologies of atomization and self-sustenance versus the Ladino ideology of interconnection.

A final set of differences lies in the distribution of the dying parent's house. In San Pedro, as I have indicated, the house is frequently left to the lastborn son. To be sure, there is considerable variation on whether, in the end, it goes to the lastborn son. Since the house is viewed as just recompense for the extra effort of having cared for the parents, it may go to the last remaining child if the lastborn son abdicates his customary responsibility, or it may go to whomever takes care of the parents and vouches for their funeral. But the general rule is clear, even if it is becoming somewhat vestigial. If the house is large, it will often be subdivided. Thus, San

Pedro children will acquire a portion of the larger parental home. In the building practices of the area, it is not uncommon for each room on the perimeter of a large house to have its own door to the street. When the estate is intact, these doors are barred and unused (except to air out the house during the rainy season). But upon inheritance, these doors make it possible for siblings to open new entrances to their own households, as they proceed to subdivide and wall off individual portions of the once-common courtyard.

In San Marcos, too, the larger patio-style homes are often used by several inheriting families. But the apartments usually take their entries from the interior patio, with all the families using a common gate to the street. Such houses are not legally subdivided, however, and children or grandchildren of the deceased may live in the central household when and if their individual economic needs demand it. Again, with houses San Pedranos subdivide and achieve separation, while Marquenses often hold houses essentially intact, sharing their use among interacting descendants. Both practices are consistent expressions of the respective ethnic ideologies.

After Inheritance

San Pedro is rife with stories of disgruntled brothers who, if they feel their lot was unequal or apparently unequal, pursue each other with suits by hired lawyers and attacks through hired sorcerers (*brujos*). Indeed, San Pedranos even talk of spiteful brothers who, though they had an exactly equal inheritance, attempt to take over a portion of their sibling's share through legal or sorcerous maneuvers. As one San Pedrano put it, "The typical family indeed fights immediately over the distribution and quantity of lands, whatever they may be, regardless of their size. Large or small, there is always going to be a fight over the possession of land and its use, even if the lands are not commercially valuable." This fervor with regard to matters of inheritance is consistent with the crucial importance of land or commercially productive property for the independence and (symbolic) self-subsistence of an Indian-oriented person or family.

In San Marcos, legal disputes over land are known but are not so often passionately discussed. In any event, except for the rich, one's principal inheritance comes in the form of an education and an acceptable ethnic (seen as racial) background. A completed education, a proper ethnic heritage, the right to use the family house, and access to family friends can ensure one a secure life as a government employee. That is an adequate inheritance for most Ladinos.

Summary

The crucial difference, then, between Indians and Ladinos is in the degree to which the bilateral inheritance is partitioned socially. Though inheritance is essentially bilateral in both ethnic groups, the San Pedro Indians rigorously subdivide inheritances for familial independence. They are more dependent on an individually owned estate for satisfying the cultural logic of independence. On the other hand, the San Marcos Ladinos more easily maintain joint rights in the larger estates, keeping them undivided for managerial purposes. Thus, they are more socially oriented in their inheritance management than the neighboring San Pedranos. In addition, Ladinos are less dependent on a material inheritance, for their cultural logic throws them more toward the pursuit of power and interdependence, a matter satisfied by education and a well-placed government job. Indeed, the social logic that facilitates joint management enables the inheriting Ladino to be mobile and to take advantage of a government position in spite of his ownership of land. The Indian, by contrast, is ideologically disposed to independent subsistence activity and hence is bound to his land. Thus, the pattern of ethnic dispositions toward land uses, derived from the fundamental ideologies of independence versus social connection, coordinates with the Indian orientation to a home community versus the Ladino orientation toward other towns and the nation, especially toward the capital city.

We see that the issue of inheritance again casts doubt on the plural-society model, for the principal behavioral difference in the inheritance system—the degree to which land is divided or jointly administered—is precisely consistent with the social positions and general ideologies of the politically, economically, and culturally interlocked ethnic groups. Moreover, the difference is certainly functional. Inheritance partition exacerbates Indian powerlessness, immobility, and social isolation; inheritance unity enhances Ladino resources, mobility, and social interconnection.

12
The Developmental Cycle of the Household

A household's composition is ultimately a synthesis of the several factors I have treated separately in prior chapters. The bonds and obligations of kinship; the notions of social positions and leadership; the results of marriage and divorce; the decisions of children to move away to work or to marry, or to stay in the household and bring in a spouse; the arrangements to send children from one household into another for school, work, experience, or companionship; the influence of ethnic ideology; the fortunes of social and economic circumstance; cultural definitions of ideal space; personality conflicts[1]—all of these combine with the basic facts of birth and death to give each household its membership at any given point in time. To be sure, each household is unique. Yet, if one considers only the formal relationships among household members, the households may be classed analytically in a limited number of types.

At any particular moment a household has a given membership and a specifiable set of principal connective relationships among its members. These relationships, however, are not static; they change and shift with time, with marriage or divorce, with birth or death, and with the numerous other decisions to be made and factors to be accommodated. Each household forms, develops, and decays, thereby transforming discrete types into linked stages. With few exceptions, the households conform to a limited number of developmental cycles consistent with the ethnic ideology and class situation in which the households are located (Fortes 1949; Smith 1956; Goody 1958). To break into the household developmental cycle for descriptive purposes is, therefore, partially arbitrary. Nevertheless, since both San Pedranos and Marquenses consider the newly married couple the common beginning of a separate household, I shall lay out the developmental cycle of the domestic group, beginning with the household composed of the one-generation newly married young couple.

The one-generation household composed of a newly married couple (usually a young couple) can mature in essentially only two directions. Barring accidents of death, it can become either a one-generation aging couple that never had children, or, by the process of having children it will turn into a two-generation expanding nuclear household. For both the San Pedrano and the Marquense, the formation of the two-generation or nuclear household is the developmental pattern expected of the one-generation new couple. Moreover, the failure to have children is, for most people, both unexpected and undesired.

Again, barring death, divorce, or separation of the parental couple, the expanding nuclear household ultimately transforms itself by a process of either dispersion or accretion. In the process of dispersion the children, as they mature, may leave the household either to work or to get married. In this case, the expanding nuclear household transforms itself into a dispersing nuclear household, reducing its membership one by one as the children marry and hive off. At the end of this cycle, the two-generation dispersing household becomes once again a one-generation household, this time composed of aged parents.

In the case of accretion, either the expanding nuclear household or the dispersing nuclear household may evolve into a three-generation household by one of two paths. One common source of the three-generation household is for one or more of the children in the nuclear household to marry and bring his or her spouse to reside with the parents, where they ultimately bear a third generation of children. Indeed, a particular household may oscillate between the two-generation and three-generation format as each child in turn marries, remains in the household, (perhaps) bears a child, locates itself suitably, and moves out after a year or more—following which a subsequent child marries and repeats the process. Alternatively, such a household might remain three-generation for a period of time, with younger children bringing in spouses before older married siblings leave. In most households, however, the older children hive off with their spouses to form a new nuclear family, as their succeeding younger brothers and sisters come close to the age of marriage or actually begin to marry. These three-generation households ultimately evolve into a household in which parents (and, eventually, a single surviving parent), the last child to be married, his or her spouse, and their children remain together. This is the final stage of the three-generation stem family, except for the few households in which unusual longevity admits a fourth generation of tiny great-grandchildren.

There are, indeed, four cases of four-generation households in my sample, two in each town. More often, however, these three-generation households lose one parent and finally both through death, and are thereby transformed into two-generation households advanced in the dispersion stage.

In Chapter 9, I showed that San Pedranos expect the lastborn son to remain in the household. San Marcos is, theoretically, more variable. Indeed, the San Pedrano three-generation household is more often virilocal than in San Marcos; the San Marcos households that reach the three-generation configuration tend to be more equal in the sex of the stem sibling.

There is another path by which households arrive at the three-generation terminal stem-type. A nuclear household, after having been separate, may take in its aging parents, either as a couple or as a widow or widower who would otherwise be living alone—thus forming a three-generation household by the process of adding a senior generation. This occurs commonly in both towns and is a major source of uxorilocality in the three-generation terminal stem household of San Pedro. These two stem households, though formed by different processes—the one by adding young children, the other by adding aged parents—look alike. However when aged parents are added, the household head is likely to be the husband of the couple who invites the senior parents into the house.

A variant of the three-generation household emerges when a one-generation elderly couple takes in one or more of its grandchildren. To arrive at this configuration, a nuclear household first hives off all of its children. Later, circumstances may arise that require one of these couples to deposit one or more of their children with their grandparents. For example, a young mother, who has never married or has separated from her spouse, may live with her child in the home of her parents. If such a mother secures a husband, he often will not want the responsibility for another person's child. On the other hand, if a single mother finds good work elsewhere, she often leaves her children in the grandparents' care. In a few cases, a young father is abandoned by his spouse and leaves the children with his parents for similar reasons. Or a young couple may die, leaving orphans. Often, a couple must live and work in a hinterland *municipio* where they feel the educational resources are inadequate. These couples, too, place their children with grandparents living in San Marcos or in San Pedro. In these cases, a three-generation household with no stem child may be formed. (I have cited the relative frequency of two varieties of such households in notes 9 and 16 of Chapter 9.) What is important here is the sex ratio of the absent stem children: two male to five female in San Marcos and three male to four female in San Pedro. It would appear that the culturally given openness to matrifocality in San Marcos and the prejudice against matrifocality in San Pedro affects even the subtle difference in the sex ratio of the absent stem child in these three-generation households.

Sometimes, a departed older son or daughter may leave his or her children in the grandparent household before the younger siblings marry. This leaves a three-generation household composed of parents, their remaining children, and grandchildren who are nephews to the resident siblings of the absent spouse. Again, the reasons for this are presumably similar to those given for the households with no middle generation. With time, such a household may simplify into a three-generation household in which there is no middle-generation resident—only grandparents and grandchildren—or into a stem family with attached cousins in the junior generation.

Sometimes, the three-generation household with no middle generation evolves when married children of the older couple give them a grandchild for company. In San Pedro, people say they do this to help care for the aged. It is also done to facilitate educating the grandchild, though less frequently than in San Marcos. In San Marcos the reasons are the same, but the order is reversed. Especially if the kin group has plantation land on which the middle-generation nuclear household may live, the retired generation moves to the center of San Marcos and takes in grandchildren. This facilitates the education of the grandchildren by relocating them from the lowlands coffee *municipios,* where schools are deficient, to San Marcos, where the grandparents can supervise their schooling and upbringing.

I am not sure how the grandparent-grandchild household (with no middle generation) subsequently evolves. Presumably, when the grandparents die the grandchildren return to their parents or live with other collateral relatives who could assist them in schooling or other needs. Or, when educations are complete, grandchildren return home and a one-generation aged couple remains.

There are many reasons why a household might take in collateral relatives. Perhaps a household can offer a residential location more suitable for someone to take a position or to go to school; to do so they may take in a sibling, niece, or nephew of either spouse. A household properly takes in orphaned or abandoned siblings, nieces, or nephews of either spouse.

There are other sources of complex households. If the parents of a three-generation household should die before all their children have married, then the resulting two-generation household will be complex, having both the nuclear core and the collateral siblings of the husband or wife until the siblings, one by one, marry and move away. In San Marcos, there are sixteen households where the nuclear household couple is intact and have collateral relatives living with them. These households are split equally, with eight attached through the husband and eight through the wife. Five other households have collateral relatives living with a widowed, divorced, or separated female household head, while one separated male household lives with his child and a brother. Interestingly, the patrilaterally expanded nuclear households are wealthier (mean income = $122.40, mean land value = $800.20) than the matrilaterally expanded nuclear households (mean income = $93.90, land value = $131.30) even though both spouses are present. The female-headed (widowed, divorced, or separated) matrilaterally expanded nuclear households have less income (mean = $73.40) but more valuable land (mean = $281.10). In San Pedro, there are three patrilaterally expanded nuclear households with a mean income of $141.70 and land value of $0.00, eight matrilaterally expanded households with a mean income of $61.80 and land value of $100.00, one bilaterally expanded household with an income of $546.00, and a land value of $560.00, and no incomplete couples among the collaterally expanded households. It would appear that collateral expansion on the wife's side correlates with relative poverty in both towns.

We see here that households evolve through several interconnected paths. A household actually disappears or ends its cycle only if a one-generation aging couple is not taken into another household and decomposes through the death of first one and then the other spouse. This does happen, though, for there are two male and three female elderly single-person households in San Marcos, and there are five female elderly single-person households in San Pedro.

The Impact of Cultural Premises on the Developmental Cycle

Thus far I have traced the developmental-cycle paths with only a partial discussion of the differences in the use of those paths by the people of San Marcos and San Pedro. Since, however, the two communities are mainly distinguished in certain cultural premises, these premises impact upon the frequency that each path is taken in each town.

Given the San Pedro cultural expectation and thrust toward independence, we may expect San Pedro to have more one-generation new marriages or one-generation initial couples than San Marcos, expressed as a percentage of the community total. In fact, four San Pedro newly married couples (2.0 percent of 196) are living in independent houses, with an additional couple living in a parental compound but maintaining a separate apartment and family expense. In San Marcos, only two newly married couples are completely independent (1.1 percent of 184), with a third couple also living in a parental compound with a separate apartment and separate family expense. The numbers are small, but behavior conforms to the cultural expectation.

Continuing with the implication of San Pedrano independence, we may expect there a higher percentage of nuclear households with no collateral persons attached. In San Pedro 60.5 percent of all (195) households are nuclear, whereas in San Marcos only 48.4 percent of the (184) households are nuclear.[2] We see here a solid inclination toward nuclear independence in San Pedro. This is the inverse of the Marquenses' thrust toward social connection, by which we may reason that in San Marcos there will be more households with collateral attachments. In this regard, in addition to the nuclear households just mentioned, San Marcos has an additional 22 nuclear households with additional collateral relatives (or 12.0 percent of the total), whereas San Pedro has 6.2 percent (12 of 195) such households. Finally, this bias toward social interconnection extends even through the one-generation households, where in San Marcos 3.8 percent (7 of 184) of all households are of one generation composed of a head (spouse optional) and collateral relatives, versus 2.6 percent (5 of 195) of such households in San Pedro.

The nature of the three-generation-household difference between the two communities is complex. On one hand, we have examined the San Pedro three-generation household as a response either to poverty or, in the final stages, to the existence of the lastborn son's obligation to the parents. Since San Pedranos specifically and Indians generally are expected to be poorer—and San Pedranos are indeed poorer than Marquenses—there is a good deal of economic pressure toward this format in spite of the nuclear ideal. By contrast, in San Marcos there are two paths toward this household situation: one by virtue of the Ladino ideology of maximizing linkages, and the other by virtue of the work ethic's impact on women's trust in men. In this latter case, lower-class women systematically expect their husbands to be unemployed. They generate the three-generation households with a matrifocal axis to "defend themselves." Since I have examined the San Marcos matrifocal bias in Chapter 9, we need only recall here that 20.0 percent (of 195) San Pedro households are three-generation, with a mean income of $64.20, which is 69 percent of the community's average income. By contrast, 26.6 percent (of 184) San Marcos households are three-generation (including those with an absent middle generation), with a mean income of $212.50, 123 percent of the community mean.

Finally, given the rules, we would expect more virilocality in San Pedro. In San Marcos, given the notion of opportunity maximization and the idea that women of the lower class band together to protect themselves, we expect a more mixed combination or a balance between virilocality and uxorilocality. In fact, as we saw in Chapter 9, virilocal links comprise a higher percentage of stem households in San Pedro than in San Marcos; 46.4 percent of San Pedro three-generation stem households are all or partially virilocal, compared to 36.6 percent of San Marcos stem households.

Conclusion

With regard to household composition, it is possible to talk about the impact of culture, as I have done above in general terms, and it is possible to talk about the impact of economics, as I have done here and in the previous chapters. Of course, the two do not separate so easily due to the culture shaping the economy and the economy providing the playing board—the given—for each culturally motivated decision. Moreover, since the household is the flexible and dynamic catchall for all circumstances, and since the circumstances are nearly innumerable and the cultural impulses several and complex, it is impossible to prove that a given result is the product of either cultural impulse or economic opportunism or constraint. The complexity of cultural dispositions, economic constraints and options, and social structural requirements is simply staggering.

What is reasonably certain is this: the moral bonds of kinship give every person a claim to several people's support. While these claims are ranked step-wise according to the degree of kinship connection, virtually every person has available several links into different households. Even so, people select from among the options according to their dominant ideological dispositions. We have seen this to be so for San Marcos and San Pedro residents.

If one uses crude indices, however, households are rather similar the world over. For example, the mean household size in San Marcos is 5.57 persons. In San Pedro it is 5.42. The difference is miniscule, and statistically it should be attributed to chance. Moreover, these figures are close to the average household size throughout the world. But if one were to conclude that the processes by which San Marcos or San Pedro (or any other) households are formed were about the same, one would stand in considerable error, as Figure 3 suggests.

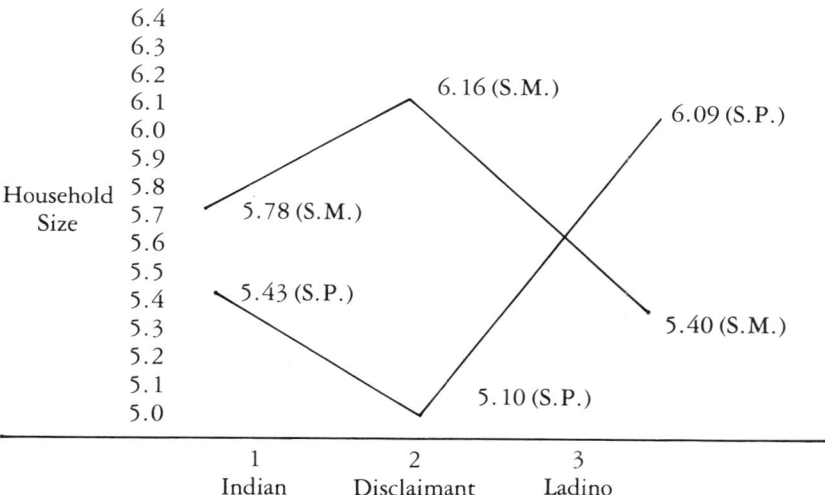

Figure 3
The Relationship of Ethnicity to Household Size

In a crude sense, the San Marcos and San Pedro household systems are inversely related as to ethnic category and family size although the causes of the differences are complex.

Another expression of difference between the communities emerges from an examination of household size and income, as shown in Figure 4.

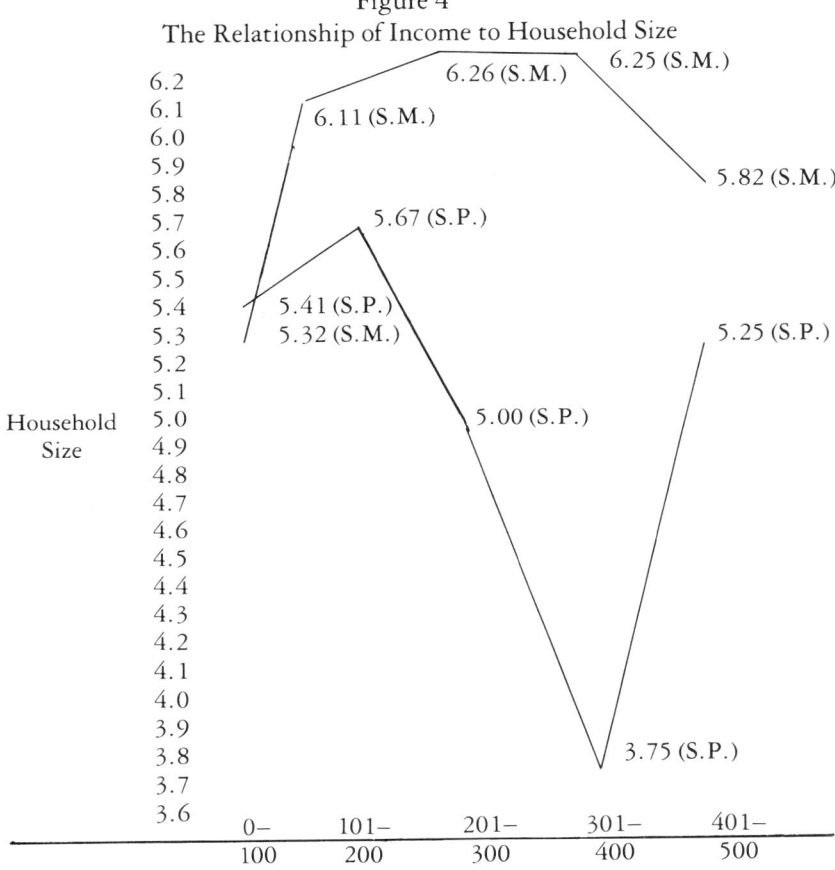

Figure 4
The Relationship of Income to Household Size

Again, San Marcos and San Pedro households display an inverse relationship, though the difference is insignificant at the lowest income level. While income and ethnic category are somewhat related (as I have shown in Chapters 4 and 6), Figures 3 and 4 are not isomorphic, manifesting a different pattern of crossover in the end categories of each figure. Again, it would appear that income here relates to household size in a nearly inverse pattern.

Throughout this book, I have attempted to unravel the complex interrelationships of San Marcos and San Pedro and of the Ladino and the Indian to each other. I have shown sets of oppositions—

patterns of inverse relationship. This has been the case for the context-free deep cultural premises, for the context-specific normative rules, and for the patterns of actual behavior insofar as these can be captured by quantitative methods. Moreover, I have established these patterns for the domains of politics, economics, and social status, as well as in detail for the domestic domain aspects of kinship, marriage and common-law union, postmarital residence, divorce and abandonment, inheritance, and household composition. In addition, I have hinted on occasion at inverse relationships in the domain of religion, although that is not the task of this book nor an area of my expertise and must therefore be left to others to explore.

What does this imply for the root issue of this book, the nature of the social juncture between Ladino and Indian? Is their relationship fundamentally a product of two cultures, the Mayan flowing down to the present with such modifications as result from cross-cultural contact under the influence of political and economic domination by Ladinos, and the Ladino derived from a European heritage? If so, then we would expect to see some similarities (by acculturation), some differences (by reaction), and vast areas of unrelated, arbitrary, unsystematic, and unanalyzable disparities that are the products of two separate and unique cultural heritages. But the differences I have shown are too systematic, too interrelated, and too pervasive to be a chance result of two separate cultures partially melded by colonialism but otherwise unrelated. Of course, no one suggests Mayan life has not changed since the conquest. But I am going beyond the usual assertion that Mayan culture adapted to the Spanish and was gradually changed by acculturation toward Spanish practice. Rather, I am suggesting that Mayan culture in the *encomienda-reducción-repartimiento* areas of Spanish dominion was fundamentally restructured at the ideological level to become an integral part of the Spanish colonial culture. No doubt the process is not yet wholly complete. But it is, I think, essentially complete. Indians subjected to the pressures of *encomienda-reducción-repartimiento* adopted the ideology expected of them by their punishing lords: that Indians were different from the Spanish in all regards. To be sure, many of the ancient sign vehicles passed through to the present because they could be used conveniently to display distinctive, oppositional, and inverse difference. But the meanings carried by the sign vehicles had been changed by being placed in inverse relationship to the ideas, symbols, and lifeways of the Spaniard. If this were so for only an item or two, little could be said. But the relationship is complex, pervasive, and multiple—penetrating political, economic, domestic, and even ritual aspects of Indian life. Far from being an accident, the pervasive inverse relationship of Indian to Ladino ideology is the essence of being Indian as well as the essence of being Ladino. Only when the ethnic ideologies are taken together, in their relationship, does the nature of the culture emerge.

13

Inverse Images: A Comparison of Postcolonial Societies and Cultures

The peculiar instance of San Marcos and San Pedro has led us to look at Guatemala from a new explanatory perspective: the Spanish idea of Indian distinctiveness—within the context of forced enslavement—forged an opposite, inverse ideology in the Indian segment of the new colonial society. Since the view helps to explain anomalies from both eastern (Pocomam, Appendix 1.A) and midwestern (Cakchiquel, Appendix 1.B) and western (San Pedro) areas of the country, the explanatory framework is generalized to the country as a whole.

If this is a general Hispanic colonial process, then wherever such Spanish ideology was brought to bear with sufficient force some closely similar, ideologically inverse social system ought to have arisen. The Canaries, the Spanish Caribbean, Mexico, Mesoamerica, Andean South America, and the Philippines are the obvious candidates for such a process. If these postcolonial societies manifest a system of inversions parallel to those of Guatemala, then Spanish ideology and the colonial process—and not the diverse aboriginal cultures—must be the dominant elements in the historical explanation of the present-day "indigenous culture" in the Spanish colonial regions. So as not to let the infinitely expandable comparative research delay the publication of my basic ethnography, I will restrict my comparison of Spanish colonialism to Peru, with a note on the Philippines.

More importantly, I contend that the factor which determines the character of Indian society is the overlord's ideology. The aboriginal culture melts down under force, to be sure, but the shape it takes depends on the idea of inversion in the lordly ideology. Given such an idea, then, in the presence of force the aboriginal culture, whatever it was, becomes an inverse subsystem.

By contrast, many approaches to colonial and postcolonial society emphasize the impact of force, asserting that the application of force to ensure colonial labor relations forms the underlying basis from which the masses derive their postcolonial ideology. If this were so, then the application of similar forms of labor control and force should result in closely similar ideologies among the postcolonial masses. Thus, from a Marxist perspective, the British Caribbean slave societies and the Spanish *encomienda* societies should have developed quite similar lowest class colonial ideologies. On the other hand, in the theory presented here, if the initial British overlord ideology is substantially different from the initial Spanish overlord ideology, then the masses of Indians should differ on those points from the masses of blacks in the postslave Caribbean societies. Thus, to test whether the approach derived from San Marcos, San Pedro, and Guatemala is generally applicable to the Western colonial process, I shall also examine the postcolonial society of Jamaica for the inverse impact of British ideology on the structure of present-day Jamaican culture.[1]

Peru: Social Structure and Ideological Inversion in the Andes

Peru affords an opportunity to explore further the thesis of ideological inversion in the colonial regime. Although, as with the Mayans, we have little documentation of the pre-Spanish Incan society, one presumes that important differences existed between the Incans and the Mayans. Some of these differences in fact have survived intact; yet the impact of the Spanish was pervasive, and the similarities of Peruvian and Guatemalan culture and society are extensive. Indeed, Gillin, van den Berghe, and others have made the comparisons explicit, and the degree to which the Mesoamerican literature is cited as a model for Andean studies further suggests the comparability of the two regions.

The similarities begin with a common history; Spanish adventurers invaded, subdued, and ruled the Quechuan peoples in essentially the same way that they conquered and colonized Mexico and Guatemala. Pizarro and his small band made use of divisions in the subject peoples to gain allies. He and his followers captured the region, executed the native leaders, spoiled the land, and raped the women. As the colony settled down, *encomienda* grants went to the Spaniards, Indians were reduced to towns *(reducciones),* and the distribution of labor by *repartimiento* began. Indeed, from Lockhart's description (1968) of the Indian condition, the fate of the Indians was worse in Peru than in Guatemala, for the presumed quick wealth in the mines left little incentive to coddle the Indians sent to the pits by *reparti-*

miento. So the Spanish subdued the Indians—savagely when necessary—and the Indians necessarily began to modify their society and ideology to accommodate to their Spanish lords' expectations. But more importantly, this small band, many of them Estremaduran Spaniards, carried with them the idea that these New World infidels were virtually the opposite of everything proper and human.

As a result, the Peruvian Indians of today are considerably changed, on the one hand because they are linked to the Spanish and on the other because their cultural premises have been changed. William Stein says of them that "it is impossible to study a Peruvian Indian community such as Hualcan without also studying the relationships of the Indians with outsiders," who, for Hualcaiños, are "the mestizo townsmen" of nearby Carhuaz and beyond (Stein 1961:10).² Moreover, because of the conquest "present-day Peruvian Indians are perhaps closer culturally to Iberian peasants than they are to the old indigenous communities" (Stein 1961:12). We shall explore the Indian ideology in Hualcan, but first, we must see the larger national and regional context of Peruvian Indian society.

Pierre van den Berghe and George Primov provide an excellent study of the Cuzco region within the context of Peruvian society in *Inequality in the Peruvian Andes* (1977). I shall depend on their material for an understanding of elite and middle *mestizo* culture, for the *mestizos* of Peru are the structural and ideological equivalents of the *ladinos* of Guatemala. For the domestic life or ideology of the Indian villagers, we must turn to Stein's sensitive *Hualcan: Life in the Highlands of Peru* (1961), an account of a Quechua peasant hamlet in the Callejón de Huaylas, Department of Ancash. An unfortunate but necessary shift in regions confronts us; however, it is clear from other accounts of towns in the Callejón, including Vicos and Huaráz, that the *mestizos* of Ancash are essentially like the *mestizos* of Cuzco.

Politically, Peru is essentially like Guatemala, with the exception that Peru, being larger, has more levels of hierarchy in every bureaucracy. The highly centralized government radiates from Lima, the capital. Each of the twenty-three departments is ruled by a "prefect" appointed by the Ministry of the Interior. The prefect has power to hurt or to help people locally, but he has no structural or financial independence from the center, for "his office is little more than a station on a long conveyor belt of *papel sellado*" (van den Berghe and Primov 1977:65). Indeed, other ministries perform the main services and make the main decisions in the departments. The departments are further divided into provinces, the provinces into districts, and larger districts into *anexos*. The districts or *anexos* are then divided into *municipios*. At each level, appointees rule (van der Berghe and Primov 1977:15).

The revolution of 1968 increased the thrust of centralization by depriving the *municipios* of elective and financial independence. As a result, centrality is even more complete in Peru than in Guatemala, and "all but the most trivial decisions flow down from the national capital" (van den Berghe and Primov 1977:14). Deviations from the will of the central government are possible only to the degree that distance and the love the rulers have for the comforts of the capital and the provincial centers make supervision incomplete.

As in Guatemala, towns are ranked by their degree of centrality, and the government concentrates in the headquarters towns, as do the ethnically superior *mestizos*. Indeed, *mestizos* run the various levels of government and capture the main services, while Indians hardly participate, except as forced draftees in the army (van den Berghe and Primov 1977:71–74, 77–79).

Ideologically, Peruvian *mestizos,* like Guatemalan *ladinos,* see themselves as inclined toward political activity, while conversely, Indians are apolitical and alienated. In Stein's description, "most agencies of social control are mestizo, . . . run by and for mestizos." The Indian finds the government "potent but prefers to avoid rather than utilize it from fear of misusing it through ignorance" and because many times he is "victimize[d]" by it (Stein 1961:218). The key phrase here is that the Indian "prefers" to "avoid." Quechua Indians have adopted the apolitical alienated ideology, thus establishing an inversion system which precisely parallels that of Guatemala.

Like Guatemala, there is an extensive pattern of absentee landlordism over large but inefficiently run estates (van den Berghe and Primov 1977:99). Unlike Guatemala, many such *mestizo* estates are located in the highland valleys, and as a result, many of the highland Indians live in varying states of dependence as wage laborers or *colono* residents of local *haciendas* (van den Berghe and Primov 1977: 86, 95). In addition, many of the Indians must migrate to the coast for seasonal labor or work seasonally on local Mestizo *haciendas* (Stein 1961:9).

While most Peruvian Indians are desperately poor agricultural laborers or small-plot owners, the *mestizos,* in contrast, dominate commerce, government, crafts, and educated professions. They either control Indians as managers and supervisors or work at jobs requiring skill, education, capital, or power (van den Berghe and Primov 1977:208–9). Furthermore, the division of labor is accompanied by a split work ethic which parallels that of Guatemala. Thus,

> One of the key values of mestizo culture is that manual labor is something to be avoided at all costs, and that Indians have a natural inclination and aptitude for hard work. Urban mestizos, for example, hire Indians to carry all but the smallest loads even for short distances. (van den Berghe and Primov 1977:171)

The *mestizos* further symbolize their disinclination for work by the use of servants in virtually every household; elites will have "several servants and retainers" while "most mestizo families in town . . . have servants of some kind" (van den Berghe and Primov 1977: 240, 235).

But do the Indians believe what the Mestizos attribute to them? On the one hand, Indians "employ passive resistance" to public works participation: "they come to work late; work slowly, inefficiently, and sullenly; show up in smaller numbers than expected; or even, in recent years, stop coming altogether" (van den Berghe and Primov 1977:171). On the other hand, Indian children manifest the central place of the work ideology by taking up adult work tasks at a very early age as their natural lot (Stein 1961:159–60). More significantly, from the Indians' point of view, the respected and good person—the ideal man—is "a hard worker who has earned the respect of all through his performance" (Stein 1961:180), and the Hualcan Indians "deprecate the mestizo because he does not like to work with his hands" (Stein 1961:230).

Thus, in both political position and economic activity, the Indians are in fact subordinate to the *mestizos*. And both groups have accepted and incorporated this subordination in their class-linked ethnic ideologies. Hierarchy is a central premise of *mestizo* ideology. Everyone is ranked. Even students and teachers, espousing an ideology of equality, march in order of rank: teachers first, then office employees, then students, and finally the *campesinos*. Van den Berghe considers the idea of rank—that is, "dominance and subordination"—"so engrained" that "scarcely anyone seems to savor the irony of the situation" (van den Berghe and Primov 1977:211, 233).

The Indians of Hualcan accept their political and economic subordination to *mestizos,* recognizing that "the individual is always subject to mestizo authority, as the ultimate political power" (Stein 1961:234). To be sure, there is hierarchy in Indian social organization, where children are subject to adults, adults are subject to older people, women are subject to and "inferior" to men (Stein 1961: 220–21), and where the civil-religious fiesta system is a model of hierarchy in which the most *mestizo* and the wealthiest rise fastest in the institution that meshes *mestizo* control and Indian piety (van den Berghe and Primov 1977:70, 151–152; Stein 1961:71–72, 58, 185, 192, 268).

Nevertheless, a countervailing principle of equality and self-sufficiency works within the Indian community, a principle opposite to the first Mestizo principle of hierarchy and dependence. Thus, van den Berghe and Primov contrast the "premise of inequality [that] suffuses most relations between mestizos" with the "strongly egalitarian" Indian "social ideology," which is asserted "repeatedly" in the phrase "we are all the same" (van den Berghe and Primov, 1977:144; see also 1977:85). In these regards, Peruvian culture embodies the same structure of *mestizo* hierarchy versus Indian egalitarianism as in Guatemalan society. Moreover, as in Guatemala, *mestizos* dictate if they can, while Indians search out consensus by painfully slow conversation and circumlocution. Indeed, the precipitation of conflict, all too easy through bold or self-confident assertion, is perhaps the greatest offense among the Indian Hualcaiños (Stein 1961:180–81).

Another inverse ideological relationship exists between *mestizo* dependency and the Indian ideal of self-sufficiency. For Indians, economic self-sufficiency means to possess enough land to minimize dependency on landlords or others (Stein 1961:18–19). Social self-sufficiency means to pare down one's social contacts and interactions to the minimum. Stein speaks of the Hualcaiños finding "no reason to combine and coordinate social activity" beyond occasional labor exchange. He asserts a "reliance on the family," "an inward-turning limitation on interpersonal investments," and an inability to "trust . . . nonrelatives" (Stein 1961:336). Neighbors are sure to be thieves, and even relatives and children will steal as opportunity permits (Stein 1961:57, 145, 160, 166). Moreover, bewitchment on account of envy is a constant threat (Stein 1961:57).

Stein captures the minimal character of social relationships in the Indian community by observing repeatedly the "aloofness," even "suspicion and hostility," between households, with each household leading its "private life . . . cut off from frequent interaction with others." Moreover, the Indians experience no "warm or deep" relationships, nor do they regularly visit each other except among kin (Stein 1961:136–37). This separation, individualism, and atomization is emphasized when Stein remarks that "the cultural emphasis is on privacy and self-sufficiency" (Stein 1961:137).[3] Although he found a number of important social ties both within the family and to protective patrons, the dominant ideology is to have "as few social ties and obligations outside the family as possible," thereby achieving the "goal of self-sufficiency and peace, . . . not [being] bothered by anyone" and "not dependent on anyone." In short, "Hualcaiños do not eagerly seek social relationships with one another," and such "strivings toward self-sufficiency lend a flavor to interpersonal relations in Hualcan" (Stein 1961:177).

The ideology of social distance and marginality is sharply and indeed contrastively symbolized in the minimal amount of body contact among these Indians, compared to the *mestizos* (Stein 1961:179). Moreover, this social withdrawal is not just local, it is national; and it is compatible with the Indian aversion to political involvement. Indeed, Hualcaiños "tend to withdraw from outside contacts if they possibly can," even though they are "intimately conjoined" with the "provincial and national spheres of existence" (Stein 1961:183).

By contrast, social contact, through a constant circulation of parties, life "crisis" celebrations, holidays, and social clubs, is a hallmark of the Mestizo (van den Berghe and Primov 1977:208–9). The degree of Mestizo social involvement may be seen in their associations through the Lions Club, the Rotary Club, Club Cuzco, Club Internacional, the Touring Automobile Club, the Bar Association, the Chamber of Commerce and Industry, the Commerce Association, "a variety of" occupational clubs, the Casa de la Cultura, the Peruvian Academy of the Quechua Language, the San Martín Institute, the Bolivian Institute, the Peruvian-North American Institute, the American Art Institute, and Alliance Française. In addition, these clubs thoroughly demonstrate the external, European, and foreign orientation of the Mestizo elite (van den Berghe and Primov 1977:25, 112, 240–41), compared to the "closed corporate" village manifestation of the Quechua Indian's ideological orientation to his own town (Stein 1961:20–21).

For the *mestizo* of Peru as for the *ladino* of Guatemala, the extension of social networks is crucial; it is both ideologically inculcated and crucial to the maintenance of power and centrality. Thus, "a vast network of informal, particularistic ties" knits together the apparently (but only formally) discrete bureaucracies, and the networks unify the various levels in the clientage system (van den Berghe and Primov 1977: 89). Through, among other means, "overlapping memberships" and "attend[ance at] each others' weddings and funerals," the Mestizos "interpenetrate, intermarry, and interact in a number of different contexts" (van den Berghe and Primov 1977: 112).[4] By contrast, van den Berghe and Primov agree with Stein in finding the Cuzco Indian "at the bottom of a class order; [in which] his cultural distinctiveness isolates and atomizes him," making his people "the most fragmented stratum in the Peruvian population" (1977:146, 147).

The ideology has been inculcated thoroughly and effectively. Although "most Indians know that they are the cultural heirs of a vast empire, . . . their sense of affiliation seldom extends beyond the local community" (van den Berghe and Primov 1977:149). Moreover, precisely this "political atomization of the Indian population into a multitude of tiny peasant communities neutralizes any power of numbers that Indians might otherwise have" (van den Berghe and Primov 1977:149).

Nowhere is the ideology of narrowed social contact more startlingly revealed than in the institution of *compadrazgo*. Both Indians and *mestizos* may call on social equals or social superiors to be *compadre* to their children, while social inferiors are rarely chosen (van den Berghe and Primov 1977:89–90). And if a social superior is chosen, certain benefits accrue: protection for an unsure Indian; contact and solidification of crucial bonds for the upwardly mobile or even the elite *mestizo*.

But the patterns of choice differ. The Hualcan Indian chooses an equal from among kin or a *mestizo* superior from whom the Indian needs protection. In choosing kin, the Indian closes off the construction of broader social networks; in choosing a *mestizo,* the Indian solidifies his subordination in a pattern of clientship (Stein 1961: 201–2). But most *compadres* are chosen from kin. As a result "compadrazgo does not have as great a community-wide integrative effect as it does in other areas of Latin America" (Stein 1961:135). Closure is further forced because the chosen kin are close kin, and because the same relatives are repeatedly chosen for the life-crisis events that occasion or require the presence of *compadres*. Thus, for baptism, "the padrinos are chosen preferably from among the husband's or the wife's parents" (Stein 1961:278). But "the same individuals usually serve as padrinos at the first haircutting" (Stein 1961:132), while "the padrinos for a marriage may be chosen from among the groom's own baptismal padrinos." Finally, "the marriage padrinos frequently sponsor the first child of the union" (Stein 1961:133). Thus, generation follows generation with relatively closed circles of *compadres*.

By contrast, *mestizos* have a broader reach in their system; their "compadrazgo is more elaborate and varied" and uses more events to generate *compadre* ties than that of the Indians uses (Stein 1961:131). In Moche, a *mestizo* community, "godparents may be blood relatives, but usually the attempt is made to secure persons who are not relatives of either of the [godchild's] parents" (Gillin 1945:107). Thus, "the real function of godparents is to broaden and, if possible, increase the social and economic resources" (1945:108). Godparents are chosen not so much for the child as for the parents, for the "sponsorship" of the child is "secondary in importance and is merely the mechanism whereby the social relationships are set up" (Gillin 1945:104). Moreover, *mocheros* have elaborated the social extensions of the system by choosing a husband from one couple as *compadre* and a wife from another couple as *comadre*. In a complex of mutual attributions, these specific *compadres,* their spouses, the parents of the child, the nurse, and the nurse's parents enter into *compadrazgo* relationships with each other (Gillin 1945:106–7). Beyond this, "the *compadrazgo* terms generalize to blood relatives of the parents and of the godparents" (Gillin 1945:107). As a result, the Mestizos of Moche achieve a dense reticulation of relationships with non-kin. Finally, in contrasting compadres "previously established" with "those established in the present ceremony," in using the metaphor of "ropes . . . spread from climber to climber in a number of directions," and in noting that even the poor end up with a "sizable group of ceremonial kinsmen," Gillin shows the multiplication rather than the closure of social relationships (Gillin 1945:107–11). One "poor man" had thirty-eight *compadres* and *comadres* and seven *padrinos* and *madrinas,* only three of whom were blood relatives. A "somewhat" richer person had sixty-seven *compadres* and *comadres*. Gillin neglected to note the number of *padrinos* and *madrinas* (1945:111–2). Thus, by contrast with Indian Hualcan, Mestizo Moche shows astonishing complexity and extension in its social relationships.

All of these oppositions—powerful-weak; central-peripheral; social-disconnected—combine to make the city the symbolic focus of the nation. This increases the power of the capital city, weakens the local governments, and guts the hinterland of talented individuals (van den Berghe and Primov 1977:86–88), a process which is quite identical to that of Guatemala. By contrast, things rural are of and for the Indian. For a Hualcaiño, it is "unthinkable that one could lead a peaceful and happy life without the means of producing the necessities of life by one's own hands" (Stein 1961:68). Given this set of inverse ideologies, a move from more rural to more urban environments is highly 'mestizoizing,' and the more central the town the faster and more thorough the effect upon the Indian. Indeed, the process of mestizoization is so built in that the Peruvians have a special word for the recently Indian: *cholo*. As in Guatemala, few remain Indian in the capital city.

Peru also shares the equation of highland equals Indian, lowland equals *mestizo*. Indeed, the southern sierra is often called the *"mancha india"* (Indian stain) (van den Berghe and Primov 1977:26). Even the elite of Cuzco feel disparaging pressure from their *costeño* (lowland) and *limeño* (Lima) fellow citizens (van den Berghe and Primov 1977: 24–25). And as in Guatemala, the symbolic value of the coast even affects the cuisine, so that *mestizos* avoid the Indian mountain foods as far as possible, preferring the "higher status" products and food styles of the coast. The Indians "favor coastal foods" also "but cannot afford them" (Stein 1961:70), thereby suggesting a common culture even at this comparatively insignificant level of food preferences.

Furthermore, within a given valley, the higher you are above the valley floor, and the further you are from a town center, the lower your status (van den Berghe and Primov 1977:124, 251–52, 204–5). The package of symbolic values, as well as the real location of prestige opportunities affects the migration process. The net flow is strongly rural to urban and highland to lowland (van den Berghe and Primov 1977:21).

The series of contrasts between Mestizo and Indian also affects clothing, in a pattern identical to that of Guatemala. The Hualcan Indian men who "own Mestizo clothing " wear it only for special occasions, and some use their mestizo clothing "only when they go to the coast," an appropriate symbolism given the highland-lowland contrast. In the highlands, however, "each community can be distinguished" by local clothing style (Stein 1961:89).

Ideology, social structure, and symbolic representation of social status each have structures that may or may not be congruent. As in Guatemala, clothing is an issue of symbolic correspondence to status. Thus,

> one of the worst social sins in Hualcan is "acting without knowing." For example, a man who put on shoes instead of sandals but could not also speak Spanish or act like a mestizo would be ridiculed or even accused of the practice of witchcraft. (Stein 1961:346–47)

The necessity of congruence is most demanding at the ends of the continuum. In the middle areas, where one's placement in several institutions may be out of phase, manipulation is frequent and mobility is rapid, perhaps even more so than in Guatemala (Stein 1961:232; van den Berghe and Primov 1977:184–224).[5] Moreover, the above quote demonstrates quite clearly that the Indian's problem is not one of simple acculturation, in which he accepts elements of a foreign culture into his own. Rather, his problem is one of establishing congruence between the several integrated social codes and social structures that include both Indian and *mestizo* forms in a unified status dictionary.

Ethnic interaction is a major topic of van den Berghe and Primov's book, and we can only touch the high points here. First, the ethnic terms stand in a hierarchy, with *indígena* at the low end, *criollo* at the high end, and *mestizo* in between. Van den Berghe contests the reality of *cholo* as a social category, asserting that it is a term used to put down a relatively acculturated person of lesser status (1977: 128–29). Stein, on the other hand, sees the term as valid and gives the hierarchy as Indian, *cholo, mestizo,* and *criollo* (1961:219). The whole matter is made more complex because official policies substitute *"campesino"* for *"indígena,"* thus obscuring some ethnic attributes of the system with a purely class terminology (van den Berghe and Primov 1977:116). What is clear, however, is that precise boundaries are nonexistent and that movement toward the center of any national institution has a mestizoizing effect in behavioral symbolism and in ethnic attribution.

Second, the degree to which Indians are subordinated to *mestizos* is recognized in pronoun usage: *mestizos* talk to Indians with *tú* forms appropriate to a child and class Indians as *hijito* (child). Indians who have learned Spanish adequately use the *Usted,* the proper term for parents and superiors, and when Indians address *mestizos,* they use parental kin terms: *"papay, tatay, mamay, papacito"* or the like (Stein 1961:170–71; van den Berghe and Primov 1977:130–31).

Third, the nature of being Indian is most distinct at the ends of the roads. One is most Indian when one lives where the roads peter out (van den Berghe and Primov 1977:17–20, 23–30, 105–12, 117–25, 147–49). Now, one could argue that this is best explained with a refuge-region hypothesis. But I would suggest that Cuzco and environs provide a foil to the argument. As late as 1906, Cuzco was a two-month horseride away from Lima, in the heart of the mountains. Today, no Peruvian Indian highland community is that inaccessible. Yet Cuzco was then, as it is now, a Mestizo center with mestizoizing impact on its inhabitants (van den Berghe and Primov 1977:228–29). Given Cuzco's *mestizo* character in spite of isolation, one can see that the social and cultural categories attributed to a place or to a region are more important than the degree of isolation of the region.

Finally, "the very permeability of ethnic boundaries . . . keeps those who remain Indians at the very bottom of the social pyramid. The Peruvian stratification system might be described as one of open ethnic lines and fairly rigid class lines" (van den Berghe and Primov 1977:141). This relatively easy ethnic mobility is a major factor in the social status consistency of the entire region; for the "hundreds of thousands of people [who] do rise in status," mostly through education, "thereby cease to be Indians" (van den Berghe and Primov 1977:141).

The way that Indians appropriately modify their own behavior to maintain consistency in the system requires a single culture approach. Van den Berghe and Primov observe that "the closer one approaches Cuzco, the more Spanish is heard on the bus and vice versa in the other direction. Bilinguals of Quechua origin gradually shift over to Spanish as they enter a universe where Spanish is dominant" (van den Berghe and Primov 1977:142). The idea of separate cultures is thus difficult to maintain in Peru, as it is in Guatemala: speaking Quechua and speaking Spanish are status-linked 'words' in a single cultural dictionary.

There remains the issue of domestic life, which, if the plural-society model is right, should be largely unaffected by matters of class and status consistency. The theory I advanced for Guatemala implies that in any particular microregion, *mestizo* and *criollo* kinship extension to collaterals and depth to antecedents will be greater than that of the Indians in the region. Unfortunately, van den Berghe and Primov do not give kinship-field data for any groups, though they imply considerable extension among the elite (van den Berghe and Primov 1977:242–47). Thus, I have inadequate information on the elite or middle-level *mestizos* of both Cuzco and Ancash.

Kinship in Hualcan seems more important than in some of the Guatemalan communities (Stein 1961:113, 115), but it is difficult to tell from Stein because he refers to cooperation and diffuse aid among relatives without giving specifics (Stein 1961:114).

On the other hand, land is held individually; inheritance is bilateral, although the sons are often surreptitiously favored; fierce legal conflicts over land occur among siblings (Stein 1961:48–49); kinsmen who are not "close" (Stein never defines the term) "borrow" items contractually for a fee; patrilineal kinsmen tend to reside closely together as a father parcels out land to his marrying sons; many sons prefer to live neolocally but near their father, and, if unable to do so, they prefer to live with the groom's parents; and each individual belongs to a patrilineally acquired name category *(kasta)*, which has no functions given except that of marriage exogamy. On the other hand, "there is a strong tendency toward local endogamy" (Stein 1961:124). Finally, the kinship system is precisely bilateral; it recognizes parents and grandparents, children and grandchildren, and refers to collaterals with Spanish-borrowed terms; and it represents affines with a structure identical to the one given for San Marcos and San Pedro. In all these points, the Quechua Indian is like most of his Guatemalan counterparts.

Furthermore, while the Hualcan husband is formally in charge, he counsels with his wife; she controls the "family larder," and thus she "rules" in certain circumstances (Stein 1961:221). This consultation with the wife and with other members of the household (1961:128) suggests a considerable egalitarian thrust to the Indian family. Both Stein and van den Berghe and Primov comment on the degree to which the Indians are used and abused as mistresses of *mestizos* (Stein 1961:228–29; van den Berghe and Primov 1977:162, 220). In all these regards, the Hualcán Indian marriage compares with that of the Guatemalan Indian. Unfortunately, I have no information on whether the Peruvian *mestizo* marriage is contrastively less egalitarian, or whether women symbolize the ethnic strata through their own contrastive ideologies and symbols of work involvement versus non-involvement. Again, a field test of the hypothesis seems possible on this issue.

In contrast to his somewhat vague statements on kinship extension, Stein clearly shows that the household is the main unit of Indian production and consumption activity. While some households may be extended to three generations or may join several brothers and their wives, the more usual residence is nuclear after the first two or three years of marriage (Stein 1961:122). Beyond this, all property is individually owned, and most extra-household cooperation appears to be between brothers holding inherited adjoining fields (Stein 1961:128–29). Though it is apparently less atomized than in Guatemala, the household is the ideal unit of self-sufficiency (Stein 1961: 336, 345).

Given that no one has explicitly sought to compare the household systems of Peruvian Indians and Mestizos, these conclusions must remain tentative. But the thrust of the available material is that the culture of the Peruvian Indian family is quite close to that of the Guatemalan. Before we can be sure of the domestic comparisons, though, a good deal of directed research needs to be carried out, especially on the *mestizos* of a region where we have good data on the Indians.

There are minor differences, however. The Quechuan terminology recognizes the siblings of grandparents, while the San Pedro and many other Guatemalan terminologies do not. And Quechua conflates siblings and cousins (Stein 1961:112–65). Thus, while the kinship pattern of Hualcan is closely similar to the general pattern of the Guatemalan Indians, the nature of the Peruvian system will be uncertain until a careful comparative study of Indian and Mestizo patterns of behavior and kinship ideology is carried out or made available. Remembering that behavior that is symbolically Indian in one place in Guatemala may be symbolically Ladino in another, the argument is not that Guatemala's social system and culture will be item for item similar to Peru's, but that in both countries, and in any local region, the system of opposite ideologies will be symbolized. In any event, Peru should be an interesting place to test the thesis of this book regarding domestic-system differences.

From the literature available, though, it appears that in virtually all areas of the public domain's social structure and ethnic ideologies, Guatemala and Peru are closely parallel in spite of the presumably distinctive cultural origins among Mayas and Incas respectively. The overwhelming impact of Spain on the essence of Indianness is thus strongly affirmed.

The Philippines: Colonial Experience at the Limits of Spanish Control

The Philippines provide another potential test of the hypothesis of an inverse ideological impact of the Spanish upon their subjects. In the first place, the Spanish transported essentially the same mindset to the Philippines as they brought to the Americas: they despised manual labor, thought of themselves as *hidalgos,* and disparaged the *indios*. Second, the Spanish Filipino labor regime was similar to that in the New World: *encomiendas* were distributed, and through them the natives were subjected to various tributes and personal services. These *encomiendas* were subject to the same laws emanating from Spain through Mexico, and the royal edicts were evaded in much the same way. And the clergy was intimately connected with the *encomiendas* as the instrument of Christianization that justified the conquest.

But there were also significant differences. Indeed, the clergy was much more engrossed with the Filipino natives than it was with the Indians in the New World. The Spaniards quickly discovered that the Philippines offered far fewer opportunities for wealth than the Americas. Precious metals did not abound, and consequently there was little need for surplus agricultural products to support large contingents of miners. The cost of agricultural export to Spain or to Mexico was prohibitive. Finally, spices did not grow well in the Philippine Islands. It was easier to transship spices acquired from the mainland and other islands, regions that were more suitable climatically. Thus, the *hacienda* was not profitable in the Philippines. As a result, few of the *hidalgos* tried to venture inland, and there were only a handful of private *encomiendas*. So, without need of land or labor, the secular Spanish citizen had relatively little need to interact with the Indian hinterland. Rather, he made his fortune in trade with China and other islands from his base in Manila, and then he returned to Spain. It appears that, as a result, the Spanish *criollo* tradition did not impact on the Philippine *indios* as thoroughly as it did in the New World.

Consequently, the hinterland was left more closely tied to the clergy than in the New World. The religious orders purchased land or received the generally unprofitable private estates by donation.

As a result, most of the large estates in Luzon were operated by the regular orders. On these estates, and in the parishes generally, the clergy operated in the native languages. Again, the clergy gained power and control through the vernacular. And few Spaniards other than clergy stayed long enough to learn the native languages.

Labor for the religious estates was provided by a rather different means than in the Americas. Rather than the apportionment of a quarter of the population on a rotating *repartimiento* basis, certain households in the villages and apparently all the households on the religious estates were known as *casas de reservas*—reserved or exempt households. The *reservas* were exempted from some tributes, and in some cases the clergy protected "their" Indians from virtually all tributes, provided that they gave themselves totally to the business of sharecropping on the estates. This system made residence on the religious estates especially attractive, and it precipitated many accusations from crown officials that the clergy was encouraging the vice of "vagabondism," the term applied to Indians who left their natal village. But the most powerful reason for leaving the villages and hamlets for the clerical estates was not to escape tributes, but to escape *polo*.

Polo was the Filipino version of *repartimiento*. Consignments of Indians were forcibly recruited by the native village leaders to spend a month or more as logcutters, timber bearers, or carpenters in the shipbuilding industry. The Philippines, more than any other colony, depended on sea trade, and the Filipino Indians built the majority of the Pacific fleet galleons. Given the overwhelming urgency to build galleons for defense and trade, it is not surprising that out of the heavy tasks of shipbuilding came the worst abuses against the Indians. Indeed, so hated was this call that the records document escape by suicide or sale of oneself into slavery in order to pay the exemption fee. The occasional rebellions over the call to *polo* service were put down harshly. Thus the comparatively benign exploitation on the religious estates was doubly attractive, for it brought exemption from *polo*.

With the exception of the labor required and the force applied for the *polo*, the Filipino natives were much less harshly engaged by the Spanish. The natives were not valuable for the acquisition of private wealth, and therefore the Spanish tended to leave them alone. They were also more thoroughly protected by the clergy. On the whole, the Indians of the Philippines were considerably buffered from contact with crown and citizen and from the constant destructive labor exploitation and oppressive taxations of the New World.

A second fundamental difference between the Philippines and the Americas consisted in the *reducción* or *congregación*. The successful New World policy of forcing the Indians into town centers did not work in the Philippines. To be sure, many plaza-style town centers were established. But for reasons which I do not understand, the Filipino natives would not stay in the town centers, drifting into the hamlet *barangayas* if they had been pulled down to the towns. Apparently as a result of this population dispersion, Indian travel and Indian residence in other regions was easier in the Philippines than in the Americas. The cries against vagabondism were frequent, and the possibility of movement favored the Indians in their progression toward clientship on the religious estates. Moreover, the dispersed residential pattern resulted in greater Spanish dependence on the indigenous native elite, especially when combined with the comparatively limited number of Spaniards who braved the second ocean voyage to the Philippines. Thus the Philippine pageant confirmed and stimulated an indigenous Filipino elite that had assimilated to the Spanish model, while the American drama crushed the elite and homogenized the Indians, with power being taken back from the early native *caciques* as the *criollo* and *ladino* population expanded.[6]

These details of history help to reveal why I was unable to discover the New World pattern of ethnic ideological inversions in the literature on the Philippines. Spanish colonialism in the Philippines was soft. Given the absence of wealth motives for intense exploitation, and the degree to which the priests buffered the peasants, the rapacious civilian Spanish imprint was not made. This would imply insufficient force and contact with the civilian Spaniards to force an inverse ideological transfer.

It is possible that the failure to congregate the Filipino Indians and force them into towns led to the failure in the assumption of an inverse ideology. This would imply that the forced removal of the Latin American Indians from their homes, occasionally throwing them together with Indians of other towns and language groups, was a key to their subsequent cultural plasticity. As we shall see in the next section, the West Indies slaves, brought from several cultural backgrounds and relocated on the plantations, also became plastic to the impress of the overlords. However, the *shape* that the masses took was defined by the *culture* of the overlord, not by the *institutions* of repression.

It could also be true that the greater Spanish dependence on the Filipino natives for a native control structure disconnected the ethnic boundary from the dominance boundary, so that the controlled were not immediately distinguished from the controllers by ethnic or racial differences. Therefore, the idea of the natural difference of the Indio may not have been projected into the countryside to become a basis of oppositional distinction.

Finally, it is difficult to account for the intervening impact of American colonial administration, comprising some fifty to eighty years, depending on the date of the available ethnographies.

The above speculations attempt to account for my failure to discover a system of inversions within Philippine society. But it is possible that the rather tribal focus of Philippine ethnography obscures the discovery of such oppositions as might exist. In other words, perhaps an oppositional system lies at a level of social interaction not yet explored by anthropologists. As noted earlier, the *indio* elite succeeded to the title of filipino, which had formerly applied to the Spanish *criollo*. Is there a contrast between the present-day Westernized Filipino and some relatively unassimilated Christian or "pagan" marginal groups? Or is the inversion process projected on the plane of urban-rural? Again, as an anthropologist working at a distance, I am frustrated by a lack of data. I am unable to find adequate descriptions of the urban elite culture, and I am unable to find a monograph with a regional perspective and adequate cultural data.

Nevertheless, some hints exist in the literature. In *Ilocano Rice Farmers: A Comparative Study of Two Philippine Barrios* (1971), Henry T. Lewis examines a small rural highland hamlet *(barrio)* of Ilocanos in Ilocos del Norte Province, comparing them with a group of Ilocanos from the same region who had migrated to the lowlands on the opposite side of Luzon island. Both groups share the same bilateral kinship-field organization and neolocal nuclear family structure. They also share the same language and cultural principles. But the migrant group shows considerably stronger kinship interaction and a greater ability to form significant fictive kin ties and village associations. The nonmigrant barrio has a "social fabric" which by comparison is "but weakly developed and maintained" (Lewis 1971:179). Moreover, the migrant group is much less tied to the "conservative

Ilocano stereotype" of "being 'hardworking,' 'thrifty,' and 'industrious' that is attached to the natives of Ilocos Norte" (Lewis 1971: 175). Rather, the migrants who have gone to the eastern lowlands appear to be

> much more characteristic of the general, less intense Philippine lowland cultural stereotype. The virtues of thrift, frugality, and industriousness which characterize (or at least rationalize) life in Ilocos Norte are not especially necessary or important in Isabela. (Lewis 1971:175)

Lewis explains the difference as a result of the "penurious social and natural environment in Ilocos Norte" compared with the "less demanding social and environmental circumstances" of the lowland area to which the migrants went (Lewis 1971:175). Yet the move from the peripheral to the somewhat more central, from road's end to main highway, from hill land to lowland, and from native to migrant corresponds with precisely those symbolic features in the New World that would result in a parallel softening of a virtually puritan, non-Hispanic, New World Indian work ethic; and it would also account for the reported strengthening of social ties. When this is compared with the intense social and political linkages of the Tagalogs (Hollinsteiner 1967), the elite language group closest to Manila and through whom the Spaniards did much of their governance, then the possibilities are intriguing indeed. Yet the jury is out, for at this distance anthropology lacks data adequate to determine an answer, and in any event we would expect the fifty to eighty years of American cultural intrusion between Spain and the available monographs to make the pattern less than completely clear.

So I offer these speculations in the hope that they will generate a viable test of the hypothesis by someone going to or already returned from intense field studies of the Philippines. If the use of the inverse-ideology model stimulates a satisfying and integrative, regional study in the Philippines, I would consider the model strongly confirmed. If the model is counterproductive, then, as I suspect, the priestly protection and relative incompleteness of Spain's colonization of the Philippines blocked the process of ideology transformation. If I am in error about the relative softness of Spanish colonialism in the Philippines, then my approach is strongly refuted. On the other hand, if some areas felt the hand of Spanish force, heard the message of their distinctiveness, and developed inversion systems, while other areas, feeling little force or not subjected to the ideology, did not develop inversions, then the theory would be strongly supported.[7]

Jamaica: Colonial Inversions with a British Twist

The British plantation societies of the West Indies provide an interesting extension of the theory of inverse-ideology formation in another colonial society. To get at the potential of inversions, I shall begin with a description of the British West Indies slave society written by a participant.

On the last day of December 1820, the Englishwoman Mrs. Carmichael began a five-year period of residence and observation in the British possessions of St. Vincent and Trinidad, which she recorded and later published in 1833. Her first day's journal observations note the sharp contrasts she encountered between English and Negro behavior and culture. Before even setting foot on land, she was struck by the "novel spectacle" of slaves dressed in their finest clothes and proceeding to Sunday market, for she was "accustomed to a devout observance of the Sabbath day" (Carmichael 1833, 1:4–5). On ordinary days Mrs. Carmichael saw many Negros in rags, but the important feature here is that, in her mind, the slaves defile the Sabbath, while Englishmen do not.

When servants came on board to greet their returning masters, Mrs. Carmichael again notes they were well dressed, but they spoke excitedly in an "uncouth . . . jargon," quite "unintelligible" to her (Carmichael 1833, 1:5). They "presented their hands, giving ours a hearty shake," being "frank, full of life and spirit," and talking "to their master with a freedom" that surprised her. Indeed, she "saw none of that servile manner" which she had "anticipated" (Carmichael 1883, 1:6). None of that proper English reserve here. She describes the island town, "unlike anything to be seen in England" (Carmichael 1833, 1:8). England is the standard.

While the lack of "cleanliness and repair" in men's ordinary clothing brought on "melancholy reflections," Negro women's clothing habits were "disgusting," for they removed their clothing while washing so that "without one exception . . . from the waist upwards, all was in a state of nudity." Even in town "several such disgusting spectacles were presented; and the little children, in by far the greater number of instances, were literally in a state of nature." Moreover, the attire of the "coloured women (that is, Mulattoes)" in the houses "would have been elegant and graceful, had they been more modest" (Carmichael 1833, 1:10–11).

So a highly Victorian England is the standard. But the import of her description is not appreciated unless we compare it with the attire of the English plantation lords. For that, we turn to a 1790 description of a family of white Jamaican plantation owners on horseback:

> The ladies wore white and green hats, under which white handkerchiefs were pinned round their faces, meeting over their noses—this is the usual precaution for preventing the sun from blistering the skin.—The gentlemen wore white handkerchiefs, under the fore part of their hats, and rode in long trowsers, made of Russia sheeting, the little children were also pinned up, and all the company had umbrellas. (Brathwaite 1971:118)[8]

Mrs. Carmichael made some parallel observations. She "thought [it] must be very disagreeable" for the Negroes to clean their tools "in the sun." She had "a shade put up for them," but no one would work there. When asked why, her Negroes told her, "Sun good for nigger" (Carmichael 1833, 1:151). The white elite obviously contrast with the Negro workers as to the degree they clothe themselves in public, the one group exceedingly covered and the other frequently naked. Furthermore, avoidance of the sun versus reveling in it have become opposite emblems of ethnic distinction. The whole effort appears to have gone beyond the utilitarian needs of comfort versus field labor.

To return to Mrs. Carmichael's first-day account, she spent the first evening in town in "much in the same way as in England, drinking tea between seven and eight, and music filled up the remainder." She was a guest in a local "gentleman's" house, for hers was not yet ready (Carmichael 1833, 1:12). It must have been relaxing, after the hard ocean voyage, to return so easily to England. As the music played, her host told her that the unusual noise was caused by the "little negroes." "I had every inclination to take a peep," though English reserve apparently restrained her, "but I was afraid if they saw me, they would stop," as her English upbringing "told" her an English child would do. But she concluded, "I have since found by experience, . . . [that] negroes are not at any age at all abashed by the presence of a stranger" (Carmichael 1833, 1:12–13). The slave ideology is quite un-English.

Why does an Englishwoman, in the course of "the first twelve hours on shore in a West India colony" come up with so many contrasts? We would of course expect differences, but these contrasts are more than mere differences; they are near, if not exact, opposites.

Are we to believe that blind chance threw a mixture of African cultures together, which coalesced and preserved a series of Africanisms rather precisely opposite to the English, and that Spanish culture just happened to be quite opposite to the culture of the ancient Mayans as well as that of the Incans? More probably, we can presume that the oppositions developed in similar ways and were a natural evolution of the total colonial society and culture.

Mrs. Carmichael's account indeed gives evidence that both Whites and Blacks of the 1820s saw each other as totally dissimilar and nearly if not absolutely opposite:

> Their carrying manure in this way [on their heads] appears disagreeable work; but they laugh at the stranger who supposes it to be so to the negro, because it would be so to him: the truth is, in so far as cleanliness is concerned, the negro is perfectly indifferent; these sort of things do not affect their personal comfort, because their whole habits and manners of life are different from Britons: what are comforts and pleasures to them, would not be so to us; and what we esteem as the comforts and luxuries of life, they would neither thank you for nor make use of. (Carmichael 1833, 1:105)

Of course, this is the British expectation regarding cleanliness. But the Negroes "laugh" at him who "supposes" the Negro to be the same as the white. Both groups seem to mutually agree "their whole habits and manners of life" are not only "different" but nearly opposite, with the one's "comforts and luxuries" receiving neither "thanks" nor "use" from the other, and vice versa.

On another occasion, Mrs. Carmichael questioned a slave who had been flogging his wife. He had done it because, in his words, "no man could bear he wife to behave so as mine do, and not punish well." Mrs. Carmichael suggested that he should have reproved her "calmly" and "she would have begged your pardon," for "it is dreadful to see how you negroes flog your wives; no white man dare do so." The slave replied, "Massa, they no need; they wive quite differ from we wive" (Carmichael 1833, 1:266–67). Even the slaves, in their own words, felt themselves to "differ." Given how little was apparently recorded of slave thought and speech, this taste of inverse logical organization will have to suffice for the colonial period.[9] The character of such a relationship is summarized in the more considered sociological opinion of Braithwaite:

> But if the slave system enslaved the whites, it damaged the free and unfree non-white even more. These elements of the population appear, in general, not only to have accepted the white stereotypes of themselves, they seem to have acted (self-fulfilling the 'prophecy'), within these images of themselves. (Brathwaite 1971:193)

One might argue that the Negro plantation culture derives from the relations of its bearers to the means of production, giving an economic and materialistic explanation to the resulting slave ideologies. But if this were so, then the culture of slaves should in many regards be like the culture of the Guatemalan *indios:* they were both allowed colony parcels on the estates and given time to work them, yet they were forced to work for masters and subjected to harsh and discriminatory practices. To be sure, there were differences: for example, the *indio* couldn't be sold away, just rented away (unless he ran away, which thereby permitted enslavement). And the colonial Indian *possibly* had more free time between turns of *repartimiento* and after meeting the *encomienda* tax quotas. But the tributes and labor demands kept both Indian men and Indian women working quite diligently to survive. So the labor enslavement was in many ways substantially similar. And by a materialist or labor-relations analysis the Guatemalan *indios* and British Caribbean Blacks should have become substantially similar.

But the fact of the matter is that the English were quite the opposite of the Spanish in certain crucial premises. As a result the Negro slaves, in taking on the opposite qualities of their English masters in the island system, became rather like the Spanish lords. Conversely, Indians and Englishmen share some surprising characteristics. Such a result must be attributed to the logic of colonial ethnicity, not to the necessity of belief arising out of a peculiar labor structure. To see how this is so, we must examine briefly the historical background of the Jamaican colony and then explore the rich detail of family variation and ideological opposition in Fernando Henriques's studies of class and color in present-day Jamaica.

The Spanish colonization of Jamaica, after its discovery in 1494, was neither enthusiastic nor successful, for the lack of quick mineral riches sapped Spanish interest in the place. By 1611, the census records a total population of 1,510 persons, of whom 523 were adult Spaniards, 107 were free negroes, 558 were black slaves, 74 were native Indians (of an estimated 60,000 at contact), and 173 were children (non-tallying figures {sic}, Henriques 1968:25–26). As a result of little interest and low population, the island was indefensible when the British attacked with eight thousand soldiers in May of 1655. Only mustering four to five hundred Spanish colonists to arms, the island fell to the English.

England, however, placed more value on the island's possession, both for its strategic naval position vis-à-vis the Spanish gold fleets and for its agricultural potential. And in spite of poorly chosen and therefore disease-ridden town sites, the island prospered. Not yet twenty years after capture, Jamaica supported some 7,700 mostly English Europeans (4,054 men, 2,000 women, and 1,712 children), as well as about 10,000 black slaves (Henriques 1968:27). By 1791, the population had increased to 30,000 Whites, 10,000 "free people of colour and freed negroes," and 250,000 slaves (Henriques 1968:31). One can assume from this explosive population shift that the Spanish cultural impact had been essentially dissipated, swallowed up by the organization of society according to British ideals.[10]

Much has been written about the nature of slavery on the British colonial plantations, both contemporaneously and currently. It is not my intent here to define the nature of the plantation, but to note that the British succeeded in imposing a labor regime upon their African charges, with sharp conceptual distinction between the White Englishmen and the Black Africans.[11] These two conditions should be sufficient, according to the theoretical perspective given here, to generate a system of inversions between Jamaican elites and Jamaican Blacks. Mrs. Carmichael's account gives some hint of such opposition, but it is difficult to depend on her due to the possibilities of a polemical justification of her way of life. We need to turn to more disciplined modern observers.

Among the professional anthropologists who have explored the problem of Jamaican social origins, Herskovits and others contend that the maternally oriented character of modern-day Caribbean society derives from the matrilineal organization of the African societies that lost their population to slavery. For certain, there are elements of folklore and religious practice of Akan (Ghanan) origin. But the matrifocal family organization and high illegitimacy rates are also standard on those islands which drew their slaves mostly from patrilineal or at least patrifocal peoples. And in any event, the tribal mixing was considerable. In light of this, Henriques enunciates the dominant anthropological position: that "differences in language and customs prevented [the slaves] carrying on their original patterns of behavior," and this, "coupled with the pressure" to "fit into the mould of the estate was sufficient to destroy most of their tribal culture" (Henriques 1957:23).

But what is the character of Jamaican society today? And can a persisting pattern of inversions be seen now? Moreover, if there are inversions, are they the same as in Guatemala, indicating that the institutional requirements of the labor regime determine the ideology of both elites and workers in *encomienda-repartimiento* as well as on slave plantations? Or do differences in Black and Guatemalan Indian ideologies arise as inverse projections of different elite cultures, the English and the Spanish?

Of course, I recognize the strong impact of social structural factors in creating a number of similiarities between the two societies. The sexual accessibility of lower-class females among Jamaican Blacks and Indian servants is a closely parallel product of the concentration of power, status, and male settlement in the two societies. But let us first explore the outlines of inversion between Jamaican elite and commoner. Then we will try to tease out a few complexes which are clearly culturally unique rather than institutionally induced. To this end we must depend upon Fernando Henriques's *Family and Colour in Jamaica* (1968), one of those few works that explores the whole range of belief and behavior among the different classes of a modern society.

Except in the decade just before Henriques's second-edition reassessment in 1968, Jamaican politics and power have been clearly in the control of English Whites and the Jamaican-born Whites and "Fair". Miscegenation proceeded on a different course than in the United States, with the Mestizos moving up and out of the category of Black, becoming various shades of "Browns" and "Fair," with varying degrees of "good" or "bad" features depending on their closeness to European or African stereotypes. Nevertheless, something close to an ethnic boundary prevails between "white bias" values that are "good," and black traits which are "bad." While a Guatemalan Indian can become Mestizo or Ladino by modifying his ideology and behavior, a Black cannot become other than black. But a Black can improve his or her class evaluation by rigorously adhering to the normative moral values expressed (though not necessarily lived) by the White elite. As a result, while the class system is overwhelmingly Black in the lower class, "Coloured" in the middle class, and "Fair" and "White" in the upper class, each color has some members in the other classes. Blacks rise through money, a stable job, or assiduously correct "Christian" family morality, and Coloureds rise—or fall—according to the same.[12] But given the "white bias," immoral behavior by the whites has become a privilege of rank, and a fall from upper-class prestige is infrequent.

Since class and color coordinate closely, one can surmise from the above that the jobs and economic rewards are closely allied to color. Quite so. With only a few recent exceptions, positions of power, prestige, and economic centrality are allocated to the White and Fair; middle level positions go to Browns and correct Blacks; while common labor, peasant agriculture, small-scale market "higgling," odd jobbing, and unemployment befall the majority of Blacks (Henriques 1968:50).

Unfortunately, there is no direct statement from Henriques on the nature and distribution of the work ethic. I was unable to determine from Henriques just how the elite felt about work in general, although it is clear that all felt that "manual labour" conveys "degradation." However, it is also apparent in several passages that being a good worker is valued by the lower and middle classes and that the attribute is considered to raise your class (Henriques 1968:133, 136). Thus, it appears that steady manual work is better than no work at all and that the prestige sectors of the society value work, in the English tradition, although they no doubt know how to take such leisure as their means may afford. Moreover, Henriques makes clear that a shiftless attitude toward work is one of the attributes that lowers a person of "better color," and characterizes as well as stereotypes the lowest-class Blacks.

We can see in this aspect of Jamaican economic ideologies a pattern of opposites, but the most interesting aspect of the pattern is that it is close to a mirror image of the Guatemalan and Peruvian work ethic. Starting with the English culture's positive evaluation of work, we find a negative attitude toward work in the most disparaged segment of the Jamaican lower class. (And, as we shall see, there is a whole series of family structure adjustments to protect the domestic unit against the impact of this ideology and the limited work that it, in fact, generates for the Blacks.) Conversely, starting with the negative evaluation of work by the Guatemalan, Spanish-derived elite, the ethnically despised Guatemalan Indian adopts a highly positive evaluation of work. Since both the Guatemalan Indian and the Jamaican Negro historically had work forced upon them, it is difficult to see how a relation to the means-of-production model can account for this supposedly epiphenomenal difference. Dependence, enslavement, and other power and resource models are insufficient. One concludes that the initial culture of the overlords indeed determines important characteristics of the colonized masses.

Turning now to matters of kinship, marriage, and family, we find other opposites within Jamaican society—and one sharp contrast with the overall structure of kinship in the Hispanic kinship tradition. Elite Jamaican society follows the English middle class's relative lack of interest in extensions of kinship beyond the immediate family[13] (Henriques 1968:159, 160, 162–63). Conversely, "one of the distinctive features of Jamaican lower class family life is the strong sense of kin which extends beyond the immediate family" (Henriques 1968:139).

Again, this total-society Jamaican pattern of upper-class disinterest versus lower-class kinship interest contrasts with the total-society pattern in Guatemala, where the elite have a higher level of interest in kinship extensions than do the comparatively individualistic and nuclear-family oriented Indians.[14] Again, it would appear the pattern must be attributed to differences in the initial ideologies of the overlords.

There exists another inversion within Jamaican society. While the kin-field and family organization of the Jamaican lower class is strongly "maternal," the kin and family orientation of the upper class is strikingly male-centered. But this structure apparently has no opposite counterpart in Guatemalan society, where the matrifocal element is lower-class Ladino but where even lower-status Indians maintain a male-focused family system with equalitarian overtones apparently due to the availability of work as craftsmen and farmers, and the ritual place of Indian males.

The Jamaican system of domestic alliances holds marriage (legal and religious), the central criterion of the "Christian family," to be the prestige pattern. The upper class and the aspiring middle class upholds this tradition rigidly. The upper class upholds the requirement for its women and socially for its men. But the system allows, and even rewards, the elite men for taking paramours from middle- and lower-class women. These women are supported as a second household or are entertained in more casual relationships. The lower-class Blacks with no class-mobility aspirations engage almost exclusively in common-law unions, some of which are enduring and many of which are not, usually depending on the economic fortunes of the male. But given the "white bias" and the cultural expectation of economic uncertainty for most Black men (which acts as self-fulfilling prophecy), many middle- and lower-class persons are quite pleased if a daughter becomes an on-the-side paramour of someone of a higher class and of "better" features and color. There are, of course, certain definite similarities here with the Guatemalan patterns of sexual access, and these similarities are one of the very real results of structural similarities in the hierarchy of the societies.

Henriques, writing in 1953, did not use the concept of the developmental cycle so usefully exploited by Raymond T. Smith and others since *The Negro Family in British Guiana* (1956). Clearly Henriques's "Grandmother Family" is the three-generation extension of the matrifocal system now well described. And presumably most of the unstable "Keeper Families" as well as a good share of the "Concubinage Families" (what we now prefer to call common-law unions) turn into the Grandmother (or matrifocal) family at the statistically probable crises that plague even the stably employed Black laborers. But we do not have statistical data on the process from Henriques. In any event, a similar pattern occurs, though less frequently, among the poor Ladinos. Guatemalan Indians, on the other hand, usually transfer household leadership to a son in the event of a father's death or incapacity, although a well-to-do household may attract a very poor male into uxorilocal residence.

Yet other aspects of Jamaican family life contrast diacritically between upper and lower classes, although they present no clear relation to the Guatemalan material. For example, Henriques describes the afternoon

> parade of nannies with their upper class charges. The mothers are preoccupied with tennis, bridge, or cocktails at this time. It is only on very special occasions that a mother will accompany an infant out of doors when it is at the preambulatory stage. This is in complete contrast to the other classes where the women are seen everywhere with their children. This dislike of public demonstration of motherhood may be due to the unconscious

reaction to the excessive display of the lower class in this matter. (Henriques 1968:157)

The system of oppositions and diacritical distinctions penetrates not only deeply, but in surprising ways. This passage highlights the degree of "contrast" or "reaction" in the symbolic and, presumably, ideological systems.

Perhaps other distinctive inversions in Caribbean society will be apparent to those who have done their own fieldwork in the area or may do so in the future. And perhaps more contrasts between the total British Caribbean and the total Hispanic mainland systems can be discovered, given the initial contrasts between English and Spanish overlord ideologies. Indeed, a careful comparison and contrast of English and Spanish elite cultures is needed, and is certainly not attempted in this exploratory essay. The next step requires critically penetrating historical and documentary research, and above all, directed comparative field research.

Inverse Images and Postcolonial Instability

Even so, the apparent reversal in the class distribution of kin interest and work ethic between English and Spanish colonial societies forces us to see the importance that the distinctive colonial ideologies of the overlords have in defining the character of colonial societies. Clearly, we are faced with colonial societies and colonial cultures, not with colonial society or colonial culture. There is much variety within the type.

The process of inverse-ideology formation may be the distinctive and most important cultural aspect of colonial societies, if for no other reason than because inverse-ideology formation is so destructive. Framed as opposites of the high lords, the bulk of the natives who inherit the postcolonial nation-states hold precisely the opposite ideology from that held by the new elites and nation-leaders, for these new elites will, for the most part, adopt the values of the prior colonists. The conflict savages the new states: the ideology of the masses is not the ideology valued in the society, and for this reason the masses can never wholly accept their own motivations and beliefs. This ambivalence surely lies at the heart of the social tension and the instability in the emerging postcolonial societies. Marx was right about one thing: capitalist colonialism would, through internal contradiction, generate its own collapse. The inverse ideologies, created in the conceptual climate of racial difference and with harsh labor and taxation regimes, ultimately became the trigger of rebellion. And Euroamerican political colonialism has almost disappeared. But Marx was wrong about the essential reason. The colonial peoples have not accumulated the power of a class consciousness by slowly coming to perceive unity in the injustice of their exploitation and material condition. Rather, colonial peoples have had an inverse, hence oppositional, and ultimately revolutionary ideology forced upon them by virtue of their masters having *conceptually* defined them as different, usually by virtue of racial categories. Then, under the pressure of enslavement in various forms, the colonialized masses have become inverse images, yet different from surrounding colonies by virtue of being opposite to the distinctive cultural templates of the several European colonial powers.

Now the once-colonial powers must deal with the whirlwind instability in the postcolonial societies. Nor can the Euroamerican response to the postcolonial Third World be simple or of a single type. For, while inverse-ideology formation, labor exploitation for export products, ethnic hierarchy, and colonial bureaucracy may account for many social structural similarities (the colonial society as a social type), nevertheless, the cultural import of differences in the overlord status ideologies—and the degree to which the overlords were effective or ineffective in imposing their wills on the native peoples—also leaves each colony and postcolonial society unique.

Appendices

Appendix 1.A
Ethnic Inversion Among the Pocomam of Eastern Guatemala

Items are quoted unless summarized in [brackets] from (Gillin 1952).

Page	Line	Indian	Page	Line	Ladino
196	7	effect a peaceful adjustment or adaptation of men to the universe	196	8–9	effect control of the universe by man
196	9–10	wishes to come to terms with the universe	196	10	wishes to dominate it [the universe]
196	13–17	man is in a world [of] law [which is supernaturally controlled] ongoing and immutable	196	27–28	universe . . . can be manipulated by man
196	17–21	man must learn certain patterns of action and attitude to bring himself into conformity with the scheme of things . . . [to] receive the minimum amount of punishment and misfortune and the maximum rewards	196	29–38	control and power . . . over things . . . animals . . . other men; . . . man has a will of his own . . . destructive force . . . is the legitimate and ultimate technique for the removal of barriers to the individual's control
197	5–7	individual . . . counts less than the group. Individual exists as a member of the group	197	10	individual personality . . . has the higher value . . . group, . . . family, . . . exist to promote the individual
197	16–17	uninterrupted routine practice of traditional patterns	197	18–22	routine is intensely boring . . . periodic change of power . . . adds zest to life. Oscillation of power
197	23–27	universe . . . restricted	198	12–40	universe . . . expanded

Page	Line	Indian	Page	Line	Ladino
		[to] local community or region			both in space and time. . . . Have kinship, political, and economic connections with the capital and other towns. Cultivate a concept of nationality [as] part of the republic
198	3–9	restricted time space . . . a timeless present	198	29	strong sense of history
199	12–20	interested in owning land so that they personally can work on it. . . . No Indian ever tries to acquire wealth or skill so that he can retire from the land, but rather the reverse	199	21–26	personally works the land only when all other means of livelihood are unavailable. . . . Control of land . . . enables the owner to master the lives of his tenants and workmen
199	36–39	[from] physical toil . . . one receives the approval of his fellows	200	3–4	toil is not only unbearably wearisome, but also disgraceful
200	7–8	adjustive and permissive	200	8	ordering, dominating
200	8–9	ranking or stratification . . . not characteristic	200	10	[ranking or stratification] always present
200	11–13	leadership [positions] thought of as obligations [not] striven for	201	28–30	political advancement [in] own interest
200	17–18	envy and competitiveness . . . an anomaly or a crime	201	21	competition or conflict [appropriate]
200	30	group decisions . . . by consensus	201	12–14	domineering or ordering behavior [with unequals] . . . factions [among equals]
201	38–39	husband is officially dominant [but] patterns require a reciprocal division of labor and of authority	202	29–30	husband's authority is definitely superior
201	1	wife shares the honors . . . the responsibilities [of public life]	202	32	does not expect his wife to share . . . public life
203	15–17	religion . . . tends to permeate all of life	203	18	much more secular
204		[religious devotions with group orientation]	205	7–8	organized support for the Church is striking by its absence

Page	Line	Indian	Page	Line	Ladino
204		[men and women religiously involved]	205	4–5	In contrast to Indian women, Ladino women show more devotion than men
206	16	relatively more secure [personality structure]	209	18	much less secure [personality structure]
206	19–22	compulsive following of the approved patterns without any strong motivation	209	18–20	no feeling of certainty that any of his available culture patterns will produce satisfactions
206	32–33	calmness and comparatively little affect, or show of emotion	209	13–15	much more emotionalism . . . likes and dislikes more demonstratively expressed . . . mood swings
207	1–9	little show of aggressiveness [except with alcohol or special offense]	209	25–26	much more aggressive . . . both toward themselves and toward members of the other caste
207	18–20	child rearing . . . quite permissive	210	13–14	the higher one goes in the Ladino class system, the greater is the rigidity of child training

Appendix 1.B
Ethnic Inversion Among the Cakchiquel of Central Guatemala

Alexander Moore (1973) richly documents the life-cycle "careers" and educational systems of Indians and Ladinos in Atchalán, a Cakchiquel-Indian/Spanish-Ladino community near Antigua.[1]

Moore's book was not intended to compare and contrast Indian and Ladino ideologies over all of their cultural domains; rather, it focuses on life-cycle patterns. There, however, he finds explicit contrasts which I think merit designation as inversions:

> The patron-client [Ladino] process very closely resembles that of the initiator-initiate relationship of the Indians. . . . The great difference is that the Indians do their initiating impersonally, publicly, and collectively. The patron-client relationship initiates clients into new roles, but does so personally, individually, and often quite privately. (Moore 1973:116)

The thrust of Moore's chapters in comparing the two ideologies is that Ladinos seek after, value, and construct circles of interpersonal and kinship alliance and patronage interdependence in an open, choice-filled status hierarchy that admits the possibility of both rising and falling in status. By contrast, Atchalán Indians move through their lives as age-sets—as gangs rather than as distinctive individuals—and they do so by official community call and recruitment rather than by individual initiative and luck. Thus, Moore summarizes:

> Unlike the Indian Atchaleños, their Ladino neighbors participate in an open system of life chances. Careers are not directed in concert by a closed group of initiators. On the contrary: careers are not directed in any concert and are often in conflict. (Moore 1973:95)

In addition, Moore draws attention to the rich historical texture of Ladino lives "in contrast to my nearly ahistorical treatment of Atchaleño Indians" (Moore 1973:95).

The remaining contrasts are more implicit in Moore's work. On the one hand, Atchalán Ladinos are indeed guided by the Ladino national culture, whose impact works out in the daily practice of their lives. Moore presents the Ladinos, compared to the Indians, as more socially and politically interested, more interconnective, more urban and urbane, more inclined toward elite professions and toward owning the land but not working the land, disinclined toward manual labor, interested in differences of status, and ranked vis-à-vis each other but all ranked above the Indians.

The Indians "would agree with everything Gillin had to say about the 'basic values' of the Indians he studied" (Moore 1973:198), and they, too, play out their lives in the construction of symbolically consistent worlds: agricultural subsistence isolation in the rural margins, relative distance and independence of siblings once out of the parental household, a life spent in mass categories—as Indian, initiate, and, with effort and luck, even as *principal*—rather than as an individual.

To repeat Ewald's observations (1954), the differences between the Indians of San Luis, Atchalán, and San Pedro are much less significant than their similarities.

Appendix 2.A
Principal Occupation of Urban Household Heads Comparing San Pedro and San Marcos

Occupation of Household Head	San Pedro			San Marcos		
	No. of S.P. Households	% of S.P. Household Heads in Trade	S.P.'s % of Trade	No. of S.M. Households	% of S.M. Household Heads	S.M.'s % of Trade
White Collar & Professional:						
Agricultural technician	1	0.5	33.3	2	1.1	66.7
Agri-surveyor	1	0.5	50.0	1	0.5	50.0
Finca administrator	0	0.0	0.0	2	1.1	100.0
Finca paymaster-accountant	0	0.0	0.0	1	0.5	100.0
Judge	0	0.0	0.0	1	0.5	100.0
Lawyer	1	0.5	100.0	0	0.0	0.0
Court secretary or clerk	1	0.5	33.3	2	1.1	66.7
Doctor	2	1.0	66.7	1	0.5	33.3

	San Pedro			San Marcos		
Occupation of Household Head	No. of S.P. Households	% of S.P. Household Heads in Trade	S.P.'s % of Trade	No. of S.M. Households	% of S.M. Household Heads	S.M.'s % of Trade
Nurse	0	0.0	0.0	3	1.6	100.0
Midwife	0	0.0	0.0	1	0.5	100.0
High school teacher	0	0.0	0.0	2	1.1	100.0
Grade school teacher	6	3.1	20.0	24	13.0	80.0
Radio station technician	0	0.0	0.0	1	0.5	100.0
Minister	1	0.5	100.0	0	0.0	0.0
Accountant	2	1.0	28.6	5	2.7	71.4
Mayor	1	0.5	33.3	2	1.1	66.7
Health inspector	0	0.0	0.0	1	0.5	100.0
Secretary	2	1.0	25.0	6	3.3	75.0
Office employee	1	0.5	16.7	5	2.7	83.3
Telegrapher	1	0.5	33.3	2	1.1	66.7
Military officer	0	0.0	0.0	3	1.6	100.0
Police	1	0.5	20.0	4	2.2	80.0
Subtotal	(21)			(69)		
Business and Commerce:						
Industrialist	1	0.5	50.0	1	0.5	50.0
Wholesaler	2	1.0	66.7	1	0.5	33.3
Retailer	18	9.2	72.0	7	3.8	28.0
Traveling salesperson	1	0.5	100.0	0	0.0	0.0
Lottery ticket seller	0	0.0	0.0	1	0.5	100.0
Subtotal	(22)			(10)		

Agriculture:						
Agriculturalists (size undifferentiated)	15	7.7	55.6	12	6.5	44.4
Agricultural wage laborers	7	3.6	63.6	4	2.2	36.4
Subtotal	(22)			(16)		
Transportation:						
Driver (taxi or chauffeur)	7	3.6	36.8	12	6.5	63.2
Truck driver	3	1.5	50.0	3	1.6	50.0
Trucker's assistant	0	0.0	0.0	2	0.5	100.0
Subtotal	(10)			(17)		
Skilled Service:						
Mechanic	4	2.1	57.1	3	1.6	42.9
Radio repair	0	0.0	0.0	1	0.5	100.0
Electrician	0	0.0	0.0	1	0.5	100.0
Clock repair	0	0.0	0.0	1	0.5	100.0
Subtotal	(4)			(6)		
Crafts:						
Thread winder	1	0.5	100.0	0	0.0	0.0
Weaver	12	6.2	92.3	1	0.5	7.7
Knitter	8	4.1	100.0	0	0.0	0.0
Tailor	21	10.8	100.0	0	0.0	0.0
Seamstress	4	2.1	66.7	2	1.1	33.3
Shoemaker	15	7.7	71.4	6	3.3	28.6
Carpenter	13	6.7	59.1	9	4.9	40.9

	San Pedro			San Marcos		
Occupation of Household Head	No. of S.P. Households	% of S.P. Household Heads in Trade	S.P.'s % of Trade	No. of S.M. Households	% of S.M. Household Heads	S.M.'s % of Trade
Mason	11	5.6	57.9	8	4.3	42.1
Smith	0	0.0	0.0	1	0.5	100.0
Painter	0	0.0	0.0	2	1.1	100.0
Tilemaker	2	1.0	100.0	0	0.0	0.0
Soapmaker	1	0.5	100.0	0	0.0	0.0
Butcher	3	1.5	100.0	0	0.0	0.0
Baker	8	4.1	88.9	1	0.5	11.1
Musician	3	1.5	75.0	1	0.5	25.0
Subtotal	(102)			(31)		
Miscellaneous:						
Photographer	2	1.0	100.0	0	0.0	0.0
Janitor	0	0.0	0.0	1	0.5	100.0
Barber	1	0.5	50.0	1	0.5	50.0
Dry cleaner	1	0.5	100.0	0	0.0	0.0
Subtotal	(4)			(2)		
Domestics:						
Cook	1	0.0	0.0	0	0.5	100.0
Washerwoman	0	0.0	0.0	3	1.6	100.0
Servant	1	0.5	33.3	2	1.1	66.7
Unpaid management of own household	8	4.1	22.2	28	15.2	77.8
Subtotal	(10)			(33)		
Total	195	100.0	51.5	184	100.0	48.5

Appendix 2.B

Value of Agricultural Land Owned by Household Comparing San Marcos with San Pedro (Urban Residents) (M = San Marcos; P = San Pedro)

Land Value in $ times 10	Percentage of Households 1 2 3 4 5 6 7 8 9 0 0 5 0 5 0 [a] 6 6 7 8		Percent of Cases[b]	No. of Cases
0 thru 25	MMMMMMMMMMMMMMMM	M =	67.0	127
	PPPPPPPPPPPPPPPPPPPPPPPPPPPPPPPPPPPPPPPP	P =	81.0	158
25+ thru 50	MMMMMMMMMMM	M =	10.3	19
	PPPPPPPP	P =	7.7	15
50+ thru 75	MMMM	M =	3.3	6
	PPPPPPPP	P =	4.1	8
75+ thru 100	M	M =	0.5	1
	PPP	P =	1.5	3
100+ thru 125	MM	M =	1.1	2
	P	P =	0.5	1

Land Value in $ times 10	Percentage of Households 1 2 3 4 5 6 7 8 9 0 1[a] 6 0 6 5 7 0 7 5 8 0		Percent of Cases[b]	No. of Cases
125+ thru 150	MMMMM PPPPPP	M = P =	3.3 3.0	6 6
150+ thru 175	MMM P	M = P =	1.6 0.5	3 1
175+ thru 200	MM	M = P =	1.1 0.0	2 0
200+ thru 225	M P	M = P =	0.5 0.5	1 1
225+ thru 250	M P	M = P =	0.5 0.5	1 1
250+ thru 275	P	M = P =	0.0 0.5	0 1
275+ thru 300		M = P =	0.0 0.0	0 0
300+ thru 325	PPP	M = P =	0.0 1.5	0 3
325+ thru 350	P	M = P =	0.0 0.5	0 1
350+ thru 375	M	M = P =	0.5 0.0	1 0
375+ thru 400	M	M = P =	0.5 0.0	1 0
400+ thru 425		M = P =	0.0 0.0	0 0
425+ thru 450	M	M = P =	0.5 0.0	1 0

450+ thru 475		M =	0.0	0
		P =	0.0	0
475+ thru 500	M	M =	0.5	1
	P	P =	0.5	1
500+ and above[c]	MMMMMMMMM	M =	7.1	13[b]
	PPPPP	P =	2.1	9

[a] Note the discontinuity between 10 and 60 percent.
[b] $N = 184$ for San Marcos; $N = 195$ for San Pedro.
[c] The mean land values for this category are $278,245.40 for San Marcos and $34,617.30 for San Pedro.

Appendix 2.C
Total Monthly Household Income
Comparing San Marcos with San Pedro (Urban Residents
(M = San Marcos; P = San Pedro)

Income in $	Percentage of Households								Percent of Cases[a]	No. of Cases
	5	10	15	20	25	30	35		
0 thru 25	MMMMMMMM							M = 13.0	24
	PPPPPPPPPPPPPPPP							P = 15.3	29
25+ thru 50	MMMMMMMMMMMMM							M = 17.9	33
	PPPPPPPPPPPPPPPPPPPPPPPPPPPPPPPPP							P = 33.7	64
50+ thru 75	MMMMMMMMM							M = 13.0	24
	PPPPPPPPPPPP							P = 12.6	24
75+ thru 100	MMMMMMMMM							M = 12.5	23
	PPPPPPPPPPPPPPPPP							P = 18.9	36
100+ thru 125	MMMMM							M = 9.2	17
	PPP							P = 4.1	8

125+ thru 150	MMMMM	M =	6.5	12
	PPP	P =	2.6	5
150+ thru 175	MMMM	M =	3.8	7
	P	P =	1.1	2
175+ thru 200	MMM	M =	3.3	6
	PPP	P =	2.6	5
200+ thru 225	MMM	M =	3.3	6
	PP	P =	2.1	4
225+ thru 250	MMMM	M =	4.3	8
	PP	P =	1.6	3
250+ thru 275	MM	M =	2.2	4
		P =	0.0	0
275+ thru 300	M	M =	0.5	1
	P	P =	1.1	2
300+ thru 325	MMM	M =	2.7	5
	P	P =	1.1	2
325+ thru 350	M	M =	1.1	2
	P	P =	0.5	1
350+ thru 375	M	M =	0.5	1
		P =	0.0	0
375+ thru 400		M =	0.0	0
	P	P =	0.5	1
400+ thru 425		M =	0.0	0
		P =	0.5	1
425+ thru 450	M	M =	0.5	1
		P =	0.0	0

	Percentage of Households								Percent of Cases[a]	No. of Cases
Income in $	5	1 0	1 5	2 0	2 5	3 0	3 5			
450+ thru 475								M =	0.0	0
								P =	0.0	0
475+ thru 500								M =	0.0	0
								P =	0.0	0
500+ and above[b]	MMMMM							M =	4.9	9
	PP							P =	2.1	4

[a] N = 184 for San Marcos; N = 190 for San Pedro.
[b] The mean incomes for this category are $1,404.70 for San Marcos and $873 for San Pedro

394

Appendix 3

Ethnic Definitions: Abbeviated Quotes from San Pedro (P1 Through P75) and San Marcos (M1 Through M49)

Abbreviation Key: oao (on account of); = (*to be* verb in some form); I (Indian); M (Mestizo); L (Ladino); "I" (first person singular); bcz (because); p (person) or ps (persons), may be tied with w (who) and = (*to be* verb); T = (that is); G (Guatemalan, or Guatemala).

Invariant Translations: *raza* = race, *sangre* = blood, *natural* = native, *persona* = person, *gente* = people.

Case No.	What is an Indian?	What is a Ladino?	What Are You?	Why?
P1	A resident belonging to this race	Descendants of foreign race	M:	We are neither Indians nor Ladinos[1]
P2	A native person[2]	A foreigner	I:	"I" am native
P3	Guatemalan people bcz we are all Indians	Foreign persons	I:	Oao = entirely (*propio*) from Guatemala
P4	Oao = I in race or a native of this place	According to the style of dressing	I:	That is my race[3]
P5	An aborigine from these lands	A cross of Spanish and *indio*[4]	L:	I am of European descent
P6	The native race	Oao the clothing which he has	I:	Bcz parents were of Indian origin
P7	A native of the country	By the manner of dress	I:	Oao being of this country
P8	A native of a place	A person of foreign extraction	L:	By [my/our] customs
P9	They are all equal	Oao clothing	I:	Oao being a San Pedrano
P10	A tradition which uses *corte y huipil*[5]	People distinguished by their dress	M:	[We have] a little of each race
P11	Psw can be seen by their clothing	Psw = distinguished by their clothing	I:	My parents were Indians

395

Abbreviation Key: oao (on account of); = (to be verb in some form); I (Indian); M (Mestizo); L (Ladino); "I" (first person singular); bcz (because); p (person) or ps (persons), may be tied with w (who) and = (to be verb); T = (that is); G (Guatemalan, or Guatemala).
Invariant Translations: *raza* = race, *sangre* = blood, *natural* = native, *persona* = person, *gente* = people.

Case No.	What is an Indian?	What is a Ladino?	What Are You?	Why?
P12	Oao clothing	Oao having better clothing	I:	That = my birth and "I" cannot progress more
P13	By the style of dress	He who can dress well	I:	Oao my parents
P14	A native person	A more civilized person	I:	Bcz such were the fathers or aborigines
P15	A person native of his country	A person with greater civilization	M:	Oao the origin of the surnames
P16	A native person	A civilized p, one who understands[7]	I:	Being descended[8] of the Indian race
P17	It has something to do with race	He is more civilized in studies	M:	Because we were conquered by the Spaniards
P18	Psw have customs of the ancient ones	Wide knowledge and highly advanced customs	M:	We have Indian and Ladino customs
P19	A descendent of the Mayan race	People who are more civilized and have more modern ideas	M:	Oao the mixture of two bloods
P20	Person descended of an ancient race	A more knowing[7] person	M:	Because now we are civilized
P21	Blood of Tecún Umán	A L is distinguished by economics	I:	[We are] of the blood of Tecúm Umán[9]
P22	An Indian person	Oao economic means[10]	I:	Oao not being Ladino
P23	Pw = rooted in the customs of forefathers, not wanting to lose his sense of autochthony	Pw has a more adequate way of life, who lives in the city	M[44].	Our antecedents[11] were Indian
P24	Oao being a native of the country	An educated person	M[45]:	Oao having Indian and Ladino blood
P25	A native person	Civilized persons	I:	Oao being from here
P26	A native of the country & the descendants of the hero Tecúm Umán[9]	An astute person	M:	"I" belong to the two social groups
P27	The Mam and Guatemalan race	Asute and sagacious	M:	We are between Spain and Guatemala
P28	A person who is quite poor	A rich person	I:	We are of the native race
P29	Limited economic alternatives[10] usually illiterate, with bad customs, bad housing	A well-taught person who has more possibilities of bettering his life	M:	We descend[6] from the Indian race
P30	Pw little civilization	He who is more ahead[12]	L:	We do not have any relatives (*familias*) who dress Indian
P31	Particularly a working man	A man of much studies, more civilized	M:	By virtue of the union
P32	Devote themselves to heavy labor[13]	A Ladino is more civilized	M:	The mixture of the two races

P33	Rooted[14] here, a native of the particular country. And we are stupid (*mamasos*)	Knows how to express himself and is smart	L.[15]	Oao being Spanish blood
P34	A person with little culture	A prepared person[16]	L:	My parents were Ladinos
P35	More humble pw does not have much civilization	Pw has the means to study and live better	M:	I don't know
P36	They are the uncivilized people	Educated men (*hombres de estudio*)	I:	Our parents were natives of this country
P37	Pw works in the field and has to eat	Intelligent and they dress well	L:	Oao descending[6] from the Indian race
P38	Pw speaks dialect, psw = more behind[17]	Psw speak Spanish and by virtue of race	L:	It's according to the races
P39	P native[18] of this place, who lacks studies, education, and orientation,[19] who = derived from[20] the Maya race	Mixture of L and I, of foreign blood	M:	Oao descending[6] from the two races
P40	The Indian race	Only on account of what he studies	I:	Oao not having any education
P41	A native of the place	Oao having much education and the means of dressing	I:	Oao living in the native place and being of limited means[10]
P42	The native race	People more prepared and with more capacity than an Indian	I:[46]	We are not as capable[21]
P43	The first men living in our country[22]	An educated person	M:[45]	Oao being educated
P44	The first men living in our country[22]	Any man who uses any modern thing	L:	Oao favorable circumstances
P45	Psw = distinguished by ancient customs	Educated people who dress well	M:	By education and blood, we are now almost Ladinos
P46	A native of his country	By his clothing and by his civilization	I:	Because of my economic means
P47	By the manner of dress	Oao being more monied[23]	I:	Because of my economic means
P48	Psw represent[24] their place, such as San Pedro or some other	Psw civilize themselves by the career that they take up	L:	By being linked to advanced things and by forgetting the [Indian] customs
P49	Native-born in Guatemala	Pw = superior to the Indian	M:	We are neither Ladinos nor Indians
P50	A native of the town	An honor (*distinción*) of people	I:	Because that is what my parents are
P51	Oao being inferior	A person who is more civilized	I:	Thus was the descent of the fathers
P52	Pw has not a bit of education, who lives in ancient times	An educated high status[25] person	I:	Oao being a native of the country
P53	P with few recourses[10] in his economic problems	Pw has high social status[26] such as in his style of dress, and in his education	M:	Oao having a mixture of the two bloods
P54	A person who dresses[27] native	High status[28] and very well dressed	M:	Because our parents are mixed
P55	A person native of the country	A more distinguished person	M[29]	We are sons of the Spaniards
P56	A descendant of Indians from before	P of higher (*más elevada*) culture	I:	Oao not having a higher culture, or in other words, not having the means[30]

Abbreviation Key: oao (on account of); = (*to be* verb in some form); I (Indian); M (Mestizo); L (Ladino); "I" (first person singular); bcz (because); p (person) or ps (persons), may be tied with w (who) and = (*to be* verb); T= (that is); G (Guatemalan, or Guatemala).
Invariant Translations: *raza* = race, *sangre* = blood, *natural* = native, *persona* = person, *gente* = people.

Case No.	What is an Indian?	What is a Ladino?	What Are You?	Why?
P57	A native of the country	Pw = greater than[31] the I	I:	Oao being more short of money
P58	Individual coming from the native race	Coming from a family of high society	M:	Oao my being civilized
P59	Oao the manner of dress	Oao the manner of dress	I:	We do not come up to being superior
P60	Pw do not know Spanish and are illiterate	Foreign people and those of blue blood	M:	Oao having a mixture of the two bloods
P61	They are the forefathers	Oao living in the center of the city	I:	Oao being of the Indian race
P62	A working man	A man of science[41]	L:	"I" am an I, but "I" associate with persons having a scientific background
P63	Pw fights to get ahead[12]	Ps on a high level (*de alto nivel*)	I:	We are struggling to get ahead[12]
P64	Psw do not have the capacity to perform social acts	Have the capacity to fill the requirements	I:	We are of that same status
P65	A peasant who cultivates the earth	Ps who hold a post in an office	M:	Oao being a little bit civilized
P66	A person who works in the field	Oao having better conditions	L:	Oao having better thoughts
P67	Pw works in the field	According to their way of thinking and their intelligence	L:	Oao possessing a magnificent idea
P68	P of few resources	P of various resources	I:	"I" am a p of limited resources
P69	Oao not being educated[16]	P prepared[16] as to studies	I:	Oao not being so educated[16]
P70	A homebody (*doméstica*) who devotes himself to his own work (*trabajos propios*)	Pw devotes himself to studies	I:	My work permits only that
P71	A poor person	A person with money	I:	Oao earning very little. "I" am not rich
P72	A person lacking in studies	A more educated person	I:	"I" am lacking in studies
P73	A p of few economic resources, lacking studies or knowledge	Oao their way of behaving by virtue of having greater economic possibilities	M:	["I" am a] person with few resources
P74	Pw devotes himself to work in the fields	A well-instructed psw has a magnetic discipline	M:	Because we are civilized and are a little bit ahead
P75	Pw will do any work, whatever it may be	They are the psw have means[42]	I:	We must do all the work and less study
M1	A p tied to the I race	A pw = mixed with a Spanish race	M[43]	Bcz we have the two origins of the races
M2	Psw = called "Mayas"	Mestizo persons	M:	We belong to the two bloods
M3	Pw uses distinctive (*típico*) clothing	Pw uses different clothing	L:	Oao clothing

398

M4	Psw speak dialects and oao costumes (*traje*)	Pw speaks Castilian language	M:	Oao speaking a little bit better and style of dress
M5	A representative of our race	The Mestizo race	L:	By my forefathers (*antepasados*)
M6	Representatives of the country	L = the word used for a M	L:	According to the descent of our fathers
M7	P born in Guatemala, native (*originario*) of a plot of their own land	They do not exist, there are only M	M:	We are of different families
M8	The dark-skinned race	The white race	L:	Because my parents were legitimate Ladinos
M9	From being Indian in race	A person who is not Indian	L:	The origin of my parents is Mexican
M10	A native person of another race	Does not speak [one of the] tongues	M:	Oao not knowing whether ["I" am] L or I
M11	Another nationality. Belongs to I family	Belongs to L family, speech more developed	L:	Parents were of the L family
M12	A brother in race	= different in surnames and life customs	L:	T = the descent of my grandparents
M13	It is a race	Distinguished by the difference in the way they live	M:	Descend[6] from other races, or in other words, the two—L and I
M14	Pw still abides by tradition	Pw does not abide the traditions of before	M:	For being of the G and Italian race
M15	Customs of forefathers and form of life	Ps whose customs and blood are different	M:	For being a mixture of the two races
M16	By their words (*vocabularios*)	The M race	M:	[I am a] descendent of two races
M17	By manner of dress and vocabulary	Expresses better than an I, and by L dress	L:	Descended of L parents
M18	By manner of speaking and dressing	Does not know a tongue, and by clothing	L:	[We are] descended of Ladino persons
M19	I don't know	According to the manner of speaking	M:	Being a mixture of the two bloods
M20	Style of dress	Style of dress	M:	By the descent of my parents
M21	A p representative of the place	A M descended of another nation	L:	By descent of my fathers
M22	P according to his clothing	Only oao speaking better language	M:	Oao being a Guatemalan
M23	Pw has primitive customs, who has his own language and clothing. Sociocultural group	Customs in accordance with European ones, speaks Spanish, and customs related to modern life. Sociocultural group	L:	By virtue of speaking Spanish and by clothing
M24	P equal to us except they live far from town and because of their clothing	A more squared-away[32] person	L:	Because of race
M25	P equal to any one else	Same[33] as the I, with more instruction	M:	Because our race is not pure
M26	P native to Guatemala	An able, quick person (*lista*)	M:	Our race is a mixture of the two
M27	Native descendant of America	P crossed with Spanish and native, who has achieved personal improvement[12] and keeps in the rhythm of the civilization	L:	By descent
M28	Like[33] everyone; only difference is race	Pw has instruction[19] and ideas	L:	By descent
M29	Just like[33] any human being, the difference is only of habits	Oao having more culture	L:	Oao having Spanish origins
M30		Pw has more advantage than an I	M:	Oao two origins
M31	Valuable element in G culture—also of using native[18] dress[27]	A principal element in the development of national and technical culture	L:	Oao using ordinary clothing[27]

Abbreviation Key: oao (on account of); = (to be verb in some form); I (Indian); M (Mestizo); L (Ladino); "I" (first person singular); bcz (because); p (person) or ps (persons), may be tied with w (who) and = (to be verb); T = (that is); G (Guatemalan, or Guatemala).
Invariant Translations: *raza* = race, *sangre* = blood, *natural* = native, *persona* = person, *gente* = people.

Case No.	What is an Indian?	What is a Ladino?	What Are You?	Why?
M32	Oao having native dress[34]	An educated person	L:	Oao having L dress
M33	Pw = the pure race the Spanish encountered	Live in town, they receive more teachings	M:	We are crossed with the Spaniards
M34	Pw dresses less well	Pw dresses better and eats better food	L:	My parents were Ladinos
M35	Pw does not understand anything	A person who understands more	L:	The descent of the fathers
M36	Human beings, a little bit ignorant, but friendly	Have more education, they are more prepared	L:	Descent of my fathers; they are foreigners
M37	A useful person	A more understanding person, who has more dignity[35]	L:	Oao the origin of my parents
M38	Possess a lesser degree of culture because the majority of them are illiterate	Of higher culture than the I, but they are always the same value	L:	Oao having a different surname, and the descent of my parents
M39	P of stronger blood, a p tied to manual things[36]	Nonmanual[37] people[38]	M:	By descent[39]
M40	P like us but with fewer aspirations	Has achieved[12] and has changed customs	L:	Oao having two families: Spanish, native
M41	An underdeveloped individual	A mixed person	L:	Spanish origin
M42	Pw is native to a certain place	Pw has had basic instruction which makes him able to develop fully, whether or not he originates in that place	L:	Oao the instruction acquired and given to others, and for living in a decent way
M43	Pw uses the dress and the vocabulary of that area, a humble p	Pw uses clothing, different vocabulary, p of status[25]	L:	Oao surnames and our form of speaking
M44	P inferior to oneself, one who works	They usually study. Not all of us are L because our forefathers were I	L:	My antecedents[40] were Ladinos
M45	Very humble p in the community	P with greater comprehension	L:	My parents were Ladinos
M46	P with another way of life, short of money	Pw uses costly furniture	I:	Oao economic circumstances that do not permit me
M47	Pw does not understand very well oao studies	Pw understands more bcz of his studies	L:	Oao having a good mind
M48	Pw has no schooling	An educated p	I:	Haven't much schooling
M49	A common and ordinary p as to his way of thinking, living, and acting	Pw dresses with more taste, more hygienic	L:	Because of our way of life

[1] The social circumstances of such denials of ethnicity are treated in Chapter 6.

[2] The word *natural* is translated throughout as "native". However, one must note that a dominant connotation is that of uncultivated, unsophisticated or unembellished by national culture.

[3] This may also be translated, "That is how race is (*Así es la raza*)."

[4] *Indio* is now a highly derogatory form of *indígena*.

[5] An ankle-length skirt (*corte*) and square-cut blouse (*huipil*) are held to be distinctively "Indian."

[6] *dependemos*

[7] *entendida*

[8] *Depender* and *dependencia* imply the notion of kinship descent and parallel the English cognate of dependents. But, it also carries the connotation of submission, subjection, or subjugation to a higher authority.

[9] Tecún Umán was the leader of the Indians in the battles against Pedro de Alvarado for the Quiché territory and people.

[10] *recursos*

[11] *antecesores*

[12] *superado, superarse*

[13] *trabajo material*

[14] *originario de*

[15] It is not uncommon for a person to class himself or herself collectively with "we" Indians but to identify oneself specifically as different.

[16] *Preparado* implies educated.

[17] *atrasadas*

[18] *nativa*

[19] *orientación* = bearings, direction, understanding

[20] *procedentes de*

[21] "Capability is acquired, again in part through the educational system. The phrase might also be translated as "We do not have the capacity." The Spanish strongly implies acquired rather than native ability.

[22] *patria*

[23] The native phrase, "*por ser de mayor dinero*," translates into colloquial English as "having more money." It is interesting, however, that the Spanish verbal choice implies that wealth is a rather permanent condition as well as a product of descent (*de*). Hence, the more adequate, though awkward, translation given in the text.

[24] *representan su lugar*

[25] *de categoría*

[26] *un alto grado social*

[27] *traje*

[28] *de calidad* = quality

[29] *Mezclado* = mixed

[30] *posibilidades*

[31] *más grande que*

Abbreviation Key: oao (on account of); = (to be verb in some form); I (Indian); M (Mestizo); L (Ladino); "I" (first person singular); bcz (because); p (person) or ps (persons), may be tied with w (who) and = (to be verb); T = (that is); G (Guatemalan, or Guatemala).
Invariant Translations: *raza* = race, *sangre* = blood, *natural* = native, *persona* = person, *gente* = people.

Case No.	What is an Indian?	What is a Ladino?	What Are You?	Why?

[32] *más construida* = more formed, more structured, more built up
[33] *igual que* or *como*
[34] *Vestuario* appears here in its unmarked, encompassing form. The usage, however, is quite uncommon.
[35] The word *dignidad* implies high esteem.
[36] *cosas materiales*
[37] *desmaterializadas*
[38] *Trabajos materiales* ("material labors") involves intensive manual labor. A thing or a person described as *material* is closely linked to heavy physical effort.
[39] *por la generación*
[40] The word *desendiente* may refer either to progeny (descendents) or to parentage.
[41] Less literally, "a knowledgeable man."
[42] "*facilidades*"
[43] "*mixto o mestizo*"
[44] "*mestizo*, or in another word, *ladinos indígena*"
[45] "mestizoized"
[46] *naturales*

Appendix 4
Prospects for Further Research

A worthwhile theory implicitly directs its users toward even more fruitful studies of additional topics and different sites. Moreover, as Karl Popper (1959, 1962) has noted extensively, a worthwhile theory can be tested, with some possibility of refutation. To be sure, anthropology tends to be more interpretive than explanatory, and theories, approaches, perspectives, and paradigm models are more easily spawned than passed by. Nevertheless, the approach that I have offered in this book lends itself to a considerable degree of testing on additional topics and in different ethnographic areas.

The theory is testable and explicit:

Given
(1) the presence of a colonizer's ideology that focuses on the colonized people as different, distinct, not like the colonizers, in a word, their opposites, and

(2) the impact of sufficient colonial force to require the colonized to change their social structure and culture,

then,

the colonized people will acquire an ideology inverse to that of their colonial lords.

To be sure, one can at present quibble over how much force constitutes hard colonialism or just how explicit the lordly notion of their oppositeness from the colonized must be. I do not know the answer to these questions now. I assume that if the general proposition clarifies the character of some postcolonial societies but not others, then the "quantitative" aspect of both degree of force and degree of oppositeness will begin to emerge. To help establish these boundaries, and to see if this approach might fruitfully clarify the nature and process of colonialism and its aftermath, I offer the following thoughts on possible research sites and topics.

Topics and Sites in Guatemala

Of the topics, religion is the most important. In terms of the theory offered, one would expect to find significant inversions in religious ideology, symbolism, and behavior between Ladinos and Indians. Barbara Tedlock, in a recent piece (1983), suggests that there are dialectical inversions within Indian religious thought. Would these dialectical contradictions be better understood if they were considered as a component of a larger system that included Ladino religious thought and symbolism in Momostenango? My theory would suggest this to be the case. The theory could be tested in Momostenango or in virtually any other town, but it must be done by someone controlling both Spanish and the local Mayan language. I do not wish to downplay the complexity of the task: within both Ladino and Indian religious ideology and symbolism there will be expressions of their fundamental oppositeness, of the place of each within the multifaceted national status continuum captured in the word *modernization,* and of the unique local ecology and social dynamic. Because Indians are the ideological inverse of Ladinos does not mean that Indians are all alike.

Another topic, touched on but not thoroughly documented in this book, concerns social networks. I have offered qualitative evidence of network difference between Ladinos and Indians. I have not given, however, a rigorously detailed network analysis, documented in the style appropriate to models as given by Mitchell (1969), Barnes (1972), and their successors. Clearly, a comparison of social networks in San Marcos and San Pedro, both urban and rural, would offer a significant opportunity for either strengthening or devaluing the theory offered in this book. One such test should be conducted in San Marcos and San Pedro, but other towns are equally acceptable.

There are, indeed, other sites in Guatemala, Latin America, and other parts of the world where the perspective that I have offered might be used. In Guatemala, for example, there are other complexes of towns, what might be called "binary ethnic municipalities," which are similar to San Marcos and San Pedro. In Alta Verapaz, Cobán may stand in a similar relationship with San Pedro Carchá. Of these two towns, Cobán is the Ladino center and San Pedro Carchá,

Indian. In western Guatemala, the Ladino weaving town of Salcajá may have a similar relationship with nearby San Cristóbal Totonicapán. To the north of San Marcos, San Lorenzo (Ladino) may have such a relationship with Comitancillo (Indian), and Rio Blanco (Ladino) perhaps with Cabicán (Indian). Except for Salcajá and San Cristóbal Totonicapán, the town centers of these pairs are not as closely contiguous as those of San Marcos and San Pedro. They offer, nevertheless, the opportunity for interesting comparative studies of ethnic inversion. Are these towns related in quite such tightly binary ways as San Marcos and San Pedro? If so, then San Marcos and San Pedro are examples of a process more common than is reported.

However, towns do not need to be binary for the theory to apply. It should work in ordinary municipalities, in those with both a dominant Ladino town center and an Indian periphery, as is common throughout Guatemala, and also in those communities where (if such is to be found) there is no Ladino presence in the community at all. I submit that Ladinos do not have to live in a municipality for the Indian ideology to be substantially contrary to that of the national Ladinos. The presence of Ladinos simply makes it easier for an ethnographer to document the system.

At a rural level, there are further opportunities for contrastive studies of rural Indian people sharing the same ecological niche and performing the same activities as rural Ladino people. For example, the hamlet of San José de las Islas, municipality of San Marcos, is contiguous with the hamlet of San Pedro Petz, municipality of San Pedro Sacatepéquez. Alternatively, San Rafael Soche, a hamlet formerly of San Pedro that was annexed to San Marcos, could be compared with the Ladino hamlets of Las Lagunas or El Rincon.[1] A thorough comparison of these hamlets might be particularly rewarding. The simplicity and similarity of agricultural production in these pairs of hamlets should address the relative merits of production relations versus ethnic inversion as the source of ideology.

Another approach to sorting out the impact of relation to the means of production versus ethnic ideology offers itself by comparing the Ladino weavers of Salcajá with the Indian weavers in either San Cristóbal Totonicapán, or Quezaltenango, or even the more distant San Pedro Sacatepéquez. A third possibility of study in this genre would be to compare Ladino merchants with Indian merchants in the city of Quezaltenango. Any of these studies offer the opportunity of a sharp test of production relations versus ideological inversion approaches to social explanation. No doubt there are many other suitable locations.

Norman Schwartz (personal communication 1979, and 1983) has commented that this approach may shed light on rural Ladinos in eastern Guatemala. If in eastern and Petén Guatemala rural Ladinos are fundamentally different *ideologically* from urban Ladinos, then ethnicity is indeed reduced to a less significant issue—as a mask hiding the importance of urbanity. Alternatively, one might find that rural Ladinos are different only in the sense that rural conditions modify their application of an ideology fundamentally like that of the urban Ladinos. If this latter is the case, then this theory is appropriate throughout Guatemala.

Language is another topic that may be fruitfully researched in relation to the theory proposed in this book. My fieldwork was conducted entirely in the Spanish language, for this was the household language of all the San Pedro and San Marcos residents. What is the character of ideology among Indians in communities that are entirely Mam-speaking? If the ideology inversions exist, are they more prominent in the entirely Mam-speaking communities, such as Comitancillo or Concepción Chiquirichapa? Or does it work the other way: if the externally visible or obviously diacritical markers (Nadel 1951), such as clothing and language differences, are lost (as in urban San Pedro), does this cause an Indian community to accentuate (or create) ideological differences at the level of fundamental premises?

The community of San Mateo, Department of Quezaltenango, offers another opportunity for significant research in language and ideology. In San Mateo, it is said, people speak Mam in some hamlets, while in others people speak Quiché. The center is (presumably) largely Spanish-speaking and probably has mostly Ladinos for permanent residents. If there are ideological inversions between Ladino and Indian, just how are these affected by the difference between the Mam and Quiche language traditions? At what level are the Mams and Quiches different from each other within this municipality: in fundamental premises, normative rules, symbols, diacritical markers, institutional involvements, social position, or otherwise? Or, not at all? At what levels are there substantial similarities between Mams and Quichés in this village? Are the similarities and differences consistently located at one or another level of social analysis? Could such a study yield fundamental information on the underlying categories of social analysis? Anyone agile enough to learn Spanish, Mam, and Quiché deserves whatever theoretical lode the territory offers.

Important issues link language change, ethnicity, and ideological systems. As noted above, do Indian communities that change to the Spanish language increase their inversion at the premise level to compensate for reduced differences in the diacritical level? Parallel to this are other issues of ethnic category change. Under what conditions do people who are San Pedrano by birth and Indian by family heritage begin to call themselves Ladino? Do they do so in any temporal relation with a change of ideology? The San Pedranos who claimed to be Ladino in my survey appear to be insufficiently studied in this monograph, because, I suspect, under survey conditions one is more easily able to label himself Ladino to an outsider. San Pedranos who made a permanent ethnic change and remained in San Pedro, and openly label themselves as Ladinos, in fact did not appear in my qualitative-research experience. Outside of San Pedro looms the larger issue of ethnic-category change. What processes are involved when Indians from hinterland agricultural municipalities move to the city? Do they move in stages, successfully obscuring their roots time after time? When and how do they make the ethnic recategorization? This needs to be studied further, using individual life-history techniques more extensively, with attention to any relation between ideological, categorical, geographical, and occupational change.

The three paragraphs above on language suggest (to me) interesting studies, but they are not phrased as tests of my approach. I return to the issue of tests. My approach suggests that Indian self-categorization and Indian ideology are fundamentally linked, as are Ladino category and ideology. Mestizo is in some measure an atypical Indian or an atypical Ladino; the Indian-Mestizo is superior to the Indian in certain national symbols, while the Ladino-Mestizo is inferior to the Ladino. However, do there exist, for any substantial lengths of time, self-designated Indians who hold Ladino premise systems? Such a situation, well documented, would constitute an important refutation of this study.

Beyond Guatemala

Mexico also provides ample opportunities for studies that relate to this book. For example, the Hispanic center of San Cristóbal de la Casas should be studied in relation to Zinacantán, and vice versa. Indeed, the principle criticism one can make of Vogt's impressive opus (1969, 1976) is that it is done without adequate relation to the surrounding Hispanic culture. Other sites include the reputedly Ladino town of Teopisca next to the Indian town of Amatenango del Valle, and the Ladino town of Las Rosas near Indian Aguacatenango. Within the Tarascan area, one might fruitfully study Pátzcuaro, the *mestizo* administrative center, in relation to Tzintzuntzan, the changing Indian community studied by Foster (1979), and Izalco, the more peasant Indian community studied by van Zantwijk (1967). Those acquainted with the social complexion of other areas of Mexico can no doubt select additional locations to rigorously test the theoretical construction of this book.

The comparison with Peru, raised in the concluding chapter, moves toward a general theory of Spanish colonial impact. What will be the result of studies in Peru, Bolivia, or Ecuador which are addressed to the propositions raised in this book? Am I correct in trying to extrapolate a theory of Spanish colonial impact based on the template of the overlord's mind, given a notion of social distinctiveness and a colonial regime of sufficient pressure? In short, how does this theory affect the understanding of and future study of ethnicity, family, and religion in Peru, Bolivia, Ecuador, and in other regions subjected to the Spanish colonial enterprise?

Also, in the final chapter I explored a pattern of differences between upper- and lower-class Jamaicans, which suggests that an ideological theory of colonialism may apply more widely than just to the Spaniards. The issues raised apply to the entire Caribbean. For example, what were the continental and elite French Caribbean ideas concerning Blacks and Frenchmen? What were their other major cultural premises and social institutions like? And what are the cultural and social relations between the present-day elite and lower class on the French Caribbean islands now? Did the French have a notion of social, racial, or other distinctiveness between the colonizer and the colonized? And did they impose a punitive social regime upon the slave population of these islands? If both, then the theory offered here would suggest that the elite and the lower class, to the degree that they claim their categorical heritage from French cultural connections, should participate in a series of inversions related to the template of elite French culture. Similar questions should be raised and documented for the Dutch, Spanish, and English Caribbean islands, in order to explore and refine the issues discussed in this book.

Finally, what are the differential consequences of British indirect rule in Africa versus British slavery in the Caribbean? Are there parallel differences in Spanish, French, or English administrative practices in Africa versus those in the Caribbean? Is there a tribal group or a culture area in Africa that was divided by a European cultural and administrative frontier, such as the one between modern-day Ghana and Togo? A comparison of the modern result of such divisions in both Africa and the Caribbean would provide an intriguing opportunity to explore the differential impact of British and French colonial practice as well as the merits of the theory offered here. Perhaps such studies already exist. If so, then someone can address critically the issues I raise; if not, then the studies can fruitfully be undertaken.

Obviously, I am not an expert on French, Spanish, Dutch, and English colonialism in the Caribbean or in Africa. In raising the issues I simply hope that someone knowledgeable and experienced in these areas, or someone embarking on a study of these regions, might explore the applicability of inverse ideologies for whatever merit it might have. Moreover, there are several lifetimes of research outlined in these speculations, even in those concerning Guatemala alone. The field study, analysis, reflection, and writing for this book, however, have taken much of my time for ten years. At that rate, with luck, I might get three more studies done, given the many obligations that override one's deepest research interests. The solution seems to be to give research possibilities away to whomever will take them, improve them, apply them in the field, judge them, and report accordingly. In that regard, I would be delighted if I were to be kept informed by anyone exploring these possibilities. To the extent humanly possible, I would be willing to correspond concerning field notes, interim reports, and developing manuscripts. If it is both feasible and desirable for some candidate, I might be able to serve occasionally as an external doctoral-committee member. With or without such participation, I hope that the ideas advanced in this book can be strengthened and refined or adequately discounted in the next decade.

Notes

Chapter 1

1. Given the fluidity of individual claim and attribution in modern-day Guatemala, it is questionable whether the Indians or Ladinos constitute "groups." For the colonial period, when Indian and Ladino were legally defined statuses and towns were legally limited to a particular ethnic kind, the term "group" is certainly appropriate. Nowadays, some Indian communities have management institutions that give the Indian segments of a community sufficient unity that they may be called groups at the municipal level. In other communities, composed of multiple ethnic populations, the Indian population lacks either an institutional base of ethnic unity or a corporate estate reserved to them exclusively. Because of this, I have used the terms *ethnic segment* and *ethnic sector* to avoid implying too much cohesion among the people classed in a single ethnic category.

2. Dick Papousek (1976) critiques Barbara Margolies's *Princes of the Earth* (1975) for blurring the distinction between Indian and poor *mestizo*. He kindly brought the similarities in our analyses (Hawkins 1983) to my attention following a presentation of my work at the International Congress of Americanists (1979).

3. This brief statement neglects exceptions and obscures the richness of the literature. For a more detailed exploration of the literature and the issues raised in the previous four paragraphs, see "Robert Redfield's Culture Concept and Mesoamerican Anthropology" (Hawkins 1983).

4. Goodenough (1981:59) also feels that Geertz has erred in conflating ideas with symbols.

> We shall reserve the term culture for what is learned, for the things one needs to know in order to meet the standards of others. (Goodenough 1981:50; see also p. 51)

> Geertz . . . has taken issue with the position that culture is located in human minds. (Goodenough 1981:53)

> For Geertz, culture is both the acts as symbols and their meaning. He focuses on the artifacts—exposure to artifacts is what people share—and states that these artifacts as

public symbols and the public meaning they have acquired in social exchanges constitute culture. (Goodenough 1981:59)

Goodenough then draws conclusions different from mine as to the impact of Geertz's approach.

5. This reference to television may be difficult to interpret outside American culture and in a few years even in our own. "The Waltons" was a popular television program about an honorable, easygoing, caring, problem-solving family, set in a nostalgic period forty or fifty years ago.

6. I do not develop a complete theory of meaning. Rather, I shall draw on a few principles that seem essential to a theory of meaning.

7. I am guessing that it would be acceptable in reference, say, to a homosexual partner in a men's prison.

8. Of course there are exceptions. Many of the Indian inhabitants of San Pedro Sacatepéquez and several communities in the region of Quezaltenango-Totonicapán-San Francisco el Alto are more successfully commercial. Yet because their inhabitants do not fit the marked expectation, they are remarkable and remarked-upon communities. Moreover, as my explanation emerges, it will become clear that Indians are not opposite in absolute across-the-country terms. Rather, they are opposite in local regional terms. Thus, the Quezaltecans can be commercially famed and still be seen as the inverse of the locality's Ladinos. In Chapter 4, I present additional reasons why commercial wealth is not such an exception.

9. The town center together with its hamlet-dotted countryside is called a *municipio,* of which there are 326 in Guatemala as of 1974. Guatemalan *municipios* are officially ranked from first through fourth rank *(categoría),* depending on their degree of urbanity. The residents themselves also judge the *municipios* as vibrant *(alegre)* or sad *(triste)* and as important and desirable or unimportant, depending also on degree of urbanity. An area is urban when it has a cluster of paved or cobbled streets, and houses that abut the streets and whose walled compounds enclose the blocks formed by the streets. Houses which abut the outside of the perimeter streets, and which do not, therefore, surround a block are also urban. The countryside, with its scattered hamlets, is thought of as *triste* compared to the central administrative town. Indeed, the agricultural lands and disorderly hamlets surrounding the town headquarters *(cabezera municipal)* are made hinterland, rather than just farmland, by virtue of the urban symbolic focus. Thus, the culturally correct translation of *municipio* is "municipality," rather than the often used "county," which seems to focus on the countryside rather than on the issue of urbanity.

10. At a second level of categorization, wealth differences do emerge in the quality and materials of the *corte* (skirt) and *huipil* (blouse) of each community. And change in the clothing style is proceeding rapidly. A

tie-dyed skirt in shades of blue, green, black, and white is being marketed out of the Quezaltenango Basin, which makes community identification by variation in skirt design virtually impossible. The backstrap-woven *huipil* of each community is rapidly giving way to a generalized brocaded *huipil* woven on footlooms in San Pedro Sacatepéquez and also in the Quezaltenango region. While the community diversity suggested in this observation is diminishing, the blurring of individual differences is becoming even sharper, for wealth differences show even less obviously in the generalized Indian dress.

11. Again for convenience, I have displayed the inverse structure between the Atchaleño Indians and the region's Ladinos in Appendix 1.B, as these emerge from Moore's *Life Cycles of Atchalán* (1973). The nature of Moore's presentation was more conducive to a summary than to a tabular presentation, so the two appendixes are not as parallel as would be desirable.

12. J. Clyde Mitchell (1969) and John Barnes (1972) effectively use the concepts of density and stars to analyze social networks. Of course, these concepts may be used to explore the structure of road connections between communities. What is interesting, though, is that the contrast between the structures of the road networks in Indian highlands and Ladino lowlands somewhat parallels the contrast between the ethnic sectors in the structure of their interpersonal networks. See Chapter 3 of this work and also Carol Smith (1975).

13. There have been Indians in the coastland since precolonial times, but colonial practices seem to have had very severe effects on their population (MacLeod 1973). Lowland hamlets linked to a parent Indian-highland town seem to be a recent reintroduction. This is so for those cases listed by McBryde (1947:90-91) and for two coastal hamlets that I found linked to Concepción Chiquirichapa and San Martín Sacatepéquez.

14. This was the case in 1973-1974. However, three factors have recently combined to make the northern region considerably more important to the western highlands and to the country as a whole: (1) highland land shortage and the resulting voluntary pioneering as well as (2) government resettlement projects that have begun to compete with (3) recent oil exploration and development that has resulted in considerable conflict, dissatisfaction, and unrest. This is, however, a rather speculative assessment of the current northern Indian rebellion arrived at mostly by analysis of newspaper reports.

15. As detailed in note 10, clothing behavior is undergoing rapid changes.

16. I will begin to account for them in Part 3 of this book.

17. Comments on status and ethnic categories abound in most of the works. On political structure, consult Nash (1958b) and R. N. Adams (1967, 1970), and compare to Siverts (1969). The classics on Indian eco-

nomics are McBryde (1947) and Tax (1953). On the civil-religious hierarchy, Nash (1958b) summarizes Guatemala, while Cancian (1965) gives perhaps the best discussion of a single village's system. W. R. Smith (1977) addresses the issue of fiesta breakdown. Notes in numerous other monographs are also available. Vogt's *Tortillas for the Gods* (1976) is still largely descriptive, although there is some penetrating structural analysis of meaning in portions of his work. Kay Warren's *Symbolism of Subordination* (1978) acknowledges the impact of national stratification on Indian religion but still neglects the analysis of Ladino religion. A significant comparative study of family and kinship is R. N. Adams's work (1960), which depends on government statistics and therefore has severe limitations. Nutini (1976:3) had lamented the dearth of studies on kinship. But rather than view the paucity of kinship studies as a professional failure, we must see it as a consistent aspect of Indian ideology. Indeed, Tax has recently reaffirmed the Guatemalan Indian's lack of interest in kinship: "It did not take long after our arrival in Guatemala to understand that the people there were not interested in kinship terms or standardized proper behavior among relatives classified in a special way" (Tax 1975:509).

Chapter 2

1. Kamen (1965) deserves a generic citation in addition to particular references throughout the following text.

2. This is my translation of the passage cited by Kamen (1965:117):

> Yo soy un hombre
> Aunque de villana casta,
> Limpio de sangre y jamás
> De Hebrea o Mora manchada.

Taken from act three, scene twenty-seven, the punctuation may vary slightly. In scene eighteen, "*Yo lo abono. No es villano, es caballero; . . .*" is an explicit contrast of rural and genteel through "I vouch for him. He is not a villager but a gentleman. (de Vega 1614:178, 189)

3. Kaman cites *Don Quijote,* Book One, chaps. 21 and 28. Some of the sources cited by Kaman, two of which are reproduced here (Cervantes and Lope de Vega), are actually somewhat postconquest. This fact, however, does not debilitate the argument. In the first place, it would be extraordinary if the culture of Spain in 1525-1550 were radically different from the culture of Spain in 1580. Second, Latin America did not receive a one-time cultural infusion from Spain. On the contrary, Spain maintained contact through political control and exerted a strong cultural influence up to the nineteenth century. Even after independence, Spain remained the symbolic center and source of ideas for Guatemala.

4. Hanke cites, on p. 90, Vial Correa Gonzalo, "Teoría y practica de la igualdad en Indias," *Revista Historia* (Universidad de Chile) 3(1964): 87-163, as the source for this quote.

5. Among the exceptions, see Carmack (1981) on witchcraft and on commoner genealogies (p. 150), on altar distribution (p. 190), and on ceremonial centers in the rural areas (pp. 57-58).

6. Carmack has "not deemed it necessary to cite all the specific sources" when insights were gained by checking documents with "aged natives" (Carmack 1981:xvii). It is possible insights not sufficiently contained within the ethnohistorical record have been imported into his text. Only someone intimately associated with all his ethnohistorical sources could determine the extent of this possible error. Such a task passes beyond both the intent of this book and the extent of my expertise.

7. Recent archaeological and ethnohistorical research is making some progress in decoding preconquest documents. This may eventually lead to an independently established cultural description for the preconquest Mesoamericans. If such a cultural picture unfolds, this argument will be strengthened by a preconquest culture (categories and ideology) substantially different from present-day Indian culture. If the preconquest-elite picture substantially parallels the ideas present in Spain, and the preconquest peasants' situation is *already* an inverse, then the notion of historical derivation is problematic. Meaning would still derive from relations to Spanish/Ladino, but the notion of Spanish institutions "forging" the inverse Indian would not be necessary.

An anonymous reviewer considered my discussion of Sanders and Price, Carmack, and Adams a straw-man attack. While there may be some truth to the assertion, I have not intended it to be so. Rather, I intended to show a style of argument and the problems inherent in it. Partly because I do not believe a preconquest culture can be reconstructed unless richly cultural preconquest writings are available and deciphered, and partly because the task would require another lifetime for an already long-delayed book, I have not attempted to present the Mayan preconquest culture as this has been archaeologically reconstructed.

8. See Simpson (1950) or Martinez Pelaez (1971) for a thorough documentation of these provisions and the subsequent contentions.

9. This is not a native term.

10. Nowadays, the civil-religious fiesta system symbolically replicates the fusion of civil and clerical components of government. It symbolizes Indian submission and Indian municipal orientation. Furthermore, the obligatory expenditure of funds for civil-religious fiestas re-creates and continues the conditions of colonial tribute. Accordingly, the present-day maintenance of a fiesta system correlates with "traditional" Indianness.

11. Many of the combinations had specific and quite intriguing names.

See León (1924) for a list and commentary. Subsequently the system broke down.

12. From the heading "Colonial Society" to this point, the description of social process is a summary of Martinez Pelaez's elegant work (1971). From this point on, structural interpretations and all the data from San Marcos and San Pedro Sacatepéquez are my own. Nevertheless, I am absolutely indebted to Martinez Pelaez for his brilliant analysis of Guatemalan social history.

13. The children were indented under the name of their father, presumably because men were (and are) the axis of social and political status within the nation.

14. The sheet is undated but is presumably bound into the record in approximately serial order.

15. One *caballería* equals 1,033 *cuerdas,* although most people today round off and talk of 1,000 *cuerdas* to the *cabellería*. One *cuerda* equals 0.108 acres. See also Chapter 4, note 9, for further conversion tables.

16. Just how much land San Marcos was allowed to incorporate from the 39 *caballerias* that became 406, or at what price, is not recorded.

17. Jones (1940) cites Paul Burgess, *Justo Rufino Barrios* (New York: Dorrance, 1926), for this quote, which may also be found in fuller form in Burgess (1972:150-51). Jones omitted an instructive passage, which I here translate:

> It is also apparent that the only way to improve the situation of the Indians and remove them from their state of misery and abjection is to create among them needs which they will acquire by continuous contact with the *ladino* class, accustoming them also to work so they can fill these needs, thereby converting this immense majority of the republic into something useful for the agriculture, commerce, and industry of the country.

More internal colonialism.

18. Jones (1940) here cites *Memoria de los labores del ejecutivo en el ramo de agricultura* (Guatemala: Tipografía Nacional, 1921), pp. 3-5, 32-33.

Chapter 3

1. During the course of my fieldwork, the general structure of government became apparent through interviews and newspaper reports. These impressions were checked for accuracy with Dombrowski et al. (1970) and with Siverts (1969). However, this presentation is not intended as an unimpeachable statement on the mechanics of central government. Rather, I present a view of the central government from the perspective of the provinces.

2. These comments on department government are based on observations from the Department of San Marcos. Nevertheless, Siverts (1969: 182ff.) and others confirm the wider validity of these local observations.

3. Santiago Chimaltenango, Huehuetenango, is an exception. There are no doubt others.

4. Significantly, the guest was a leader of one of the opposition parties. This suggests San Pedro's place in the government hierarchy as a member of the opposition and highlights the Indian as the opposite of Ladino.

5. Totonicapán and Quezaltenango are exceptions. Quezaltenango used to be much more of a Ladino center than it now is. The transition apparently took place on account of two factors. First, there have been persecutions of the Ladino power elite by the central government following their attempted secessions and the formation of *El Estado de los Altos,* the Highland State. Second, transportation improvements have more recently facilitated a life in the capital with a business in the departments. This has drained off much of the Ladino elite. But in 1974 it was still in Ladino governmental hands, although they nearly lost the 1974 elections to an Indian candidate for mayor. I do not know Santa Cruz del Quiché personally, but Carol Smith refers to it as a "Ladino Town Center" (C. A. Smith, 1975:107), and census figures seem to corroborate that attribution.

6. The cost in 1973 was five cents per issue. For a day laborer, this would be one-third to one-half of an hour's pay. During the second half of my fieldwork, the price went up to ten cents. Wages remained stable. The papers are distributed by street vendors throughout the nation's main cities.

7. In the sixth office, I was only able to secure information on part of the employees before being told to cease, as my questions were perceived as offensive. Obviously, this is not a complete listing of government employees in San Marcos. In the five offices completely surveyed and in the one partially surveyed, I asked for the name, job title, salary, residence, and birthplace of the employees. I did not get birthplaces for two of the sixty-five employees canvassed, hence the total of sixty-three for birthplace and sixty-five for current residence.

8. Many more such contacts for San Marcos could doubtless be found, but I did not pursue this topic as systematically as I should have liked since a high official in San Marcos strongly implied that I had permission to work in that town provided that I did not investigate politically related topics. Thus, the information presented here is limited to whatever was freely brought to my attention. Based on informal chats with the mayor of San Marcos, the piecing together of the comments of others, the casual remarks of a U.S. State Department officer, and the official contacts and itineraries outlined in the local newspaper, it appears that the mayor of San Marcos could get access to virtually every ministry or branch of the

national government in no more than two links of kinship, affinity, or friendship (kin of friend, friend of kin, and so on). Unfortunately, I felt unable to explore the matter adequately due to a general official reluctance to discuss politically sensitive topics.

9. See Ingham (1974) for other aspects of the asymmetrical relationships of *compadrazgo,* and Kendall (1974) for a review of the literature and a counterexample.

10. The term *social network* refers to a section of the system of social relations viewed from the perspective of an individual, community, or other point of reference. By contrast, the term *social structure* refers to the relational system in the abstract, viewed as organized by the social facts of native categories, rules, rights, duties, and expectations.

I use the term *network* in a metaphysical rather than a technical sense; no attempt is made here to use the more rigorous developments of network theory as they have been elaborated in the papers brought together by J. Clyde Mitchell (1969) and Boissevain and Mitchell (1973) or in the review by Barnes (1972). However, some technical comments about this episode are appropriate. Mentioning the names of those in one's primary star and discussing those in one's secondary star would appear to enhance the secondary and tertiary stars of the listeners. Indeed, it could help add primary-star members: if enough information is given, an individual could make a new primary-star contact out of a reachable secondary-star contact by mentioning the mutual friend in the primary star of both. More probably, name dropping makes the speaker, heretofore a casual primary-star member and into a useful primary-star member, and into a broker through whom one can access a secondary- or tertiary-level person. Through this behavior, the information density of the network is increased. With this information, it is possible to increase the interaction density of the network. The number of links between persons is either reduced or made apparent, increasing reachability. Furthermore, discussing the occupations or positions of those in one's network increases the range or social dispersion of the listeners' network by the addition of potential first-order and actual second-order members having different positions in the social system.

The speaker probably does not lose anything by discussing his network. On the contrary, he positions himself regarding his centrality of access, makes himself available as a broker, and accrues to himself a social debt if he is used as such. By means of such conversations, the listener can presumably estimate the probability of achieving a desired result through the network and negotiate his own social network as collateral to the social debt incurred by working through the speaker.

Unfortunately, the conceptual tools of network theory were not used in this fieldwork, and hence these comments cannot be properly exemplified. I did not realize until later how valuable these party conversations were.

Therefore, the term "network" will be used to indicate the relative interconnectedness among persons without further concern for the technical modes of describing that interconnectedness. However, a rigorous technical application of network theory among Latin American elites and in a cross section of the two ethnic groups would be richly rewarding in documenting the relational system that ethnicity status ideologies generate. Two studies that approach this goal and offer fascinatingly compatible results are Anthony Leeds's (1974) article on Brazilian careers and Stone's (1974) article on elite genealogies in Costa Rica. In San Marcos and San Pedro, clearly, the social consequences of the inverse ideologies concerning interconnection are considerable.

11. Three years later I discovered that the wife of the rector of the University of San Carlos was the sister of a prominent Marquense. This probably was the connection through which the educational superiority of San Marcos was insured.

12. The clipped, telegram style leaves an ambiguity. The solution was to be *"conforme ofrecimiento entrevista sostenida su despacho."* This could be read "in conformity with offering in interview held your office." Whether this indicates "in conformity with [the] interview [that was] held in your office," or "in conformity with [an] interview [to be] held [in] your office," I do not know. The most likely way to suggest futurity in a telegram would be to use *sostenerse* and not *sostenida*. This would suggest that there was a previous, probably informal meeting not appended to the case documentation. However, the futurity reading is possible due to the fact that immediately thereafter the municipal corporations of both towns were ordered to reply to the governor on the case.

13. Currently, San Pedro supplies the electricity to residences, and San Marcos maintains the roads, the water system, and the street lights on the main avenue.

14. The 1974 election was a bit complex. An opposition deputy to the congress was elected from San Pedro. The opposition mayoral slate lost, by a few votes, I am told.

15. Sub-rosa contacts by the San Marcos mayoralty through other channels of friendship would be likely, but I cannot document them in this instance.

16. *"En el nombre de los alcaldes del departamento, la municipalidad de San Marcos y el pueblo de San Marcos."* Note that he emphasized the special place of the San Marcos municipality. The term *el pueblo* can be translated in two ways. One meaning is "the people or citizens" and is synonymous with *la gente*. This could apply either to the people of the department or of the town. But the other meaning is "the urban center or town" and is synonymous with *el centro* or *la cabezera*. This latter meaning is the more likely because the descending order of department to municipality to town is

cognitively appropriate. In this reading, the importance of the San Marcos urban center and its residents is stated very crisply indeed! Regardless, the ambiguity has its impact.

17. Flowers are also given to the saints and to the dead on sacred occasions. While the visit of the president would not be seen as a sacred event, the flowers do communicate respect (in the sense of recognition of power and authority and allocation of esteem) and appreciation in either sacred or profane contexts. As in many other societies, symbols having sacred connotations help to identify the center of political authority.

18. As an individual fieldworker, I was unable to evaluate the relative political access of the lowland Ladino municipalities. I hypothesize that in consequence of their ideological bias toward politics and interconnection that should exist as Ladinos, they will generate more extensive networks than the Indians. However, both the existence of the ideology and the nature of their networks in the lowland communities must be ascertained by fieldwork. The absence of an ideology of interconnection among the lowland Ladinos would constitute a refutation of the core of this thesis, although I would be greatly surprised (but not refuted) if any of the lowland municipalities of San Marcos had the extensive linkages of the San Marcos municipality.

Chapter 4

1. This line of reasoning has close parallels to Aguirre Beltrán's notion that Indians persist and even thrive in "refuge regions" made economically marginal by a severe physical setting (Aguirre Beltrán 1967).

2. This observation is a generalization that should be treated with caution as I did not visit all the *municipios* in the department, and those that I did visit were not subjects of intensive investigation. However, it is consistent with what I have seen and read of the San Marcos department and of the highland region. For San Marcos, see Ewald (1954: chap. 7) and W. R. Smith (1973:48-50). For Guatemala, see McBryde (1947:83-87). For Mexico, see Pi-Sunyer (1973), Siverts (1969), and Stavenhagen (1970).

3. It is not convenient at this point to give a detailed definition of the term *household*. See Chapter 12 if immediate access to this issue is desired.

4. For complete details, the interested reader is encouraged to consult Lila M. O'Neal's works (1965; 1:121-24; also available in English) and Arturo Méndez Cifuentes (1967). The latter work gives an instructor's guide to the parts and processes of foot-loom weaving.

5. Sol Tax reports that in the 1930s women were more involved (Tax 1953: 26 n.2). Once again, a few women today (1973-1974) are becoming weavers in San Pedro. Whether this is due to a labor shortage or to an inflation-induced pressure to reduce wages is not known.

6. That is, one room plus kitchen and outhouse. Many houses are, of course, larger, and in such cases, looms are usually placed in a workroom or in an outside-covered corridor.

7. These data and those in subsequent tables are taken from a sample survey that I conducted in the urban centers of the two towns. *Urban* was taken in the native conceptual sense, which for them included all the houses in blocks circumscribed by maintained streets and all houses facing the perimeter street around the area of circumscribed blocks. By this definition, the urban area is somewhat smaller in size and population than the urban zone used in the national census, for the latter includes several detached rural *caseríos* close to the urban center.

To define the sample, each block (or, on the perimeter, street segment) was assigned a number, and 25 percent of them were drawn by lottery. All households on each sample block were contacted repeatedly until interviewed. Absolute refusal to cooperate was less than 1 percent in San Marcos and less than 2 percent in San Pedro. The survey questionnaire form was developed and administered during the last three months of my twenty months of fieldwork, by which time I felt that I had a reasonable understanding of both the native categories and some crucial theoretical as well as native cultural questions deserving quantitative attention.

In the tables that follow, the sample size varies between 190 and 196 for San Pedro as a result of incomplete data for any particular variable. The occupational tables used in the text make no attempt to list the full range of occupations or account for 100 percent of the community. Rather, they are designed to highlight salient features of the system. For the full table, see Appendix 2.A.

8. The Kolmogorov-Smirnov two-tailed test of differences between San Marcos and San Pedro, contrasting government employment with self-employment, was statistically significant at the 0.000 level. Note that weavers who work for a *patrono* usually consider themselves self-employed since they can work as much or as little as they wish and are paid by piece rather than by wage.

9. In San Marcos Department, the *cuerda* is a unit of area equal to a square of 25 *varas* per side. The *vara* is a unit of length variously reported as 32 inches or 0.83 meters (32.9 inches) in length. The *caballería* is technically equal to 1,033 *cuerdas*, though most people say it is 1,000. Thus, the English and metric conversion rates are as follows (using 0.83 meters per *vara*):

Cuerdas	Acres	Hectares
1.00	0.108	0.04
9.27	1.000	0.41
22.90	2.470	1.00

10. Household land value was computed by multiplying the number of *cuerdas* of each type of land owned (*plano,* level; *laderoso,* hilly) by the expressed value for each type, and adding the results. Where the informant for a household did not know the value per unit of land, the mean value for the type of land in that community was computed and used in calculations. Per capita value of lands owned is obtained by dividing the household land value by the number of persons in the household.

11. The probability that these figures could be derived, if in fact San Marcos and San Pedro were from the same population, is indicated below for each factor explored in Table 4. The Mann-Whitney/Wilcoxon and Kolmogorov-Smirnox tests reject the null (equality) hypothesis. However, the Kolmogorov-Smironov test shows greater similarity of distribution shape when the high values are deleted.

	Mann-Whitney/Wilcoxon One-Tailed Test for Separation of Means	Kolmogorov-Smirnov One-Tailed Test for Differences in Frequency Distribution
	Significance	Significance
Total land value	0.0029	0.022
Per capita land value	0.0027	0.010
Total land value of those < 10,000	0.0037	0.115
Per capita land value of those < 10,000	0.0029	0.067

These and all succeeding calculations of nonparametric statistics derive from the procedures contained in the Statistical Package for Social Sciences, *SPSS Update* (Hull and Nie 1979).

12. The impact of the large landowners is considerable. If, for example, one deletes all landowners with more than $200,000 in land value, the figures for San Pedro are unchanged (i.e., no such values exist in the San Pedro sample). But six such cases exist in San Marcos, which, when deleted, leave the remaining Marquenses with a mean land value of $2,515.90 and a mean per capita land value of $481.10. While these are still double the figures for San Pedro, the impact on means of the few rich landowners is clear. Nevertheless, the Mann-Whitney/Wilcoxon and Kolmogorov-Smirnov statistical tests are unaffected by the extreme values as they test on the basis of rank order only. Even if one deletes all owners with a land value of $10,000 or more (deleting fourteen cases from San Marcos and four cases

from San Pedro), the household mean land value for urban San Marcos is $582.20 and for urban San Pedro is $355.60. This is still significant for both land value (P = .0315, one-tailed) and per capita land value (P = .0285). Obviously, the difference is becoming progressively less marked as one moves toward the field of lower land values.

13. Note that the format of Table 5 is shifted to focus attention first on San Marcos.

14. As noted earlier, my sample suggests that some 2.1 percent of San Marcos household heads class themselves as merchants, which amounts to only 30.8 percent of the combined merchants in the two towns.

15. One San Pedro family operated a pair of buses in 1973-1974, but they had gone out of business by 1979.

16. The crispness of this division is somewhat eroded by the fact that San Marcos buses carry a good deal of cargo in their overhead racks or belly bays, while San Pedro trucks often carry highland Indians to and from their coastal labors. Nevertheless, the cargo on the buses is often quite personalized, as belongings, and the people on trucks are quite depersonalized, as freight, with the trucks being hired to bring squads *(cuadrillas)* of Indians to a *finca* as though they were so many nonpaying but self-propelled sacks of cement. Moreover, in other areas of Guatemala, Ladinos no doubt control or dominate the truck-freight industry. Perhaps urban centrality is a sufficiently strong symbol that load hauling, an Indian activity, is not threatening.

17. Reported monthly receipts of various kinds to all household members plus one-twelfth of estimated agricultural income based on reasonable management of reported property, plus one-twelfth of any income from migratory wage labor.

18. The probabilities that my samples from San Marcos and San Pedro were drawn from the same population are in the following table:

	Mann-Whitney/Wilcoxon One-Tailed Test for Separation of Means	Kolmogorov-Smirnov One-Tailed Test for Differences in Frequency Distribution
	Significance	Significance
Total household income	< .0000	< .000
Per capita household income	.0003	.005

These figures indicate that the null hypothesis of equality of means is soundly rejected.

19. At least in 1973-1974. By 1978, one European immigrant to San

Marcos and his Marquense wife had built a mansion and furnished it in the finest *Better Homes and Gardens* tradition.

20. The negative value of work and the positive value of landownership have been written about in many places. So far as I am aware, they have not been seen as interconnected in the form of absentee administration of owned lands. Nor has anyone accounted for the distinction in administrative styles between the efficiently run, profit-motivated agrofactories that are called "plantations" by Wolf and Mintz (1957) versus the inefficiently run, status-motivated family estates that they called "haciendas." I believe that the inverse relationship between rent and work, and the connection of work-idleness to status in the colonial society accounts for much of the difference between "plantation" and "hacienda" administration. Note that I have not adopted the Wolf and Mintz analytical typology; rather, I have used the native term *finca*.

The economics of coffee production is beyond the scope of this work, but a note or two in verification of "the phenomenally inefficient management of Guatemala's *latifundia* economy" is in order.

I had the good fortune and pleasant association of spending a week with a well-known coffee buyer for one of Guatemala's largest coffee-export houses. We spent time on his plantation, where I saw and had explained in detail the amount of management necessary and the complexity of the tasks involved in economically efficient production and maintenance of a coffee *finca*. We also visited other *fincas*, several of which were owned by San Marcos absentee landlords. The *fincas* of the absentee landlords were in obvious states of utter mismanagement and low productivity. The coffee buyer's records of coffee purchases on adjacent *fincas* confirmed that the absentee landlords produced from one-third to one-half of what could be and was being grown in the same ecological zone on *fincas* under reasonably constant ownership supervision. Proper management, I discovered, is tiresome work, for it involves daily hiking over rough mountain terrain.

Even more difficult than the exhausting task of physically covering the land are the management decisions required in planting, pruning, shade control, fertilization, pest and fungal control, and harvest management. Each of these operations is independently crucial to high production, and each operation requires up-to-the-minute knowledge of the varied status of each ecological zone of a *finca*. The only solution is for the owner to scout his lands almost daily. Where *fincas* are too large for this, competent administrators can be hired, but then they must be checked on. The absentee owner pursuing a profession or government post in San Marcos or Guatemala City is ill-disposed and unable to do this.

Exact production figures are hard to arrive at. The coffee buyer-*finca* owner had recently acquired his *finca* and in the course of two years had raised its production threefold to twice the national average yield per *cuerda*

(Direccion General de Estadistica 1971a:241-50). He was aiming to triple the national yields in the next year or so. But this man was extremely industrious, and he was a European immigrant not steeped in the status ideology enjoining work. Indeed, according to his account, and using the Wolf and Mintz terminology, the Europeans ran the "plantations" and the Guatemalans ran the "haciendas."

Independent confirmation of this experience comes from the United Nations Food and Agriculture Organization publication, *Coffee in Latin America* (1958). Chapter 3 of the section on coffee in El Salvador confirms in detail the managerial complexity of coffee production. Only now (1973-1974), it is perhaps more complex in the chemical-management aspects. A quote in this respect will be helpful:

> From the same table [which lists percentages of plantations performing certain tasks in the year under study] it can be deduced that other operations [than weeding and harvesting, which were effected on 99 percent and 100 percent of the plantations, respectively] relatively widely performed are those relating to disease and pest control and the pruning of shade trees which are carried out on rather more than 50 percent of the area under coffee—and the pruning of the coffee trees themselves (effected on slightly under 50 percent of the area planted). On the other hand, operations of supreme importance to plantation yields, such as the application of organic fertilizers and the protection of soil against erosion, are undertaken only on a very small fraction of the total area under coffee. Other tasks which are of great importance in the improvement of cultivation techniques—application of mineral fertilizers and re-sowing—are also performed over a relatively small proportion, equivalent in 1954-55 to approximately one-third of the total area. (United Nations Food and Agriculture Organization 1958:120)

This study also shows that increased labor input is profitable even beyond that presently used on the most labor-intensive *fincas* in El Salvador. Unfortunately, the study did not differentiate between labor versus management time inputs. As a measure of low production in El Salvador, the report shows that 75.1 percent of the total units, covering 44.6 percent of the total area under coffee, produce less than one-half the yield per hectare of the top production category, which includes 9.8 percent of the producers and 22.2 percent of the area cultivated (United Nations Food and Agriculture Organization 1958:121).

A most interesting comment on profitability in relation to labor intensiveness and yield is given. If one takes into account operating costs plus the interest on the investment in land, then a yield of 400 kilograms per hectare is necessary to break even. (A one-half *quintal* yield per *cuerda*, quite common on the unmanaged absentee-owner *fincas* of Guatemala, would give 520 kilograms per hectare; a one-third *quintal* per *cuerda* would yield 345 kilograms per hectare. Under good management, 1.0 to 1.5 *quintals* per *cuerda* is expected, and higher yields are possible.)

"On the other hand," according to the U.N. study, "if the only factors taken into account are the depreciation of the initial investment and direct or current expenditure, and the interest on the capital is not recovered as an outlay, it would seem that, broadly speaking, plantations of all types obtain a profit on the crop" (United Nations Food and Agriculture Organization 1958:128).

These economic observations tend to confirm my assertion that coffee land has status value because it produces income without work. Especially if it is acquired by inheritance, a coffee *finca* is likely to support the owner no matter what his management effort. He can indeed "live by his rents" and not worry about management, for status derives more from one's cultivated position in the social network than from wealth per se.

21. The tradition of the picaresque novel—about the young buck who does not work but merely manipulates his way through a series of funny but despoiling adventures—is a common theme throughout Latin America and captures this phenomenon in much more delightful terms than my cold rendition.

22. Note that this information on Salcajá is casually acquired. It stands as a hypothesis and suggests a location where the argument of this book might be severely tested. Moreover, Salcajá would provide an excellent test of the thesis of cooperative household organization and women's work involvement. Compared to women in the surrounding communities, Salcajá women should be less involved in household production or in weaving support, even though San Pedro demonstrates the production efficiency of women doing so.

Chapter 5

1. The word *criollo* is principally used to refer to an American-born European. It usually has a connotation of "elite." However it can also take the simple meaning of "native." Peasant farmers contrast seed and corn varieties issued by the Peace Corps volunteers with inbred *maíz criollo,* which is more subject to wind damage on account of its shallower and more clumped root structure. Eggs are also called *criollo* if they have been laid by hens that have scavenged for their own food. Thus, the word *criollo* has a connotation not only of "native" but also of "inbred" and "unrefined." (Perhaps this pejorative connotation was significant in the minds of the Spanish crown officers when they contrasted themselves with the native-born Spanish elite, as discussed in Chapter 2.)

2. *"los indígenas se les pone a trabajar."* In this construction, the Indians are the object *(les)* in an impersonal verb form *(ponerse).* The Indians are the acted-upon rather than the actors.

3. The verb form *distinguirse* in my question is slightly leading. It has a connotation of hierarchy beyond mere differentiation. This is manifest in

such forms as *un hombre distinguido* (a distinguished man). This likely forced the respondent to highlight the aspect of hierarchy. However, it is not a serious distortion. The native-introduced term, *diferenciarse,* leads to a parallel though less-elaborated distinction in passages 4-8.

4. The use of the plural form, *las tierras,* implies many units and points to the small-plot agriculture characteristic of the Indians.

5. *Conocimientos,* here rendered as "knowledge," might also have been translated as "understandings," thereby preserving the Spanish plural form. Indeed, the phrase *no entiende* is frequently used to characterize Indians. However, the word *conocimientos* also implies "acquaintance" or "familiarity," suggesting Indian inadequacy at a more surface, even behavioral level (education, etiquette, training) rather than at a deep conceptual level (understanding, comprehension).

6. When the natives of San Marcos and San Pedro use the word *cultura,* they mean "cultivated," "refined," or "Europeanized." Thus, the word "culture" in native texts bears this meaning, rather than my technical definition from Chapter 1.

7. Unfortunately, this material could not be transcribed: everybody was talking at once.

8. The native phrase, *tiene descendencia,* implies descent from parents or ancestors.

9. The anatomical racial descriptions in passages 30 and 32 were offered by the Indian student living in the outlying hamlet. This is significant in that Indian race and urban marginality will be shown to be equivalent codes.

10. *Traje,* costume, is a word that refers to the distinctive apparel worn by the Indians. In contrast, the Ladinos wear clothing *(vestido* or *vestuario)* and are said to be *de vestido.*

11. A *profesión* is a job that requires some schooling. The word is sometimes used to refer to occupations learned by apprenticeship, although usually the native word *arte* (trade) contrasts here. Agricultural labor is the archetype of work that does not require school learning. Indeed, no school learning whatsoever is offered to this end except in a postsecondary school outside the department. With this schooling one is never involved in *trabajo del campo* but in *agronomía,* a *profesión.*

12. More idiomatically, "are native to—*son propios de.*"

13. *Gente inculta* is a particularly difficult translation. "Uncultured" is far too mild. "Ill-mannered" is close, but the command *"no seas inculto"* can be applied to a child who shies away from a visitor or to a child who defecates where he should not. Thus, the word has latent connotations of gross, despicable, bumpkin or hick, and also ignoramus. A person who is *culto* or *muy culto* is refined, proper, educated, urbane, and polite where he or she should be.

14. *Padre de familia* could also be rendered "household head."

15. This passage contradicts the notion of Ladino disdain for labor that will be developed in subsequent chapters. To a degree, this informant may be making the best of his difficult life circumstances. However, this expression places him in a lowered status position, closer to Indians. Indeed, the Ladino artisans are nearly at the bottom of the social scale in San Marcos.

16. In this 1971 sample survey, urban blocks of San Marcos and San Pedro were randomized with a 25 percent sample taken, but because of a breakdown in record keeping by my assistants, no information is available on the number of missed households. One San Pedro *aldea* was covered 100 percent. This, however, was part of a different sampling than that conducted in 1973, from which the other numeric data for this book are drawn. Thus, the sample-management breakdown in 1971 does not affect the other data in this book.

17. The unabbreviated originals are given in Hawkins (1978:55-60, 65-77).

18. P10 and P11 are subtly tinged with the notion of hierarchy since the Spanish *distinguido* or "distinguished" implies outstanding in the sense of superior and not just distinct in the sense of distinguishable or visible. See note 3, this chapter.

19. Lévi-Strauss has been justly critiqued for his indiscretions with the ethnographic data. My intent here is not to depend on the correctness of Lévi-Strauss's ethnographic analysis but to clarify the roots of a certain kind of sociological thinking that will be applied with modifications to Guatemala.

20. Table 8 does have blanks in that no one who defined themselves in institutional terms defined Ladinos in origin terms. I do not know why this is so.

21. This expression was used by the natives of both towns.

22. Interesting in this regard, the hamlet here referred to, El Rincón of San Marcos, hired a Comitancillo Indian to instruct them in the dance of the *paach*, the Indian corn-twin dance, during their 1973 patron-saint fiesta. A *paach* is a double or siamese ear of corn, considered to be a set of twins and symbolic of increased fertility and productivity. This and other data suggest that El Rincón is under considerable pressure as to its ethnic status because it is rural in location and occupation. Yet ample genealogical materials and other discussions confirm that this hamlet of "Ladinos" has a highly social and politically coercive ideology like the town center of San Marcos.

Chapter 6

1. As mentioned in the previous chapter, a reverse stress is also apparent: failure to acquire education, combined with a small-farm rural-

agricultural dependence is making many San Marcos *aldea* Ladinos increasingly nervous about their ethnic categorization.

2. In this region of Guatemala, *indio* has a disparaging connotation approximately equivalent to the use of "nigger" in American English.

3. A highland "Indian" town north of San Marcos identified by pseudonym. This interview took place as I pretested the 1971 survey form, and hence is not included in Appendix 3.

4. Pierre van den Berghe uses "cultural commuting" (1974:323) to refer to the process of oscillating categorically when one moves or, rather, reverberates geographically. For van den Berghe, however, the notion of culture is one that shades heavily into behavior. In my view, the behavioral switching is not a cultural change but a selection of differing portions of the total symbolic system according to the interaction circumstances. Social scientists behave similarly when they speak jargon at the office and ordinary English at home. Each mode of speaking serves to orient them toward a set of relationships. However, the modes take sociological meaning not from their intrinsic content but from their structural opposition. The individual who is Indian at home and Ladino away from home is not changing between cultures. Rather, he is using symbols to reorient the categorical map with which he orders relations. It is the same map, whether one uses it right side up as an Indian or upside down as a Ladino. Whether commuting or permanent, "ladinoization" (R. N. Adams 1956) consists of a reorientation of culture over relations rather than of a change of culture. To his credit, van den Berghe put emphasis on the social-relational aspect of the Indian situation throughout the article. Thus, he concludes,

> Ethnic fluidity is not only a function of long-range, irreversible movement across the ethnic line, but also of the repeated and sometimes quite rapid oscillations on both sides of it. Clearly, this commuting has both a cultural and a social dimension, and the latter is frequently the more important or relevant one. (1974:324)

5. An interesting dissertation project for someone would be to determine if self-proclaimed *mestizos* of Indian parentage are symbolizing their discordant social or economic circumstances, while *ladinos* of Indian parentage are symbolizing a changed ideology, with or without changed circumstances.

6. I have checked the informants answering "I don't know" with those answering "neither Indian nor Ladino" for statistical similarity or difference. For all variables checked, and in all four samples (urban and rural subdivisions of both San Marcos and San Pedro), the Mann-Whitney/Wilcoxon test did not discriminate, and the null hypothesis of no difference is reasonably accepted. Therefore, the grouping of these two responses under the general analytical term "disclaiming applicability" is statistically reasonable.

7. A word or two of caution is needed regarding the interpretation of the figures in Table 9. First, the survey-interview situation does not have the same symbolic and situational constraints as does the natives' daily interaction. This may increase the frequency of the non-Indian/non-Ladino "disputing" responses relative to the symbolic claims that would occur in the ordinary interpersonal transactions among natives that lead to ethnic definition. Second, providing the four categories was a methodological mistake that rigidified what is essentially a fluid system of symbols. However, I have voluminous open responses and commentary, from the first survey used for Appendix 3, and from throughout the fieldwork period as to the kinds of categories chosen as an alternative to Ladino or Indian. Among San Pedranos, the responses other than Indian or Ladino in descending order of frequency are *mestizo; no sé; nada, no existen,* or *todos son iguales;* and *Guatemalteco.* In San Marcos, the order is *mestizo* and *no sé.*

Of course, the possibility of survey-induced distortions in the symbolic range and interaction constraint of the offered terms warn that one should not assume the figures in Table 9 represent a sociologically real distribution of categories of people, whether Ladino, Indian, Mestizo, or other disclaimant. The figures are real for this census context, but they only point toward the reality of uninterrupted native life, evidencing, as they do, the qualitative and quantitative interplay of several components of category and interaction.

8. The Mann-Whitney probability of the actual San Marcos Indian mean income not being lower than the San Marcos Ladino income is 0.0046. The probability of the actual San Pedro Indian mean income not being lower than that of San Pedros Ladinos is less than 0.0000.

9. Again, the disparity is created by the extremely high values of a few Ladinos.

10. The probability that San Pedro is equal to San Marcos given this sample is <0.0000 for household income, 0.0003 per capita income, 0.0029 for land value, and 0.0025 for per capita land value.

11. P-value in testing that San Pedro mean household income is less than San Marcos is 0.3805 between Indians, and 0.3915 between Ladinos; P-value that San Pedro mean land value is less than San Marcos is 0.1450 between Indians, and 0.1648 between Ladinos. Similar figures that can be cited for commercial assets, vehicles, and other goods are omitted here.

12. Here, the probabilities of incorrectly concluding that the San Pedro "disclaimants" are not less than the San Marcos disclaimants are 0.003 for household income and 0.029 for land value.

13. Here are the relevant figures for San Pedro Indians and disclaimants compared with those for San Marcos disclaimants and Ladinos by the Mann-Whitney/Wilcoxon one-tailed test:

| | San Pedro | San Marcos | |
Variable	N	N	P-Values
Household income	159	166	<0.0000
Per capita income	159	166	<0.0000
Land value	162	166	0.0032
Per capita land value	162	166	0.0026

The hypothesis that the San Pedro mean is equal to the San Marcos mean is necessarily rejected in favor of concluding San Marcos is greater than San Pedro.

Chapter 7

1. Here *culture* has the eclectic meaning, since the discussion treats usage in the Latin American literature. In contrast to Colby and van den Berghe (1969), Furnivall (1944) sees the economy also as multiple.

2. If this attribution is reasonably fair, then it becomes clear that the plural-society model is dependent on the rather weak Malinowskian "function" rooted in the assumption of universal needs. Thus, all variations will be evidence of plurality if one cannot think of a structural or cultural reason for the variation. Unless one vigorously shows that there are no connections, the plural society is the default model of failed analysis.

3. Thus, the Guatemalan data tend to confirm the Schneider and Smith model in *Class Differences and Sex Roles in American Kinship and Family Structure* (1973), which combines the social-structural view of Raymond Smith (1956) with the culture-as-category-and-ideology view of David Schneider (1968).

4. Nur Yalman's *Under the Bo Tree* (1967) was especially helpful in developing the idea of status-linked transformations of a basic culture. Yalman, however, did not see the Ceylonese (now Sri Lanka) variations as status-linked. However, there is some evidence that variations in Ceylonese family and kinship might well be status transformations. In this regard, an ideological focus on the females is less prestigious than an ideological focus on the males. Thus, the highest prestige castes permute the bilateral culture toward patrilineality while the lowest prestige Muslim caste permutes toward matrilineality.

5. This pattern is common throughout linguistic systems. As expressed by Jerzy Kuryłowicz, "The unmarked member has two functions, *negative* and *neuter,* according to whether it is used in opposition to the positive member or outside such opposition. Thus *he killed the lion and the lioness*

(*lion* 'exclusive': male only) but *he hunts the lion (lion* 'inclusive': male and female)" (Kuryłowicz 1964:16).

6. In addition to Kuryłowicz, quoted in note 5, examples of hierarchies of a polysemic term are given by Palmer (1976:76-78), including this tree diagram:

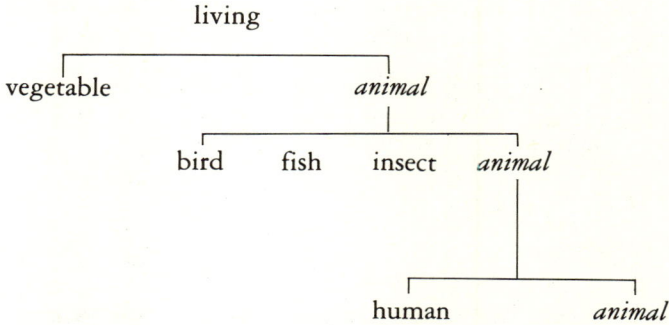

Moreover, according to Waugh (1979), such hierarchies are implicit in all triads of the unmarked, marked, opposite-of-marked sort.

7. The conceptual proximity of *cariño* to "diffuse enduring solidarity," "prescriptive altruism," or "the axiom of amity" seems readily apparent.

8. House-site inheritance is modified in the town center if it is a valuable commercial site.

9. Although it does occasionally happen, it is not felt that a daughter should impose on her husband by having her parents live in.

10. The key cultural term here is to "recognize" a child. This involves a social statement of obligation by signing its birth record and thereby giving notice that one is "responsible." A biological connection not validated by subsequent caring behavior *(cariño)* engenders no moral obligation at all.

11. I never found a case of union discouraged on account of relationship, in order to determine the relation of the theory of practice. Alternatively, some informants suggested that a same first surname was sufficient to prohibit marriage. But on questioning, each admitted that unrelated persons of the same surname could marry or live in common-law union.

12. The rural Indian genealogies can be quite extensive if one uses David Schneider and Raymond Smith's (1973) method of encouraging the respondent to name the successively extending relatives of each person mentioned. But in the hamlets, the range of such genealogies is an artifact of the knowledge of neighbors, engendered by close residence in a highly stable community. When one asks who of the known network is considered related by any kind of obligation or esteem different than that of just *particulares,* then the rural kin-field becomes very narrow indeed, including descend-

ants of one's grandparents. Moreover, when someone leaves the rural *aldea* to migrate to the coast or even to the capital, that person's descendants (and even the person) tend to drop out of the hamlet genealogies.

13. I have not visited *El Gallito* and cannot, therefore, confirm or modify the native assertion.

14. So say the natives of both towns. The *shecas* are certainly unique regionally, but I have no idea if that is true for the country as a whole. San Pedranos call themselves *shecanos* freely, and may or may not be pleased if others call them that, depending on context.

15. This is the case for all class levels of Marquenses. Because of the difficulty of getting enough unelicited instances of the natural use of *familia* at every class level, my data are not sufficiently complete for the middle-class government employees. There is some evidence that the San Marcos elite is more prone to use the kin-field meaning of *familia* than the San Marcos poor. It is possible that a class-linked gradient of focus exists. Nevertheless, poor Marquenses easily used the extended meaning in interviews and in natural conversation, and they included affinal kin as *familiares*. San Pedranos seldom and only formally used the extended meaning of *familia* and excluded affines from *familiares*.

16. San Pedro also has house compounds in which there live more than one cooking group. Unfortunately, I neglected to interview a San Pedro family on this matter so I do not have a native quote distinguishing between a cooking group as *familia* and *los de la casa* as two or more related cooking groups. I rather think, however, that San Pedranos would make the same distinction. They certainly distinguish related cooking groups with their *gasto diferente* from the larger *familia de la casa*.

17. The social childhood of Indians is also commented on in Chapter 9, note 3. Joseph Gross (1976; personal communication, 1979; Gross and Kendall 1983) is exploring the extended Indian residential arrangements in Santiago Atitlán. Here the problem of partition relates to social prestige through control. For these Indians, control is manifest in the domestic domain in the ability to control and subordinate children. This feature of Atiteco life is made more intelligible in the context of the wider system given here.

18. The Latin-derived legal system does not use prior-case precedence but a proof-text method of legal-code applicability. Thus, a revision could be made that would correspond with customary practice and belief.

19. "*Article 190 (Kinds of Kinship)*—The law recognizes consanguineal relationships to the fourth degree, relationship of affinity to the second degree, and civil relationship, which arises from adoption and exists only between the adopter and the adopted. Conjugal partners are kinsmen, but they do not create degree" (Guatemala 1972:42).

20. "*Article 199 (Paternity of the Husband)*—The husband (*marido*) is

father of children conceived during a marriage, even though the latter be annulled. Conception during the marriage is presumed for (1) a child born 180 days after the marriage ceremony or [after] the reunification of legally separated spouses and (2) a child born within 300 days following the dissolution of marriage" (Guatemala 1972:43).

"*Article 222 (Presumption of Paternity)*—It is presumed that (1) those born after 180 days from the initiation of common-law union and (2) those born within 300 days of the cessation of co-residence are children of the couple who have lived in consensual union" (Guatemala 1972:48).

21. "*Article 203 (Adultery by the Mother)*—The husband *(marido)* cannot contest the paternity of a child conceived or born during the marriage, alleging adultery by the mother, even when the latter [that is, the mother] testifies to the nonpaternity of her husband, unless the pregnancy and the birth had been hidden from him, in which case he can repudiate paternity by proving the facts which justify the repudiation" (Guatemala 1972:46).

22. Apparently because the kinship relation with a spouse does not create degree, one cannot make a claim on in-laws.

Chapter 8

1. This is the legal definition, which is analytically distinct from a native cultural definition. The native cultural definition contains the same ideas. Much to my chagrin, when I turned to my fieldnotes to find a coherent corroborative statement, I had none. In effect, I had either acquired their definition or imported mine without noting the development of the construct. However, since I have native statements on the duties of parents toward their children, on the axiom of helpfulness within the household, on the propriety of durable unions whether married or common-law as the context for procreation, and on the legal distinction between *matrimonio* and *unión,* I feel confident in proceeding.

In a homily delivered in a San Pedro marriage mass, the priest, a Guatemalan national, said: "Marriage is a mutual agreement to help each other, to accept each other. . . . You have no reason to go looking at others. . . . [You are bound] until one of the two die. In the church one cannot divorce. It is indissoluble, whether you are happy beings thus united, or whether you are miserable."

Cosmologically, marriage may be indivisible. But the natives get divorced civilly and account this effective for practical purposes.

2. And as we shall see, the same terms for marriage and union are used by the Marquenses and other Spanish-speaking Guatemalans, with the same legal options for change of category.

3. Again these distinctions apply to both San Pedro and San Marcos,

and appear to be pan-Guatemalan, in Spanish. The translation of *marido* as mate is only approximate.

4. As required by law, the portions read include Article 78 and Articles 108 through 114 of the *Código Civil* (Guatemala 1972). The legally specified obligations will be detailed later in this chapter.

5. The couple did not unite residentially or sexually, I was told, until after the church ceremony.

6. This was the mission of the group whose conversation is quoted on page 244.

7. Perhaps acquires its meaning from its prepositional phrase usage, *de roca,* meaning, according to the dictionary, "hard," "hardened," "hardhearted," or "constant."

8. Chi-square = 8.88 with 12 degrees of freedom and a significance of 0.713, strongly suggesting no deviation from chance. The Tau C measure of rank correlation is significant at $P = 0.014$, but the value, 0.105, suggests little association is present. The Mann-Whitney/Wilcoxon test of the separation of mean household income suggests the common-law unions are indeed lower in income than the legal-plus-ecclesiastical marriages, with a M-W/W one-tailed p-value of 0.0224. The Kolmogorov-Smirnov test of distribution difference also (barely) separates common-law from legal-plus-ecclesiastical marriages (one-tailed $P = 0.049$). On the other hand, if the civil marriages are tested against the ecclesiastical marriages for income difference, there is little evidence of mean (M-W/W) or distribution (K-S) difference (M-W/W one-tailed $P = 0.4335$, K-S one-tailed $P = 0.238$). Finally, ecclesiastical marriage shows no difference from the combination of civil marriage and common-law union (M-W/W one tailed $P = 0.4478$, K-S two-tailed $P = .648$).

9. Kendall's tau, M-W/W, and K-S on all the combinations listed for note 8 yield no reason to reject the hypothesis of similarity. The M-W/W one-tailed probability that the common-law mean income is the same or greater than the legal marriage mean under an assumption of no difference is .057, the only probability coming close to calling for rejection of the null hypothesis.

10. While it is perhaps unusual for the low-status sector to espouse vigorously the ethic of work as good, we are dealing with a postcolonial society in which the ideology was imposed. Because of the bifurcation into ethnic groups of opposed ideology throughout the system, and because the dominant sector of Spanish and then Ladino elite brought with them the ideology of nonwork, the Indians became both the workers and eventually the lovers of work. (See Chapter 2 for historical derivations.) By contrast, in the United States the middle class seems to have established the central ideology as one of work and achievement. To a lesser degree because the system is much less rigid, the lower class in America has

adopted in certain respects an opposite ideology or orientation toward security (Schneider and Smith 1973).

11. As discussed in Chapter 6.

12. Chi-square = 21.99 with 12 degrees of freedom and a significance of 0.0376, though there is a problem with empty cells, which makes the statistic potentially meaningless. M-W/W probability of incorrectly concluding that the mean income of common-law unions is less than legal marriage (civil or ecclesiastical), if in fact they are the same, is 0.0005, while the K-S P is 0.010 (one-tailed). The M-W/W one-tailed probability that ecclesiastical marriages are not higher than civil marriages in household income is 0.0043, while the one-tailed K-S probability is 0.009. The M-W/W one-tailed probability that ecclesiastical marriage is not of higher income than unions and civil marriage is less than 0.0000. K-S probability is less than 0.000.

13. For example the M-W/W one-tailed probability that mean land values of common-law unions and legal marriages is the same is 0.0003. There is no probable separation of civil from ecclesiastical marriage (M-W/W two-tailed P = 0.9216). The probability that the mean land value of ecclesiastical marriages is not greater than the mean of all others is 0.023.

14. San Marcos household heads are 87.5 percent Catholic, 4.9 percent *evangélico*, 2.7 percent other (principally Mormon and Jehovah's Witness), and 4.9 percent with no religion *("nada")*; San Pedro household heads are 80.6 percent Catholic, 11.2 percent *evangélico*, 1.0 percent other, and 3.1 percent with no religion *("nada")*, and 4.1 percent claiming not to know *("no se")*.

15. In 1975, I thought that the legal wife had divorced the doctor, but in 1978, I learned that the divorce had been dropped. Moreover, the man visited the wife while he lived with the consort; the women lived in different towns.

16. Another major aspect of the explanation is that the woman is the symbolic locus of kinship purity and continuity for the household. What a man does, does not affect the symbolic endowment of his social-status heirs. (See Chapter 7.)

17. This is Moore's (1973) pseudonym for a community near Antigua, Guatemala.

18. The go-between also shows the open, public, and respectable nature of the hoped-for relationship.

19. Among the Maya, alcohol plays a part in rituals of social reorganization. It has specialized native meanings and sacramental associations with the body of Christ in Catholic practice. Wine is itself transformed in the mass to symbolize the social and spiritual transformations that a mass brings about. But one suspects there is more. Can alcohol also be a physiological

solvent of the inhibitions to change that appear to be an aspect of the concept of restrictedness and fixity in Indian positional ideology?

20. For details, consult Collier (1968).

Chapter 9

1. In the previous chapter, "marriage," following the native meaning for *matrimonio,* was specifically limited to legally sanctioned unions. This makes the customary anthropological usage of "postmarital" residence a bit of an anomaly. We could, of course, coin a word—say, postconjugal residence (no doubt it has already been coined and used with gusto somewhere)—but that seems like verbal excess. I would rather ask the reader to keep in mind that from here on, "postmarital" refers to the period after *any* union of intended durability, whether legal or consensual.

2. In this chapter, the word "marriage" refers to either state legalized unions or consensual unions. Where I wish to precisely distinguish, I will use the appropriate term, *matrimonio,* or *unión,* in Spanish.

3. The fusion of status and family and the fact that Indians never reach full adulthood except among their peers or before the law is emphasized in the Ladino use of *tú* and other second-person familiar pronouns to refer to Indians. Such pronouns are properly used by parents and other adults in reference to youngsters, the essence of which is carried across the ethnic boundary. In contrast, the *vos* form is used for equalitarian familiarity and for its implied permissive sense among Ladinos. *Vos* may also be used to refer to a decided inferior and connotes with irony a sure knowledge of absolute license deriving from one's status superiority.

4. This book does not attempt to deal with religion, but in this context a comment is appropriate. The "symbolism of subordination," to use Kay Warren's title (1978), is apparent in provincial Catholic ritual. Given that religious activity subordinates, Indians are free to work out their community hierarchy in the civil-religious fiesta system. So church and religious participation belong to the poor, the oppressed, the Indians, and that other subordinate category: Ladino women. Moreover, is there a possible inverse relation between the multiple shamans serving individual clients with rituals performed in the margins and boundaries of the Indian communities versus the single priest serving the Ladino community from the center? Although this book critiques plural-society analysis predominantly through an analysis of domestic life, these facts and others, such as the existence of the Earth Lord in Ladino imagery and the interpreted substance of Warren's book, suggest that the ritual domains of Indians and Ladinos are not independent either.

5. See Joseph Gross (1974, 1976) and Gross and Kendall (1983) for a

jural analysis of household relations in the Indian community of Santiago Atitlán. Gross shows more clearly than anyone else the degree to which the domestic domain is manipulated in order to raise one's community social status.

6. *Uxorilocal residence* refers to the postmarital residence of a man in the household of his wife and her parent or parents. *Virilocal residence* refers to the postmarital residence of a woman with her husband and his parent or parents. *Independent residence* is used instead of the term *neolocal residence* to describe residence in a household differentiated from the parents or relatives of either spouse by both a separate entryway and a separate accounting of expenses. These terms apply only to the actual instances of behavior and are not intended to type the society or its ethnic segments.

7. The natives of both towns use expressions of verticality as metaphors for the existence of both authority and inequality of status.

8. The idea of norms as compromises arises out of David Schneider's discussion of conglomerate roles of *American Kinship* (1968). While my debt to Schneider is considerable, especially with respect to the idea of culture, my dependence upon the empirical and theoretical approach of Raymond T. Smith is even greater. Although there is no obvious place to footnote his *Negro Family in British Guiana* (1956), his notion of the implications of status for the constitution of household has fundamentally affected my thinking. Expanding on Fortes (1949) and flowing into Schneider and Smith (1973), Smith's *Negro Family* is a classic explication of the relations between the politico-jural domain, social status, and domestic life in a complex society.

9. An additional 5.6 percent (11 of 196) of the households were three-generation, but the middle connecting generation was either entirely absent (5 households) or the third generation comprised a child or children of a parent who had moved out, leaving the absent parent's younger siblings as uncles of the only third generation child (6 households).

10. These figures match the direction estimated by the native theory. However, the one-tailed M-W/W probability of making an error when assuming that household values are less than non-three-generation households is 0.1174 for household income, 0.0002 for per capita income, and 0.4403 for land value. One might accept the hypothesis that three-generation households have lower incomes, but the separation is not quite statistically compelling. However, because the three-generation households have more members, their per capita incomes are compellingly lower.

11. Delayed fission for occupational cooperation is noted by Waldemar Smith in his dissertation (1973) and more recent book (1977), but he gives no figures and does not discuss household composition in detail.

12. This does not apply to the Indians living in urban San Marcos, who are invariably recent immigrants from either San Pedro or one of the

predominantly Mam-speaking *municipios* of the department. Ladinos in rural San Marcos express a lastborn-son residential preference.

13. Due to space limitations I could not include material on a Ladino hamlet, although the rural Ladino is a thorough test of the adequacy of my approach to ethnicity. This must await separate treatment. My own evidence shows that even the rural agricultural Ladinos have some kinship or other connection into the urban center and ultimately to local people in power and that they have an expectation that they can tap the government by these connections. In addition, their residence in the Ladino town is symbolic of a particular social category and gives access to social services. Thus, in spite of their agricultural vocation carried out by manual labor, they have many of the symbolic attributes of the Ladino status category. Politically and socially and hence symbolically, they are Ladinos, but many of the other symbols of their status (such as wealth, occupation, education, and dress) are discordant with their symbolic background of claimed ancestry and municipal affiliation. This dissonance apparently explains the frequency with which my queries on the matter of ethnic status in the Ladino hamlets were met with nervous laughter.

14. An additional 4.3 percent (8 of 184) of the households were three-generation, with the middle generation either entirely absent (5 households) or with the third generation comprised of a child or children of a parent who had moved out, leaving the absent parent's younger siblings as uncles of the only third-generation children (3 households).

15. In contrast with San Pedro's statistical separation by household income, the three-generation San Marcos households (including those with no middle generation) are not statistically distinct from the non-three-generation households (two-tailed M-W probabilities of difference are 0.2262 for income and 0.2597 for land value). Moreover, the direction of the difference is reversed in San Marcos, with three-generation households having an income mean rank higher than non-three-generation households.

16. One of these thirteen had children of three absent siblings of the in-resident son. If this household is deleted, the twelve single child virilocal stem households had a mean household income of $406.00.

17. Given the hypothesis that advantageous social connections are pursued in San Marcos, but that matrifocality contains two countervailing processes of self-protection (among poor women) and social connection (among the better off), we would expect virilocal households to have a higher mean income and assets than the community as a whole. Excluding the one household mentioned in note 16, the hypothesis is confirmed at a significance level of 0.0240 for income and 0.0448 for land value.

18. A discussion of Comitancillo, Department of San Marcos, might appear out of place in the general comparison of San Marcos and San Pedro. The justifying circumstance is this: Comitancillo is a community where,

by virtue of its general use of Mam as a domestic language, its hinterland isolation, and its comparatively simple subsistence base (highland agriculture plus seasonal plantation labor), I could more fully and forcefully test the hypothesis of interconnection throughout the Guatemalan system.

Once fieldwork was well under way in San Marcos and San Pedro, I made several journeys further north in the highlands, particularly to Comitancillo. But I quickly foresaw that the time and effort required to learn Mam so as to avoid the national political language and thereby work out the Comitancillo Indian context of domestic culture, social relations, and symbols would so dissipate my efforts that I would end with no depth anywhere. I resolved, therefore, to use the then available notes in the literature, in the hope that I at a future date, or someone else in the meantime, would work out a careful domestic analysis of a more "traditional" *municipio*. Fortunately, Joseph Gross has begun to do this (Gross 1974).

The Comitancillo material included here is an artifact of this frustrated intention. But, in view of its qualitative consistency with what is reported in other communities, I thought it worth passing on, although it must be viewed as quite provisional.

19. I spent four days interviewing and poking around in the trade language (Spanish) rather than in the domestic language (Mam).

20. W. R. Smith's (1973) dissertation analyzes social change in the ritual fiesta system and gives an elegant and readable comparison of San Pedro and San Miguel Ixtahuacán, a *municipio* bordering on the north of Comitancillo. San Miguel and Comitancillo appear to be quite similar. The quoted phrase approximates, I believe, a sentence in an early draft of a chapter in W. R. Smith's dissertation that he had sent to me. But I can no longer find the source in his dissertation (1973) or in his book (1977).

21. Community endogamy also keeps the family estate's bilaterally inherited lands from being scattered beyond the reasonable working range of a man. In this way, it tends to keep the lands out of the commercial market, dominated in Indian perception and historical fact by unscrupulous Ladino agents. Friedl (1959) provides a description of the land tenure consequences of village exogamy. Historically, endogamy would have helped to maintain rights in the communal *"ejido"* lands as usufruct for potential claims on other *municipios* were thus minimized, given bilateral transmission of usufructuary access. But, then, why a *bilateral* inheritance system? Why not patrilineal inheritance and exogamy, given the probable predominance of patrilineality among pre-Columbian Mayans. The answer, I think, lies in the fact that people were the most important asset of an *encomienda* grant in a particular *reducción* town. The generally reciprocal expectation of a return in in-marrying women for out-marrying daughters would not work if the *encomendero* were so careless as to kill off his male

laboring force in the process of extracting wealth. Many *encomenderos* were more than careless. (See Martinez Pelaez (1971) and Simpson (1950) for tie-ins to the voluminous historical literature.) Furthermore, the bilaterality of both ethnic sectors constitutes the common cultural idiom in terms of which both atomization and interconnectivity could be enacted as symbols of status and institutions of status group maintenance.

22. Caution is again advised as the normative information was acquired from only one male informant and was only partially checked with one other.

23. For a more thoroughly researched study of land-size reduction in the neighboring *municipio* of San Miguel Ixtahuacán, see Waldemar Smith (1977:73-91). For a wider account of the problem, framed in the idiom of necessary political action, see the work of Humberto Flores Alvarado (1971).

24. Waldemar Smith captures the heart's passions when he reports having overheard an Indian from San Miguel Ixtahuacán say that he was not afraid to enter any government office in San Marcos, thus exemplifying his extraordinary bravery (1977:115).

25. While inheritance is said to be bilateral, my impression was that sons saw the father as having administrative control over the combined estate of the father and mother. But as I have tried to indicate, my exposure to the community does not allow a definitive statement.

26. My category, not theirs; let us say forty years of age and older.

27. This observation derives from an afternoon spent on a hillside overlooking one hamlet of Comitancillo where I discussed the households one by one with an informant. Thus, caution is again advised. See also the jural analysis of Santiago Atitlán inheritance and residence given by Gross (1974).

28. The task of enriching the cultural description and of testing these assertions numerically would make a fine research topic.

Chapter 10

1. In this chapter we shall again have to carefully distinguish between marriage, common-law union, and my analytical cover terms for both: domestic alliance or conjugal union.

2. A couple may live apart from each other so that the husband or, less often, the wife may make a living. Financial support by the husband and sexual fidelity by the wife are the other key symbols, but the couple must have been known to have been living together publicly for these latter two symbols to assume full meaning.

3. Some occasional gossip suggested that sexual relations and domestic services would be entertained even though the *obligation* was in abeyance.

4. I only caught this once in natural conversation with a man I knew had abandoned home, so the generalization is a bit speculative.

5. This quote concerning work does not contradict the Ladino's negative work ethic. For the poor there is no way to fulfill the conjugal expectation of financial provision except by work, while the last two of the three reasons for separation are directly related to the contradiction between manual work and Ladino status.

6. The Mormon missionaries in San Pedro faced a similar problem. They boarded with a family composed of a widowed woman, her marriageable spinster daughter, and other younger children. While I am reasonably certain a limited contract was adhered to, the townspeople thought that incomprehensible and improbable.

7. I am not sure what proportion of the poor Ladinos actually act this way, but I ran into a number of cases.

8. The willingness to lose income seems to affirm the proposition that centrality is more important than income in the complex of ideology and behavior that enters into one's claims of status. Indeed, because class is less important than other aspects of ethnic symbolism and status consistency, the market is the least restricted domain of Indian activity. The *"indios millonarios"* (a common refrain) do not contradict the system as harshly as *indios educados* or *indios poderosos*. (I have not heard the latter two terms.) The social persecutions that San Pedro's native doctor has faced are considerable; the rich merchants of San Pedro have felt almost nothing by comparison.

9. A few single women gain independent status by pursuing a postgraduate education and taking on a respected professional job. Friends of mine in Guatemala City had done this, but no one from San Marcos or San Pedro. A few women in San Marcos and San Pedro who would probably remain unmarried took schoolteaching or secretarial positions.

10. Since she married beneath her class and since the man abandoned her, absconding with a sizable amount of cash, I do not class this case as a contradiction of the principle that women themselves have difficulty in getting a divorce or in controlling their men.

11. This does not contradict the argument in Chapter 8 that the primary cultural impulse in maintaining a *casera* is dominance.

12. In this regard, Ladino women are like Indians. They symbolize this resemblance through the subordination symbols of Catholicism. Ladino women and Indians, both male and female, are the primary religious participants.

13. *"Pájaro verde dondequiera se halla."* The green bird is the quetzal, printed in green on the unit denomination bills.

14. The frequency of matrifocality at some point in the developmental

cycle of the domestic group, however, is less pronounced in San Marcos than in Smith's report for Guyana.

15. I suspect that the early surge in San Marcos is related to lower-class matrifocality. However, exploring the time of divorce in relation to other social and economic factors is a topic that awaits both further research and future publication.

Chapter 11

1. The limitations of a single field worker in two towns precluded going to funerals in evangélico, Mormon, and Jehovah's Witness congregations in both towns. From those few that I did attend, the Protestant chapel service is different from the mass, but the preparations and processions both before and after the sectarian service appeared to be essentially the same, except for the absence of liquors and the chanted *novenas*.

I must note here that I recognize inadequacies in my own fieldwork concerning funerals. I felt inhibited in investigating thoroughly this area of the peoples' lives because of the emotional content of the event for the participants. I seldom felt comfortable in inviting myself to funeral events. Even when accompanied, I found it awkward to inquire concerning relationships among persons present, to make counts, or to pursue discussions. This was rectified by discussions with trusted informants, and by participation in and discussion of one funeral with a close friend in San Pedro. Nevertheless, I would expect that a careful enumeration of participants, relationships, costs, and beliefs would establish further differences consistent with the general ideological frameworks of the two ethnic groups.

2. If a death takes place late at night or early in the morning, then an evening *velación* and nighttime vigil is impractical. In such cases the *velación* chants are more truncated and less well attended, while relatives arrange for mass and interment on the same day.

3. Though not strictly adhered to, there is a tendency in San Pedro for the men of the family cluster to walk before the women and for the old to walk before the young relatives in this central group of close *familiares*. In San Marcos there is a tendency, though again not strictly adhered to, for household family groups to walk together rather than to divide by age and sex.

4. Although neither I nor my student assistant in a 1979 field school recollect seeing caskets hanging from the ceiling or wills designating funeral responsibility in return for land, it appears that my field method was a bit weak here because I have no record of having asked specifically about either practice among the Ladinos. Thus, the most cautious statement would be that there appears to be a lessened or less emphatic interest or anxiety since

these behavioral manifestations, if present at all, are certainly less obvious than in either urban or rural San Pedro.

Chapter 12

1. Personality is (mercifully) a subject untouched in this book; nevertheless, it has an impact in any given household.
2. These figures include two-generation households with one spouse missing, as follows:

	San Marcos			San Pedro		
	N	Mean Income	Mean Land Value	N	Mean Income	Mean Land Value
Nonnuclear	95	204.4	28189.6	73	90.15	(77) 533.7
Nuclear complete, male-headed	74	146.6	13620.9	95	100.3	(96) 1638.2
Nuclear complete, female-headed	5	106.0	4821.4	3	152.0	0.0
Male-headed, spouse absent	1	233.0	10000.0	8	36.3	253.1
Female-headed, spouse absent	7	63.6	557.4	11	51.7	545.0
Nuclear complete, + male spouse's prior children	1	185	1500.0	0	—	—
Nuclear complete, + female spouse's prior children	1	123	700.0	0	—	—
	N = 184 for both income and land value			N = 190 for income N = 195 for land value		

Chapter 13

1. In addressing Peru, the Philippines, and Jamaica, I recognize that I am stepping beyond my area of direct expertise. Thus, I do not intend to assert the definitive character of these regions. Rather, I would invite those with greater experience to comment on the argument, and I hope to stimulate some who are about to depart for fieldwork to collect the comparative ethnic data needed to affirm or to discredit this approach.
2. See also Stein (1961), p. 20.
3. See also Stein (1961), pp. 169, 176-77, 202-3. The theme of self-sufficiency and of narrow social relationships is pervasive in the book.

4. See also van den Berghe and Primov (1977), pp. 85, 149, and 239 for parallel references.

5. One wonders why this might be so. Perhaps the greater degree of *colono*-type clientage in the highlands of Peru is more mestizoizing than the more independent small-plot land tenure of highland Guatemala. If so, there should be more mobility out of the haciendas than out of the predominantly free-holding communities, a hypothesis which could easily be checked through fieldwork.

6. The above description is a condensation of materials found in Dennis M. Roth, *The Friar Estates of the Philippines* (1977); John A. Larkin, *The Pampangans: Colonial Society in a Philippine Province* (1972); Nicholas P. Cushner, S.J., *Spain in the Philippines: From Conquest to Revolution* (1971); Frederick L. Wernstedt and J. E. Spencer, *The Philippine Island World: A Physical, Cultural and Regional Geography* (1967).

7. With a research grant from Brigham Young University, I spent three weeks in the Philippines—around Manila, on Panay Island, and in Ifugao—trying to see the system firsthand. But I came away considerably more impressed with the need for knowing the languages and engaging in long-term immersion than with data concerning the empirical merit of my model.

8. Braithwaite here quotes from an anonymous source, *A Short Journey in the West Indies,* 2 vols. (London, 1790), vol. 2, pp. 26-34.

9. It is impossible to tell how accurate Mrs. Carmichael's renderings are. She claims she kept a daily log of the vernacular speech and of events. Whether she later imputed this logic to the slaves is difficult to tell. She was, in any event, a constant apologist and defender of the good inherent in slavery and cannot be used for anything more than to alert us to a possible system of inverse thought in the colonial period.

10. Henriques (1968) is the principal source of this historical brief.

11. To be sure, miscegenation made the society a good deal more complex than the first cut in the categories.

12. The three classes—upper, middle, and lower—are of course but an analytical convenience (and thus somewhat dangerous) as well as a mode of shortcutting description. Henriques recognized that Jamaican society was a continuum of degrees of social, political, and economic access, without observable boundaries. Adam Kuper (1976) emphasizes the importance of analyzing the system as a continuum. Thus, the use of three class terms is useful for describing conditions roughly at the top, middle, and bottom, but it does not suggest that groups as such exist.

13. Presumably the interest in kinship that one might surmise for English nobility was not transferred to Jamaica because the royalty would have had little reason to risk their lives or health by going to Jamaica to set the model. Beyond this undocumented historical surmise, the mobility of those

who rose from ordinary risk-taking Englishman to elite planter would imply some shearing of kinship ties.

14. Of course, all segments of both societies maintain some interest in kinship. The issue is one of contrastive degree.

Appendix 1.B

1. Norman B. Schwartz (1983:351), in commenting on my analysis of culture and Guatemala (Hawkins (1983)), suggests a possible inversion of Ladino and Indian life cycles in Atchalán might be fruitfully explored. The original remark, made in 1979 at the International Congress of Americanists, Vancouver, B.C., Canada, encouraged my efforts in comparative analysis. Prior to the conference, as I recall, a take-home final examination invited students in my class on Mesoamerica to explore *Life Cycles in Atchalán* (Moore 1973) for confirmation and/or negation of my theories.

Appendix 4

1. In 1979, Bonnie Lynn Mitchell accompanied my field school group to Guatemala. In the course of two months research she attempted to refute my approach and establish the essential similarity of rural peasant Indians and Ladinos in San Marcos and San Pedro since she considered material production similarity to be the essential basis of life ways. She found, however, that in important ideological aspects of work ethic, merchandising, and social interconnection ideologies there were significant inversions and behavioral repercussions. (Mitchell 1982)

References

Adams, Richard E. W.
1977   *Prehistoric Mesoamerica.* Boston: Little, Brown & Co.
Adams, Richard Newbold
1956   "La ladinización en Guatemala." In *Integración social en Guatemala,* edited by Jorge Luis Arriola, pp. 213–44. Seminario de Integración Social Guatamalteca, Vol. 3. Guatemala: Seminario de Integración Social Guatemalteca.
1960   "An Inquiry into the Nature of the Family." In *Essays in the Science of Culture,* edited by Gertrude Dole and R. Carneiro, pp. 30–49. New York: Crowell.
1967   *The Second Sowing: Power and Secondary Development in Latin America.* San Franciso: Chandler.
1970   *Crucifixion by Power: Essays on Guatemalan National Social Structure, 1944-1966.* Austin: University of Texas Press.
AGG [Archivo General de Guatemala]
   Manuscript documents are catalogued by *legajo* (bundle number) and *expediente* (item number).
Aguirre Beltrán, Gonzalo
1967   *Regiones de refugio: El desarrollo de la comunidad y el proceso dominical en mestizoamerica.* México, D.F.: Instituto Nacional Indigenista.
Alvarado, Pedro de
1525a *An Account of the Conquest of Guatemala in 1524.* Edited by Sedley J. Mackie. New York: Cortés Society, 1924.
1525b *Relación hecha por Pedro de Alvarado a Hernando Cortez, en que se refieren las guerras y batallas para pacificar las provincias del Antiguo Reino de Goathemala.* México, D.F.: José Porrua e Hijos, Sucs., 1954.
Arensberg, Conrad M.
1937   *The Irish Countryman: An Anthropological Study.* New York: Macmillan Co.
Arita Figueroa, Jesús Oliverio
1973   "Diagnóstico socio-económico de un hospital de area de la Re-

pública de Guatemala." Tesis de Licenciatura, Universidad de San Carlos.

Barnes, John A.
1972 "Social networks." Addison Wesley Modular Publications, Module 26.

Bendix, Richard
1962 *Max Weber: An Intellectual Portrait*. Garden City, N.Y.: Doubleday & Co.: Anchor Books.

Boissevain, Jeremy, and J. Clyde Mitchell,
1973 *Network Analysis Studies in Human Interaction*. The Hague: Mouton.

Boon, James A.
1973 "Further Operations of 'Culture' in Anthropology: A Synthesis of and for Debate." In *The Idea of Culture in the Social Sciences*, edited by Louis Schneider and Charles Bonjean, pp. 1–32. Cambridge: Cambridge University Press.

Brathwaite, Edward
1971 *The Development of Creole Society in Jamaica: 1770-1820*. Oxford: Clarendon Press.

Bunzel, Ruth
1952 *Chichicastenango: A Guatemalan Village*. Seattle: University of Washington Press.

Burgess, Paul
1972 *Justo Rufino Barrios*. Translated into Spanish by Ricardo Letona Estrada. San José, Costa Rica: Editorial Universitaria de Guatemala.

Burns, Robert Ignatius
1975 *Medieval Colonialism: Postcrusade Exploitation of Islamic Valencia*. Princeton, N.J.: Princeton University Press.

Burridge, Kenelm
1969 *New Heaven, New Earth: A Study of Millenarian Activities*. Oxford: Basil Blackwell, 1980.

Cancian, Frank
1965 *Economics and Prestige in a Maya Community: The Religious Cargo System in Zinacantán*. Stanford, Calif.: Stanford University Press.

Cardaillac, Louis
1979 *Moriscos y cristianos: Un enfrentamiento polémico (1492-1640)*. Translated by Mercedes García Arenal. Madrid: Fondo de Cultura Economica.

Carmack, Robert
1981 *The Quiche Mayas of Utatlan*. Norman: University of Oklahoma Press.

Carmichael, Mrs.
1833 *Domestic Manners and Social Conditions of the White, Coloured, and*

Negro Population of the West Indies. Vol. 1. London: Whittaker, Treacher, and Co.

Chejne, Anwar G.
1974   *Muslim Spain: Its History and Culture.* Minneapolis: University of Minnesota Press.

Colby, Benjamin N., and Pierre L. van den Berghe.
1969   *Ixil country: A Plural Society in Highland Guatemala.* Berkeley: University of California Press.

Cole, John W., and Eric R. Wolf
1974   *The Hidden Frontier: Ecology and Ethnicity in an Alpine Valley.* New York: Academic Press.

Collier, George
1975   *Fields of the Tzotzil: The Ecological Basis of Tradition in Highland Chiapas.* Austin: University of Texas Press.

Collier, Jane Fishburne
1968   "Courtship and Marriage in Zinacantán, Chiapas, Mexico." In *Contemporary Latin American Culture,* edited by Margaret A. L. Harrison and Robert Wauchope, pp. 138–201. Middle American Research Institute, Publication no. 25. New Orleans: Tulane University.

Consuegra, Sfelino
1969   *Monografía del municipio de San Pedro Sacatepéquez, Departamento de San Marcos, República de Guatemala, Centro América.* San Pedro Sacatepéquez, Guatemala. n. p.

Contreras R., J. Daniel
1951   *Breve historia de Guatemala.* Guatemala: Ministerio de Educación Pública.

Cooper, Rex Eugene
1976   "Social Inequality in Western Guatemala: The Indian and the National Domain." Master's thesis, University of Chicago.

Cushner, Nicholas P.
1971   *Spain in the Philippines: From Conquest to Revolution.* Institute of Philippine Culture, Quezon City, Philippines: Ateneo de Manila University.

de Vega, Lope
1614   *Peribáñez y el Comendador de Ocaña.* Santiago de Chile: Empresa Editora Zig-Zig, 1954.

Díaz del Castillo, Bernal
1967   *Historia verdadera de la conquista de la nueva España.* México, D.F.: Editorial Porrua.

Dirección General de Cartografía
1961   *Diccionario geográfico de Guatemala.* 2 vols. Guatemala: Tipografía Nacional, 1961–1962.

Dirección General de Estadística
1971a   *II censo agropequario, 1964.* 5 vols. Guatemala: República de Guatemala.
1971b   *VII censo de población, 1964.* 3 vols. Guatemala: Dirección General de Estadística, 1971–1972.
1974   *Anuario estadística.* Guatemala: Ministerio de Economía.
1975   "San Marcos: Cuadro número 48." Punto focal, Dirección General de Estadística, Guatemala City, Guatemala. Computer printout.

Dombrowski, John, Elinor C. Betters, Howard I. Blutstein, Lynne E. Cox, and Elery M. Zehner
1970   *Area Handbook for Guatemala.* Washington, D.C.: U.S. Government Printing Office.

Douglas, Mary
1966   *Purity and Danger: An Analysis of Concepts of Pollution and Taboos.* London: Routledge & Kegan Paul.

Durston, John W.
1972   *La estructura de poder en una región ladina de Guatemala.* Seminario de Integración Social Guatemalteca, Estudios Centroamericanos numero 7. Guatemala: Seminario de Integración Social Guatemalteca.

Early, John D.
1983   "A Demographic Survey of Contemporary Guatemalan Maya: Some Methodological Implications for Anthropological Research." In *Heritage of Conquest: Thirty Years Later,* edited by Carl Kendall, John Hawkins, and Laurel Bossen, pp. 73–91. Albuquerque: University of New Mexico Press.

Ewald, Robert H.
1954   "San Antonio Sacatepéquez: Culture Change in a Guatemalan Community." Ph.D. diss., University of Michigan.

Flores Alvarado, Humberto
1971   *Proletarización del campesino de Guatemala.* Quezaltenango, Guatemala: Editorial Rumbos Nuevos.

Fortes, Meyer
1949   "Time and Social Structure: An Ashanti Case Study." In *Time and Social Structure and Other Essays,* 1–32. New York: Humanities Press, 1970.
1958   "Introduction." In *The Developmental Cycle in Domestic Groups,* edited by Jack Goody, pp. 1–14. Cambridge Papers in Social Anthropology, no. 1. Cambridge: Cambridge University Press.

Foster, George M.
1979   *Tzintzuntzan: Mexican Peasants in a Changing World.* Rev. ed. New York: Elsevier.

Friedl, Ernestine
1959 "Dowry and Inheritance in Modern Greece." In *Peasant Society: A Reader,* edited by Jack M. Potter, May N. Diaz, and George M. Foster, pp. 57–62. Boston: Little, Brown & Co., 1967.
Furnivall, J. S.
1944 *Netherlands India: A Study of Plural Economy.* Cambridge: Cambridge University Press.
Garcia-Arenal, Mercedes
1975 *Los Moriscos.* Madrid: Editora Nacional.
1978 *Inquisición y moriscos: Los procesos del Tribunal de Cuenca.* Madrid: Siglo XXI de España, 1983.
Geertz, Clifford
1973 *The Interpretation of Cultures.* New York: Basic Books.
Gibson, Charles
1966 *Spain in America.* New York: Harper & Row.
Gillin, John
1945 *Moche: A Peruvian Coastal Community.* Institute of Social Anthropology Publication no. 3. Washington, D.C.: Smithsonian Institution.
1952 "Ethos and Cultural Aspects of Personality." In *Heritage of Conquest: The Ethnology of Middle America,* edited by Sol Tax, pp. 193–222. Glencoe, Ill.: Free Press.
González, Julio
1951 *El repartimiento de Sevilla.* Madrid: Consejo Superior de Investigaciones Científicos.
Goodenough, Ward
1981 *Culture, Language, and Society.* 2d ed. Menlo Park, Calif.: Benjamin/Cummings.
Goody, Jack
1958 *The Developmental Cycle in Domestic Groups.* Edited by Jack Goody. Cambridge: Cambridge University Press.
Gossen, Gary H.
1974 *Chamulas in the World of the Sun: Time and Space in a Maya Oral Tradition.* Cambridge, Mass.: Harvard University Press.
Gross, Joseph J.
1974 "Domestic Group Structure in a Mayan Community of Guatemala." Ph.D. diss., University of Rochester.
1976 "Residence Patterns in a Mayan Community: An Issue of Prestige." Paper presented at the Western Social Science Association Conference, Arizona State University, April 30, 1976.
Gross, Joseph J., and Carl Kendall
1983 "The Analysis of Domestic Organization in Mesoamerica: The Case of Postmarital Residence in Santiago Atitlán, Guatemala."

In *Heritage of Conquest: Thirty Years Later,* edited by Carl Kendall, John Hawkins, and Laurel Bossen, 201–28. Albuquerque: University of New Mexico Press.

Guatemala
1972   *Código civil.* Guatemala: Editorial del Ejército.
1973   *Manual de instrucciones para el empadronador.* Guatemala: Dirección General de Estadística.

Guzmán Böckler, Carlos
1975   *Colonialismo y revolución.* México, D.F.: Siglo Veintiuno Editores.

Hull, C. Hadlai, and Norman H. Nie
1979   *SPSS Update: New Procedures and Facilities for Releases 7 and 8.* New York: McGraw-Hill.

Hanke, Lewis
1974   *All Mankind Is One: A Study of the Disputation Between Bartolome de las Casas and Juan Gines de Sepulveda in 1550 on the Intellectual and Religious Capacity of the American Indians.* De Kalb: Northern Illinois University Press.

Hawkins, John P.
1978   "Ethnicity and Family in Western Highland Guatemala." Ph.D. diss., University of Chicago.
1983   "Robert Redfield's Culture Concept and Mesoamerican Anthropology." In *Heritage of Conquest: Thirty Years Later,* edited by Carl Kendall, John Hawkins, and Laurel Bossen, pp. 299–336. Albuquerque: University of New Mexico Press.

Heath, Shirley Brice
1972   *Telling Tongues: Language Policy in Mexico, Colony to Nation.* New York: Teachers College Press.

Henriques, Fernando
1957   *Jamaica: Land of Wood and Water.* London: Macgibbon and Kee.
1968   *Family and Colour in Jamaica.* 2d ed. London: Macgibbon and Kee.

Hinshaw, Robert E.
1975   *Panajachel: A Guatemalan Town in Thirty-year Perspective.* Pittsburgh, Pa.: University of Pittsburgh Press.

Hollinsteiner, Mary R.
1967   "Tagalog Social Organization." In *Brown Heritage: Essays on Philippine Cultural Tradition and Literature,* edited by Antonio G. Manuud, pp. 134–48. Quezon City: Ateneo University Press.

Imamuddin, S. M.
1965   *Some Aspects of the Socioeconomic and Cultural History of Muslim Spain 711-1492 A.D.* Leiden: E. J. Brill.
1969   *A Political History of Muslim Spain.* 2d ed., rev. and enl. Dacca, Pakistan: Najmah Sons.

Ingham, John M.
1974 "The Asymmetrical Implications of Godparenthood in Tlayacapán, Morelos." In *Contemporary Cultures and Societies of Latin America,* 2d ed., edited by Dwight B. Heath, pp. 395–403. New York: Random House.

Jones, Chester Lloyd
1940 *Guatemala: Past and Present.* Minneapolis: University of Minnesota Press.

Kamen, Henry
1965 *The Spanish Inquisition.* New York: New American Library, Plume ed., 1971.

Kendall, Carl
1974 "Filiation and Brotherhood: Compadrazgo in Esquipulas, Guatemala." Ph.D. diss., University of Rochester.

Kuper, Adam
1976 *Changing Jamaica.* London: Routledge and Kegan Paul.

Kurylowicz, Jerzy
1964 *The Inflectional Categories of Indo-European.* Heidelberg: C. Walker.

Ladero Quesada, Miguel Angel
1969 *Los Mudejares de Castilla en tiempos de Isabel I.* Valladolid: Instituto "Isabel la Católica" de Historia Eclesiástica.

Larkin, John A.
1972 *The Pampangans: Colonial Society in a Philippine Province.* Berkeley: University of California Press.

Lawrence, Peter
1967 *Road Belong Cargo: A Study of the Cargo Movement in Southern Madang District New Guinea.* Atlantic Highlands, N.J.: Humanities.

Leeds, Anthony
1974 "Brazilian Careers and Social Structure: A Case History and Model." In *Contemporary Cultures and Societies of Latin America,* 2d ed., edited by Dwight B. Heath, pp. 285–307. New York: Random House.

León, Nicolás
1924 *Las castas del Mexico colonial o nueva Espana; noticias etno-antropológicas.* Mexico, D.F.: Museo Nacional de Arqueologia, Historia, y Etnografia.

LePlay, Frederic
1871 *L'organisation de la famille selon le vrai modele signale par l'histoire de toutes le races et de tous le temps.* Paris: Bibliothécaire de l'Oeuvre Saint-Michel.

1872 *The Organization of Labor in Accordance with Custom and the Law of the Decalogue.* Translated by Gourverneur Emerson. Philadelphia: Claxton, Remsen, & Haffelfinger.

Lévi-Strauss, Claude
1962 *La pensée sauvage.* Paris: Plon.
1963a "The bear and the barber." *Journal of the Royal Anthropological Institute* 93:1–11.
1963b *Structural Anthropology.* New York: Doubleday & Co.
1963c *Totemism.* Boston: Beacon Press.
1966 *The Savage Mind.* Chicago: University of Chicago Press.

Lewis, Henry T.
1971 *Ilocano Rice Farmers: A Comparative Study of Two Philippine Barrios.* Honolulu: University of Hawaii Press.

Lockhart, James
1968 *Spanish Peru 1532–1560: A Colonial Society.* Madison: University of Wisconsin Press.

MacLeod, Murdo J.
1973 *Spanish Central America: A Socioeconomic History 1520–1720.* Berkeley: University of California Press.

McBryde, Felix Webster
1947 *Cultural and Historical Geography of Southwest Guatemala.* Washington, D.C.: Government Printing Office. Reprint, Westport, Conn.: Greenwood Press, 1971.

Mangin, William
1959 "The Role of Regional Associations in the Adaptation of Rural Migrants to Cities of Peru." In *Contemporary Cultures and Societies of Latin America,* 1st ed., edited by Dwight B. Heath and Richard H. Adams, pp. 311–23. New York: Random House, 1965.

Margolies, Barbara
1975 *Princes of the Earth: Subcultural Diversity in a Mexican Municipality.* Washington, D.C.: American Anthropological Association.

Martínez Pelaez, Severo
1971 *La patria del criollo.* Guatemala: Editorial Universitaria.

Méndez Cifuentes, Arturo
1967 *Nociones de tejidos indígenas de Guatemala.* Guatemala: Editorial "Jose de Pineda Ibarra."

Mitchell, Bonnie Lynn
1982 "Indian and Ladino Women in Rural Western Highland Guatemala." M.A. Thesis, Brigham Young University.

Mitchell, J. Clyde
1969 "Introduction." In *Social Networks in Urban Situations: Analyses of Personal Relationships in Central African Towns,* edited by J. Clyde Mitchell, 1–50. Manchester: Manchester University Press.

Monroe, James T.

1966 "A Curious Morisco Appeal to the Ottoman Empire." *Al-Andalus* 31:281–303.

Moore, Alexander
1973 *Life Cycles in Atchalán: The Diverse Careers of Certain Guatemalans.* New York: Teachers College Press.

Morales Urrutia, Mateo
1961 *La division politica y administrativa de la Republica de Guatemala.* 2 vols. Guatemala: Editorial Iberia-Gutenberg.

Motolinía, Fray Toribio
1555 *Carta al Emperador: Refutación a Las Casas Sobre la Colonización Espanola.* Mexico: Editorial Jus, 1949.

Nadel, S. F.
1951 *The Foundations of Social Anthropology.* London: Cohen & West.

Nash, Manning
1958a *Machine Age Maya: The Industrialization of a Guatemalan Community.* Chicago: University of Chicago Press, 1967.
1958b "Political Relations in Guatemala." *Social and Economic Studies* 7:65–75.

Nutini, Hugo G.
1968 *San Bernardino Contla: Marriage and Family Structure in a Tlaxcalan Municipio.* Pittsburgh: University of Pittsburgh Press.
1976 "Introduction: The Nature and Treatment of Kinship in Mesoamerica." In *Essays on Mexican Kinship,* edited by Hugo G. Nutini, Pedro Carrasco, and James M. Taggart, 3–27. Pittsburgh, Pa.: University of Pittsburgh Press.

O'Callaghan, Joseph F.
1975 *A History of Medieval Spain.* Ithaca, N.Y.: Cornell University Press.

O'Neale, Lila M.
1965 *Tejidos de los altiplanos de Guatemala,* 2 vols. Translated by Edith Recourat. Seminario de Integración Social Guatemalteca, nos. 17 and 18. Guatemala: Seminario de Integración Social Guatemalteca.

Palmer, F. R.
1976 *Semantics: A New Outline.* Cambridge: Cambridge University Press.

Papousek, Dick A.
1976 Review of *Princes of the Earth: Subcultural Diversity in a Mexican Municipality,* by Barbara Luise Margolies. *Boletín de estudios Latinoamericanos y del Caribe,* 21:90–91.

Paul, Benjamin
1950 "Life in a Guatemalan Indian village." In *Patterns for Modern*

Living, Division 3, *Cultural Patterns.* Vol. 2, pp. 467–515. Chicago: Delphian Society.

Peristiani, Jean G.
1976 *Mediterranean Family Structures.* Cambridge Studies in Social Anthropology, no. 13. Cambridge: Cambridge University Press.

Pi-Sunyer, Oriol
1973 *Zamora: Change and Continuity in a Mexican Town.* New York: Holt, Rinehart & Winston, Inc.

Popper, Karl
1959 *The Logic of Scientific Discovery.* New York: Harper Torchbooks, 1968.
1962 *Conjectures and Refutations: The Growth of Scientific Knowledge.* New York: Harper Torchbooks, 1968.

Redfield, Robert
1941 *The Folk Culture of Yucatán.* Chicago: University of Chicago Press.

Reina, Ruben
1959 "Two Patterns of Friendship in a Guatemalan Community." *American Anthropologist* 61:44–50.

Roberts, Bryan R.
1973 *Organizing Strangers: Poor Families in Guatemala City.* Austin: University of Texas Press.

Roth, Dennis M.
1977 *The Friar Estates of the Philippines.* Albuquerque: University of New Mexico Press.

Sahlins, Marshall
1976 *Culture and Practical Reason.* Chicago: University of Chicago Press.

Sanders, William T., and Barbara J. Price
1968 *Mesoamerica: The Evolution of a Civilization.* New York: Random House.

Saussure, Ferdinand de
1959 *Course in General Linguistics.* Translated by Wade Baskin and edited by Charles Bally and Albert Schehaye, in collaboration with Albert Riedlinger. New York: McGraw-Hill, 1966.

Schneider, David M.
1965 "Kinship and Biology." In *Aspects of the Analysis of Family Structure,* edited by Marion J. Levy, pp. 83–101. Princeton, N.J.: Princeton University Press.
1968 *American Kinship: A Cultural Account.* Englewood Cliffs, N.J.: Prentice-Hall.
1972 "What Is Kinship All About?" In *Kinship Studies in the Morgan Centennial Year,* edited by Priscilla Reining, pp. 32–63. Washington, D.C.: Anthropological Society of Washington.

1976 "Notes Toward a Theory of Culture." In *Meaning in Anthropology,* edited by Keith H. Basso and Henry A. Selby, pp. 197–220. Albuquerque: University of New Mexico Press.

Schneider, David M., and Raymond T. Smith
1973 *Class Differences and Sex Roles in American Kinship and Family Structure.* Englewood Cliffs, N.J.: Prentice-Hall.

Schwartz, Norman B.
1983 "The Second Heritage of Conquest: Some Observations." In *Heritage of Conquest: Thirty Years Later,* edited by Carl Kendall, John Hawkins, and Laurel Bossen, pp. 235–46. Albuquerque, N.M.: University of New Mexico Press.

Simpson, Leslie Byrd
1950 *The Encomienda in New Spain.* Berkeley: University of California Press.

Singer, Milton
1972 *When a Great Tradition Modernizes.* London: Pall Mall Press.

Siverts, Henning
1969 "Ethnic Stability and Boundary Dynamics in Southern Mexico." In *Ethnic Groups and Boundaries: The Social Organization of Culture Difference,* edited by Fredrik Barth, pp. 101–16. Boston: Little, Brown & Co.

Smith, Carol A.
1975 "Examining Stratification Systems Through Peasant Marketing Arrangements: An Application of Some Models from Economic Geography." *Man* 10:95–102.

Smith, M. G.
1974 *The Plural Society in the British West Indies.* Berkeley: University of California Press, 1964.

Smith, Raymond T.
1956 *The Negro Family in British Guiana.* London: Routledge & Kegan Paul.
1970 "The Nuclear Family in Afro-American Kinship." *Journal of Comparative Family Studies* 1(1):55–70.

Smith, Waldemar Richards, Jr.
1973 "The Mesoamerican Fiesta System: A Behavioral Analysis." Ph.D. diss., University of California, Santa Barbara.
1977 *The Fiesta System and Economic Change.* New York: Columbia University Press.

Stack, Carol B.
1974 *All Our Kin.* New York: Harper & Row.

Stavenhagen, Rodolfo
1970 "Classes, Colonialism, and Acculturation: A System of Interethnic Relations in Mesoamerica." In *Masses in Latin America,* edited

by Irving L. Horowitz, pp. 235–88. New York: Oxford University Press.
1975 *Social Classes in Agrarian Societies*. Translated by Judy Adler Hellman. New York: Doubleday, Anchor Press.

Stein, William W.
1961 *Hualcán: Life in the Highlands of Peru*. Ithaca, N.Y.: Cornell University Press.

Stone, Samuel Z.
1974 "Aspects of Power Distribution in Costa Rica." In *Contemporary Cultures and Societies of Latin America*, 2d ed., edited by Dwight B. Heath, pp. 404–21. New York: Random House.

Tax, Sol
1937 "The Municipios of the Midwestern Highlands of Guatemala." *American Anthropologist* 39:423–44.
1942 "Ethnic Relations in Guatemala." *America Indígena* 2:43–48.
1947 "Notes on Santo Tomás Chichicastenango." Microfilm Collection of Manuscripts on Middle American Cultural Anthropology, no. 16. Chicago: University of Chicago Library.
1953 *Penny Capitalism: A Guatemalan Indian Economy*. Smithsonian Institution, Institute of Social Anthropology, Publication no. 16. Washington, D.C.: U.S. Government Printing Office. (Photo-reproduction, New York: Octagon Books, 1972).
1975 "The bow and the hoe: Reflections on hunters, villagers, and anthropologists." *Current Anthropology* 16:507–513.

Tedlock, Barbara
1983 "A Phenomenological Approach to Religious Change in Highland Guatemala." In *Heritage of Conquest: Thirty Years Later*, edited by Carl Kendall, John Hawkins, and Laurel Bossen, pp. 235–46. Albuquerque: University of New Mexico Press.

Tumin, Melvin M.
1952 *Caste in a Peasant Society*. Princeton, N.J.: Princeton University Press.

Turner, Victor W.
1969 *The Ritual Process: Structure and Anti-structure*. Chicago: Aldine.

United Nations Food and Agriculture Organization
1958 *Coffee in Latin America: Productivity Problems and Future Prospects*. Vol. 1, *Colombia and El Salvador*. New York: United Nations.

Van den Berghe, Pierre L.
1974 "Ethnic Membership and Cultural Change in Guatemala." In *Contemporary Cultures and Societies in Latin America*, 2d ed., edited by Dwight B. Heath, pp. 316–27. New York: Random House. (First published in *Social Forces* (1968) 46:514–22.)

Van den Berghe, Pierre L., and George P. Primov

1977   *Inequality in the Peruvian Andes: Class and Ethnicity in Cuzco.* Columbia: University of Missouri Press.

Van Zantwijk, Rudolf A.
1967   *Servants of the Saints: The Social and Cultural Identity of a Tarascan Community in Mexico.* Atlantic Highlands, N.J.: Humanities.

Vogt, Evon Z.
1969   *Zinacantán: A Maya Community in the Highlands of Chiapas.* Cambridge, Mass.: Harvard University Press, Belknap Press.
1976   *Tortillas for the Gods: A Symbolic Analysis of Zinacantán Rituals.* Cambridge, Mass.: Harvard University Press.

Wagley, Charles
1957   "Plantation America: A Cultural Sphere." In *Caribbean Studies: A Symposium,* edited by Vera Rubin, pp. 3–13. Jamaica: Institute of Social and Economic Research, University College of the West Indies.

Wagley, Charles, and Marvin Harris
1955   "A Typology of Latin American Subcultures." *American Anthropologist* 57:429–51.

Warren, Kay B.
1978   *The Symbolism of Subordination: Indian Identity in a Guatemalan Town.* Austin: University of Texas Press.

Waugh, Linda R.
1979   "Marked and Unmarked: A Choice Between Unequals in Semiotic Structures." Unpublished paper. Available from author, Department of Linguistics, Cornell University.

Weber, Max
1968   *Economy and Society.* 3 vols. New York: Bedminster Press.

Wernstedt, Frederick L., and J. E. Spencer
1967   *The Philippine Island World: A Physical, Cultural, and Regional Geography.* Berkeley: University of California Press.

Wisdom, Charles
1940   *The Chorti Indians of Guatemala.* Chicago: University of Chicago Press, Reprint ed., Midway, 1974.

Wolf, Eric R., and Sidney Mintz
1957   "Haciendas and Plantations in Middle-America in the Antilles." *Social and Economic Studies,* 6: 380–412.

Worsley, Peter
1968   *The Trumpet Shall Sound: A Study of Cargo Cults in Melanesia.* New York: Schocken.

Yalman, Nur
1967   *Under the Bo Tree: Studies in Caste, Kinship, and Marriage in the Interior of Ceylon.* Berkeley: University of California Press, 1971.

Index

Adams, Richard E. W., 42, 43
Adams, Richard N., 166
agriculture, 18, 20, 36, 153, 157, 184
Aguirre Beltrán, Gonzalo, 4
Alcaldías Mayores, 57
aldeas, 96, 145, 162, 228, 289
Alvarado, Pedro de, 48–53
anthropology: focal changes in, 4, 40, 415n7
Arana, Carlos, 126, 130
Arensberg, Conrad M., 297
Arita Figueroa, Jesús Oliverio, 107
army, the national, 103
artesanos and artisans, 152, 161, 184
Atchalán, 12, 263
Audiencia, 69
Aztecs, 45

baking, 146
Banco Nacional de Desarrollo Agrícola (BANDESA), 106
Barrios, Justo Rufino, 81, 86, 236
behavior: conjugal failure and, 324; culture as, 4, 12; ethnographic data from, 42; ideology and, 113, 185; indexical, 11; landownership and, 168; Peruvian, 360; residency rules and, 270–77, 279–85; social freedom and, 169; status/performance separations of, 7
Belize, 93
Bendix, Richard, 166
Betanzos, Domingo de, 46
blacks, 373
boca costa, 18
Boon, James, 5
Brathwaite, Edward, 369, 371
British, the, 368, 372
Bunzel, Ruth, 96, 240, 295
Burns, Robert I., 34, 35, 36
Burridge, Kenelm, 40
bus system, 162

cacao, 56, 61
Cakchiquel, the, 13, 53, 263, 382
campaña, 98
Cancian, Frank, 21, 266
Cardaillac, Louis, 38
cariño, 220, 234
Carmack, Robert, 40–42
Carmichael, Mrs., 368–70
Carrera, Rafael, 81
Casa de Cultura, 115
centrality, 183, 194
Chejne, Anwar G., 31, 32, 36
Chiapas, 3, 21, 81, 296
Chichicastenango, 240, 241, 295

children, 221, 235, 238
chronicles, 58, 64; postconquest tests, 40
Ciudad la Unión, 124
clergy, 55, 56, 63, 64, 363
clothing: contrast of, 11, 182; funeral, 330; perspectives on, 177, 179–81, 194; the status index of, 141, 166, 202–3, 288, 358, 359, 368
Club Shecana, 228
Códizo Civil, 244
coffee, 81, 108, 157
Colby, Benjamin N., and Pierre van den Berghe, 5, 137, 215, 216, 289
Cole, John W., and Eric R. Wolf, 296, 297
Collier, George, 296
Collier, Jane F., 265, 266
colonial documents, 50, 66; of San Marcos, 69, 70, 72; of San Pedro, 53, 57, 60, 62, 71, 72, 74
colonialism: institutions of, 54; internal, 5, 33; inverse ideologies from, 377; in Jamaica, 371; New/Old World comparison of, 38, 80; in Peru, 349; in the Philippines, 363
comercientes, 151
Comitancillo, 180, 286, 291
common-law union, 244, 246, 249, 253, 256, 266, 308; termination of, 302, 305
communication services, 108, 114
communities: atomization of, 295; coastal, 18; ethnicity and status of, 205–6, 210–11; finca, 18; particulares and, 219; Peruvian rank of, 352; status of persons and status of, 99, 203–4. *See also* municipios and municipalities
compadrazgo, 21, 116, 194, 356
composición, 59
congregaciones, 58
congress, the national, 91, 92
conocimiento, 177
conquistadores, 45, 47, 49, 54, 63, 65
Consuegra, Sfelino, 156
Contreras R., J. Daniel, 81
Cooper, Rex Eugene, 150, 166
courts, 91, 92, 103, 235, 238
courtship, 225, 245, 253
criollos, (Creoles), 58, 63, 64, 66, 85, 176, 359, 366
crown, the, 55, 57, 58, 63
cultural commuting, 204
culture: class homoginization, 28, 35, 85, 86, 365; distinction in, 12, 13, 135, 166, 169, 183, 200; function and ideology, 294; idea and form, 6, 7, 13, 42; Indian as molded, 346; inverse subsystem, 349; meaning in context, 178; meltdown pressure, 25, 26, 29, 30, 38, 80, 370, 373; Peruvian congruency, 359; point/counterpoint, 38; survivals, 41
Culture and Practical Reason (Sahlins), 135
Cuzco, 358, 360

debt peonage, 82, 83
Defender of the Indians, 46
departments, 92, 93, 97, 99, 351, 352
depopulation, 49, 61
Diario Oficial, 108
Díaz del Castillo, Bernal, 39, 45, 48, 51, 52

diputados, 91
disinheritance, 292
divorce, 304
Dombrowski, John, 83
domestic alliance: categories of, 243, 244, 253; conjugal behavior and wealth, 248, 255, 256, 258, 259, 260; courtship, 245, 253; endogamy, 290, 296; illicit or secondary, 251, 259, 311; Jamaican, 375; norms for, 251, 258, 262; in other Indian communities, 263; premarital sex, 261; reasons for failure of, 322; terminations of, 301, 305, 313; timing of terminations of, 322; uxorical residency and, 270, 279, 339; virilocal residency and, 270, 339, 343
domestic domain, the: contrasts in, 11, 21; cultural models tested in, 212; economic symbols in, 165; ethnicity and, 5, 312; the funeral in, 327, 330; in Jamaica, 372, 374; origin symbols in, 184; in Peru, 360. *See also* households
Dominican order, 46
Don Quixote, 27
Douglas, Mary, 67

Early, John D., 100
economic domain, the: agriculture and, 153, 157; banking and, 105, 108; building new markets, 119; commercial activity in, 116, 160; contrasts in, 20, 138, 312; cottage industry in, 139, 161; currency for, 56; domestic conflict and, 301; domestic domain and, 217, 315; income and status, 167; independence and, 86; kin ideology and, 233; market structure in, 137; merchandising and, 150, 152, 161; the mestizo in, 67; perspectives on, 135–38; in Peru, 352, 353; plural society and, 216; postwar shift in, 175; production, 140, 142, 147, 164, 168; Spanish Christian, 29; transportation in, 140, 152, 162; the wheat cooperative, 129. *See also* employment
education: economics and, 156; institutions for, 106; labor and, 290; language and, 43; locating the university, 118; perspectives on, 176, 177, 179–81; residency and, 270, 277, 340; status index of, 184
ejidos, 59
elections, 111
El Gallito, 228
el gobierno, 91
elopement, 225, 244, 264, 265, 266
empleados del gobierno, 158
employment: civil service or governmental, 109, 115, 157, 158, 164; compared, 147–50, 161; Indian ideology and, 310; job transfer and conjugal failure, 307; Ladino ideology and, 313; occupations, 147, 183; professions, 156, 162; residency and, 269, 277, 293, 296, 298; self-employment, 150, 156; as servants, 165; underemployment, 164. *See also* labor
encomienda, 23, 30, 39, 45, 49,

54–58, 87; endogamy and, 440–41n21
"Encomienda America," 87
endogamy, 290, 296, 440n21
Estrada Cabrera, Manuel, 83
ethnicity, 9, 14, 87; functions of ideal types of, 173; government enhancement of, 113; households and, 164, 165; idioms for, 187, 188, 193; indices of, 167; institutional hierarchy and, 195, 197; interaction system and, 204, 211; in Jamaica, 373; municipal, 97; perceptions of, 176, 395; in Peru, 359; in the Philippines 366; recategorization of, 407; symbols of, 184, 185, 193
ethnic mobility, 193
"Ethos and Cultural Aspects of Personality," 11
Ewald, Robert H., 97

familia and family, 217, 229, 240, 328; affines and, 237; close, 230; familiares and, 217, 229, 329; parientes and, 219, 231; particulares and, 219, 231; in Peru, 361. *See also* children; fatherhood; grandparents; kinship
Family and Colour in Jamaica (Henriques), 373
fatherhood, 224, 234, 238, 239, 252, 308
ferias, 95
fiesta system, 19, 40, 65, 258, 354, 415n10
Fiesta System and Economic Change (Smith), 258
fincas, 18, 83, 164, 168, 333;
finqueros, 157

Folk Culture of Yucatán, The (Redfield), 4
Fortes, Meyer, 217, 337
Friedl, Ernestine, 297
friendship, 10, 92, 98, 110
Fuentes y Guzmán, Francisco Antonio de, 64
Furnivall, J. S., 216

Gálvez, Mariano, 81
García-Arenal, Mercedes, 37, 38
García Granados, Miguel, 81
Geertz, Clifford, 6
Gibson, Charles, 47, 48, 52, 54
Gillin, John, 11, 350, 357
Ginés de Sepúlveda, Juan, 45, 47
González, Julio, 30
Goodenough, Ward, 7
Goody, Jack, 337
Gossen, Gary, 21
governors, 93, 95, 97, 99, 109, 128, 132
grandparents, 225, 237, 291, 339, 362, 376
Gross, Joseph J., 21, 264, 295
Guatemala: conquest of, 48–53; independence of, 80; future research in, 404
Guatemala City, 15, 97, 98, 228, 290
Guzmán Böckler, Carlos, 20

haciendas, 56, 60, 352, 363
Hanke, Lewis, 39, 46
Harris, Marvin, 40
health services, 107, 156, 163; accident insurance, 107
Heath, Shirley, 43
Henriques, Fernando, 372–77
Heritage of Conquest: The Ethnology of Middle America, 11
Heritage of Conquest: Thirty Years Later, 4

Herskovitz, Melville, 372
hidalgos, 45
Hinshaw, Robert E., 97
Hollinsteiner, Mary R., 367
households: accretion/dispersion of, 338; cooking groups in, 218, 229; crafts in, 141, 145, 147; development of, 268, 278, 285, 291, 294, 337; division of labor in, 164; doublestem, 280; expansion of complex, 341; heads of, 193, 339; isolation of, 150; kin responsibility and, 221, 234; kinship terms and, 218, 219, 229, 233; matrilocal, 310, 322, 340, 343; in Peru, 354, 362; secondary, 252, 260; stem types of, 271, 279, 296, 338–40; symbolic initiation of, 266. *See also* residency
Hualcan, 351–55
Hualcan: Life in the Highlands of Peru (Stein), 351

ideology. *See* oppositions; status ideology; symbols
Ilocano Rich Farmers: A Comparative Study of Two Philippine Barrios (Lewis), 366
Imamuddin, S. M., 31, 32, 36, 37
incompatabilidad, 305, 323
independence ideology, 185
independence movements, 64
Indians and indígena: as a colonial product, 80, 346; as a study group, 3–5; craft specialization by, 150; economic freedom of, 136; independence reforms and, 81–84; Mam alliance, 50–53; Moors compared to, 39; in Peru, 352, 354; Spanish description of, 45

indigo, 61
Inequality in the Peruvian Andes (Van den Berghe and Primov), 351
inheritance, 221, 296, 330, 332, 361
Inquisition, the, 25–27, 30, 36
institutional hierarchy, 190
Instituto Nacional de Fomento Municipal (INFOM), 119
Ixil Country (Colby and Van den Berghe), 289

Jakobson, Roman, 8
Jamaica, 368
jefes políticos, 82
Jones, Chester L., 81–83
jueces de milpas, 61

Kamen, Henry, 26–30
kinship: affines, 237; categories of, 217, 229; courts and, 235, 238; field structures for, 224, 232, 236; Indian status and, 269; inequalities and permutations of, 240; in Jamaica, 375; norms for, 220, 234, 343; in Peru, 356, 360–62; plural society and, 215; siblings, 237; status ideology and, 237. *See also* familia and family
knitting, 145

labor: agricultural, 153–56; baking, 146; debt peonage, 82, 83; encomienda, 55, 56; household division of, 164; in Jamaica, 371, 374; knitting, 145; perspectives on, 176, 177, 179–82; in Peru, 353; in the Philippines, 364, 367; repartimiento, 60; status

symbols of, 184; tailoring, 146; Vagrancy Law and, 83; weaving, 142; work ethics, 165, 169, 353, 367
labor service, 34
Ladero Quesada, Miguel Angel, 34, 35
ladinization, 84
Ladinos: as an ethnic group, 3, 9, 44; marginality and, 198; native definition of, 187; Indian village residency of, 291
landownership: absentee, 10, 157, 168, 352; colonial disputes of, 74–77; conjugal status and, 258; encomienda, 56; inheritance of, 292, 335, 336; land values and, 58, 59, 158, 422n10; in Peru, 361; reducción and, 58, 59; San Marcos and, 157; San Pedro and, 153–56; San Marcos/San Pedro disputed, 121; Spanish, 30; symbols of, 133, 134, 168. *See also* fincas
language: as colonial ethnic marker, 66; contrasted use of, 11; Indians and, 43, 44, 139, 288; perspectives on, 178, 179, 180, 194, 202; in the Philippines, 364; as a research field, 406; status index of, 182, 202–3, 359
la reconquista, 25
La Reforma, 81
las Casas, Bartolomé de, 46, 55
Lawrence, Peter, 40
lawyers, 162
leisure display, 164, 168
León Cardona, Juan de, 53, 56
LePlay, Frederic, 296
Lévi-Strauss, Claude, 8, 189, 200
Lewis, Henry T., 366, 367

limpieza de sangre, 27
Lockhart, James, 350

McBryde, Felix Webster, 97
MacLeod, Murdo J., 53, 56, 58, 61, 66, 67, 79
Malinowski, Bronislaw, 190
mandamiento, 61, 82, 83
Mangin, William, 290
marginality: colonial, 67; Indian, 315; Ladino, 198, 309, 310; mestizo, 206; in Peru, 355; Spanish, 27
marketing, 21
marriage: colonial, 64; comparisons, 116, 117; the domestic alliance of, 243, 245, 248, 253, 254, 258, 261, 266; familia and, 219; kinship and, 222; structure field for, 224, 236; termination of, 302
Martínez Peláez, Severo, 24, 44, 56, 58, 60, 64–67, 80, 83, 85
Marx, 377
Méndez Montenegro, Julio César, 121
Mercedarian order, 57
Mesoamerica, 3, 39, 44
mestizo, 65, 66, 84, 85, 170; in Jamaica, 373; the middle ground of the, 174, 185, 198; perspectives on being, 177, 178–81, 203–6, 209; in Peru, 351, 359; as symbolic, 210, 211
military service, 11, 103
ministries, the national, 91, 92, 98, 99, 131; in Peru, 351
Moche, 357
Monroe, James T., 33
Montesinos, Antonio de, 46
Moore, Alexander, 12, 263
moriscos, 36

mudéjar, 34
municipios and municipalities: central government and, 97, 99, 123, 127; councils and the wheat cooperative, 129; described, 10, 95, 96; developmental projects and, 117, 118, 119; funding in, 98; kinship in, 228; officials of, 97; in Peru, 352; unification of, 124. *See also* communities
muwalladun, 32

Nash, Manning, 12, 97
National Geographic Institute, 122
Negro Family in British Guiana, The (Smith), 316, 322, 376
New Laws, the, 55, 56, 57
New World, 38, 39, 79
Nutini, Hugo G., 241

O'Callaghan, Joseph F., 25, 28, 30
oppositions: access competition, 117–33; analogy for meaning continuum, 7–9; descriptive terms of, 45–47, 73; household, 342; ideological, 10; incongruency confusing the, 202; inheritance, 334; institutions as symbolic, 174; in Jamaica, 369, 374; kinship, 225, 231; kinship-term, 218, 219, 230–33; land wealth, 158; Mesoamerican, 44; mestizo, 66; Moorish, 38; Mudejar, 34; in Peru, 354, 357; Spanish, 27, 29, 37, 38; Spanish Old/New World ideological, 79; symbolic systems of, 170, 182; work ethic, 165, 354, 374. *See also* origins; status ideology
origins: birthplace and status, 107; domestic/social domain link by, 199; founding of San Marcos and San Pedro, 68–70; Moorish, 32; perspectives on, 187–88, 193; recategorizing, 202; residency and, 290; Spanish value of, 25–29; symbolism of, 14, 19, 65, 73, 182, 183, 185, 201

Paul, Benjamin, 264
Peristiani, Jean G., 7
Peru, 290, 350
Petén, 19
Philippines, 363
plural society model, 5, 199, 212; conjugal union and the, 262, 312, 324; defined and discussed, 215–16; inheritance and the, 336; kinship and the, 215, 233; postmarital residence and the, 267
Pocomam, the, 13, 379
police, 91, 101, 113
political domain, the: access to, 117–33, 184, 203, 204; careers in, 109, 110; colonial, 63, 66, 71, 78; contrast in, 11, 20, 66; debt and favor in, 98, 127; departments of, 93, 97; domestic domain and, 217; encomienda and, 55, 57; government jobs in, 158; Indians and, 123, 133, 297; information flow in, 95, 128; kinship and, 233; Ladinos in, 98, 99, 110, 312; municipalities of, 95, 97, 129; national government and, 91, 97, 110; patronage and party in, 111,

122, 312; in Peru, 351;
receiving the president and, 97,
130; Spanish Christian, 25;
units of government in San
Marcos, 100
"Political Relations in Guatemala"
(Nash), 12
population: colonial, 71, 72, 79;
departmental, 93; in Jamaica,
372; municipal, 96; of San
Marcos, 100; of San Pedro, 113
postal service, 114
presidency, the, 91, 92, 97, 110,
130
Price, Barbara J., 40
Primov, George, 351–62 passim
Pueblo de Indios, 59
putting-out system, 140

Quezaltenango, 52, 73, 76, 100,
145, 150, 228

race: categories for, 65, 66, 85,
86; Islam and, 31, 32;
perspectives on, 176–78,
179–80, 186; Spanish ideology
and, 25, 29, 30, 34, 37;
symbolism of, 183, 199
realenga, 59, 60, 74
Recordación Florida, 58
Redfield, Robert, 4, 12
reducción, 23, 39, 58–60, 87,
365
Reina, Ruben, 10
religious domain, the: colonial,
64; contrasted, 11, 21;
domestic alliances and, 245,
249, 254, 256, 258, 266, 312;
funerals and, 327; Indians and,
269; Moorish, 31; in the
Philippines, 363; as a research
field, 404; Spanish, 25, 31–39,
43

repartimiento, 23, 30, 39, 45,
56, 58, 60, 62, 364
residency: collateral relatives and,
340–42; colonial, 68–73, 78;
comparisons of, 39, 293, 295,
342; government employment
and, 109, 115; inheritance and,
331; in Jamaica, 376; Moorish,
31; Mudejar, 34; municipal,
96; in Peru, 358, 361; in the
Philippines, 364, 365;
professionals and, 162;
registration and, 107; segregated,
66; social security and, 269,
292, 298; Spanish, 27, 29;
status and, 268, 278;
uxorilocal, 266. *See also*
households
revolution, 378
roads, 15, 18, 19, 83,
109
Roberts, Brian, 290

Sahlins, Marshall, 135, 294
Salcajá, 169
Sanders, William T., 40
San Marcos: colonial, 66, 67,
71–73; government offices in,
101–9; mestizo status in, 175;
the municipality of, 100;
self-perspectives for, 176–78,
186, 193, 195, 196, 198,
202–3, 206, 209; social
interconnections in, 109, 118;
velación in, 327
San Pedro la Laguna, 264
San Pedro Sacatepéquez: colonial,
53, 67, 71; governmental
offices in, 113, 129; mestizo
status in, 175; the municipality
of, 113, 150; self-perspectives
for, 178–81, 193, 194, 197,
203, 205, 210; social

interconnections in, 115, 118, 127; velación in, 328
San Rafael Soche, 100
Santiago Atitlán, 264
Saussure, Ferdinand de, 7, 13, 42
Schneider, David M., 6, 13, 185, 217, 231
Schwartz, Norman B., 20
settlement, the colonial system of, 58
sexual access, 65, 144, 301–4, 310, 311, 315, 373, 376
Simpson, Leslie, 49
Singer, Milton, 6
Siverts, Henning, 137
slavery, 55, 373
Smith, Carol A., 137
Smith, M. G., 216
Smith, Raymond T., 6, 217, 316, 322, 337, 376
Smith, Waldemar R., 123, 133, 138, 175, 258, 298, 313
social domain, the; advancement in, 12, 27; atomization of, 295 356; class and category in, 19, 20, 166, 190, 195, 202–11, 216; cultural programs, 115; debts in, 116, 165; domestic domain and, 216, 217, 278; equality in, 10, 11, 63, 66, 72, 86, 144, 190; highlights of, 19; homogeneity in, 28, 35, 85; ideals and congruency in, 174; interconnection in, 10, 24, 32, 164, 332; in Jamaica, 374; market structure and, 137; Mesoamerican, 40–43; Moorish, 25, 30–32; Morisco, 36–38; Mudejar, 34–36; origin and, 190; in Peru, 354, 355; in the Philippines, 365; postwar, 175; purifying the Spanish, 26–29; reform and, 81, 84–87; social distance, 219, 224, 231, 265, 355; social networks, 118, 133, 355, 366, 404, 418n10; social pressures on, 25, 29, 30, 33, 38, 41; social security, 269, 292, 298; urban/non-urban, 9–10
Sociedad de Obreros de San Pedro, 123
Soconusco, 61
Sofra. *See* labor service
south coast, the, 18, 19
Spain: Creole dependence on, 86; Islam in, 31
Spain in America (Gibson), 47
Stack, Carol B., 217
status ideology, 13; colonial, 65, 71, 78; community, 99, 115, 131; domestic, 116, 217, 255, 262, 270; ethnic continuum for, 184; Indian independence, 268, 330; institutional, 184, 185, 195; kinship, 229, 233, 240, 413n17; Ladino dominance, 112, 312; male/female, 239, 259, 261, 262, 270, 280; origin and, 199; in Peru, 353; political enablement, 98; residency, 268, 278, 288, 292, 297. *See also* oppositions; symbols
Stavenhagen, Rodolfo, 5, 80, 137
Stein, William, 351–62
superación, 156
Symbolism of Subordination (Warren), 21
symbols: acculturation and, 84; adjustments to, 133; analogy for meaning through, 7–9; bus system as, 162; center/periphery, 183, 194; Christianity as, 26, 30, 49, 65; church marriage as, 246; clothing, 166; cultural,

6–7, 115; economic, 135–38; ethnic, 9; food, 161, 358; incongruency in, 175, 185; labor, 164–66; land, 127, 133, 158, 168; life-style, 168; mestizo, 175, 185; office location as, 103, 119, 128; origin, 14; political seating as, 97, 130; racial, 29; redundancy in, 189; residency as, 107, 267, 279, 292, 301; social status, 14, 72, 73, 78, 86, 176; the threshold as, 246, 253, 266; time display as, 167; totemism, 189; urban/city, 228, 358; women as, 239, 259, 262; work ethic, 29, 62, 353

tailoring, 146
taxation and tribute, 30, 31, 34, 45, 55–59, 86, 106, 137
Tax, Sol, 85, 96, 97, 166, 175, 241, 295
Telling Tongues (Heath), 43
Third World, the, 378
tiendas, 119
time, 167
totemism, 189
Tovar, Prudencio, 62, 78
tribute. *See* taxation and tribute
trucking, 152, 162

Ubico, Jorge, 83
United States, the, 117
Universidad de San Carlos, 118
urban affiliation, 9–10, 27, 30, 71
uxorilocal residency, 270, 279, 339

vacant-town phenomenon, 10, 96
Vagrancy Laws, 83
Van den Berghe, Pierre, 350, 351–62 passim
Vasco de Quiroga, 47
vecinos, 69, 73
velación, 327, 330
virilocal residency, 270, 339, 343
Vogt, Evon, 21, 296

Wagley, Charles, 87
Warren, Kay B., 11, 21
Waugh, Linda, 8
wealth, 19; conjugal failure and, 309, 311, 315; domestic alliance and, 248, 255, 256, 310; ethnicity and, 209–11; households and, 341, 345; independence and, 116; Mayan, 40; merchandising, 150, 159; perspectives on, 176, 186, 194; poor nobleman, 27–29; residency and, 268, 271, 279; as a symbol, 184, 197
weaving, 139–45, 161, 169
Weber, Max, 14, 167
weddings, 220
wheat cooperative, 129
work ethic, 29, 36, 39, 165, 169, 353, 367
world view, 13
Worsley, Peter, 40

Yalman, Nur, 267, 295

Zapata, Luis, 50
Zinacantán, 265, 266